"For anyone feeling overwhelmed in helping a friend or family member through abuse, an addiction or any other challenging problem, now you can feel much more confident. The *Counseling Through Your Bible Handbook* is a handy, practical and, best of all, biblical guide that will lead you to God's solutions. It's about time!"

—Dr. Woodrow Kroll,
President, Back to the Bible International

"June's *Handbook* includes everything of importance to me for counseling. It emphasizes the sufficiency of Scripture, the pre-eminence of Christ, and it is a treasury of practical help to those in distress."

—Lee LeFebre,
President, Exchanged Life Ministries, Denver, Colorado

"June Hunt has been addressing the root issues for hurting hearts for as long as I have known her. God has given her an insightful sensitivity not only to identifying human problems but also to uncovering biblical solutions. She has done it for me more than once! All who have hurting hearts or who minister to wounded spirits need this resource, which is efficiently arranged and ready to provide answers and tools for healing. No human resource has more 'hope for the heart'!"

—Dr. Dorothy Kelley Patterson,
Professor of Theology in Women's Studies,
Southwestern Baptist Theological Seminary, Fort Worth, TX

"The *Counseling Through Your Bible Handbook* provides a virtual lab in biblical counseling. Through practical application, June shows us how to use biblical truth to change minds, change hearts, and change lives in the power of the Spirit."

—Dr. Mark L. Bailey,
President, Dallas Theological Seminary

"You hold in your hands a treasury of biblical hope and practical help. While it won't equip you to change people (that's God job), it will help you handle the Word of Truth accurately and speak its timeless wisdom into the lives of others."

—Dr. Tim Clinton,
President, American Association of Christian Counselors

D0112469

Counseling
Through
Your Bible
Handbook

JUNE HUNT

HARVEST HOUSE PUBLISHERS

EUGENE, OREGON

Cover by Garborg Design Works, Savage, Minnesota

Cover photo © Chris Garborg

COUNSELING THROUGH YOUR BIBLE HANDBOOK
Copyright © 2008 by Hope for the Heart, Inc.
Published by Harvest House Publishers
Eugene, Oregon 97402
www.harvesthousepublishers.com

The Library of Congress has cataloged the edition as follows:

Library of Congress Cataloging-in-Publication Data
    Hunt, June.
    Counseling through your Bible handbook / June Hunt.
       p. cm.
    Includes bibliographical references.
    ISBN 978-0-7369-2181-7 (paperback)
    ISBN 978-0-7369-2818-2 (Deluxe)
    1. Pastoral counseling—Handbooks, manuals, etc. 2. Bible—Psychology—Handbooks, manuals, etc.
    I. Title.
    BV4012.2H8335 2008
    253.5—dc22

                               2007044121

Printed in the United States of America

11 12 13 14 15 16 17 18 / DP-SK / 11 10 9 8 7

Periodically I've felt like that proverbial ox in the ditch…stuck and unable to free myself. I've had times when I needed a helping hand to pull me out. For over 30 years I've been part of a uniquely fun and fascinating group of friends who have faithfully met with each other…cared for each other…prayed for each other.

Thank you, TMMC…

— Randy and Lana Dodgen

— Tom and Rita Smith

— Precious prayer partner Eleanor Briley

…for the times you have pulled me up with your strong hands. Your friendship reminds me of Ecclesiastes 4:9-10: "Two are better than one…If one falls down, his friend can help him up. But pity the man who falls and has no one to help him up!"

Acknowledgments

As I look back on the beginnings of this *Handbook,* I see a tiny path—a footpath so small that it wasn't on anyone's map except God's. It was 1989 and I was leading conferences and Bible studies. People were asking question after question about problems in their lives, wanting biblical answers. But where would I take them? The Bible isn't organized topically...so I began searching the Scriptures, piecing together topical guidance.

As I felt my way along this uncharted path, a host of hardworking, talented, and persevering sojourners came alongside me—the staff of Hope for the Heart. Together, we designed our *Biblical Counseling Keys* on 100 topics. For this *Counseling Handbook,* we have distilled 50 of them down into chapters.

With a heart of deepest respect and gratitude, I especially acknowledge the following for their contribution:

From the beginning:

— Beth Stapleton and June Page, who, in the early days, researched and poured their lives into the *Biblical Counseling Keys,* and

— Kay Deakins, who for years has "kept the ox out of the ditch."

For this Handbook:

— Elizabeth Gaston and Angie White, who took turns guiding this project along a twisting path

— Jill Prohaska, Carolyn White, Mary Peppers, Barbara Spruill, and Ginger Swann, whose editorial input was indispensable at every turn

— Connie Steindorf, Jeanne Sloan, Laura Lyn Benoit, Karen Williams, and Bea Garner, who painstakingly keyed and proofed countless drafts along the journey

— Titus O'Bryant, whose diligent research will keep the mud from flying

— Steve Miller of Harvest House, whose patient leadership ensured we arrived at our destination with 50 chapters to help even the most road-weary traveler, and

— Above all, the Shepherd of my soul, who—even when I've strayed—has put me back on the path (sometimes the same path again and again), and has kept me on the road of inner freedom and fulfillment—the Road to Transformation.

CONTENTS

A HELPFUL NOTE FROM JUNE

Dear Friend,

Oddly enough, when we've been heading in the wrong direction, the painful result of being on the *wrong road* can be the most persuasive motivator to get us on the *right road*.

But what do we do if we don't know what to do?

At times, I've been stuck, stymied, and totally stumped…not knowing what to do or which way to turn. How I longed for wise counsel—someone to pull me "out of the ditch," to pivot me toward the right path, to put me on the right road. But…sometimes that special someone wasn't in my life.

You, too, know what it's like to feel the strain of a perplexing problem and to seek a fitting solution. You ask for help, but the answers aren't helpful. You want wisdom, but the counsel isn't wise. You feel no confirmation, no spirit of peace, no sense of "Yes!"

What should you think when you don't know what to think?

When your mind is mired in the mud, you can't move forward, you can't move backward. You're bogged down in the ditch and see no way out, with no one to help.

That is the *why* of this handbook:

- to offer step-by-step solutions for climbing out of a ditch (actually, 50 difficult ditches) and…

- to offer powerful hope, help, and healing from God's holy Word.

And why rely on the Bible? When King David careened off course, he found himself in the "ditch of adultery." Trying to get himself out of that muddy hole, he dug a deeper ditch—into the mire of murder. But after a complete change of heart—the deepest dedication of his life to the Lord—David made this strong declaration: "Your

Word is a lamp to my feet and a light for my path" (Psalm 119:105). He learned that the wisdom of God's Word would keep him walking on the right road, in the right direction.

At different times in our lives, we've all found ourselves caught in a quagmire—whether self-propelled or by accident or by an unwelcomed shove! No matter the depth of the ditch, we all need a helping hand to pry us out of the pit. However, Jesus warned, "Can a blind man lead a blind man? Will they not both fall into a pit?" (Luke 6:39). Therefore, our helper needs to see the situation and the solution accurately and to take a stand on solid ground, *being solidly grounded in truth*.

In reality, the Lord always offers His hand, saying, "Do not fear, for I am with you; do not be dismayed, for I am your God. I will strengthen you and help you; I will uphold you with my righteous right hand" (Isaiah 41:10).

My prayer is that throughout your lifetime, the timeless truths in this handbook will...

- provide a strong hand to pull you out of the ditch,
- provide a guiding hand to guide you down the right path,
- provide a helping hand to help you help others.

Realize that each chapter in this handbook is one separate path. And each of the 50 paths is distinctly different, with its own "map." Every map contains step-by-step directions, concluding with ten relevant passages (for the Scripture Prayer Project described later). These mapped paths ultimately lead to "the Road." Being on the Road means you are moving toward Christlike maturity—spiritually, mentally, and emotionally. On this Road you will find inner freedom and true fulfillment.

Everyone wants guidance from someone who is wise—especially someone the Lord has freed from a pit. Indeed, it is He who "redeems your life from the pit" (Psalm 103:4). Once you're out of your own ditch and walking the Road—look around! By sharing your journey with strugglers who are stuck, *you can be that wise person*...called by Christ to speak His words of wisdom into their lives.

Because all these maps are biblically based, I believe this how-to handbook will divinely help you help others. And toward what end? That, being conformed to the character of Christ, we all reach His designed destination—*total transformation!*

Enjoy the journey.

Yours in the Lord's hope,
June Hunt

Your Scripture Prayer Project

"Set up road signs; put up guideposts.
Take note of the highway, the road that you take"
(JEREMIAH 31:21).

At the end of each chapter, you will see a list of relevant scriptures. These Bible verses pertain to the chapter's topic (such as Rejection) and they serve as "road signs" revealing God's heart on that topic. They are guideposts to show how God wants us to think and act.

To turn these passages into *Your Scripture Prayer Project,* simply look up each of these verses, write them down, and personalize each verse with words you would naturally speak from your heart. These personal prayers, when applied to your life, will be especially powerful because...

— the Word of God possesses unique power (Hebrews 4:12), and,

— the Word of God renews your mind, producing a transformed life (Romans 12:2).

The following sample prayer is a model:

Your Scripture Prayer on Decision Making

Proverbs 3:5-6	Lord, I trust in You with all my heart and I won't rely on just what I understand. In all my ways, I will rely on You, because You will direct me in the way I should go.
Psalm 32:8	Thank You for being willing to instruct me and teach me the right way to go—even to counsel me and watch over me.
Psalm 25:9	I humble my heart so that You will guide me and teach me Your way.
James 1:5	When I need wisdom, I will ask You for it. Thank You for not faulting me for asking, but rather wanting to make me wise.
Proverbs 16:9	Even when I plan my future, I'm so glad that You determine my steps.
Psalm 40:8	Oh, God, I truly desire to do Your will. Thank You for putting Your truth in my heart!
John 16:13	I yield myself to Your Spirit of Truth, who will guide me into *all* truth.

Matthew 6:10   I pray that whatever is Your perfect will for me in heaven will also be accomplished in my life here on earth.

1 Corinthians 10:31   And, Lord, may whatever I do be truly for Your glory… and Yours alone.

In Jesus' name I pray. Amen.

COUNSELING

How to Give Biblical Hope with Practical Help

"I need to...talk with you!" says the caller in a tense, hesitant voice. The words are spoken a bit haltingly. "I'm...I'm worried...I may lose someone I love. I want to be reconciled. Would you be willing...to help me?"

Your heart responds—you want to help. But how can you make sure your help is actually helpful? What if the "presenting problem" isn't the *real* problem? For example, what if the real problem isn't a lack of reconciliation, but a lack of truthfulness on the part of the one calling for help?

When people come to you for counsel, what are the basic principles and approaches you need to know to pull them out of the ditch and guide them onto the Road to Transformation? First, make a commitment that your counsel be biblical. The starting point is stated in 1 Kings 22:5: "First seek the counsel of the LORD."

WHAT IS BIBLICAL COUNSELING?

Everyone has sincere opinions, but opinions aren't always right. In fact, we've all been sincere...and been sincerely wrong! That is why you should ask, "What is my foundation for truth?" The Bible should be your foundation. If your thinking doesn't line up with God's thinking, then *change your thinking!* Isaiah 40:8 says, "The grass withers and the flowers fall, but the word of our God stands forever."

- *Counseling* is help and hope given by one knowledgeable person to another person or group. The counsel given can range from personal comfort and encouragement,[1] with general advice and guidance, to a group crisis intervention. We are called by God not only to "carry each other's burdens," but also to "encourage one another and build each other up" (Galatians 6:2; 1 Thessalonians 5:11).

- ***Biblical counseling*** means you rely on truths from the Word of God as you seek to give wise counsel. Hebrews 4:12 says, "The word of God is living and active. Sharper than any double-edged sword, it penetrates even to dividing soul and spirit, joints and marrow; it judges the thoughts and attitudes of the heart."

- ***Christ-centered counseling*** is giving advice, encouragement, and hope to others based on biblical truth while relying on Christ to provide the power for change. Second Corinthians 5:17 says, "If anyone is in Christ, he is a new creation; old things have passed away; behold, all things have become new" (NKJV).

What Qualifies You to Offer Biblical Counsel?

If you are in a growing relationship with God, and...

— You have personally sought and received the comfort of God (2 Corinthians 1:3-4).

— You love Christ and care about the needs of others (Galatians 6:2).

— You accurately handle the Word of Truth (2 Timothy 2:15).

— You are called by God to counsel others (2 Corinthians 9:8; Hebrews 10:24-25).

The Lord says,

> *"I will instruct you and teach you in the way you*
> *should go; I will counsel you and watch over you"*
> (PSALM 32:8).

What Is Your Major Responsibility When Giving Counsel?

For your counseling to have maximum effectiveness, you must live in *total dependence* on Christ, seeking His will. Jesus said, "I am the vine; you are the branches. If a man remains in me and I in him, he will bear much fruit; apart from me you can do nothing" (John 15:5).

The Seven S's of Spiritual Wisdom

With a heart of humility, realize:

1. The *solutions* are not your solutions (John 14:26).
2. The *self-sufficiency* you lean on should be replaced with *Christ-sufficiency* (John 15:5).
3. The *Spirit of Christ* is your counselor, enabling you to counsel with truth (John 16:13).

4. The *sinful* person should never be confronted with condemnation
   (1 Peter 3:15-16).

5. The *success* of your counseling is not dependent on your knowing all the
   answers (Proverbs 3:5-6).

6. The *Scriptures* will light the way as you help others walk out of darkness
   (Psalm 119:105).

7. The *secret* of victory over sin is relying on the power of the indwelling
   presence of Christ (Philippians 4:13).

WHAT ARE YOUR GOALS WHEN GIVING BIBLICAL COUNSEL?

The more you know God's Word, the more you will know God's will. When someone comes to you with a problem, first ask yourself, *Has God already spoken specifically about this in His Word? If so, what has He said? If not, is there a general biblical principle that needs to be considered?* The greater your dependence on the Word of God, the wiser you will be. Psalm 119:105 says, "Your word is a lamp to my feet and a light for my path."

As a biblical counselor who is sincerely serving Christ, you will want to:

— Help those who are off course get on a "correction course" to move toward wholeness and spiritual maturity. The Bible says, "If one of you should wander from the truth and someone should bring him back, remember this: Whoever turns a sinner from the error of his way will save him from death and cover over a multitude of sins" (James 5:19-20).

— Lead an unbeliever into a personal relationship with Jesus Christ. Jesus said, "If anyone would come after me, he must deny himself and take up his cross and follow me. For whoever wants to save his life will lose it, but whoever loses his life for me will find it" (Matthew 16:24-25).

— Present wisdom from God's Word in order to enable strugglers to live in victory. "Listen to advice and accept instruction, and in the end you will be wise" (Proverbs 19:20).

PRACTICAL COUNSELING: HOW DO YOU DO IT?

Be wise in how you walk through the doors of opportunity God brings your way. You may spend many days, weeks, or months helping the heart of one in need, or you may sow only a few seeds in the life of someone who briefly crosses your path.

Pray regularly that God will direct both your words and actions. Colossians 4:5-6 says, "Be wise in the way you act toward outsiders; make the most of every opportunity.

Let your conversation be always full of grace, seasoned with salt, so that you may know how to answer everyone."

1. Prepare the Physical Setting

— Provide a private, relaxing place to talk (safe for all parties involved).

— Eliminate distractions (radio, TV, music, other voices, or annoying noises).

— Prevent interruptions (hold phone calls, activate the answering machine, utilize a "Do Not Disturb" sign, place a notepad by the door for messages).

— Avoid physical barriers (don't sit behind a desk unless you need to appear firmly authoritative to someone who is belligerent or abusive).

— Change lighting to reduce glare (adjust blinds, curtains, or overhead lights as needed).

— Keep counseling aids handy (Bible, paper, pen, and referral phone numbers).

— Place facial tissues and drinking water within reach (replenish prior to meeting).

"The wisdom of the prudent is to give thought to their ways"
(Proverbs 14:8).

2. Promote Personal Nonverbal Nurture

— Smile upon greeting the person (a friendly face can disarm a fearful disposition).

— Shake hands or use another appropriate greeting (human touch conveys warmth and care).

— Situate chairs in close proximity (if at a 90-degree angle, turn your body to face the other person).

— Slant your body slightly forward (leaning forward signifies, "I'm interested in what you are saying").

— Sustain good eye contact (refuse to be distracted—if necessary, move to another location).

— Show an occasional nod of the head (this simple movement signifies acceptance versus rejection).

— Stay open and approachable (don't sit with arms folded or fists clenched. Folded arms signify, "I'm not convinced you want help").

"A cheerful look brings joy to the heart"
(Proverbs 15:30).

3. Probe for the *Real* Problem

How to Get Started

— Call the person by name—several times:

   "Hi, David! Come on in."

— Don't engage in small talk. Off-the-subject comments delay getting to the point and may decrease the person's willingness to be vulnerable.

— Ask a direct question...

   "How can I help you?" or *"What would you like us to talk about?"*

   Answer: "How can I get her to stay with me...to be reconciled?"

— Realize, the *presenting problem* (what someone *assumes* is the cause of the trouble) is *very often* not the *real problem*. If the real problem relates to a lack of trustworthiness due to a lack of truthfulness, probe with pertinent questions to gain insight and understanding.

   "The purposes of a man's heart are deep waters,
   but a man of understanding draws them out"
   (Proverbs 20:5).

How to Probe into the Past

— Ask why the problem exists...

"What has she actually said is the reason for the trouble?"

   "She says I lie."

"Do you ever twist the truth?"

   "Only sometimes."

"Does she say this is a major problem?"

   "Yes."

"Do you want to be a man of integrity?"

   "Yes."

— Ask background questions regarding family, home, school, dating, work.

"David, what was it like growing up in your home?"

   "We all walked on eggshells. Mother had a lot of fear."

"*What was your mother afraid of?*"

— Listen to what is not shared. If one parent is not mentioned at all, ask about that parent.

"*What was your relationship with your father?*"

"He was cold and harsh."

— Ask for the earliest memories of that habit.

"*When was the first time you remember lying? What caused you to lie back then?*"

"If I upset Dad he would hurt my Mom, so I would lie to keep him from getting angry."

— Encourage further talk.

"*Could you tell me more?*"

"He would threaten divorce…"

"*Go on…*"

"He'd take everything…"

"*M-m-m…*"

"…leaving us with nothing."

— Primarily ask open-ended questions that cannot be answered with yes or no.

"*David, when are you most tempted to lie today?*"

"When someone could become upset with me."

— Explore the impact of significant people (such as parents, siblings, other relatives, friends).

"*What messages did you receive about you from what your father said and did?*"

"It's like he said, 'You're nothing. You're a zero.'"

"*How did that make you feel?*"

4. Pose the Question, Why Do We Do What We Don't Want to Do?

Those who are stuck in the ditch of negative habits (such as lying) can lose all hope of personal change. They don't know *what* to do, much less *why* they do what they do. The apostle Paul expressed what we have all experienced: "What I do is not the good I want to do; no, the evil I do not want to do—this I keep on doing" (Romans 7:19).

We have all been created with three God given inner needs: love, significance, and security:

> *Love*—to know that someone is unconditionally committed to our best interest (John 15:12)
>
> *Significance*—to know that our lives have meaning and purpose (Psalm 57:2)
>
> *Security*—to feel accepted and have a sense of belonging (Proverbs 14:26)

At the heart of our negative behavior is an attempt to get our legitimate needs met in illegitimate ways. The Bible calls this sin. Proverbs 14:12 says, "There is a way that seems right to a man, but in the end it leads to death."

5. Present the Ultimate Need-meeter

Why did God give us these deep inner needs, knowing that "people fail people"? (For example, some parents are harsh, cruel, and abusive.) While every person has been *created* with these three inner needs, no person is *able* to meet our three needs.[2] Realize that if one person *could* meet all our needs, we wouldn't need God!

The Lord planned that *He would be our Need-meeter.* The apostle Paul revealed this truth by exclaiming, "What a wretched man I am! Who will rescue me from this body of death?" Then he answered his own question in a strong way: "Jesus Christ our Lord!" (Romans 7:24-25).

All along, the Lord planned to meet our deepest needs for...

> *Love*—He says, "I have loved you with an everlasting love" (Jeremiah 31:3).
>
> *Significance*—He says, "I know the plans I have for you...plans to give you hope and a future" (Jeremiah 29:11).
>
> *Security*—He says, "Never will I leave you; never will I forsake you" (Hebrews 13:5).

Sometimes the Lord will meet certain needs by Himself, and other times He will use other people as an extension of His care and compassion.

═══ *Share These Steps with Those Who Are Struggling* ═══

You can be pulled out of any ditch, any negative pattern keeping you from being all God created you to be. How? Romans 12:2 says, "Do not conform any longer to the *pattern* of this world, but be transformed by the *renewing of your mind.*" Therefore, with a renewed mind, you can be set free. John 8:32 says, "You will know the truth, and the truth will set you free." Here is the path to becoming F-R-E-E:

F—Face the truth of your own negative habit.

Pray Psalm 139:23: "Search me, O God, and know my heart; test me and know my anxious thoughts."

Evaluate: Focus on or write down your area of struggle: "My biggest struggle has been lying."

R—Recognize the inner need(s) you are trying to meet through this negative habit.

Are you trying to meet your own need for *love,* or *significance,* or *security,* or a combination of these?

Psalm 51:6 says, "Surely you [God] desire truth in the inner parts; you teach me wisdom in the inmost place."

Evaluate: Do you make up stories to impress people because you feel *insignificant?* Or do you lie when you are afraid because you feel *insecure?* "I lie because I feel insecure."

E—Exchange trying to meet your own need for allowing Christ to meet that need.

Philippians 4:19 makes it plain: "My God will meet all your needs according to his glorious riches in Christ Jesus."

Solution: "Jesus is my security. People were angry with Jesus, yet He was totally truthful—so if someone gets angry with me, I can be totally truthful. He is the Way, the TRUTH, the Life. I will replace my fear with faith because I have the TRUTH inside me."

E—Experience Christ's inner strength as your source for change.

Claim Philippians 4:13: "I can do everything through him who gives me strength."

Solution: "Instead of relying on my lies to 'keep the peace,' I will rely on Christ's power to tell the truth. That, in turn, will produce inner peace. I will live with a new plan through His power. I will be a person of honesty, integrity, and truth."

CONCLUSION

When dealing with a person's negative habit, turn to the topical chapter addressing that problem and learn how to pull that person out of the ditch and guide that struggler down a step-by-step path leading to the Road to Transformation. See the table of contents for all the topics. By the way, before you can effectively guide others down their individual paths, first you need to apply the preceding steps to your own life—choosing the area(s) where you have personally struggled.

In the power of Christ, *we all can change*—we all can be *transformed* to be like Christ because Colossians 1:27 says it is "Christ in you, the hope of glory." He is our hope of freedom—for, "if the Son sets you free, you will be free indeed" (John 8:36).

As a Christian giving or receiving counsel, you have the most awesome resource available: the presence of Christ living in you, the power of Christ working through you, the character of Christ reflected by you (1 Corinthians 3:16; 2 Peter 1:3; Romans 8:29).

—JH

Your Scripture Prayer Project

John 14:26

Isaiah 59:2

Proverbs 3:5-6

Hebrews 4:12

Galatians 2:20

1 Samuel 12:23

2 Peter 1:3

2 Corinthians 13:5

Psalm 51:5

Psalm 119:11

For additional guidance on this topic, see also *Codependency, Crisis Intervention, Critical Spirit, Decision Making, Forgiveness, Hope, Identity, Marriage, Premarital Counseling, Reconciliation, Salvation, Suicide Prevention* and other related topics.

ABORTION RECOVERY
Healing and Restoration After an Abortion Decision[1]

Those who have had an abortion are often weighed down by deep hurt and intense shame. Their "ditch" is deep and wide, as they struggle with a host of issues such as guilt, anxiety from grief and guilt, to depression or even suicidal thoughts and the hope of developing healthy emotional and sexual relationships. Understanding and accepting God's truth may not come quickly for these wounded women—and even men—crippled by the pain of past destructive choices. They need someone compassionate to help them through their pain in order to receive the healing God offers. No sin is so great that the sinner cannot be made right and brought into close relationship with God. Psalm 34:18 says...

> *"The LORD is close to the brokenhearted and*
> *saves those who are crushed in spirit."*

WHAT ARE THE CONSEQUENCES OF ABORTION?

Abortion often leads to serious, though sometimes delayed, emotional consequences. Post Abortion Stress (PAS) is a traumatic stress disorder that many experience after an abortion. A woman suffering from PAS may find she is unable to...[2]

— process her painful thoughts and emotions involving the abortion

— grieve the loss of her baby

— be at peace with God and those involved in the abortion decision

— realize and accept her God-given worth

> *"My guilt has overwhelmed me like*
> *a burden too heavy to bear"*
> (PSALM 38:4).

WHAT ARE THE STAGES OF POST ABORTION STRESS (PAS)?

There are four stages a woman generally experiences following an abortion.[3] Each provides an opportunity to either become further entrenched or to reach up for God's hand of grace. Therefore, her decisions during these stages either lead further into bondage or closer to freedom.

Relief: She feels relieved the "crisis" is over and the pressing problem has disappeared.

Rationalization: This period of uncertainty occurs when the moral dilemma resurfaces, resulting in a mental rehearsing of logical explanations and excuses for having had the abortion.

— "I wouldn't have been a good mother. It's better that the baby wasn't born."

— "I may have been upset at the time, but I'm okay now."

— "It's legal…therefore, it is certainly okay."

Repression: The guilt and grief can seem so overwhelming that a woman can block the details and painful memories, even to the point she actually "forgets" she had an abortion.

— "That's ridiculous. Why would my medical records indicate I had an abortion?"

Resentment: Left unresolved, hidden or repressed anger results in bitterness that will greatly hinder a woman's relationship with God and her interactions with others. Having consistently resisted God's grace at each stage, she now experiences the "bitter root" warned against in Hebrews 12:15: "See to it that no one misses the grace of God and that no bitter root grows up to cause trouble and defile many." Hidden or repressed anger toward herself and those involved in the abortion results in depression and bitterness. If this anger is not dealt with, her relationship with God and her interaction with others become hindered.

WHAT OTHER DEFENSE MECHANISMS ARE UTILIZED?

Defense mechanisms shield a person from frightening thoughts, feelings, and memories, providing a way to lie to oneself when the truth seems too painful to face. This delusion delays freedom because God uses truth to set captives free. What we fear most is what we need most to face.

Denial: Refusing to accept the reality of the situation.

— "I did nothing wrong; I feel nothing."

Avoidance: Avoiding or dismissing unacceptable truths.
  — "I'm not going to church today—it's Sanctity of Life Sunday. My abortion doesn't affect me, and I refuse to dwell on it."

Compensation: Trying to make up for real or imagined defects by exaggerating a strength.

  — "We're all human…this good thing that I do makes up for the bad thing I did."

Reaction: Pushing down whatever feelings are causing anxiety and adamantly professing the exact opposite of those feelings, often with tears.

  — "I have never, ever regretted my decision to have an abortion. In fact, the times since the abortion have been among the best years of my life."

The natural human reaction to fear and anxiety is to fight against it or flee from it, not to embrace it and walk through it with God's help. To believe that truth can be denied, avoided, camouflaged, or replaced with a lie is to walk in blindness and remain in the dark. Only that which is brought into the light can be forgiven. Acknowledging our sin and asking forgiveness pulls us onto the road to freedom. God's purpose in this is not to shame us but to reveal His loving and forgiving heart.

> *"Nothing in all creation is hidden from God's sight. Everything is uncovered and laid bare before the eyes of him to whom we must give account"*
> (HEBREWS 4:13).

WHAT ARE SYMPTOMS OF PAS?

God desires that no one live with PAS, but He uses it to draw people to Him in search of relief from pain, release from guilt, and removal of all the destructive and heartbreaking side effects of sin.

Guilt: Heavily burdened because of violating a personal moral code or God's law

Anxiety: A state of apprehension (tension, a pounding heart, an upset stomach, and disturbed sleep patterns)

Avoidance Behaviors: Steering clear of situations or objects that are reminders of abortion (such as baby showers or children)

Psychological Numbing: Keeping emotions controlled (refusal or inability to form and maintain close relationships)

Depression and Thoughts of Suicide: Flattened emotions, low self-esteem, and thoughts of suicide

Re-experiencing: Having recurring nightmares or flashbacks of the abortion caused by certain triggers (such as vacuum cleaners or commercials featuring babies)

Fertility and Bonding Issues: Preoccupation with becoming pregnant again, anxiety over fertility, an interruption in bonding with present or future children

Survival Guilt: Making attempts to atone for a choice perceived to be selfish or sinful

Self-abusive Behaviors: Some may develop eating disorders, or engage in alcohol or substance abuse, or other self-punishing or self-degrading behaviors

Anniversary Reaction: Increased symptoms around the anniversary of the abortion, or what would have been the due date of the aborted child

Brief Reactive Psychosis: A brief break with reality (usually within two weeks of the abortion) and, in most cases, a subsequent rapid recovery to normalcy

Those suffering from the disruptive effects of PAS struggle to live a fulfilling life. However, they are unable to achieve the full life that is found only in a right relationship with Jesus.

> *"I have come that they may have life,*
> *and have it to the full"*
> (John 10:10).

Who Can Suffer from PAS?

— Women who were pressured to have the abortion

— Women who were raised in a strict religious home environment who have had an abortion

— Women who were raped and had an abortion under duress

— Women who are returning to an environment where the abortion must be kept a deep, dark secret

— Men who were excluded from the abortion decision

— Men who coerced their partner to abort

— Men whose spouses aborted against their will

— Men who are ambivalent about the abortion decision

Although poor choices were made, God pursues us and repeatedly gives us second chances.

*"I will search for the lost and bring back the strays.
I will bind up the injured and strengthen the weak"*
(Ezekiel 34:16).

Maintaining a healthy relationship is extremely difficult while experiencing the stressful symptoms of PAS. Anyone striving to survive has limited emotional energy to invest in intimacy with someone else.

Breakup of the Relationship: A woman can become disillusioned when a man fails to be her "protector" by insisting she have an abortion. If the decision was made against the man's wishes, he may feel like he failed to protect his unborn child. Because abortion involves a death, this stress on a relationship can lead to feelings of isolation.

Threat to Family Structure: The sense of oneness is destroyed by the woman's legal right to make this death decision on her own. The woman's decision to abort a man's child can cause the loss of his identity as a protecting "father," leaving him weak and powerless.

Sexual Dysfunction: Female sexual desire is usually drastically reduced after an abortion. However, the woman's need to boost her sense of self-worth may drive her to compulsively search for sexual encounters. The man may push to resume sexual relations immediately to receive confirmation that his partner still loves him. If the woman resists his overtures, this can lead to further feelings of emasculation and failure.

Communication Problems: Feelings of resentment may develop on both sides, building walls that hinder intimacy.

These negative reactions aren't anticipated, and those involved may not be prepared to work through them. The barrier that rises can seem impossible to breach and becomes catastrophic to the relationship. When the heart is hurt and spirit crushed, relationships with others cannot be healthy or healed.

*"My spirit grows faint within me;
my heart within me is dismayed"*
(Psalm 143:4).

What Part Does Denial Play in PAS?

Denial of whom or what has been lost through abortion helps buy time psychologically...until the realization that the death of a baby has really occurred and the man or woman bears much of the responsibility for causing that death. Layers of denial need to be peeled back, much like an onion, revealing soft, thin, almost transparent layers of stress and pain that must be examined and grieved before going to the next layer.

Coming out of denial is the work of the Holy Spirit in the postabortion man or woman. Frequently those who are hurting from abortion will get "stuck" in their hard places. These places should be considered "holy ground." This is where they feel they are fighting for their very lives and where they need to know someone is walking with them shoulder to shoulder to help them find God's grace.

How Can You Heal After Having an Abortion?

Spend all the time necessary at these junctures on the path to recovery, so that one day the Road to Transformation will be reached, where healing and wholeness wait.

Admit Personal Responsibility

— Stop blaming other people or circumstances for the abortion
— Realize the decision is ultimately the mother's choice
— Agree with God that abortion is wrong

> *"Nothing in all creation is hidden from God's sight.*
> *Everything is uncovered and laid bare before the*
> *eyes of him to whom we must give account"*
> (Hebrews 4:13).

Awaken Painful Memories

— Choose to work through the denial
— Relive the negative feelings surrounding the abortion
— Talk about the experience with a trusted friend or sensitive counselor

> *"The purposes of a man's heart are deep waters,*
> *but a man of understanding draws them out"*
> (Proverbs 20:5).

Acknowledge the Anger

— Learn that it is okay to express anger
— Determine with whom you are angry, and why
— Write (but don't mail) an appropriate anger letter to each person with whom you are angry

> *"In your anger do not sin.*
> *Do not let the sun go down while you are still angry,*
> *and do not give the devil a foothold"*
> (Ephesians 4:26-27).

Address Issues of Guilt/Shame

— Stop self-condemning language

— Stop self-abusive behavior

— Overcome self-hatred

— Put to rest "survival guilt"

> *"I acknowledged my sin to you and did not cover up*
> *my iniquity. I said, 'I will confess my transgressions*
> *to the LORD'—and you forgave the guilt of my sin"*
> (PSALM 32:5).

Agree to Forgive

— Choose to forgive; it is not a *feeling* but an *act of the will*

— Determine whom you need to forgive

— Write a letter to God forgiving each person with whom you have been angry

> *"Bear with each other and forgive whatever grievances you may*
> *have against one another. Forgive as the Lord forgave you"*
> (COLOSSIANS 3:13).

Acknowledge the Grief

— Recognize the loss of the pregnancy

— You may want to name your child, realizing that a real live baby was aborted

— Write out your feelings for your child

— Conduct a short memorial service

— Commit your child into the loving hands of God

> *"[There is] a time to weep and a time to laugh,*
> *a time to mourn and a time to dance"*
> (ECCLESIASTES 3:4).

Acquire a Ministry of Sharing Hope

— Express compassion to others in similar circumstances

— Advise others who are considering an abortion

— Be the light that leads a hopeless heart to Christ

*"Praise be to the God and Father of our Lord Jesus Christ, the
Father of compassion and the God of all comfort, who comforts
us in all our troubles, so that we can comfort those in any
trouble with the comfort we ourselves have received from God"*
(2 CORINTHIANS 1:3-4).

Q: What happened to your child after the abortion?

A: Although the Bible doesn't specifically address this question, in principle you can know that your baby went to heaven. For example, consider the situation with King David, who was described as "a man after his [God's] own heart" (1 Samuel 13:14). When David's seven-day-old baby died, he said, "I will go to him, but he will not return to me" (2 Samuel 12:23). Like David's baby, your precious child is in the presence of God—our just, merciful, compassionate God.

=== *Your Grateful Prayer to God* ===

Heavenly Father,

Thank You for taking care of my child, who is living in heaven with You. I bring all my guilt and grief and lay them at Your feet. From Your heart of mercy I accept Your full forgiveness. Thank You, Jesus, that You are now in me to live Your life through me. You've given me a new heart, and You will heal all my heartaches. You've given me a new life that is cleansed, forgiven, and free. Thank You, Lord, for Your unconditional love. I choose to release my life to You so You can work Your will in me. I choose to rely on the Spirit of Christ living in me to guide me from this day forth. Lead me to love others as You love me. In the Savior's precious name I pray. Amen.

When God is willing to forgive you but you are not willing to forgive yourself, realize you are setting yourself up as a higher judge than God. Because God forgives you, you can forgive yourself.

—JH

Your Scripture Prayer Project

Jeremiah 1:4-5

Psalm 139:2-4

Luke 15:20

Acts 3:19

Mark 11:25-26

Psalm 30:11-12

2 Corinthians 4:2

Romans 8:1-4

2 Corinthians 5:17

John 8:31-36

For additional guidance on this topic, see also *Anger, Decision Making, Forgiveness, Grief Recovery, Guilt, Hope, Identity, Marriage, Pregnany...Unplanned, Suicide Prevention.*

3

ADULTERY

The Snare of an Affair

Has your life been gripped by the agony caused by adultery? Has it been forever changed because of the snare of an affair? The "ditch of adultery" can cause countless lives—families, friends, even entire churches—to become mired in the muddy fallout. Marriage was God's idea...and He designed it to be a lifelong covenant commitment. Adultery violates that commitment, for it is voluntary extramarital sexual activity between a married person and another person who is not his or her lawful spouse. Any impurity in marriage violates the law of God and grieves the heart of God.

> *"Marriage should be honored by all, and the*
> *marriage bed kept pure, for God will judge the*
> *adulterer and all the sexually immoral"*
> (HEBREWS 13:4).

WHY ARE PEOPLE DRAWN INTO ADULTERY?

Those who walk through the door of adultery assume, *I won't get caught...it's no big deal.* They have no clue their wrong choices will reap severe repercussions even though the Bible warns, "Do not be deceived: God cannot be mocked. A man reaps what he sows" (Galatians 6:7). Then after the affair they say, "What was I thinking?" How about...

— They focused on what they thought would meet their needs.

— They rationalized that God understands their situation.

— They blamed their marriage partner for their problems.

— They failed to look at the lifelong consequences.

— They assumed their mate would never change.

— They believed it would make them happy.
— They opened the door of compromise.
— They thought they wouldn't get caught.
— They hardened their heart.
— They were lured by lust.

Q: Why does anyone get involved in adultery?

A: Typically people get into adulterous relationships because they rationalize their wrong actions as right. Then they indulge in selfish pleasures to the extent they develop a heart that is hardened toward the desires of God.

"All a man's ways seem right to him,
but the LORD weighs the heart"
(PROVERBS 21:2).

WHAT ARE TYPICAL SIGNS OF INFIDELITY?

Justification. Excuses. Rationalization. Those who have illicit affairs are quick to spin the truth in order to cover their tracks, yet this biblical proverb presents an eye-opening perspective: "The man of integrity walks securely, but he who takes crooked paths will be found out" (Proverbs 10:9).

Frequent signs of affairs are a combination of the following:

— Change in behavior
— Change in mood
— Change in spending patterns
— Change in schedule
— Changes in physical appearance: clothes, jewelry, cologne
— Less personal conversation
— Less vulnerability (sharing from the heart)
— Less discussion of future plans
— Less spontaneity
— Less sexual intimacy
— More out-of-town "business" trips

— More unaccounted-for time away from home
— More faultfinding
— More emotional distance
— More unexpected gifts ("guilt gifts")
— More anger at being questioned

What Are Reasons to Stop Committing Adultery?

There are ten great reasons:

— Your Bible forbids it
— Your mate is wounded
— Your peace is forfeited
— Your health is jeopardized
— Your future will not be blessed
— Your morality is compromised
— Your children lose their hero
— Your conscience is scarred
— Your integrity is destroyed
— Your God condemns it

> *"The integrity of the upright guides them,*
> *but the unfaithful are destroyed by their duplicity"*
> (Proverbs 11:3).

What Enables an Adulterer to Truly Change?[1]

Commit to follow this course on your pathway to recovery and find restored trust in your marriage. Becoming trustworthy before others is a signpost that you're on the Road to Transformation and growing in Christlike maturity.

Confess the adultery and seek forgiveness from God and your spouse. To put the affair in the past, the truth must be revealed for God to bring healing. "Confess your sins to each other and pray for each other so that you may be healed" (James 5:16).

Commit yourself completely to your covenant partner. Children are not the glue that holds a marriage together;[2] commitment to the marriage covenant is the tie that binds a husband and wife. "Do not break faith with the wife of your youth" (Malachi 2:14-15).

Cut all ties with the third party. Affairs are not "okay" as long as no one knows.

Like any other sin, adultery cannot be hidden because God knows, the illicit partners know, and in time, others will know. Ultimately, the affair will burn the participants. "Can a man scoop fire into his lap without his clothes being burned?" (Proverbs 6:27).

Choose where to place your thoughts when tempted. People who have affairs can still love their spouses. It is possible to still feel a love for one person yet be infatuated with another at the same time. "Whatever is true...noble...right...pure...lovely... admirable...excellent...praiseworthy—think about such things" (Philippians 4:8).

Consider the difference between love and lust. "How can it be wrong if it feels so right?" is the excuse many give. But love is not merely a feeling. The supreme test for determining if something is right is not how it feels, but what God says about it. If sin never felt good, no one would ever be tempted to sin. Love is a choice—for you to do what is best for another person, and for you to make a personal sacrifice. "Husbands, love your wives, just as Christ loved the church and gave himself up for her" (Ephesians 5:25).

Count the cost. The excuse "As long as no one knows, no one will be hurt" is a myth. Adultery hurts everyone involved. Guilt and God's judgment is brought not only upon one person, but both parties involved. Adultery destroys truthfulness, credibility, and one's testimony. "A man who commits adultery lacks judgment; whoever does so destroys himself" (Proverbs 6:32).

Communicate godly sorrow. Admitting an affair doesn't automatically make everything okay. The Bible says there is a vast difference between worldly sorrow and godly sorrow. Worldly sorrow is being sorry for getting caught. Godly sorrow is a change of mind with a change of direction that results in a change of behavior. Godly sorrow causes you to hate your sin so much that you turn from it and never turn back to it again. "Godly sorrow brings repentance that leads to salvation and leaves no regret, but worldly sorrow brings death" (2 Corinthians 7:10).

Continue to rely on God's strength to help you resist repeating the sin of adultery. After "coming clean," it remains important to be on guard. Repetitive sin is often an easy trap because it's familiar territory. The Bible warns against habitual sin: "Watch and pray so that you will not fall into temptation. The spirit is willing, but the body is weak" (Matthew 26:41).

WHAT ARE DO'S[3] AND DON'TS[4] FOR THE FAITHFUL MATE?

"My world is gone...I feel so helpless, so powerless." How typical these feelings! While you are powerless to change your mate, you are not powerless in the way you respond. Regardless of your spouse's response—or lack of—you have the choice to find your significance and security in the Lord. Isaiah 54:5 says, "Your Maker is your husband—the LORD Almighty is his name."

Do use "I" statements to express your feelings. If you are suspicious, don't think bringing up the subject might put the thought in your mate's mind. Discussing your honest feelings may relieve your thoughts, be a deterrent for the future, or be used by the Holy Spirit to convict your partner. Don't attack; don't blame. You could say, "I feel you are keeping something from me." "I feel hurt your affection has turned from me." "I need you to be totally honest with me." Scripture tells us how to handle such an encounter: "If your brother sins against you, go and show him his fault, just between the two of you. If he listens to you, you have won your brother over" (Matthew 18:15).

Do express your anger in a nondestructive way. Anger is not always wrong. Anger is a natural response to hurt, injustice, fear, or frustration. But, "in your anger do not sin" (Ephesians 4:26).

Do pray for the Spirit of God to guide your decisions about possibly leaving an adulterous spouse. Must a person stay married even if his or her mate continues to commit adultery? Marital unfaithfulness is a ground for divorce. Jesus does not *demand* divorce in such a case, but rather, *permits* it: "Anyone who divorces his wife, *except for marital unfaithfulness,* and marries another woman commits adultery" (Matthew 19:9).

Do rely on the Lord to be your Savior, Completer, and Healer if an estranged spouse chooses to leave. It is not necessary to have a mate to be whole. One is a whole number—not a half, not a fraction. You can be whole in Christ: "Heal me, O LORD, and I will be healed; save me and I will be saved, for you are the one I praise" (Jeremiah 17:14).

Do choose as an act of will to forgive. Forgiving someone does not necessarily mean you must forget. The key is how the offense is remembered. Forgiving is remembering without bitterness, hatred, or resentment.[5] "Bear with each other and forgive whatever grievances you may have against one another. Forgive as the Lord forgave you" (Colossians 3:13).

Don't try to find ways to change your mate. This is not your responsibility. In fact, you can't change your mate—you don't have that power. "The LORD will fight for you; you need only to be still" (Exodus 14:14).

Don't bring up specifics in order to convict your mate. The Holy Spirit is the One who convicts. "He will convict the world of guilt in regard to sin and righteousness and judgment" (John 16:8).

Don't blame yourself for the adultery.[6] Almost all wounded mates struggle with false guilt, feeling responsible for the mate's affair. However, anything you did or didn't do did not cause your spouse to sin against you. You can't make another person sin. The actions of adulterers were based on their personal choices. The Bible says, "Each of us will give an account of himself to God" (Romans 14:12).

Don't minimize or deny the seriousness of the situation. Minimizing or denying the seriousness of the situation does not change the fact it is sin. Call sin what it is. "All other sins a man commits are outside his body, but he who sins sexually sins against his own body" (1 Corinthians 6:18).

Don't seek ways to meet all your mate's needs. You can never meet all your mate's needs. If you could, your mate would never sense a need for God. God did not create anyone to meet another person's every need. God Himself promises to meet all our needs. "God will meet all your needs according to his glorious riches in Christ Jesus" (Philippians 4:19).

Don't believe you can't make it alone and that you are completely dependent on your spouse. Your sufficiency is to be in the Lord alone, not in another person. "Find rest, O my soul, in God alone; my hope comes from him. He alone is my rock and my salvation; he is my fortress, I will not be shaken" (Psalm 62:5-6).

> Why is adultery so deceptive? Because it gives
> the illusion of being loved...a flawed feeling of
> connection...a false sense of security. Instead of living
> in a fantasy world, live by the facts of God's holy Word:
> "God did not call us to be impure, but to live a holy life"
> (1 Thessalonians 4:7).
>
> —JH

Your Scripture Prayer Project

Proverbs 6:27

Mark 7:21-23

1 Corinthians 6:18

Proverbs 6:32

Hebrews 13:4

Malachi 2:15-16

Colossians 3:13

Isaiah 54:5

Psalm 62:5

Exodus 14:14

For additional guidance on this topic, see also *Anger, Depression, Domestic Violence, Dysfunctional Family, Forgiveness, Guilt, Hope, Identity, Manipulation, Marriage, Reconciliation, Rejection, Self-worth, Sexual Addiction, Sexual Integrity, Worry* and other related topics.

4

ALCOHOL AND DRUG ABUSE

Breaking Free and Staying Free

D rug or alcohol addiction is a modern-day demon that can take over and radically alter a person's behavior, health, family, and future. Most people with a drug dependency insist they are not dependent. However, when they try to stop the habit, they cannot...because they continue to sink deeper. Beneath the surface of self-delusion, this "ditch of drug abuse" is filled with quicksand and its victims feel that they just can't free themselves. Second Peter 2:19 says, "A man is a slave to whatever has mastered him." Nevertheless, there is hope for deliverance, for lasting change.

WHAT ARE THE MAJOR DRUG CLASSIFICATIONS?[1]

Drugs are generally classified into four major groups depending on their effect on the body. In all four, excessive usage can cause death! Proverbs 14:12 says, "There is a way that seems right to a man, but in the end it leads to death."

Depressants produce a calming effect and slow down the central nervous system.

> *Prevalent types:* alcohol, sedatives, tranquilizers, barbiturates, and organic solvents
>
> *Psychological symptoms:* poor concentration, distorted thinking, lack of judgment, aggressiveness
>
> *Physical effects:* drowsiness, slurred speech, lack of coordination, tremors, decreased energy, coma, impaired vision, decreased pulse rate and blood pressure, respiratory depression, death

Isaiah 28:7 refers to those who "stagger from wine and reel from beer...and are befuddled with wine...they stagger when seeing visions, they stumble when rendering decisions."

Stimulants excite bodily functions and speed up the central nervous system.

> *Prevalent types:* cocaine, crack, meth, and amphetamines
>
> *Psychological symptoms:* excitability, increased energy, exaggerated self-confidence, heightened sexual drives, temporary exhilaration, emotions
>
> *Physical effects:* hyperactivity, restlessness, insomnia, loss of appetite, dry mouth, bad breath, itchy nose, dilated pupils, rapid and unclear speech, perspiration, headaches, dizziness, elevated blood pressure and heart rate, psychosis, death

The book of Proverbs describes those who walk without wisdom: "Disaster will overtake him in an instant; he will suddenly be destroyed—without remedy" (Proverbs 6:15).

Hallucinogens alter and distort reality.

> *Prevalent types:* LSD, marijuana, PCP, and mescaline
>
> *Psychological symptoms:* hallucinations, heightened sensitivities, anxiety attacks, lowered inhibitions, out-of-body experiences
>
> *Physical effects vary with the drug:* LSD acts as a stimulant; marijuana acts as a depressant; sleeplessness, loss of appetite, increased energy, increased pulse rate and blood pressure, eyes fixed in a blank stare or rapid involuntary eye movements, slurred or blocked speech, higher rate of accidents and violence, disorientations, death

Although the Bible does not directly mention hallucinogens, it does address the frightening and disturbing hallucinogenic effects of alcohol: "Your eyes will see strange sights and your mind imagine confusing things...'They hit me,' you will say, 'but I'm not hurt! They beat me, but I don't feel it! When will I wake up so I can find another drink?'" (Proverbs 23:33-35).

Narcotics reduce pain and elevate a person's mood.

> *Prevalent types:* opium, morphine, codeine, heroin, methadone, and meperidine
>
> *Psychological symptoms:* temporary euphoria, dulled senses, lethargy, and confusion
>
> *Physical effects:* relief of pain, droopy eyelids, constricted pupils, slowed reaction and motor skills, drowsiness, lack of coordination, depressed reflexes, dry mouth, constipation, scars or abscesses at injection sites

When you are in pain, rather than turning to drugs, turn to the Lord. Be dependent on Him and seek His direction for pain relief: "I am in pain and distress; may your salvation, O God, protect me" (Psalm 69:29).

WHAT IS THE DOWNWARD SPIRAL OF DEPENDENCY?

Intoxication occurs when the influence of a substance in your body causes changes in your behavior—including mood changes, faulty judgment, slurred speech, poor coordination, unsteady gait, sexual impropriety, aggressive behavior, and impaired social functioning. Intoxication may result in becoming comatose or even death.

> *Dorland's Illustrated Medical Dictionary* defines *intoxication* as "poisoning; the state of being poisoned."[2] How interesting that Moses said, "Their grapes are filled with poison…Their wine is the venom of serpents, the deadly poison of cobras" (Deuteronomy 32:32-33).

Abuse occurs when your use of drugs results in your failure to fulfill responsibilities or to maintain healthy relationships, or when you put yourself or others at risk of potential harm.

Addiction occurs when you experience these three leading indicators:

— *Drug tolerance:* you need increasingly more to obtain the same effect
— *Physical dependence:* you suffer from withdrawal symptoms such as nausea, sweating, shaking, anxiety
— *Craving:* you develop a pattern of compulsive drug use

Withdrawal occurs when the distress caused by a lessening or lack of the drug severely disrupts your daily life. "No longer do they drink wine with a song…In the streets they cry out for wine; all joy turns to gloom, all gaiety is banished" (Isaiah 24:9,11).

Q: How can I be held responsible for my drug dependence when most drugs are addictive and actually cause the addiction?

A: Your drug dependence has been created both by your choice to use drugs and by the drug itself. Intoxication results from the makeup of the drug you use and the way it is metabolized by your body. The only way to avoid addiction is to make a deliberate choice to stop abusing drugs. First Samuel 1:14 says, "How long will you keep on getting drunk? Get rid of your wine."

A Checklist for a Chemical Dependency[3]

C   Do you ever attempt to *conceal* your habit from others?

H   Do you ever think about getting *help* for your habit?

E   Do you have problems at your place of *employment* because of your habit?

M   Do you ever experience a loss of *memory* as a result of your habit?

I   Do you ever become severely *intoxicated*?

C   Do you ever feel unfairly *criticized* because of your habit?

A   Do you ever feel your habit is *abnormal*?

L   Do you ever *lose* friendships or *leave* relationships as a result of your habit?

L   Do you ever *lower* your intake yet end up returning to your previous level?

Y   Do you ever neglect your *young children* or other loved ones because of your habit?

D   Do you become *defensive* or argumentative about your usage?

E   Do you fail to get in touch with your *emotions* because of your usage?

P   Is your *physical* health affected by your usage?

E   Do you *enjoy* only functions where alcohol or other drugs are available?

N   Is your *need* for the substance affecting your finances?

D   Do you *deny* that you experience any consequences from your habit?

E   Do you *evade* difficult situations by indulging in your habit?

N   Is your *need* to feed your habit affecting your relationships?

T   Is your *tolerance* level for the substance getting higher?

If you answered yes to five or more of the above questions, you may have a serious dependency. Isaiah 5:22 says, "Woe to those who are heroes at drinking wine and champions at mixing drinks."

> **Q:** Is alcoholism an inherited disease over which a person has no control?
>
> **A.** Medical professionals continue to debate whether or not alcoholism is a disease. Because of the strong and lasting changes alcohol can have on the brain and other organs, many consider it a disease. Others take the position that it is more behavioral.

A disease is *an abnormal condition of the body* caused by...[4]

- infection (i.e., catching the flu or smallpox from outside the body)

- genetic defect (i.e., being born with diabetes or with a genetic makeup where alcohol is not processed normally)

- environmental factors (i.e., being exposed to toxins and pollutants or developing cirrhosis of the liver, where excessive alcohol has caused so much stress on the liver that it no longer functions properly)

While alcoholism can be influenced by genetics and by chemical alterations, the vital fact to remember is that you do have control over whether you succumb to alcoholism or whether you are restored from alcoholism. Your family background and genetics can make you more susceptible to alcoholism; however, these influences can be resisted (1 Peter 1:13).

HOW CAN A PERSON FIND DELIVERANCE FROM DEPENDENCY?[5]

Just as chemical dependency does not develop overnight, neither does deliverance from dependency typically occur quickly. Yet just as a sequence of events can lead you into quicksand, another sequence can lead you into freedom.

By putting one foot in front of the other, you can begin your journey on the path to recovery. One day you may find yourself running down the Road to Transformation in full freedom…and even pulling others out of the quicksand along the way.

Admit to being powerless over your dependency.

> "I am unable to manage or control my life." No matter what the trial, 2 Corinthians 1:9 says we are not to "rely on ourselves but on God."

Realize that the God who made you has the power to restore you.

> "I am asking Christ to be my Redeemer, and to restore every area of my life" (see Psalm 71:20-21).

Yield your will to the will of the Lord.

> "I am asking Christ to take control of my life" (see Matthew 16:24-25).

Face reality—face your true self.

> "I will take an honest look at my life, asking God to uncover my sins and character flaws" (see Psalm 139:23-24).

Admit your struggle with sin, both to God and to someone else.

> "May I see my sin as God sees it and hate my sin as God hates it" (see 1 John 1:8).

Accept God's help to change your patterns of the past.

> "I will commit my life into the care of Christ" (see 1 Peter 5:6-7).

Confess your failings and flaws.

> "I'm willing to see myself as God sees me" (see Psalm 51:10-12).

Ask forgiveness of those whom you have offended.

> "I will find those whom I've hurt, and from my heart ask forgiveness" (see Matthew 5:23-24).

Make restitution where you have wronged others.

> "I will make amends…with the help of God" (see Ezekiel 33:15-16).

Keep a clean slate by acknowledging when you have been wrong.

> "Each day I will take responsibility for my irresponsibility" (see Titus 2:11-12).

Pray for God's direction for your life.

> "I want to be led by the Lord, and walk only on His path" (see Psalm 25:4-5).

Reach out to others with your hand and your heart.

> "I will care for those who need care, and will help with a heart of compassion" (see Galatians 6:2).

What Are the "Don'ts" for Deliverance?[6]

Don't fight addiction on your own. Rely on God and participate in a legitimate drug recovery program (see Ecclesiastes 4:9-10).

Don't be blind about your ability to lie to yourself and to others! Ask someone to help you be accountable (see Jeremiah 17:9).

Don't socialize with those who encourage or tolerate your habit. Forge new friendships and helpful, healthy habits (see 1 Corinthians 15:33).

Don't worry about the future. Walk with God one day at a time (see Matthew 6:34).

Don't give up if you relapse. It is never too late to get back on track. "If we confess our sins, he is faithful and just and will forgive us our sins and purify us from all unrighteousness" (1 John 1:9).

Don't be prideful as you succeed in the recovery process. Be grateful for God's grace and power to achieve change. "Pride goes before destruction, a haughty spirit before a fall" (Proverbs 16:18).

Don't be surprised at temptation—flee from it! "No temptation has seized you except what is common to man. And God is faithful; he will not let you be tempted beyond what you can bear. But when you are tempted, he will also provide a way out so that you can stand up under it" (1 Corinthians 10:13).

WHAT ARE THE SPIRITUAL TIPS FOR RECOVERY?[7]

Realize that the time to begin recovery is today.

> "Today, if you hear his voice, do not harden your hearts" (Hebrews 3:15).

Accept that recovery is a lifelong process, not a onetime event.

> "Not that I have already obtained all this, or have already been made perfect, but I press on to take hold of that for which Christ Jesus took hold of me" (Philippians 3:12).

Pray daily for victory. It is through prayer that God protects you.

> "Watch and pray so that you will not fall into temptation. The spirit is willing, but the body is weak" (Matthew 26:41).

Read your Bible every day to get strength from God.

> "My soul is weary with sorrow; strengthen me according to your word" (Psalm 119:28).

Meditate on Scripture to fight against falling into sin.

> "I have hidden your word in my heart that I might not sin against you" (Psalm 119:11).

Attend church every week to worship God and to grow with others.

> "Let us consider how we may spur one another on toward love and good deeds. Let us not give up meeting together, as some are in the habit of doing, but let us encourage one another" (Hebrews 10:24-25).

Share your struggles with caring loved ones.

> "Confess your sins to each other and pray for each other so that you may be healed" (James 5:16).

Have confidence in God and prioritize growing in your relationship with Him.

> "Seek first his kingdom and his righteousness, and all these things will be given to you as well" (Matthew 6:33).

Depend on Christ's strength to stay drug- or alcohol-free.

> "I can do everything through him who gives me strength" (Philippians 4:13).

Know that permanent change is possible.

> "With God all things are possible" (Matthew 19:26).

You may say, "I can't...I've tried...I just can't do it!"

Well, maybe it's true you don't have the stamina to stop...and stay stopped. But understand that Christ hasn't called you to stay sober alone. The Bible reveals the secret: "Faithful is He who calls you, and He also will bring it to pass" (1 Thessalonians 5:24 NASB).

Q: Why do people have a personal conviction to abstain from alcohol?

A: First, the Bible gives us warnings like this one: "Wine is a mocker and beer a brawler" (Proverbs 20:1).

Second, the Bible gives us "the stumbling argument"—the concern that someone might stumble because of your example. "It is good not to eat meat or drink wine or do anything that causes your brother to stumble" (Romans 14:21 ESV).

Your Scripture Prayer Project

1 Corinthians 6:19-20

Deuteronomy 29:19

Isaiah 24:11

Proverbs 23:20

Isaiah 28:7

Proverbs 23:33

Psalm 69:29

Romans 6:12

Philippians 2:13

Psalm 25:5

For additional guidance on this topic, see also *Anger, Codependency, Crisis Intervention, Domestic Violence, Dysfunctional Family, Forgiveness, Guilt, Habits, Hope, Identity, Self-worth, Verbal and Emotional Abuse, Victimization, Worry* and other related topics.

5

ANGER

Facing the Fire Within

Firefighters know the danger of letting a fire get out of control. They are trained to respond quickly. You, too, must respond quickly to control the flames of anger before they consume your life and leave a smoldering ditch of destruction.

"An angry man stirs up dissension,
and a hot-tempered one commits many sins"
(PROVERBS 29:22).

WHAT ARE THE DEGREES OF ANGER?

Anger is an emotional agitation that occurs when a need or expectation is not met.[1] Like heat, anger has many degrees, ranging from mild irritations to hot explosions.

Indignation—simmering anger provoked by something unjust and often perceived as justified

Wrath—burning anger accompanied by a desire to avenge

Fury—fiery anger so fierce that it destroys common sense

Rage—blazing anger resulting in loss of self-control, often to the extreme of violence and temporary insanity

WHAT ARE MISCONCEPTIONS ABOUT ANGER?

Is it a sin for a person to be angry? No, the initial feeling of anger is a God-given emotion. The way you *express* this emotion determines whether your anger becomes sin. Ephesians 4:26 says, "In your anger do not sin."

How can a person keep from feeling guilty when he is angry?[2] Your anger is a signal that something is wrong. The purpose of the red warning light on a car dashboard is to propel you into action—to cause you to stop, evaluate, and do what is needed. For example, Jesus became angry at the hypocritical religious leaders who interpreted "resting on the Sabbath" to excess: "He looked around at them in anger and, deeply distressed at their stubborn hearts, said to the man, 'Stretch out your hand'…and his hand was completely restored" (Mark 3:5).

What Are the Four Sources of Anger?

Hurt[3]—Your heart is wounded. Everyone has a God-given inner need for unconditional love.[4] When you experience rejection or emotional pain of any kind, anger can become a protective wall that keeps people and pain away.

Injustice[5]—Your right is violated. Everyone has an inner moral code that produces a sense of right and wrong, fair and unfair, just and unjust. When you perceive that an injustice has occurred against you or others (especially those whom you love), you may feel angry. If you hold on to the offense, the unresolved anger can begin to make a home in your heart.

Fear[6]—Your future is threatened. Everyone is created with a God-given inner need for security.[7] When you begin to worry, feel threatened, or get angry because of a change in circumstances, you may be responding to fear. A fearful heart reveals a lack of trust in God's perfect plan for your life.

Frustration[8]—Your effort is unsuccessful. Everyone has a God-given need for significance.[9] When your efforts are thwarted or do not meet your own personal expectations, your sense of significance can be threatened. Frustration over unmet expectations of yourself or of others is a major source of anger.

What Is the Root Cause of Anger?

When we feel that our real or perceived rights have been violated, we can easily respond with anger.[10]

Wrong Belief:

"Based on what I believe is fair, I have the right to be angry about my disappointments and to stay angry for as long as I feel like it. I have the right to express my anger in whatever way is natural for me."

Right Belief:

"Because the Lord is sovereign over me and I trust Him with my life, I have yielded my rights to Him. My human disappointments are now God's appointments to increase my faith and develop His character in me. I choose to not be controlled by anger, but to use anger to motivate me to do whatever God wants me to do" (see 1 Peter 1:6-7).

How Can Past Anger Be Resolved?

Unresolved anger is a bed of hidden coals burning deep wounds into your relationships with God and with others. This powerful emotion robs your heart of peace and steals contentment from your spirit. So how is this anger resolved?[11]

Realize Your Anger

— Willingly admit that you have unresolved anger.

— Ask God to reveal any anger buried in your heart.

— Seek to determine the primary reason(s) for your past anger.

— Talk out your anger with God and with a friend or counselor.

(Proverbs 21:2)

Revisit Your Root Feelings

— Did you feel *hurt* (rejected, betrayed, unloved, ignored)?

— Did you experience *injustice* (cheated, wronged, maligned, attacked)?

— Did you feel *fearful* (threatened, insecure, out of control, powerless)?

— Did you feel *frustrated* (inadequate, inferior, hindered, controlled)?

(Psalm 139:23-24)

Release Your Rights

— Confess that harboring anger in your heart is sin.

— Give your desire for revenge to God.

— Refuse to hold on to your past hurts by releasing them to God.

— Pray for God to work in the life of the one who has wronged you and to change your heart toward that person.

— Release the one who hurt you into the hands of God—forgive as God forgave you!

(Colossians 3:13)

Rejoice in God's Purpose

— Thank God for the ways He will use this trial in your life.

— Know that God can use your resolved past anger for your good and for the good of those around you.

— Praise God for His commitment to use all the circumstances in your life to develop Christ's character within you, making you strong, firm, and steadfast.

(Romans 8:28-29)

Restore the Relationship When Appropriate

Forgiveness looks at the offense; reconciliation looks at the relationship. Forgiveness can be done without the other person changing, but reconciliation requires trust to be rebuilt by both. When there is refusal to admit sin, reconciliation cannot happen. In the case of infidelity in marriage, the innocent party can forgive, but full restoration requires the adultery to stop. Spousal abuse can be forgiven, but it must stop before there can be reconciliation. The anger fueling an abusive attitude does not develop quickly and it will not dissipate immediately. Do not force reconciliation until there is truly a change of heart by the offender.

(2 Corinthians 5:20)

How Can I Release "Present Anger" Constructively?

"Anger is one letter short of danger." More than a catchy phrase, these words reflect the painful truth. And because too many times the tongue has not been tamed, conversations escalate out of control. These steps will help you learn to handle your anger constructively and biblically.

As you follow these eight guideposts down the path of peace, soon you'll be on the Road to Transformation, with fertile ground for new growth at every turn.

Acknowledge Your Anger

— Be willing to admit you are angry.

— Be aware of when you feel angry.

— Become aware of suppressing or repressing your anger because of fear.

— Be willing to take responsibility for any inappropriate anger.

(Proverbs 28:13)

Analyze Your Style

— How often do you feel angry?

— How do you know when you are angry?

— How do others know when you are angry?

— How do you release your anger?

(Psalm 139:23-24)

Assess the Source

— Hurt, injustice, fear, frustration (see page 52)

"Surely you desire truth in the inner parts;
you teach me wisdom in the inmost place"
(Psalm 51:6).

Appraise Your Thinking

— Are you expecting others to meet your standards?

"She *should* take better care of her children."

"He *ought* to notice what I do for him."

"He *must* be here before 7:00 P.M."

"She'd *better not* call during dinner!"

— Are you guilty of distorted thinking?

Exaggerating the situation

Assuming the worst

Labeling one action based on other actions

Generalizing by saying, "You never..." or "You always..."

(Proverbs 21:29)

Admit Your Needs

Anger is often used as a tactic to get inner needs met.

— Do you use anger as a manipulative ploy to demand certain "musts" in an attempt to *feel loved*?

— Do you use explosive anger to get your way in an attempt to *feel significant*?

— Do you use controlling anger, insisting on certain conditions in order to *feel secure*?

— Do you know that only Christ can ultimately meet all your needs?

(Philippians 4:19)

Abandon Your Demands

Instead of demanding that others meet your inner needs for love, significance, and security, learn to look to the Lord to meet your needs.

—"Lord, though I would like to feel more *love* from others, I know that You love me unconditionally."

"I have loved you with an everlasting love;
I have drawn you with loving-kindness"
(JEREMIAH 31:3).

—"Lord, though I would like to feel more *significant* to those around me, I know that I am significant in Your eyes."

> *"'I know the plans I have for you,' declares the*
> *LORD, 'plans to prosper you and not to harm*
> *you, plans to give you hope and a future'"*
> (JEREMIAH 29:11).

— "Lord, though I wish I felt more *secure* in my relationships, I know I am secure in my relationship with You."

> *"The LORD is with me; I will not be afraid.*
> *What can man do to me?"*
> (PSALM 118:6).

— "Lord, though I wish others would be more responsive to my needs, I know that You have promised to meet all my needs."

> *"His divine power has given us everything we need*
> *for life and godliness through our knowledge of him*
> *who called us by his own glory and goodness"*
> (2 PETER 1:3).

Alter Your Attitudes

Take the following steps, which are outlined in Philippians 2:2-8:

— Have the goal to be like-minded with Christ.

— Do not think of yourself first.

— Give the other person preferential treatment.

— Consider the other person's interests.

— Have the attitude of Jesus Christ.

— Do not emphasize your position or rights.

— Look for ways to demonstrate a servant's heart.

— Speak and act with a humble spirit.

— Be willing to die to your own desires.

Address Your Anger

— *Determine* whether your anger is really justified.

— *Decide* on the appropriate response.

> How important is the issue?
>
> Would a good purpose be served if I mention it?
>
> Should I acknowledge my anger only to the Lord?

— *Depend* on the Holy Spirit for guidance.

— *Develop* constructive dialogue when you confront.

— *Don't* speak from a heart of unforgiveness. Think before you speak.

— *Don't* use phrases such as, "How could you?" or "Why can't you?"
    Use personal statements, such as "I feel..."

— *Don't* bring up past grievances. Stay focused on the present issue.

— *Don't* assume the other person is wrong. Listen for feedback from another point of view.

— *Don't* expect instant understanding. Be patient and keep responding with gentleness.

— *Demonstrate* the grace of God by saying the following to yourself:

> "I placed my anger on the cross with Christ."

> "I am no longer controlled by anger."

> "I am alive with Christ living inside me."

> "I will let Christ forgive through me."

> "I will let Christ love through me."

> "I will let Christ reveal truth through me."

> *"I have been crucified with Christ and I*
> *no longer live, but Christ lives in me. The life I live*
> *in the body, I live by faith in the Son of God,*
> *who loved me and gave himself for me"*
> (GALATIANS 2:20).

THE QUICK ANSWER TO ANGER

When you sense a surge of anger, ask, "Can I change this situation?" If you can, change it. If you can't, release it.

—JH

===== *Your Scripture Prayer Project* =====

James 1:19-20

Proverbs 29:22

Proverbs 29:11

Proverbs 15:1,18

Proverbs 22:24

Proverbs 19:19

Ephesians 4:26-27

Ecclesiastes 7:9

Psalm 4:4

For additional guidance on this topic, see also *Alcohol and Drug Abuse, Codependency, Depression, Evil and Suffering...Why? Fear, Guilt, Hope, Self-worth, Stress Management, Verbal and Emotional Abuse, Worry.*

6

ANOREXIA AND BULIMIA

Control that Is Out of Control

Anorexics stop eating, and bulimics keep overeating. But all this has little to do with food. Both groups of strugglers are actually starving—for unconditional love and acceptance. Those hiding in the ditch of an eating disorder are seeking to conceal their shameful struggle. Tragically, these sufferers believe the ditch is what they deserve. They do not know the depth of God's boundless love for them (Ephesians 3:17-19).

WHAT ARE ANOREXIA AND BULIMIA?

— *Anorexia* is a psychological eating disorder characterized by chronic self-starvation, rooted in a distorted body image and an abnormal fear of gaining weight.

— *Bulimia* is a psychological eating disorder characterized by repeated binge-and-purge episodes. Food is eaten to meet emotional needs, resulting in guilt and fear of weight gain, which prompts self-induced vomiting.

WHAT ARE THE UNDERLYING PROBLEMS?[1]

Why are anorexics so determined to destroy themselves? Anorexics are convinced they don't deserve to live—they have made too many mistakes. In the acute stage, many try to burn themselves in hot showers, jump out of buildings, or cut themselves.[2] Others become so exhausted from fighting the mental battles that they see no hope and give up trying to get better.

— *Confusion:* Valuing brains vs. beauty, intelligence vs. thinness, achievement vs. appearance

— *Deception:* Stealing food/laxatives, lying about eating, pretending to swallow, spitting it out later

— *Depression:* Feeling "fat" though weight is appropriate for the height or though looking like "skin and bones," logical thinking becomes virtually impossible, life becomes an unconscious or conscious and deliberate attempt at suicide.

— *Compulsion* for some area of control: "Eating is the *one* part of life I can control."

— *Loneliness:* "I can't talk to anyone about this problem."

— *Low self-worth:*[5] "I'm a fat pig"; "I'm a bad person"; "I don't deserve to live."

— *People pleasing:* "If I'd just done better...been better...weighed less, then I would have been loved."

— *Perfectionism:* "I must have a perfect body, like the actors and actresses in the movies, to be happy." "I must look like magazine models." "I must perform perfectly, or no one will love me."

Ask yourself: "Am I now trying to win the approval of men, or of God? Or am I trying to please men? If I were still trying to please men, I would not be a servant of Christ" (Galatians 1:10).

WHAT ARE THE WARNING SIGNS?

Don't be deceived. Not all sufferers appear greatly underweight. Be alert to other warning signs. Don't be misled about the danger of these disorders—both can be deadly. Those who suffer can say, "My life is consumed by anguish and my years by groaning; my strength fails because of my affliction, and my bones grow weak" (Psalm 31:10).

— *Blood cell abnormalities:* Anemia and low counts of white blood cells cause a deficiency in the immune system.

— *Bone problems:* Deficiency in calcium causes bone deterioration, fractures, osteoporosis.

— *Bowel dysfunction:* Excessive use of laxatives causes bowels to become totally dependent, unable to function without laxatives, causing long-term stomach problems.

— *Dental problems:* Purging of food brings up hydrochloric acid from the stomach that washes across the teeth. Gastric juices cause erosion of tooth enamel, cavities, pain, discoloration, and tooth loss.

— *Digestive problems:* Forced vomiting causes bleeding esophagus, bloated stomach, stomach cramps, chronic constipation, and other digestive complications.

— *Glandular problems:* Thyroid irregularities cause decreased energy, decreased reflexes, lethargy. Water imbalance and retention cause chronic swelling of feet, hands, glands. Other potential problems include low body temperature, dry skin, brittle nails.

— *Hair loss:* Poor nutrition and inadequate protein cause thinning of hair and balding.

— *Heart problems:* Malnutrition causes an imbalance of the heart's essential minerals, which, in turn, causes irregular heartbeats and possibly death (mortality rate of 5.15 percent among bulimics).

— *Hypoglycemia:* Low blood sugar causes fatigue, anxiety, dizziness, headaches.

— *Kidney failure:* Chronic dehydration causes kidney failure.

— *Menstrual problems:* Deficiency in fat (essential to good health) causes menstrual cycles to stop for two to three months at a time. When fat levels drop below 22 percent of normal weight, menstruation ceases.

— *Mental difficulties:* Malnutrition (deficiency in vitamins, minerals, proteins, fats) causes slow thinking, extreme forgetfulness, seizures.

— *Musculoskeletal problems:* Deficiency in potassium causes muscle spasms, pain, atrophy, premature aging.

— *Vision problems:* Deficiency in vitamin A causes deterioration of eyesight.

— *Weight swings or drops:* This is the most ominous sign of all. Binging or purging of the bulimic causes extreme weight fluctuation within short periods of time. The self-starvation of the anorexic causes the body weight to go so low that the kidneys and other organs start to shut down, leading to death.

WHAT ARE THE CAUSES OF THIS STRUGGLE?[4]

Anorexia and bulimia are the consequence of an attempt to satisfy the inner hunger for unconditional love and acceptance by having a "perfect" body. But why? Those who have these disorders struggle with...

Feeling worthless because of abuse in the home

— verbal assaults or emotional starvation

— physical or sexual abuse

— alcoholism or drug abuse

Feeling inadequate because of unrealistic expectations of others

— perfectionist parents

— acceptance based on performance

— conditional love

Feeling driven in a high-performance atmosphere
— models and ballerinas (60 percent have eating disorders)

— dancers, actors, actresses

— athletes, particularly wrestlers and gymnasts

Feeling hopeless as a result of depression after an abortion
— denial of reality

— deep sadness with no apparent explanation

— guilt over taking an innocent life

Feeling powerless because of obesity in family
— one or both parents

— a propensity for gaining weight

— fear of being fat

What Is the Root Cause?

Both the anorexic and the bulimic have an obsessive focus on being thin. The bulimic does not love food any more than the anorexic loves to starve. The bulimic hates food just as much as the anorexic does, using food as a means to numb feelings and to lose weight by purging.

Wrong Belief:

"I'm so fat no one could love me. I hate who I am. The only way I can be loved is to be in control of my body and get it to the right size."

> *"There is a way that seems right to a man,*
> *but in the end it leads to death"*
> (Proverbs 14:12).

Right Belief:

"The issue in life is not my size, but to see myself through God's eyes. The Lord loves me just as I am. Instead of being consumed by control, I'm choosing to release control of my life and trust the Lord Jesus with every part of my heart."

> *"Trust in the Lord with all your heart and lean not on*
> *your own understanding; in all your ways acknowledge*
> *him, and he will make your paths straight"*
> (Proverbs 3:5-6).

What If This Is Your Struggle?

As a struggler, you must begin by admitting that there is a problem. To non-strugglers, this may seem a simple step…however, specialists agree this can be the most difficult one of the entire recovery process.

Follow these eight signs on your path to recovery, all leading to the road to inner freedom and fulfillment.

Agree to get a thorough medical checkup. This condition is life threatening!

> *"The prudent see danger and take refuge,*
> *but the simple keep going and suffer for it"*
> (Proverbs 27:12).

Attend weekly (or regular) sessions with a knowledgeable, professional counselor.

> *"Apply your heart to instruction and your*
> *ears to words of knowledge"*
> (Proverbs 23:12).

Acquire as much knowledge about eating disorders as possible—for yourself and for those close to you.

> *"Know also that wisdom is sweet to your soul;*
> *if you find it, there is a future hope for you,*
> *and your hope will not be cut off"*
> (Proverbs 24:14).

Admit your inability to control the eating pattern.

> *"Confess your sins to each other and pray for each*
> *other so that you may be healed. The prayer of*
> *a righteous man is powerful and effective"*
> (James 5:16).

Abandon the idea that you just need more willpower. This is not a diet problem.

> *"The weapons we fight with are not the weapons*
> *of the world. On the contrary, they have divine*
> *power to demolish strongholds…take captive*
> *every thought to make it obedient to Christ"*
> (2 Corinthians 10:4-5;
> also read 2 Corinthians 12:9-10).

Allow yourself to forgive those who have hurt you, and even to forgive yourself.

> *"Bear with each other and forgive whatever*
> *grievances you may have against one another.*
> *Forgive as the Lord forgave you"*
> (Colossians 3:13).

Act in total faith on God's power to rescue you.

> *"In you, O Lord, I have taken refuge; let me never*
> *be put to shame. Rescue me and deliver me in your*
> *righteousness; turn your ear to me and save me. Be*
> *my rock of refuge, to which I can always go; give the*
> *command to save me, for you are my rock and my fortress"*
> (Psalm 71:1-3).

Accept your true worth.

Know that you are worth Jesus' dying for you—you are dearly loved (John 3:16)! If you have come into a personal relationship with the Lord Jesus, your *true identity* is in Christ Himself. You are a new creation in Christ. You are no longer what you were. If you allow Jesus to become the focus of your life—not food, not compulsion, but Christ—you will increasingly find freedom.

> *"If anyone is in Christ, he is a new creation;*
> *the old has gone, the new has come!"*
> (2 Corinthians 5:17).

How Can You Help?[5]

When the sufferer relapses and seeks refuge in the ditch, provide a strong, steady hand that doesn't let go.

Learn everything you can.

Knowledge is your friend; ignorance is your enemy (see Proverbs 19:20).

Confront in a loving way.

Confrontation is not easy, but doing nothing is the opposite of love (see Proverbs 12:18).

Encourage seeking professional help.

A mark of wisdom is acknowledging a need for help (Proverbs 15:22).

Talk about emotions to reach deeper levels of communication.

> As part of your dialogue, ask, "Why do you feel that way?" Seek to uncover the underlying causes behind this crisis (Proverbs 20:5).

Listen, listen, listen with your heart.

> People love to hear their words repeated: "So what you are saying is _____." Listening and repeating helps build trust and opens up communication, which, in turn, can lead to healing (Ecclesiastes 3:7).

Verbalize genuine, heartfelt love.

> Terms that convey compassion and concern, such as *precious* or *dear,* often help someone feel nurtured (Proverbs 25:11).

Express love with appropriate physical affection.

> Look into the person's eyes, touching the hand or shoulders. In relationships with parents, siblings, and spouses, hugging, holding, or kissing can be especially meaningful.

> *"A friend loves at all times, and a brother is born for adversity"*
> (Proverbs 17:17).

Be honest about the dangers.

> The debilitating effects of eating disorders wreak havoc on the body. Help an anorexic or bulimic learn to think long term, not short term, about the very real dangers (1 Thessalonians 5:14).

What Are the Don'ts?

Don't be forceful or controlling.

> This will not work. Try distracting the person from negative thoughts by giving constant praise and unconditional love (Proverbs 12:18).

Don't be unrealistic about your expectations for change.

> It has taken the person nearly a lifetime of negative thinking to reach this point. It will take many months or longer for healing to take place (Proverbs 19:11).

Don't assume that all doctors who treat anorexics and bulimics are equally capable.

Find a competent, compassionate specialist who ministers to the inner needs and can develop a bond of trust. If necessary, seek a second or third opinion (Proverbs 15:22).

Don't let anorexics see their weight when being weighed.

Whatever the number, their negative thinking tells them it's too high. If they don't have a number to fight, that's one less negative they have to contend with (Proverbs 16:21).

Don't fail to request help from a former anorexic.

Former anorexics know all the tricks, such as poisoning their food, exercising under the sheets, and slipping food up their sleeves to discard it later. Nothing is more reassuring to someone with an eating disorder than a helping hand from someone who's been there—someone now living in victory (Proverbs 27:17).

Don't assume you are helpless if anorexics won't eat. Offer to hand-feed.

Because anorexics possess a negative mind-set that tells them not to eat, hand-feeding can relieve their self-imposed pressure of guilt and fear of overeating (Galatians 6:2).

Don't give up.

Patience, persistence, and perseverance are essential to helping restore wholeness (1 Corinthians 13:4,7-8).

People with eating disorders are love-starved. Express your love by keeping eye contact and spending time with them—much time. They spell love T-I-M-E. They also don't feel valuable, and when you tangibly reach out and touch them, you demonstrate they *do* have value. Even if they don't seem to respond, they desperately seek your acceptance. They desperately long for unconditional love, the Lord's love, your love.

Those who struggle with eating disorders feel they have no control—so their focus of control is on food. But their true need is not gaining control, but giving control to Christ.

—JH

Your Scripture Prayer Project

Hebrews 4:13

Proverbs 15:32

Proverbs 18:15

Proverbs 16:20

Colossians 3:9-10

Romans 6:6

1 Corinthians 6:19

1 Corinthians 10:31

1 Corinthians 10:13

Galatians 2:20

For additional guidance on this topic, see also *Alcohol and Drug Abuse, Codependency, Crisis Intervention, Critical Spirit, Depression, Fear, Habits, Hope, Identity, Illness, Manipulation, Overeating, Rejection, Self-worth, Worry* and other related topics.

7

CHILDHOOD SEXUAL ABUSE

The Secret Storm

Nothing penetrates the core of a child's inner being like sexual abuse. Its long tentacles reach deep within the child, wrapping around the young heart, choking and killing innocence and trust. This violation leaves its victims in a dark, dirty ditch...a place no child should have to experience.

WHAT CONSTITUTES CHILDHOOD SEXUAL ABUSE?

Just to clarify its broad reach, childhood sexual abuse is any physical, visual, or verbal interaction with a minor by an older child or adult whose purpose is sexual stimulation or sexual satisfaction. A victim of such abuse is any boy or girl under the age of 18 who has suffered one or many experiences of sexual abuse. Such abuse results in emotional, mental, spiritual, or physical harm.

Sexual abuse of a child is almost always committed by someone the child knows or with whom the child has frequent contact. Such familiarity sets the stage for a child to be all the more vulnerable to victimizers.

The Bible is not silent about the deceitful schemes of victimizers:

> *"He lies in wait like a lion in cover;*
> *he lies in wait to catch the helpless; he catches the*
> *helpless and drags them off in his net"*
> (Psalm 10:9).

WHAT CONSTITUTES INCEST?

Incest is sexual interaction with a child or an adolescent by a person who is a member of the child's family—a blood relative, an adoptive relative, or someone related by marriage or remarriage. Incestuous relationships usually continue over a long period of time. Incest occurs primarily in the following types of relationships (in order of predominance):

— A girl with her father or stepfather, grandfather, uncle, male cousin, older brother, half-brother, or brother-in-law

— A boy with his father or stepfather, grandfather, uncle, male cousin, brother, half-brother, brother-in-law, sister, or mother

The Bible is not silent about the act of incest: "No one is to approach any close relative to have sexual relations" (Leviticus 18:6).

Many people blame children for either being abused or staying in an abusive relationship. However, these uninformed critics are unaware that a child victim of sexual abuse feels overwhelmed and powerless. A child has no choice about being abused, does not have the ability to stop the abuse, is defenseless against the emotional pain, and feels helpless and totally alone.

The Bible is not silent about God's concern for victims:

> *"You, O God, do see trouble and grief; you consider it to take*
> *it in hand. The victim commits himself to you; you are the*
> *helper of the fatherless...You hear, O Lord, the desire of the*
> *afflicted; you encourage them, and you listen to their cry"*
> (Psalm 10:14,17).

What Is the Typical Course of Childhood Sexual Abuse?

Typically childhood sexual abuse is not a onetime, isolated incident, but rather a premeditated plan resulting in repeated abuse by a perpetrator. While the details of each victimization are different, perpetrators follow a typical pattern of behavior: first *seducing,* then *stimulating, silencing,* and *suppressing* the child. Once suppressed, the child loses all hope.[1]

Seduction—The perpetrator emotionally seduces the child by developing intimacy, progressively building trust and giving pleasure. This is accomplished by becoming an attentive "friend," showing preferential treatment or giving money, gifts, bribes, or rewards.

Stimulation—The child feels pleasure in physical touch that seems appropriate, affirming, and warm (playful wrestling and tender touching such as hugs and gentle back rubs). Over time the child becomes desensitized and vulnerable to a progression of more advanced sexual activity. The increased physical encroachment may not be enjoyable, but the increased sexual stimulation can be enjoyable. (By God's design, the body naturally responds to sexual stimulation. While children eventually feel conflicted over the mixture of pain and pleasure, no guilt should ever be attributed to the child—the guilt belongs to the abuser alone.)

Silence—The perpetrator moves to ensure the victim's silence through intimidation and fear-inducing threats. A warped sense of loyalty has already been cultivated within the child through special attention, gifts, and privileges. Although the abuse may be a onetime event or continue for years, few victims ever tell. The destructive secret remains imbedded for years in a quagmire of ambivalent feelings such as love and hate, pleasure and shame, tenderness and terror. The victims feel rage at the reality of being in the relationship and rage at the possibility of losing the relationship. Meanwhile, abusers are keenly aware of their power over their innocent prey.

Suppression—When no one rescues the child from the abusive relationship, the child feels doubly betrayed. Any hope of ever being "saved" by anyone, including God, is destroyed. The child, feeling no choice but to bow to the supreme power of the perpetrator, slips quietly into emotional enslavement. Then, when hopelessness reigns, the soul is suppressed and the light within the spirit is snuffed out.

The Bible describes men of deception:

> *"There is no fear of God before his eyes. For in his own eyes he*
> *flatters himself too much to detect or hate his sin. The words*
> *of his mouth are wicked and deceitful; he has ceased to be*
> *wise and to do good. Even on his bed he plots evil; he commits*
> *himself to a sinful course and does not reject what is wrong"*
> (Psalm 36:1 4).

How Do Perpetrators Play "the Guilt Game"?

After an act of sexual abuse, victimizers fear being found out. They seek to shift the blame to the victim by unloading a truckful of guilt. This strategy is a game.

Most games are fun, and most games require some level of strategy. In the case of child abuse, perpetrators use one of the most powerful weapons in existence—guilt. In fact, most perpetrators possess an expertise at playing the guilt game—a game of deceit. For victims, this game is not fun; it is cruel. The Bible says, "Deceit [is] in the hearts of those who plot evil" (Proverbs 12:20).

— "If you share our secret, it will break my heart. They won't let me see you again; I will kill myself."

— "If you share our secret, Mother's feelings will be so hurt. She won't understand; she will leave us."

— "If you share our secret, your mother will divorce me. Our family will be destroyed, and it will be your fault."

— "If you share our secret, I'll tell them you wanted it, you started it. No one will believe you."

— "If you share our secret, I won't love you anymore. I will kill the family, and I will kill you."

What Are the Do's and Don'ts of Awareness?

When it comes to abuse of any kind, too many people become like an ostrich, hiding their heads in the sands of denial. Although it is terribly hard to do, facing the truth that child abuse is taking place is the first step to healing. Take comfort in the fact that "when justice is done, it brings joy to the righteous but terror to evildoers" (Proverbs 21:15).

Do's[2]
— Be aware child abuse is illegal, a crime, and must be reported.

— Be aware children are usually abused by people they know.

— Be aware children seldom lie about abuse.

— Be aware most often, physical abuse is violent, but sexual abuse may not be.

— Be aware children may deny or change their stories because of fear.

— Be aware sexual abuse is progressive and will get worse if not stopped.

Don'ts
— Don't be in denial, no matter how difficult it is to believe what you hear.

— Don't assume that if it happened only once, it is not serious.

— Don't minimize the abuse.

— Don't let the offender go without confrontation.

— Don't blame other family members.

— Don't keep abuse a family secret.

What Do You Do First?

If You Suspect Child Abuse

Seek the help of a professional who is trained to work with children to...

Verify or to relieve your suspicions
— Contact a child advocacy program to discuss your concerns privately.

— Consider having someone there do an evaluation of the child and make recommendations as to a course of action.

Further inform yourself (not in the presence of the child)
— Contact Child Protective Services.

— Contact a family attorney.

— Contact a shelter for women and children.

— Contact a pastor or spiritual leader.

— Contact the local police or a law enforcement agency.

— Contact the local district attorney's office.

> *"A wise man has great power, and a man of*
> *knowledge increases strength; for waging war you*
> *need guidance, and for victory many advisers"*
> (PROVERBS 24:5-6).

If a Child Discloses Abuse

Stay calm.

— Take time to sensitively answer any questions from the child.

— Be available to the child at all times.

— Remain with the child, and leave the child only with another adult whom you and the child trust.

— Respect the privacy of the child from those who have no need to know.

— Make no promises you can't keep, such as, "Your mom won't be angry," or "He won't get into trouble."

— Explain that the law enforcement agencies must be informed and what will happen next.

— Be prepared to provide protection, arrange for a medical exam, and obtain professional counseling. First Thessalonians 5:14 says, "We urge you...encourage the timid, help the weak, be patient with everyone."

How Do You Take Action with Follow-up?

— Take the child to a pediatrician or the local hospital emergency room for immediate examination and documentation.

— Relate why you suspect possible child abuse, and state that a child abuse case should be turned over to a caseworker.

— Ask for a copy of the medical report in writing and for copies of photographs if they are taken. (If necessary, an attorney can subpoena them.)

— Keep a paper trail of all contacts you make: calls, reports, and photographs.

— If a caseworker's file disappears, supply duplicates of your copies of photographs and reports.

— Follow up with caseworkers on a regular basis, asking about the status of the case and how you can be of assistance.

— If the local services are not responsive, keep appealing to higher authorities by contacting a state or federal agency. First Peter 2:13-14 says, "Submit yourselves for the Lord's sake to every authority instituted among men...who are sent by him to punish those who do wrong and to commend those who do right."

How Do You Surface the Secret?

Children victimized by sexual abuse are in bondage to "the secret." Revealing the truth is the only strategy for breaking the power of the secret. It involves gently drawing the child out...into the light of truth.

To open the hearts of victims, give them loving care and the compassion of Christ.[3]

— Pray for supernatural wisdom from the Spirit of God.

— Provide a safe atmosphere, away from upsetting people and places.

— Ask, "Have you been experiencing something uncomfortable or confusing?"

— Listen carefully, repeat what is said, and ask, "Did I get it right?"

— Be cautious about asking leading questions such as, "Did he do _____ to you?"

— Let authorities with expertise in childhood sexual abuse ask most of the questions to determine the truth.

— Communicate that you believe the child.

— Acknowledge that the offender is wrong.

— Give assurance that the child is not to blame.

— Confirm that "telling" is the right thing to do.

— Provide a safe atmosphere by displaying genuine love and compassion.

> *"The purposes of a [child's] heart are deep waters,*
> *but a man of understanding draws them out"*
> (Proverbs 20:5).

Give Children Permission to Say No to Adults

Many children do not know they have permission to take action to protect themselves. When it comes to sexual abuse, often they don't realize what is happening, and they become too frightened to react quickly. Because most children are taught to obey authority figures, they need to be empowered to protect themselves when an authority figure becomes abusive. The following statements can instill confidence and build assertiveness in a young heart and help the child to resist inappropriate sexual advances:

— "God loves you and made your body with a special plan and purpose in mind."

— "If you are asked to do something you think is wrong, I expect you to say no—even to an older relative or friend of the family." (Role-play saying no in a firm, assertive voice.)

— "Your body belongs to you, and you decide who touches it."

— "The parts of your body covered by a bathing suit are private."

— "Never allow anyone other than your doctor to touch your private parts, and then only for medical reasons."

— "If someone tries to touch your private parts, scream and run to a safe place."

— "If someone touches your private parts and says that it's okay, he or she is wrong! You must tell me or someone you trust."

— "If a person does not stop touching you, say, 'I'll tell if you don't stop!' Then when you are safe from harm, tell me or another trusted person about what happened."

— "If you are asked to keep the touching a secret, do not be afraid. Tell anyway."

— "If you try to report something wrong and a trusted adult does not believe you, keep telling no matter how embarrassed you feel—keep telling until someone believes you."

"If sinners entice you, do not give in to them"
(Proverbs 1:10).

In child abuse, "the secret"—knowing a child won't tell—
is the perpetrator's most powerful weapon.
God's strategy is to surface the secret…
the truth is what sets us free.

—JH

====== *Your Scripture Prayer Project* ======

Psalm 34:18

Psalm 30:2

Lamentations 3:22-23

Isaiah 43:18-19

Romans 12:19

Ephesians 4:32

2 Corinthians 5:17

Jeremiah 29:11

Psalm 107:21

Philippians 4:7

For additional guidance on this topic, see also *Anger, Depression, Fear, Forgiveness, Guilt, Hope, Identity, Manipulation, Marriage, Rejection, Self-worth, Verbal and Emotional Abuse, Victimization* and other related topics.

8

CODEPENDENCY
Balancing an Unbalanced Relationship

I t's an addiction—not to drugs or alcohol, but to a relationship. One person is perceived as emotionally weak, needing to be connected to someone emotionally strong, and one is perceived as emotionally strong, but is actually weak due to a need to be needed. Both are in denial.

Sometimes roles change, yet codependency is characterized by intense highs and lows as the pair negotiates the unbalanced relationship as though stuck on a seesaw—from one high to another...first suffocating one another...then distancing from each other...producing a destructive pattern of manipulation and control that drains life's joy and happiness. Dependency on God, not another person, is the remedy for such relationship addiction.

"Avoid all extremes"
(ECCLESIASTES 7:18).

How Do You Identify a Codependent Relationship?

You could be in a codependent relationship if you:

— Feel a loss of personal identity

— Violate your conscience

— Have difficulty establishing healthy, intimate relationships

— Struggle with low self-worth

— Control and manipulate

— Have difficulty setting boundaries

— Become jealous and possessive

— Fear abandonment

— Experience extreme ups and downs

— Have a false sense of security

— Have another addiction besides the relationship

— Feel trapped in the relationship

How Do You Overcome Codependency?

In an out-of-balance relationship, both individuals wind up in the ditch of co-dependency—a place detrimental to your relationships with God and others.

God wants you to depend on Him—to totally rely upon Him. He wants you to trust Him to meet all your needs, take care of your loved ones, and overcome destructive dependencies. Here are four sizable steps to set your feet on the path to recovery and your heart on the hope of healthy relationships.

Step #1: Confront Your Codependency

Confront the Fact You Are Codependent[1]

Admit the truth…

— to yourself.

— to a trustworthy person who will hold you accountable to change.

— to God.

> *"Confess your sins to each other and pray for*
> *each other so that you may be healed. The prayer of a*
> *righteous man is powerful and effective"*
> (James 5:16).

Confront the Consequences

Accept responsibility for…

— how your past experiences and reactions have hurt your relationships.

— the pain you have caused yourself by being jealous, envious, selfish, or obsessive.

— the ways in which your codependency has weakened your relationship with God and caused you to lose both quantity and quality time with the Lord and intimacy with Him.

> *"He who conceals his sins does not prosper, but whoever*
> *confesses and renounces them finds mercy"*
> (Proverbs 28:13).

Confront Your Painful Emotions
Understand that...

— you will have pain no matter what you choose. If you leave the codependent relationship, you will hurt. If you stay, you will hurt. Your only hope for future healing is leaving the codependent lifestyle.

— when the intensity of the relationship diminishes, you will experience emotional withdrawal.

— you will need the support of others to get through the initial pain and to help you avoid another codependent relationship.

> *"A friend loves at all times,*
> *and a brother is born for adversity"*
> (PROVERBS 17:17).

Confront Current Codependent Relationship(s)[2]
Acknowledge...

— your codependent role in the relationship, and stop relating through codependent patterns.

— your destructive behaviors, then replace them with constructive behaviors. It helps to write them down.

— the natural pain of emotional withdrawal, which is common to the healing of addictions. Focus instead on God's supernatural purpose, which is to conform you to the character of Christ.

Confront Your Codependent Focus
Stop focusing on...

— what the other person is doing. Start focusing on what you need to do to become emotionally healthy.

— the other person's problems. Start focusing on solving your own problems, and stop neglecting people and projects in your own life.

— trying to change the other person. Start focusing on changing yourself.

> *"The wisdom of the prudent is to give thought to*
> *their ways, but the folly of fools is deception"*
> (PROVERBS 14:8).

Confront What You Need to Leave in Order to Receive Healing
Leave your...

— childhood and your dependent thinking ("I can't live without you"), then enter into healthy adulthood ("I want you in my life, but if something were to happen, I could still live without you").

— immature need to be dependent on someone and embrace your mature need to be dependent on the Lord.

— fantasy relationships ("You are my all-in-all") and nurture several balanced relationships of healthy give-and-take.

> *"Wounds from a friend can be trusted,*
> *but an enemy multiplies kisses"*
> (PROVERBS 27:6).

Confront Your Need to Build Mature Noncodependent Relationships
Establish...

— several interdependent relationships, and not just one exclusive relationship.

— emotionally balanced relationships without being needy of the extreme highs and lows of codependent relationships.

— personal boundaries, saying no when you need to say no and then holding to your no.

> *"I will maintain my righteousness and never let go of it;*
> *my conscience will not reproach me as long as I live"*
> (JOB 27:6).

Step #2: Look at Your Past Love Addictions
One effective way to confront codependent love relationships is through the process of journaling. Writing things down over a period of time helps you to paint a more complete picture of what's happening, and enables you to gain insights. Start writing about your codependent relationships by putting the name of each person at the top of a separate page. Answer the following questions for each relationship:

Write out

— How did you meet and attract this person?

— How did you pursue him or her?

— How did you fantasize about this person?

Conclude by answering...

— How do you think God feels or felt about your choices?

— Realize the Lord is ready to meet your deepest emotional needs.

Write out
— How did the relationship progress—fascination, fantasy, fog, fear, forsaking, fixation, frenzy?
— How did you feel in each stage?
— How did you act during each stage?

Conclude by answering...
— How did you fail to involve God in your life during each stage?
— Realize how ready the Lord has been to intervene.

Write out
— How you became preoccupied with the relationship.
— How did you start neglecting yourself and start focusing on taking care of the other person?
— How did you come to expect that person to meet all your needs?

Conclude by answering...
— How did you start neglecting God...when did you stop relying on Him?
— Realize how ready the Lord has been to make you fruitful.

Write out
— How has each relationship replicated your painful childhood experiences?
— How were you mistreated in the relationship, and how did you react?
— How does the relationship impact you today?

Conclude by answering...
— How is God replacing—or wanting to replace—your self-destructive patterns with constructive, healthy, holy patterns?
— Realize how ready the Lord is to "re-parent" you to meet your deepest needs and heal your deepest hurts.

Write out
— How you experienced fear, envy, jealousy, abandonment, and anger in the relationship.
— How you assigned a higher priority to each person than to everything else.
— How you made them the focus of your thought life.

Conclude by answering...

— How you can appropriate "the mind of Christ" to overcome destructive feelings and live out of your resources in Christ.

— Realize how ready the Lord has been to give you His thinking.

Write out

— How do you feel about each person and the relationship now?

— How has your perspective changed?

— How did things, people, and circumstances become factors in changing your perspective?

Conclude by answering...

— How has God been involved in changing your perspective?

— Realize how ready the Lord is to complete His perfect plan for your life.

> *"Do not fear, for I am with you; do not be dismayed,*
> *for I am your God. I will strengthen you and help you;*
> *I will uphold you with my righteous right hand"*
> (ISAIAH 41:10).

Step #3: Pursue Interdependent Relationships

Develop an intimate relationship with God and form interdependent relationships with significant people in your life.

Commit to...

— becoming actively involved in Bible study and group prayer.

— reading God's Word on a daily basis and memorizing Scripture.

— finding an accountability group and a Christian "relationship mentor" who will be available to you, spend time with you on a regular basis, be honest with you, and coach you in your relationships.

Make a plan to move toward maturity.

Ask...

— God to help you discern where you are stuck in the relationship developmental stages.

— your mentor or another wise person to help you identify your relationship needs.

— your accountability group to help you establish appropriate goals for meeting your relationship needs.

Make your relationship with your parents complete.

Choose to…

— resolve any unhealthy patterns with your parents.

— not be emotionally enmeshed, needy, or controlled by your parents. If necessary, separate yourself emotionally until you can respond in a healthy way, with no strings attached.

— identify and process your "family of origin" problems, forgive your offenders, and grieve your losses. Say, "That was then; this is now."

Make a vow to be a person of integrity.

Learn to…

— free yourself of any family secrets, refusing to carry them.

— listen…say no…set boundaries…give and receive…and ask for what you need. Now practice these new, healthy patterns.

— feel your feelings…express hurt…withdraw and think about what you need to do or say. Write out your action plan, rehearse it, and do it.

Make a new job description.

My new job is to…

— discern the character of a person and respond accordingly with maturity.

— be a safe person and be present and attentive in my relationships.

— take care of myself and be responsible for myself without hurting, punishing, attacking, getting even, or lying to myself or to others.

Make a new commitment to yourself.

I will…

— let go of the old, self-centered me because I am growing into a new, Christ-centered me.

— exchange the lies I've believed about myself for God's truth about me as found in His Word.

— not betray myself by making immature choices. I will redeem my past by making good, mature choices.

Make maturity your highest goal.

Focus on…

— forming friendships where you are free to learn, grow, and mature.

— guarding your heart against any relationship that has the potential to trigger codependent tendencies.

— building relationships with trustworthy, mature Christians whose goal is Christlikeness.

"Let us throw off everything that hinders
and the sin that so easily entangles, and let us run with
perseverance the race marked out for us"
(Hebrews 12:1).

Step #4: Find Freedom Through Effective Communication

Finding freedom from codependent relationships requires communicating your new convictions in a consistent, loving, and straightforward way. The following guidelines can help:

Communicate the necessity for change.

"I realize I have been responding to you in an unhealthy way. I have been far too dependent on you to meet my needs as I have sought to meet all your needs. I am committed to healthy relationships and putting God first in my life. I know I have had negative responses to you and I will begin having positive responses by making decisions based on what is right in God's eyes."

Communicate your need for forgiveness.

"I realize I was wrong for _____ (not speaking up when I should have, not being the person I should have been in this relationship). Will you forgive me?"

Communicate your limits of responsibility.

"I feel responsible for _____. I am not responsible for _____ (making you happy, making you feel significant). I want you to be happy, but I don't have the power to make you happy."

Communicate your limits.

"I want to do _____ with/for you, but I don't feel led by God to do _____."

Communicate what release is not...and what it is.

Follow through by actually *releasing* the other person:

> Releasing you is not to stop loving you,
>   but loving enough to stop leaning on you.
>
> Releasing you is not to stop caring for you,
>   but caring enough to stop controlling you.
>
> Releasing you is not to turn away from you,
>   but turning to Christ, trusting His control over you.
>
> Releasing you is not to harm you,
>   but realizing "my help" has been harmful.
>
> Releasing you is not to hurt you,
>   but to be willing to be hurt for healing.

Releasing you is not to judge you,
> but letting the divine Judge judge me.

Releasing you is not to restrict you,
> but restricting my demands of you.

Releasing you is not to refuse you,
> but refusing to keep reality from you.

Releasing you is not to cut myself off from you,
> but pruning the unfruitful away from you.

Releasing you is not to prove my power over you,
> but admitting I am powerless to change you.

Releasing you is not to stop believing in you,
> but believing the Lord alone will build character in you.

Releasing you is not to condemn the past,
> but cherishing the present and committing our future to God.

BECAUSE OF HIM IN ME...

Because Christ was not codependent
…I will not be codependent.

Because Christ kept healthy boundaries
…I will keep healthy boundaries.

Because Christ was not manipulated
…I will not be manipulated.

Because Christ stood up to pressure
…I will not cave in to pressure.

Because Christ was not guilt-driven
…I will not be guilt-driven.

Because Christ refused to compromise
…I will not yield to compromise.

Because Christ lives in me
…I will conquer codependency!

—JH

════════════ *Your Scripture Prayer Project* ════════════

Jeremiah 17:5,7

Exodus 20:3

John 8:36

Colossians 3:13

Psalm 62:7

Galatians 1:10

Galatians 6:4-5

1 Peter 5:7

Philippians 4:13

For additional guidance on this topic, see also *Anger, Depression, Dysfunctional Family, Fear, Guilt, Habits, Hope, Identity, Manipulation, Marriage, Rejection, Self-worth.*

9

CRISIS INTERVENTION

Caring Enough to Confront

What can you do when someone you love is caught in the throes of a harmful habit, a dangerous addiction, and your attempts at reasoning have brought no change, no escape from the ditch of a destructive pattern? Originally associated with helping alcoholics, there is one technique that has often proven to be effective when all individual intervention has failed: a group crisis intervention. And the reason? *There is power in numbers!*

Typically, personal pleas and earnest appeals fall on deaf ears. Even when several people confront a person one at a time, each plea can be easily dismissed. The person to whom you are appealing may see each of you as little firecrackers who are simply popping off. But by coming together and confronting the person as a united group, you can become like dynamite empowered by God to move the immovable. The Bible lays out the plan of action for such a group intervention:

> *"If your brother sins against you, go and show him his*
> *fault, just between the two of you. If he listens to you, you*
> *have won your brother over. But if he will not listen, take*
> *one or two others along, so that 'every matter may be*
> *established by the testimony of two or three witnesses'"*
> (MATTHEW 18:15-16; READ ALSO EZEKIEL 3:18-19).

HOW TO CONDUCT A GROUP CRISIS INTERVENTION

If someone you love needs to be rescued from reckless living, consider the following crisis intervention roadmap, complete with its twists and turns. The goal isn't just getting your loved ones on the path of recovery, but steering them toward the Road to Transformation—toward Christlike maturity. Crisis intervention confrontations can address harmful habits ranging from being dependent on...

Objects: chemical addiction to alcohol, tobacco, cocaine, or sexual addiction to erotic items, porn magazines, videos, sex toys

Behaviors: inappropriate sex, spending, gambling, "love" or a "savior" addiction

Those who take the time to confront a person ensnared by a destructive habit do so *because they care.* Here is how you can help:

— *Pray* for wisdom and understanding from the Lord (Psalm 32:8; Proverbs 2:6).

— *Educate* yourself regarding the person's particular addiction or besetting sin, and explore any appropriate crisis intervention programs. Read materials on intervention and visit counseling centers and available treatment facilities (Proverbs 18:15).

— *Call* a counseling office, if needed, and ask for a referral to a Christian leader trained in crisis intervention procedures (Proverbs 15:22).

— *Meet* with an intervention specialist to plan the approach. Discussion needs to include counseling options (appropriate treatment program options with preadmission plans and procedures), insurance coverage, and the impact of counseling on both the individual's life and the lives of the entire family (Proverbs 19:20).

— *Enlist* the aid of key people (caring family members, friends, a doctor, an employer, a coworker, or a spiritual leader—especially those whom your loved one respects) who have been directly affected by the person's problematic behavior, those who can attest to its harmful effects on themselves and others, and who are willing to confront (Proverbs 14:25).

— *In absolute confidentiality* and without the person present, hold the first meeting with these key people (and possibly a trained leader). Each key person will rehearse *what* he or she will say regarding the negative impact of the person's behavior, *how* it will be said, and *the order* in which they will speak during the intervention (Proverbs 27:5-6).

— *Hold* a second meeting, this time with the person present. One at a time, each key person will express loving care and genuine concern, followed by the rehearsed personalized statements (Proverbs 12:18).

The Six *P*'s of Appeal

In making individual group crisis intervention statements, here are six key things to keep in mind.

1. *The Personal*

Affirm rather than attack: "I want you to know how much I care about you [love you/value you/believe in you] and how terribly concerned I am about you." Ephesians 4:29 says, "Do not let any unwholesome talk come out of your mouths, but only what is helpful for building others up according to their needs, that it may benefit those who listen."

2. *The Past*

Give recent examples describing specific negative behavior that you have witnessed. "You've been emotionally pulling away from me." "Last night when you failed to come home, I found the motel receipts." "Dad, last Saturday you stumbled in drunk in front of my friends." "You quit coming home after work." Proverbs 12:17 says, "A truthful witness gives honest testimony." Be brief, keeping your examples to three or four sentences (Proverbs 17:27).

3. *The Pain*

Emphasize the painful impact on you by using "I" statements. Use "feeling" words:

> "I felt truly hurt that _____."
>
> "I felt heartsick/heavyhearted/heartbroken when _____."
>
> "I feel so much sadness, such deep sorrow over _____."
>
> "My heart is aching/grieved/in agony because _____."
>
> "My spirit feels wounded/pierced/injured since _____."
>
> "I feel emotionally battered/bruised/defeated whenever _____."
>
> "I was shocked/stunned/stymied that _____."
>
> "I feel our marriage bed is polluted and I feel dirty because _____."

Proverbs 16:23 says, "A wise man's heart guides his mouth, and his lips promote instruction."

4. *The Plea*

Give a personal plea for your loved one to receive counseling: "I plead with you to get the help you need to overcome this destructive habit. If you do, you will have my utmost respect and deepest gratitude" (see Proverbs 18:21).

5. *The Plan*

Be prepared to implement an *immediate plan* if counseling is accepted: "You have been accepted into the counseling program at (location). (Names) have agreed to be your accountability partners, and a bag has already been packed for you" (see Proverbs 24:11-12).

6. *The Price*

Outline specific consequences if treatment is refused: "We cannot allow you to come home or be with our family until you have stopped (_behavior_) and have been free of it for (_name length of time_) or until you have completely walked away from this (_situation_) and stopped all contact with (_name_)."

> *"Stern discipline awaits him who leaves the path;*
> *he who hates correction will die"*
> (Proverbs 15:10).

The Don'ts of Dialogue

You can gently influence a person to want to change—not by what you say, but how you say it. The Word of God says, "If someone is caught in a sin, you who are spiritual should *restore him gently*" (Galatians 6:1).

When you conduct the group crisis intervention...

— *Don't* call names, preach, or be judgmental. "You were a totally selfish, insensitive jerk. I don't know how you can look at yourself in the mirror!"

Instead, "Last night I was deeply hurt when you (_state the person's actions_)."

> *"A man who lacks judgment derides his neighbor,*
> *but a man of understanding holds his tongue"*
> (Proverbs 11:12).

— *Don't* argue if your facts are disputed. "That's not at all true!"

Instead, "You may be right, but that is what I have read."

> *"The Lord's servant must not quarrel; instead, he must be kind to everyone,*
> *able to teach, not resentful. Those who oppose him he must gently instruct,*
> *in the hope that God will grant them repentance leading them to a*
> *knowledge of the truth, and that they will come to their senses and escape*
> *from the trap of the devil, who has taken them captive to do his will"*
> (2 Timothy 2:24-26).

— *Don't* come to the defense of the offender when others are making their statements.

"He really didn't mean to hurt you."

Instead, remain silent when others are speaking.

> *"There is a...time to be silent and a time to speak"*
> (Ecclesiastes 3:1,7).

— *Don't* accept promises with no commitment for immediate action. "I can't go to counseling now, but I promise to start next month."

Instead, only accept, "I am willing to do what you are asking."

> *"A simple man believes anything,*
> *but a prudent man gives thought to his steps"*
> (PROVERBS 14:15).

— *Don't* overreact—keep your emotions under control. You may be verbally attacked with, "How can you say you love me and do this to me!" Don't react with, "How can you say you love me and do what you have done to me?"

Instead, calmly state your position, and if again opposed, calmly repeat these same words again…and again: "This is in your best interest."

> *"Everyone should be quick to listen, slow to speak*
> *and slow to become angry, for man's anger does not*
> *bring about the righteous life that God desires"*
> (JAMES 1:19-20).

— *Don't* shield your loved one from facing the consequences of bad behavior. "I will continue covering for you."

Instead, "I will not lie for you anymore."

> *"A man reaps what he sows"*
> (GALATIANS 6:7-8).

— *Don't* give ultimatums unless you are prepared to follow through on them. If, after a short time in treatment, your loved one says, "I promise not to do it again. Just please let me come back this one time." Don't acquiesce; don't give in.

Instead say, "No, not until your counselor is convinced that you and I are both ready for you to return."

> *"Let your 'Yes' be yes, and your 'No,' no"*
> (JAMES 5:12).

At the end of the crisis intervention, your loved one will either take the advice given by immediately seeking counseling or entering a treatment/accountability program, or experience the consequences of refusing treatment.

Let the heart of this scripture be your guiding purpose:

> *"If one of you should wander from the truth and someone*
> *should bring him back, remember this: Whoever*
> *turns a sinner from the error of his way will save him*
> *from death and cover over a multitude of sins"*
> (JAMES 5:19-20).

As the sculptor uses the chisel and hammer to craft his valuable art…the Master Sculptor will use you to carve Christlike character in the one you confront.
—JH

Your Scripture Prayer Project

Ephesians 4:29

Proverbs 18:21

Proverbs 11:12

Proverbs 15:1

Romans 2:1

Mark 7:15

Psalm 139:23-24

Luke 14:11

Philippians 4:8

Romans 15:7

For additional guidance on this topic, see also *Abortion Recovery, Alcohol and Drug Abuse, Anorexia and Bulimia, Codependency, Critical Spirit, Cults, Depression, Domestic Violence, Manipulation, Marriage, Salvation, Suicide Prevention, Verbal and Emotional Abuse, Victimization* and other related topics.

10

CRITICAL SPIRIT
Changing the Heart of a Critic

Anyone with a critical spirit is an expert at *finding* fault and *focusing* on it. Unfortunately, faultfinders seldom find anything else! Piles of mud balls are strewn throughout their ditch of disapproval, and at the opportune moment...ready...aim... fire! They pop up and hurl one derogatory comment after another.

A critical spirit does not reflect the heart of the wise, nor does it reflect the heart of God. Jesus said, "Out of the overflow of the heart the mouth speaks. The good man brings good things out of the good stored up in him, and the evil man brings evil things out of the evil stored up in him" (Matthew 12:34-35).

WHAT IS A CRITICAL SPIRIT?

— A critical spirit is an excessively negative attitude with harshness in judging.

— A person with a critical spirit gives unfair criticism by faultfinding, nitpicking, carping, quibbling, and complaining.

— The Bible is clear about those who are judgmental:

> *"You, then, why do you judge your brother?*
> *Or why do you look down on your brother?*
> *For we will all stand before God's judgment seat"*
> (ROMANS 14:10).

WHAT IS A CARING SPIRIT?

— A caring spirit is a thoughtful, attentive attitude with a heart to help.

— One of the most important needs we all have is for someone to care about us, someone to be attentive to our dreams and disappointments, our joys and sorrows, our successes and failures, our strengths and weaknesses, our vices and virtues. How blessed we are when we have caring people in our lives!

— Those who have a caring spirit reflect the heart of our caring Savior.

> *"The LORD is good, a refuge in times of trouble.*
> *He cares for those who trust in him"*
> (NAHUM 1:7).

HOW DOES A CRITICAL SPIRIT DIFFER FROM A CARING SPIRIT?

Those who take a critical view of others are usually unaware of the extent of their negativity. Seeing their critical spirit contrasted with a caring spirit is most helpful.

A CRITICAL SPIRIT		A CARING SPIRIT
Condemns the person as well as the action	*Proverbs 12:18*	Condemns the action, not the person
Focuses on the faults of others	*Luke 6:41*	Focuses on self-examination
Ridicules others	*Proverbs 11:12*	Encourages others
Makes judgments based on appearances	*John 7:24*	Makes judgments based on the facts
Assumes the worst without first hearing from the accused	*John 7:51*	Assumes the best while waiting to hear from the accused
Tears others down without seeing their unmet needs	*Ephesians 4:29*	Builds others up according to their needs
Responds harshly when criticized or accused by others	*Proverbs 13:10*	Responds appreciatively without quarreling when others give advice, and seeks to correct personal misbehavior
Lacks mercy toward others	*James 2:12-13*	Responds with mercy toward others

FROM WHERE DOES A CRITICAL SPIRIT ORIGINATE?

A critical spirit most commonly is birthed in a home environment where criticism abounds, where parents model a critical spirit before their children. Then, after growing up in an atmosphere where criticism is daily fare, the child carries on this spirit into adulthood (see Proverbs 27:3).

To keep from being attacked, those who are unjustly criticized often stay on the attack. Harsh words can quickly hurt the hearts of both children and adults; therefore, as a form of self-defense or revenge, this can explain why *hurt people go on to hurt people!* [1] Jesus addresses our times of hurt and what we need to do:

> *"You have heard that it was said, 'Eye for eye, and tooth for tooth.' But I tell you, Do not resist an evil person. If someone strikes you on the right cheek, turn to him the other also"*
> (MATTHEW 5:38-39).

WHAT IS THE ROOT CAUSE OF A CRITICAL SPIRIT?

Isn't it interesting how shifting the blame to God or someone else is much easier than taking responsibility for our own wrong choices? We all have three inner needs: love, significance, and security.[2] Criticizing someone else makes us feel a sense of significance—a sense of power, at least for the moment.

Wrong Belief:

"My sense of significance is enhanced when I point out the wrongs of others. Like riding a seesaw, the more I push others down with criticisms, the higher I rise above them, and the more powerful I feel. The fact that I am right justifies my criticism of others."

However, the Bible says, "You, therefore, have no excuse, you who pass judgment on someone else, for at whatever point you judge the other, you are condemning yourself, because you who pass judgment do the same things" (Romans 2:1).

Right Belief:

"When I am critical of others, I am only exposing my own sin. God thought I was significant enough to create me with His plan and purpose for me. Because Christ lives in me, continually extending His mercy toward me, I will reflect His mercy by caring for the hearts and lives of others rather than criticizing their attitudes or actions" (1 Thessalonians 5:14-15).

HOW DO I CHANGE MY HEART FROM CRITICAL TO CARING?

Perhaps you've been convicted of caustic criticism and you no longer want to be a "ditch dweller," slinging your derogatory mud. Begin now to climb out of the ditch *one kind word at a time*...and you'll find yourself on the path to recovery and peace.

Identify your shortcomings (Psalm 139:23-24)

— Humble your heart to see your own sin, your imperfections, and your immense need for God's mercy.

— Help others see their significance in God's eyes.

— Pray, "Lord, may I see my sin as You see it; may I hate my sin as You hate it."

Practice compassion for others (Colossians 3:12)

— Look closely at the life of Christ to learn His compassionate way of confronting the truth.

— Pray that you will not be a critical stone thrower, but a compassionate need-meeter.

Draw out the heartfelt needs of others (Proverbs 20:5)

— Don't listen only to what people say on the surface. Listen for the needs and feelings beneath the surface—feelings of being unloved or feeling insignificant or insecure.

— Pray that God will give you a discerning spirit as you seek to draw others out.

Offer acceptance to others (Romans 15:7)

— Realize that everyone has an innate fear of rejection and a deep yearning for acceptance.

— Choose to be a channel through which God extends His acceptance to others.

See the God-given worth in others (Luke 12:6-7)

— Treat every person, especially the one most problematic to you, as someone with God-given worth. The truth judges our hearts, attitudes, and actions toward others.

— Pray that the Lord will not allow you to despise anyone whom He created and loves.

Praise the positives in others (Philippians 4:8)

— Avoid the temptation to try to catch people doing something wrong. Instead, comment on what they are doing right.

— Pray that you will see something positive in every person, then faithfully make that your focus.

— Pray that you would see others as God sees them and value them as He values them.

Refuse to wound others with words (Colossians 3:16)

— Consider the fallacy of saying, "Talk is cheap." Talk is costly when it tears others down. Prayerfully consider the possibility that what you are criticizing in someone may be something God wants to deal with directly, and that God may want you to pray and remain silent.

— Before speaking words of criticism, ask a wise friend to evaluate the content and tone of your words. Realize that after critical words are spoken, you can never take them back.

— Inspire those who need to change by sharing with them your belief that they can change. Encourage them by saying, "Don't give up. Trust God to guide you in the way you should go. I know you can make the right decisions. I believe you can experience God's best."

— Present your words to God as His instrument for good, and pray that He will put His words into your mouth.

See the unmet needs of others (Philippians 4:19)

— Instead of judging the inappropriate actions of others, seek to understand the need behind each action.

— Realize that people who speak forth cutting words reveal that they have unmet inner needs (for love, significance, or security).

— Realize that people don't always mean what they say nor understand their own deepest needs.

— Pray that your critics will allow the Lord to meet their deepest inner needs.

Rely on God's Word and God's Spirit for wisdom

— Seek God's wisdom by reading a chapter a day from the book of Proverbs.

— Write down every verse from Proverbs that pertains to the tongue. Check your words against this list and see if you are being wise with what you say.

— See God at work in every circumstance and trust Him for wisdom to know how to respond (wisdom is the ability to look at life from God's point of view).

— Pray that God's Spirit will teach you spiritual truths and lead you to speak these truths in love.

> *"This is what we speak, not in words taught us*
> *by human wisdom but in words taught by the Spirit,*
> *expressing spiritual truths in spiritual words"*
> (1 CORINTHIANS 2:13).

Is there anything that could totally eradicate all judgmental attitudes—every single critical spirit? Yes! If every person would live out these few words of Jesus:

"Do to others as you would have them do to you"
(MATTHEW 7:12 NRSV).

People with a critical spirit look like kids on a big see-saw.
They push others down just to elevate themselves.
—JH

Your Scripture Prayer Project

Proverbs 18:21

Proverbs 11:12

Romans 2:1

Psalm 139:23-24

Romans 15:7

Proverbs 15:1

Ephesians 4:29

Luke 14:11

Philippians 4:8

1 Thessalonians 5:11

For additional guidance on this topic, see also *Anger, Codependency, Depression, Domestic Violence, Dysfunctional Family, Forgiveness, Habits, Hope, Identity, Manipulation, Marriage, Rejection, Self-worth, Verbal and Emotional Abuse, Victimization, Worry* and other related topics.

11

CULTS

The Truth Twisters

They are subtle, secretive, and seductive, luring people away from friends and family, and *fundamental truth*. They prey on people's emotions, promising unconditional love and spiritual fulfillment. But their beliefs and practices distort what the Bible says about God and His divine purposes.

Those who are ensnared by cults wind up in a ditch of deception, thinking it is the closest thing to heaven on earth. And they believe the only people who can meet their emotional needs are their fellow ditch dwellers.

WHAT IS A CULT?

— A cult is a sect or religious system that promotes doctrines that deviate from those of orthodox biblical Christianity.

— Every cult V-A-R-I-E-S from one or more fundamental doctrines of the Christian faith:

V Virgin Birth: Jesus Christ was conceived by the Holy Spirit and born of a virgin (Matthew 1:18,23). By contrast, Mormons, for example, state that God the Father had sexual relations with Mary to conceive Jesus.[1]

A Atonement: Only the shed blood of Jesus Christ can pay the penalty for personal sin (Romans 5:8-9). However, the Moonies (Unification Church) teach that Jesus failed in His mission because He was crucified.[2]

R Resurrection: Jesus Christ was raised from the dead in bodily, physical form and was seen on earth by many (1 Corinthians 15:3-6). However, Herbert Armstrong's Worldwide Church of God taught that Christ was revived spiritually and was no longer human after the resurrection.[3]

I Incarnation: Jesus Christ, who is God, took on human form and was fully God and fully man (John 1:1-3,14) However, The Way International teaches that Jesus was the Logos—the expression of God, but not God Himself.[4]

E Eschatology: After Jesus Christ visibly returns to earth during the end times, a final judgment is a certainty, sending the unrighteous to eternal punishment and the righteous to eternal life (Matthew 25:46; Hebrews 9:27-28). However, Jehovah's Witnesses teach that only 144,000 Jehovah's Witnesses will inhabit heaven.[5]

S Scripture: The Bible is wholly inspired by God, without error in the original writings and revelation, and is the only authority for righteous living (Proverbs 30:5-6; 2 Timothy 3:16). However, Mormons ascribe to four holy books, with the Book of Mormon as the most "correct" book (not the Bible).[6]

WHAT CHARACTERIZES CULT LEADERS AND THEIR FOLLOWERS?

Leaders believe they alone have the one true message from God[7] and...

— *present* themselves as infallible authorities, requiring absolute loyalty.

— *persuade* through their strong, charismatic personalities.

— *prohibit* individual freedom, expecting unquestioned obedience.

— *promote* themselves as divine or as God's sole agent on earth.

— *possess* "new truth" from God, while perverting biblical truth.

— *provide* simplistic answers for complex problems.

> *"Such men are false apostles, deceitful workmen,*
> *masquerading as apostles of Christ. And no*
> *wonder, for Satan himself masquerades as an angel*
> *of light. It is not surprising, then, if his servants*
> *masquerade as servants of righteousness"*
> (2 CORINTHIANS 11:13-15).

Followers believe their leader alone has the one true message from God and...

— *follow* the cult leader blindly.

— *forfeit* individual freedom.

— *forsake* friends and family to have a new "family."

— *fear* punishment for not conforming to legalistic rules and regulations.

— *feel* misunderstood and persecuted by the outside world.

— *forego* reason for emotion.

*"The time will come when men will not put up
with sound doctrine. Instead, to suit their own desires,
they will gather around them a great number of
teachers to say what their itching ears want to hear"*
(2 Timothy 4:3).

Who Are Most Susceptible to Being Lured?

People who join cults do not knowingly submit their lives to deceit and error. They are typically intelligent, sincere seekers of truth caught in the snare of subversive spiritual forces. The following characteristics describe the average cult member:[8]

— between ages 18 and 28

— mostly males

— middle to upper class

— underachiever

— idealistic

— looking for meaning
and purpose of life

— low self-esteem

— alienated from family

— experiencing a crisis

— disillusioned with life

— naive or too trusting

— religious background, but
not spiritually grounded

*"He feeds on ashes, a deluded heart misleads him;
he cannot save himself, or say, 'Is not this thing
in my right hand a lie?'"*
(Isaiah 44:20).

How Can You Help?

Reaching Out with Care

Merely loving those who are lost will not get them through the gates of heaven, and neither will a dissertation on doctrine. Frequently a person is drawn into a cult assuming it will meet his or her emotional needs. Respect, replant, and restore are the three junctures on the path of recovery for those entrenched in the ditch of deception. If you care about loved ones caught in the clutches of a cult, realize their first need is to know you *respect* them as creations of God with God-given worth. Only then will the soil of their hearts be prepared for you to *plant* seeds of doubt and to replace false teaching with truth. Ultimately, through gentle reasoning and persistent prayer, God can use you to help open a closed heart, clear a confused mind, *restore* a damaged relationship, and set someone soundly on the Road to Transformation.

"In your hearts set apart Christ as Lord.
Always be prepared to give an answer to everyone who
asks you to give the reason for the hope that you have.
But do this with gentleness and respect"
(1 Peter 3:15).

Reaching Out Through Relationship

Respect—Take Time to Listen

As long as your loved one is in the cult, make every effort to reestablish and remain in contact. With the following guidelines, build a bridge that won't blow up into what could be a very volatile situation.

> *Don't* criticize or make fun of the cult leader and members—this only causes defensiveness.
>
> Be polite when reference is made to the cult and its leaders.
>
> *Don't* project negative emotions or get into arguments, in spite of your own discomfort.
>
> Allow Christ to control your anger, responding always with kindness.
>
> *Don't* interrupt, regardless of your disapproval. Instead, listen without interrupting.
>
> Listen more than you talk.

(Re)Plant—Sow Seeds of Doubt[9]

Plant seeds of doubt in the mind of your loved one—which, in time, can grow into bigger doubts. This helps the person become more objective and see errors in the cult's teaching. God's Spirit can cultivate the smallest seed to convict the cult member that something is terribly wrong.

> *Plant* the realization that joy does exist outside the cult.
>
> Send a scrapbook of family pictures to bring to mind happy memories prior to your loved one's cult involvement.
>
> *Plant* specific proof of cult errors.
>
> For example, show photocopies from the Jehovah's Witnesses' own writings, of prophecies they made that have gone unfulfilled.
>
> *Plant* a fresh awareness that your loved one's freedom to choose has been stifled.

Sincerely say, without sarcasm, "It's a shame that you don't have the freedom to decide for yourself when you can visit us."

Plant factual information about the cult—facts about which your loved one is probably unaware.

Provide proof of the facts about the cult or cult leader with articles from the Internet, newspapers, or magazines, or from a well-documented book.

Plant examples of inconsistencies within the cult's doctrinal teachings.

Ask, "Is it true that Mormons teach 'as man now is God once was'?"[10] Show passages from the Book of Mormon (Mormon 9:9-11 and Moroni 7:22; 8:18) that say God doesn't change. Ask, "Please help me understand which you think is incorrect—the Mormon teaching, or the Mormon writings?"

Restore[11]—Regain What Has Been Lost

Goal #1: Regain basic cognitive skills lost during cult involvement

Duration: From up to six or eight weeks after leaving a cult

Tasks:

To recall memory—the past is often suppressed.

— Recall in detail positive events prior to cult involvement.

— Talk about positive childhood friends and family members.

— Laugh about previous humorous situations. Don't "walk on eggshells."

To speak clearly—speech patterns are often broken.

— If the person's voice trails off, say, "Would you please repeat that?"

— If the person uses abstract global terms, ask what the terms mean for today.

— If the person's focus is on the future, talk about current events.

To make decisions—decision-making is discouraged or denied.[12]

— Discourage blind conformity by assuring the person of his or her ability to make good individual choices, rather than simply conforming to others.

— Encourage the person to choose his or her own food from the menu.

— Let the person choose and purchase his or her own clothing.

> *"If someone is caught in a sin,*
> *you who are spiritual should restore him gently"*
> (GALATIANS 6:1).

Goal #2: Regain a sense of God-given worth and individuality lost during cult involvement

Duration: From the first or second month to as long as 24 months

Tasks:

To diffuse rage—Unhealthy regression when in the cult can swing to unhealthy aggression after leaving the cult, with violent verbal attacks toward the cult and its leaders.

— *Help the person focus* not only on the wrong doctrines and deeds of the cult, but also on the inner unmet needs of individuals in the cult.

— *Help the person see* that polarized black-and-white thinking was the breeding ground for his or her initial cult involvement. The initial teachings of a cult must contain some grains of truth, or no one would be drawn into it.

— *Help the person list* ten important lessons he or she has learned as a result of his or her cult experience.

> *"Man's anger does not bring about the*
> *righteous life that God desires"*
> (JAMES 1:20).

To dispel taboos—the ex-cult member's attitudes and beliefs can still be in bondage to the cult's taboos.

— *Regarding the physical body*

Ask, "Since God created our physical bodies and He called everything He created 'very good,' do you think it wise to agree with those who say our bodies are bad (or mere illusions)?"

> *"God said, 'Let us make man in our image,*
> *in our likeness, and let them rule over the fish of the sea*
> *and the birds of the air, over the livestock, over all the*
> *earth, and over all the creatures that move along the*
> *ground.'...God saw all that he had made,*
> *and it was very good"*
> (GENESIS 1:26,31).

— *Regarding sex*

Say, "God created the marriage covenant, and He also created sexual intimacy for bonding in marriage. Do you think it wise to be against what God chooses to bless?"

> *"For this reason a man will leave his father and mother*
> *and be united to his wife, and they will become one flesh"*
> (Genesis 2:24; read also 1 Corinthians 7:3-5).

— *Regarding exclusion of certain foods*

Ask, "Since the New Testament repealed the dietary law and Jesus declared 'all foods clean,' do you really think it wise to place human teaching above God's teaching?" (Read Mark 7:19; Acts 10:11-16; Colossians 2:16.)

> *"It is for freedom that Christ has set us free.*
> *Stand firm, then, and do not let yourselves*
> *be burdened again by a yoke of slavery"*
> (Galatians 5:1).

To decrease insecurity—ex-cult members usually feel as though they are living in a goldfish bowl and that the eyes of all the family are on them.

— *Let go* of overprotective behavior even though your heart still fears that your loved one may return to the cult.

— *Initiate* the subject and ask, "Before you joined the cult, did you feel smothered and in need of a safe place to escape?"

— *Ask,* "Now what can I do differently that would be meaningful to you?"

> *"The purposes of a man's heart are deep waters,*
> *but a man of understanding draws them out"*
> (Proverbs 20:5).

To direct aimlessness—when a cult member finally leaves a group that seemed to have all the answers, finding purpose in life can present a huge internal battle.

— *Help the person establish* a purpose for living.

> "Let's make a short list of God's purposes for your life. Let's especially look at your God-given responsibilities."

— *Help the person establish* future-oriented goals, both short-term and long-term.

> "Let's list a few six-month goals and five-year goals to help you fulfill each of these purposes."

— *Help the person establish* priorities.

> "Let's make a plan with action steps for you to accomplish your goals. What do you think should come first?"

— *Help the person establish* a Christ-centered spiritual family.

"Let's establish some criteria and set a goal for finding a healthy, Bible-believing church. I would enjoy helping you find a safe and supportive family of believers."

"Let us consider how we may spur one
another on toward love and good deeds"
(Hebrews 10:24).

Bank tellers learn to spot counterfeits not by studying fake bills
but by continually handling real bills.
The best deterrent from being deceived by a cult is knowing biblical doctrine:
It's easy to detect the false when you know the true.
—JH

Your Scripture Prayer Project

2 Timothy 2:15

Proverbs 16:25

Proverbs 30:5-6

Ephesians 2:8-9

John 1:3,14

Proverbs 19:2

Hebrews 9:27

John 14:6

Matthew 7:15

For additional guidance on this topic, see also *Codependency, Crisis Intervention, Hope, Identity, Occult, Salvation.*

12

DATING

The Delights and Dangers of Dating

For some, dating is daunting...and for others, it's downright fun. It provides interaction with the opposite sex and the opportunity to come into contact with potential marriage partners. But dating is as much about you as it is your dating prospects, and serves as an ideal time for developing Christlike character and preparing you for a lifelong marriage commitment.

But there is a "ditch of dating." Nothing can soil a pure dating relationship like immorality—and its consequences can make for a steep climb out of the ditch.

> *"So they are no longer two, but one. Therefore what*
> *God has joined together, let man not separate"*
> (Matthew 19:6).

What Characteristics Should You Look for in a Prospective Date?

Place a check mark (√) beside each character trait present within the person you feel drawn to date.

Does your prospective date...

☐ Demonstrate wisdom and discernment?

☐ Have a heart to do what is best for you?

☐ Possess a sensitive conscience in regard to right and wrong?

☐ Refuse to use you or others to gain status?

☐ Have the approval of the significant people in your life?

☐ Have a reputation of keeping commitments?

☐ Display follow-through in meeting obligations?

- ☐ Show respect toward authority?
- ☐ Have a positive outlook on life?
- ☐ Exercise discipline and self-control?
- ☐ Manage money well?
- ☐ Maintain eye contact when talking with people?
- ☐ Interact courteously with others?
- ☐ Have an active Bible study and prayer life?

> *"Do not be misled: 'Bad company corrupts good character'"*
> (1 CORINTHIANS 15:33).

HOW DO YOU DEVELOP GODLY DATING PRACTICES?

Dating can be an exciting adventure of the heart leading to marriage, but hearts are fragile and should be treated with care. Protect your heart because it belongs to God first, then you. When a dating friendship grows into a love relationship, your heart still belongs to God, but you also place it in someone else's hands. So it is critical to:

Be Wise. Ask the Lord to...

— guide your decision to date.

— guide the decisions of your date.

— guard your heart, mind, body, and soul during the dating process.

— confirm your choices with His peace as you date. (If you don't have His peace about the person you are dating, don't go out with that person again.)

Be Safe. You deserve to be treated well and to be safe.

— Allow trusted friends, family, and coworkers to introduce you to someone who shares your beliefs and interests.

— When you begin to date, spend time together with a group as you get to know each other.

— Meet in public places as you build trust and observe character. (If you do not respect the character of the one you are dating, then don't go out with that person again.)

Be Real. Just as you want to get to know the person you are dating, be honest and real with your date.

Be Honest. Talk to your date about what you don't enjoy or appreciate.

— Don't "go along with whatever" just because it's what your date wants.

— Don't cave in to peer pressure. Be willing to say no when you know you should say no. (If you respectfully speak the truth, in the end, you will earn respect.)

> *"Do not conform any longer to the pattern of this world,*
> *but be transformed by the renewing of your mind"*
> (ROMANS 12:2).

WHAT ARE THE DO'S AND DON'TS OF DATING?

Don't focus on romance.
    Do focus on cultivating a solid friendship.

Don't lie if you don't want to accept a date.
    Do be under the authority of your parents (if living at home).

Don't confuse lust for love.
    Do reflect Christian values on your dates.

Don't date non-Christians.
    Do trust God's plan for your life.

Don't wait to determine your standards.
    Do become a good and honorable date.

Remember that your identity is not to be lost in someone else. You can be joined to another and still be a separate person. You are *one* person, and one is not a fraction—it is a *whole* number. You are complete in Jesus Christ.

WHAT IF YOU WANT TO DATE BUT MUST WAIT?

Put God in charge of the timing and pace of your dating life. Consider making this the prayer of your heart:
Heavenly Father...
— I will refuse to be desperate to find someone to date.
— I will wait on Your timing and person to date.
— I will not lower my criteria as I evaluate a prospective date.
— I will use this time to listen intently for Your voice to lead me.
— I will focus on what I *do* have, not what I *don't* have.
— I will be grateful for Your unconditional love for me.
— I will remember that I am *not* alone, unloved, or forgotten.
— I will not put my life on hold until I begin to date.

— I will look for ways that I can bless others.

"I have stilled and quieted my soul;
like a weaned child with its mother,
like a weaned child is my soul within me"
(PSALM 131:2).

HOW DO YOU BREAK OFF A DATING RELATIONSHIP?

Often, only one person realizes the dating relationship isn't working and must assume responsibility for stopping the relationship. In doing so, remember Paul's admonition in Ephesians 4:15 about "speaking the truth in love."[1]

How to Handle a Breakup

If you are the initiator of a breakup:	If you are the recipient of a breakup:
Be honest and direct. Don't lie about the reasons. The other person might try to fix any of your phantom, made-up causes.	Listen, but don't take everything that is said literally. Look at the big picture. Evaluate the validity of the reasons given.
Don't prolong the agony. Don't dangle hopes of reconciliation if you honestly don't see it happening.	Don't plead, beg, or grovel, but accept the breakup. Ask direct, honest questions. You may need to reevaluate how to conduct yourself in any future dating relationships.
Pray and think through what you are going to say. Don't use clichés such as, "It's not about you; it's about me." But don't blame the other person, either.	Don't threaten or raise your voice. Listen and think through what is being said before you respond.
Keep it as short and unemotional as possible. Sincerely apologize for any pain that might result from the discontinuance of the relationship.	Take time to think and pray before saying or doing anything. If you have offended the other person, offer a sincere apology and ask for forgiveness.
Do not check up on the other person if you have no intention of trying to reconcile.	Do not gossip about the other person.
Pray for your ex-dating partner and ask for wisdom, understanding, and discernment in choosing future dating partners.	If you've been wronged, forgive your ex-dating partner and release the person to the Lord. Ask the Lord to bless the person and to use the breakup to draw you closer to Him and teach you useful insights.

How Do You Maintain Purity over Passion?

Make purity in the dating relationship a top priority. Otherwise, it is far too easy to be misled by looks, propelled by insecurity, or lured by lust, and end up with a used body, a guilty conscience, and a broken heart.

If you've been thus misled and find yourself in the dating ditch, know that *it is not God's will* for you to give in to impurity. Instead, confess your sexual sins and ask God to guide you onto the pathway of purity.

The following acrostic, P-U-R-I-T-Y, can help you maintain a godly perspective in your dating relationship:

P Prioritize God's standard for purity in your dating.

— Make a commitment to God and each other to maintain sexual purity until marriage. Pray about this daily, and before each date. Should you ever violate this commitment, have an understanding that you will break off the relationship and seek individual counsel and healing.

— Have same-sex "his and her" accountability partners who ask explicit questions about sexual purity on a weekly basis, or more often, if needed.

> *"Marriage should be honored by all, and the*
> *marriage bed kept pure, for God will judge the*
> *adulterer and all the sexually immoral"*
> (Hebrews 13:4).

U Undertake personal accountability for how you treat your date's body.

— Avoid sensual kissing before marriage. This type of kissing is a form of sexual foreplay that prepares the body and soul for further sexual activity because of its highly arousing nature.

— Don't touch a body part on your date that a full-body swimsuit would cover.

> *"In this matter no one should wrong his brother or take*
> *advantage of him. The Lord will punish men for all*
> *such sins, as we have already told you and warned you"*
> (1 Thessalonians 4:6).

R Refrain from activities that violate God's standard by arousing sexual desires. If these standards are violated, repent and recommit to sexual purity.

— Don't use language that could arouse sexual desire—even when "joking"—and avoid discussing sexually oriented subjects.

— If you travel together before marriage, arrange for separate bedrooms.

— Immediately involve your accountability partners if you find yourself slipping morally.

> *"It is God's will that you should be sanctified:*
> *that you should avoid sexual immorality; that*
> *each of you should learn to control his own*
> *body in a way that is holy and honorable"*
> (1 THESSALONIANS 4:3-4).

I Implement goals that are pleasing to God.

— Study Scripture together. Read, for example, about role models in the Bible, such as Joseph and Ruth.

— Undertake service projects that give you an opportunity to work together to help others.

— Commit to helping each other maintain balanced lives, with time for friends, hobbies, and other priorities.

> *"We make it our goal to please him...For we must*
> *all appear before the judgment seat of Christ, that*
> *each one may receive what is due him for the things*
> *done while in the body, whether good or bad"*
> (2 CORINTHIANS 5:9-10).

T Trust in God's timing.

— Remember that God's timing can differ vastly from ours.

— As you date, allow the Lord to handle any hurts and disappointments that come your way.

— Do not consider dating as a waiting game. Use your single years to build your relationship with the Lord and with others. God has not created us to live in isolation, but to be in fellowship with others. Develop a heart of love and acceptance for those whom He has placed in your life.

> *"With the Lord a day is like a thousand years,*
> *and a thousand years are like a day"*
> (2 PETER 3:8).

Y Yield your life to the Lord.

— Surrender your expectations, emotions, and will to God.

— Don't let the pounding of your biological clock block out the voice of the Holy Spirit.

— Memorize and meditate on scriptures that are related to waiting on the Lord.
— Surrender your will. Give up your demands and expectations for marriage. Instead, focus on seeking God's will.

> *"Seek first his kingdom and his righteousness, and*
> *all these things will be given to you as well"*
> (MATTHEW 6:33).

On your next date, think about your future mate
and apply God's Golden Rule:
Do unto your date what you would have someone do to your mate!
—JH

Your Scripture Prayer Project

Psalm 119:9

2 Corinthians 6:14-15

Proverbs 22:3

1 Thessalonians 4:3-4

1 John 1:9

1 Corinthians 13:4-7

Proverbs 15:22

Proverbs 16:9

Deuteronomy 31:8

Jeremiah 29:11

For additional guidance on this topic, see also *Codependency, Decision Making, Identity, Manipulation, Marriage, Premarital Counseling, Self-worth, Sexual Addiction, Sexual Integrity, Singleness.*

13

DECISION MAKING

Discerning the Will of God

H e loves me, he loves me not; he loves me, he loves me not."
   Through the ages, people have played this simple game of trying to determine whether someone loved them or not by plucking petals one by one from a daisy. The last petal supposedly reveals the answer—but what an unreliable way to make decisions!

There's probably no faster way to end up in a decision-making ditch than depending on a daisy. Wise decisions are made by discerning the will of God, and God reveals His will to those willing to do His will. James 1:22 says, "Do not merely listen to the word, and so deceive yourselves. Do what it says."

ANSWERING KEY QUESTIONS ABOUT THE WILL OF GOD

Q: Has God already determined His will for me?

A: Yes. God's will for you was prepared in advance.

> *"We are God's workmanship, created in Christ Jesus to do*
> *good works, which God prepared in advance for us to do"*
> (EPHESIANS 2:10).

Q: Can I actually know God's will for my life?

A: Yes. God desires to reveal His will to you in a personal way.

> *"The God of our fathers has chosen you to know his will"*
> (ACTS 22:14).

Q: How does God reveal His will?

A: God reveals His will primarily through the Spirit of God and the Word of God.

"The Spirit of truth…will guide you into all truth"
(John 16:13).

"Your word is a lamp to my feet and a light for my path"
(Psalm 119:105).

Q: Will God reveal the whole blueprint of my life?

A: No, only God sees the whole picture—past, present, future. Discovering God's will is scroll-like. He unrolls the scroll one line at a time.

"I will instruct you and teach you in the way you
should go; I will counsel you and watch over you"
(Psalm 32:8).

Q: Why does God's will for me sometimes include sorrow and affliction?

A: Suffering gives us compassion for others and allows us to see God's sufficiency as we learn to depend on Him.

"It was good for me to be afflicted so that
I might learn your decrees"
(Psalm 119:71).

What Decisions Are Pleasing to God?

Be assured that God doesn't play hide-and-seek as you try to discover His will. As you sincerely place His desires above your desires, He will be faithful to point the way. Let this be the prayer of your heart:

"I desire to do your will, O my God;
your law is within my heart"
(Psalm 40:8).

God blesses decisions that…

— He initiates (Proverbs 4:11).

— line up with His Word (Psalm 119:33).

— accomplish His purpose (Philippians 2:13).

— depend on His strength (Philippians 4:13).

— result in giving Him glory (1 Corinthians 10:31).

— promote justice, kindness, and humility (Micah 6:8).

— reflect His character (Romans 8:29).

— come from faith (Hebrews 11:6).

— consider the interests of others (Philippians 2:4).

— are bathed in prayer (1 Thessalonians 5:17).

TESTS OF DECISION MAKING

From God's perspective, decisions are not to be determined by random selection, supernatural events, people's opinions, delay tactics, analytical thinking, or good feelings. God wants you to measure your decisions by His standards. Rather than testing God, test yourself against the following tests. "Find out what pleases the Lord" (Ephesians 5:10).

Scriptural Test: Has God already spoken about it in His Word?

> *"All Scripture is God-breathed and is useful for teaching,*
> *rebuking, correcting and training in righteousness"*
> (2 TIMOTHY 3:16).

Secrecy Test: Would it bother me if everyone knew this was my choice?

> *"The integrity of the upright guides them, but the*
> *unfaithful are destroyed by their duplicity"*
> (PROVERBS 11:3).

Survey Test: What if everyone followed my example?

> *"Set an example for the believers in speech,*
> *in life, in love, in faith and in purity"*
> (1 TIMOTHY 4:12).

Spiritual Test: Am I being people-pressured or Spirit-led?

> *"Am I now trying to win the approval of men, or of*
> *God? Or am I trying to please men? If I were still trying*
> *to please men, I would not be a servant of Christ"*
> (GALATIANS 1:10).

Stumbling Test: Could this cause another person to stumble?

> *"It is better not to eat meat or drink wine or to do*
> *anything else that will cause your brother to fall"*
> (ROMANS 14:21).

Serenity Test: Have I prayed and received peace about this decision?

*"Do not be anxious about anything, but in everything, by prayer
and petition, with thanksgiving, present your requests to God.
And the peace of God, which transcends all understanding,
will guard your hearts and your minds in Christ Jesus"*
(Philippians 4:6-7).

Sanctification Test: Will this keep me from growing in the character of Christ?

*"We…are being transformed into his
likeness with ever-increasing glory"*
(2 Corinthians 3:18).

How Does God Give Us Guidance?

Daisies aren't the only things that can plummet us to the bottom of a decision-making ditch. Operating on gut instinct, heeding unwise counsel, and turning to supernatural phenomena all muddy our ability to make clear, God-directed decisions.

Choose to get on the path of recovery by turning only to sound biblical methods for guidance. Soon you'll have the map of Christlike maturity marking all your decisions!

*"Let the wise listen and add to their learning,
And let the discerning get guidance"*
(Proverbs 1:5).

Here are some practical suggestions regarding G-U-I-D-A-N-C-E.

G Gifts

Discover and use the spiritual gifts, talents, and abilities God has given you to serve others. Discern His direction by noticing opportunities He brings to develop those gifts (1 Peter 4:10).

— Reflect on what you really enjoy doing and be aware of weaknesses.

— Write down past accomplishments that have brought you joy.

— Ask a friend to evaluate your strengths.

U Understanding

Take time to clearly discern what the decision is about and what is involved (Proverbs 15:21).

— Do you know all the facts?

— Are you aware of the consequences of your choices?

— Is there a deadline for the decision?

I Impressions

The Spirit of God often brings conviction or establishes truth in your heart (Psalm 16:7).

— Pray for God to speak to you and confirm your impression through another source.

— Consider a time of fasting, if led to do so.

— Spend time in quiet meditation, seeking God's heart.

D Desires

When you seek to please the Lord in all areas of your life, His desires become the desires of your heart (Psalm 37:4).

— Study Scripture so you can better know God's heart.

— Pray, "Lord, may I see my sin as You see it. May I hate my sin as You hate it."

— Find and think upon scriptures that promise His strength for your weaknesses.

A Advice

God often speaks to us through others (Proverbs 19:20). Seek counsel from those who are…

— grounded in the Word of God.

— mature in godly wisdom.

— living successfully, having overcome similar circumstances.

N Necessity

Evaluate your God-given responsibilities and choose your actions appropriately (James 4:17). Exercise great care with regard to…

— choices that would keep you away from young children at home for an extended time.

— moving a long distance from a dependent elderly parent.

— taking a vacation when your employer needs assistance in a rare emergency (consider the biblical principle of a submissive attitude toward those in authority over you).

C Circumstances

Not all doors are opened by God, but closed doors can help in decision making (Proverbs 16:9).

— Consider the obvious situations and realize they are not necessarily the final answer.

— Learn to see beyond circumstances to what God wants to accomplish.

— When unsure about an open door, ask God to close the door if it is not His will for you to go through it.

E Elimination

Even though all choices may be permissible, some may not be the best (1 Corinthians 10:23). Eliminate one by one the options available to you and choices that...

place you in tempting situations.

— would not be the best use of your time.

— require skills you don't have.

WHAT IF YOU JUST AREN'T SURE?

When time has run out and you still don't know what to do, pray:

> Lord, because You know everything, You know the decision before me and the way I should go. I want only Your will. Because I no longer have the option of waiting, I will choose one option. If this decision is not right in Your sight, I ask Your Spirit in me to put a heaviness in my heart. If this is the right direction, please confirm it with Your peace. I am willing to take whatever detours You decide to put in my path, as long as I reach the destination You have for me. In Christ's name I pray. Amen.

God plays no game of hide-and-seek—
the closer you draw to the heart of God,
the clearer you'll know the will of God.
He reveals His will day by day...He unrolls the scroll one line at a time.
—JH

Your Scripture Prayer Project

Proverbs 3:5-6

Psalm 32:8

Psalm 25:9

James 1:5

Proverbs 16:9

Psalm 40:8

John 16:13

Matthew 6:10

1 Corinthians 10:31

For additional guidance on this topic, see also *Fear, Forgiveness, Grief Recovery, Habits, Hope, Identity, Illness, Manipulation, Marriage, Parenting, Worry.*

14

DEPRESSION
Walking from Darkness into the Dawn

Heavy hearts and sustained sadness are just two characteristics of depression. The psychological condition affects the whole person—body, soul, and spirit—and generates a pervasive sense of hopelessness. For those in the ditch of depression, it can feel like the walls are closing in.

But depression doesn't have to be permanent. Healing is possible, and joy can be restored.

> *"Why are you downcast, O my soul? Why so*
> *disturbed within me? Put your hope in God, for I*
> *will yet praise him, my Savior and my God"*
> (PSALM 42:5).

IS DEPRESSION THE RESULT OF SIN?

Depression is not a result of sin when you...
— *Grieve* over normal losses.

— *Experience* natural deterioration due to the passing of years—your body chemistry can change and become compromised.

Depression can be a result of sin when you...
— *Suffer* consequences of sinful choices, yet continue without change.

— *Don't* take necessary steps for healing, seek biblical counseling, memorize Scripture, read Christian materials, get medical help when appropriate.

— *Hold* on to self-pity, anger, and bitterness instead of choosing to forgive.

— *Use* depression to manipulate others.

— *Continually* choose to blame God and others for your unhappiness.

— *Are* depressed because you choose to let others control you instead of choosing to obey Christ. Allow Him to be in control of you.

What Are the Symptoms of Depression?

Depressed persons display sad, discouraged, joyless dispositions. Major depressive episodes often involve five or more of the following classic symptoms nearly every day for at least two weeks:[1]

— Pervasive depressed mood

— Diminished pleasure in usual activities

— Significant change in appetite or weight

— Fatigue or loss of energy

— Diminished ability to think clearly, evaluate, or concentrate

— Slower or more agitated movements

— Too little or too much sleep

— Feelings of worthlessness or excessive guilt

— Suicidal thoughts/attempts

Does Taking Medicine for Depression Mean a Lack of Faith?

No. Various physical conditions can contribute to depression. In bipolar and postpartum depression, a biochemical imbalance exists that can generally be treated successfully with medication. Unfortunately, many Christians fear being labeled unspiritual if they seek medical help for depression. Yet by doing nothing, they suffer needlessly.

Sometimes medication is needed for a period of time to "level out" mountainous swings so those in the throes of depression can see truth and walk on level ground. Ezekiel 47:12 explains that God made "leaves for healing." Medicine is biblical. However, medicine should be used not to numb pain or to escape it, but to help a person process pain. Also, medication should be the last avenue tried only after all other steps have been taken—and always in conjunction with counseling.

What Are Physical Contributors to Depression?[2]

Hormonal imbalance: Depression can be caused by a chemical imbalance in the brain. Hormonal changes during puberty, postpartum (after childbirth), and perimenopause (around menopause) can lead to depression.

Medications and drugs: Certain legal and illegal drugs can cause depression, such as analgesics, antidepressants, steroids, contraceptives, and cardiac medications.

Chronic illnesses: Medical problems such as a thyroid deficiency and even a bout with the flu can cause chemical imbalances in the brain, which can cause depression.

Melancholy temperament: Orderly, gifted, and creative, the person with a melancholy temperament can, at the same time, be moody, overly sensitive, and self-deprecating. Because they are analytical, critical, and hard to please, they can take everything too seriously—too personally—and quickly become depressed.

Improper food, rest, exercise: A deficiency in the physical basics of life can contribute to a chronic sense of fatigue, lack of energy, and social withdrawal.

Genetic vulnerability: Based on statistical data, those with family members who suffer from depression are two times more vulnerable to depression than those with no family history of depression.[3] Likewise, "50% of those with bipolar have at least one parent with the disorder."[4]

If you are concerned about depression, learn what you can about your family history and treatment options.

> *"A simple man believes anything,*
> *but a prudent man gives thought to his steps"*
> (PROVERBS 14:15).

WHAT ARE EMOTIONAL CONTRIBUTORS TO DEPRESSION?

Some people say, "Depression is anger turned inward." This is not always true, but is true when anger *is repressed.* Repression occurs when unacceptable desires and emotions are blocked from a person's awareness and left to operate in the unconscious mind.[5] This stuffed or swallowed anger causes masked depression and keeps underlying bitterness from being exposed. Bitterness is a major cause of depression.

> *"Each heart knows its own bitterness,*
> *and no one else can share its joy"*
> (PROVERBS 14:10).

Are you repressing anger over the loss of...

...a loved one, expectations, self-esteem, respect for others, control, health or abilities, possessions, personal goals? If so, read Ephesians 4:31: "Get rid of all bitterness, rage and anger, brawling and slander, along with every form of malice."

Are you suppressing fear of...

...losing a job, abandonment, dying, growing old, empty nest, being alone, failure, rejection? If so, read Isaiah 41:10: "Do not fear, for I am with you; do not be dismayed, for I am your God. I will strengthen you and help you; I will uphold you with my righteous right hand."

Are you internalizing stress over...

...work difficulties, financial obligations, relocation, family responsibilities, marital problems, troubled child, workload, alcoholic spouse? If so, read 1 Peter 5:7: "Cast all your anxiety on him because he cares for you."

Even our deep disappointments must be resolved or our bitterness will cause trouble. Unresolved anger and bitterness can hurt those who are close to us.

> *"See to it that no one misses the grace of God and that no*
> *bitter root grows up to cause trouble and defile many"*
> (HEBREWS 12:15).

ARE THERE SPIRITUAL CONTRIBUTORS TO DEPRESSION?

Disobedience and guilt provide enough fertile seed to turn any white cloud into a dark storm.

> *You can't* harbor the guilt of displeasing God and still experience the full joy of His salvation.
>
> *You can't* withstand the schemes and attacks of the enemy without knowing and appropriating the Word of God.

Unless you apply the remedy of confession and repentance—a change of mind and a change of direction—you may find depression sweeping over your soul and spirit, and, like the disobedient Israelites, "you will find no repose, no resting place for the sole of your foot. There the LORD will give you an anxious mind, eyes weary with longing, and a despairing heart" (Deuteronomy 28:65).

When you ask God to forgive your sins through the power of Jesus' death and resurrection, He becomes your forever Savior.

> *You can't* lose your relationship with Him, no matter what you do, think, or feel.
>
> *You can't* destroy what God protects, and He is the One who secures your salvation and guards it.

At times, you will be disobedient and need to confess and repent. This is not a renewing of your salvation, but a maintaining of your relationship with the Lord. On the other hand, if you've never confessed your sins and asked Jesus to become your Savior...

You can't know you will spend eternity in heaven.

You can't know true joy in this life.

True joy from God is greater than a life without struggle. It's a peace that remains when life falls apart. It's an assurance deep within that enables you to find satisfaction in Him, to trust in His sovereignty through the most harrowing storm. This is possible because God, and no one and nothing else, becomes your greatest delight. And right now, He wants to share this joy with you.

> *"As the Father has loved me, so have I loved you. Now*
> *remain in my love...I have told you this so that my joy*
> *may be in you and that your joy may be complete"*
> (JOHN 15:9,11).

WHAT CAN HELP DEFEAT DEPRESSION?

Allow the light of God's love to permeate your "ditch of darkness" and guide you to the Road to Transformation. Here are the steps you can take to C-O-N-Q-U-E-R depression:

C Confront any loss in your life, allowing yourself to grieve and be healed.

> *"[There is] a time to weep and a time to laugh,*
> *a time to mourn and a time to dance"*
> (ECCLESIASTES 3:4).

O Offer your heart to God for cleansing and confess your sins.

> *"If we claim to be without sin, we deceive ourselves*
> *and the truth is not in us. If we confess our sins,*
> *he is faithful and just and will forgive us our*
> *sins and purify us from all unrighteousness"*
> (1 JOHN 1:8-9).

N Nurture thoughts that focus on God's great love for you.

> *"I have loved you with an everlasting love; I*
> *have drawn you with loving-kindness"*
> (JEREMIAH 31:3).

Q Quit negative thinking and negative self-talk.

> *"Whatever is true, whatever is noble,*
> *whatever is right, whatever is pure, whatever is lovely,*
> *whatever is admirable—if anything is excellent or*
> *praiseworthy—think about such things"*
> (PHILIPPIANS 4:8).

U Understand God's eternal purpose for allowing personal loss and heartache.

> *"We know that in all things God works for the*
> *good of those who love him, who have been called*
> *according to his purpose"*
> (ROMANS 8:28).

E Exchange your hurt and anger for thanksgiving, and give thanks even when you don't feel thankful.

> *"Give thanks in all circumstances,*
> *for this is God's will for you in Christ Jesus"*
> (1 THESSALONIANS 5:18).

R Remember that God is sovereign over your life, and He promises hope for your future.

> *"For you have been my hope, O Sovereign LORD,*
> *my confidence since my youth"*
> (PSALM 71:5).

HOW CAN YOU HELP A DEPRESSED PERSON?

Following are suggestions for how you, one gentle tug at a time, can begin helping your loved one out of the ditch of depression.

— Learn all you can about depression—read books, watch videos, attend seminars (see Proverbs 23:12).

— If suicide is a concern, ask, "Are you thinking about hurting yourself or taking your life?" The person may get mad, but it's better to have a *mad* friend than a *dead* friend (see Proverbs 18:21). (For more on this, see Suicide Prevention on page 395.)

— Take all suicide and self-injury threats seriously. Fifteen percent of those who are depressed ultimately kill themselves[6] (see Proverbs 18:4).

— Be an accountability partner and say, "I'm with you in this, and I won't abandon you" (see Ecclesiastes 4:9).

— Initiate dialogue regularly through frequent phone calls and intentional contact (see Proverbs 16:21).

— Listen and hear the person's pain. Listening affirms the person's value (see James 1:19).

— Talk about depression. Talking helps remove the stigma of depression (see Proverbs 25:11).

— Verbally encourage the person sincerely and often (see 1 Thessalonians 5:11).

— Realize the power of touch, such as a hand on the shoulder or appropriate hugs and kisses (see 1 Peter 5:14).

— Play inspirational praise music to lift spirits. Music is therapeutic (see Ephesians 5:19).

— Bring laughter into the person's life—through fun notes and cards, videos, movies, and people (see Proverbs 17:22).

— Provide "nutritional therapy." For example, vitamins B-6 and E, calcium, magnesium, and folic acid are helpful for combating depression. Ask your doctor for more information (see Ezekiel 47:12).

— Help the person set small, daily goals that require minimum effort, and check on his or her progress regularly (see Proverbs 13:4).

— Enlist help from other family and friends. Be specific about concerns (see Galatians 6:2).

— We may never understand it all, but we can know this:

> *"Though he brings grief, he will show compassion,*
> *so great is his unfailing love. For he does not willingly*
> *bring affliction or grief to the children of men"*
> (LAMENTATIONS 3:32-33).

When your heart feels weary and deeply pressed down,
let the weight of your depression press you closer to God.
—JH

Your Scripture Prayer Project

Psalm 130:5

Psalm 42:11

Psalm 54:4

Proverbs 15:22

Philippians 4:8

Isaiah 43:2

Philippians 4:6-7

Job 6:10

James 1:12

Jeremiah 29:11

For additional guidance on this topic, see also *Anger, Codependency, Critical Spirit, Dysfunctional Family, Evil and Suffering, Fear, Forgiveness, Grief Recovery, Guilt, Hope, Identity, Illness, Marriage, Rejection, Self-worth, Victimization, Worry.*

15

DOMESTIC VIOLENCE

Assault on a Woman's Worth

D omestic violence is devastating. While abusive acts are committed by both men and women, approximately 95 percent of domestic violence victims are women. And many of these women blame themselves for the abuse, which further fuels the cycle of violence. Domestic violence refers to a pattern of coercive and violent behavior exercised by one adult in an intimate relationship with another.[1]

Many victims find themselves thrown into the ditch of domestic violence. And as they repeatedly try to escape, they're violently shoved back in to suffer more abuse. The violation of a trusted relationship produces severe pain. In the midst of it all one can find comfort in Psalm 34:18: "The LORD is close to the brokenhearted and saves those who are crushed in spirit."

WHAT IS THE CYCLE OF ABUSE?[2]

Like a volcano, abuse doesn't start with a sudden outburst of physical force, but rather with intense internal pressure in need of an outlet. Abusive patterns develop in three stages that are cyclical and become increasingly violent. Family members who fall victim to these patterns can feel traumatized by the mere anticipation of a violent eruption. Unfortunately, the escalating nature of abuse is rarely curbed without intervention and adequate accountability. Psalm 10:15 says, "Break the arm of the wicked and evil man; call him to account for his wickedness that would not be found out."

Agitated Stage: An environment of tension and anxiety marks the beginning phase of abuse. The husband communicates his dissatisfaction over something small and blames his wife. Through verbal and emotional abuse, a husband maintains *passive psychological control* over his wife and creates fear of impending disaster. During this stage many women buy into the lies spoken to them and accept responsibility for their husbands' unhappiness. Then they try to adjust their own behavior in an effort to please their husbands and relieve the tension in their homes.

> *"From the fruit of his lips a man enjoys good things,*
> *but the unfaithful have a craving for violence"*
> (PROVERBS 13:2).

Acute Stage: In this phase, the pressure becomes so intense that the abuser erupts and gives full vent to his rage. When violent behavior is unleashed, family members, outsiders, or police are often called upon to diffuse the rage. This acute stage of *aggressive behavior* doesn't last long, but over time these overpowering outbursts tend to become more frequent and more dangerous.

> *"An angry man stirs up dissension,*
> *and a hot-tempered one commits many sins"*
> (PROVERBS 29:22).

Apologetic Stage: During this "honeymoon phase," the abuser becomes contrite, and the wife feels soothed by her husband's loving actions. This temporary honeymoon phase is characterized by a dramatic transformation from being villainous to virtuous. This transformation is demonstrated by a number of the following: apologies, crying, gifts, helpfulness, bargaining, penitence, peacemaking, accepting responsibility, remorse, romance, promises, pleading. With renewed hope for change and the wife's deep desire to have a successful marriage, she views her husband's overtures as apologies and extends forgiveness. But, as with all honeymoons, they don't last, and the cycle of anger occurs again…and again.

> *"The prudent see danger and take refuge, but*
> *the simple keep going and suffer for it"*
> (PROVERBS 27:12).

WHAT PROTECTION IS AVAILABLE THROUGH THE LEGAL SYSTEM?[3]

Violent outbursts can occur at any time and can escalate when a husband senses or is informed his wife is leaving. A wife who is wise will have prepared for the worst by having a safety plan for leaving. For a detailed list of strategies and legal system information, please contact Hope for the Heart toll-free at 1-800-488-HOPE (4673) or www.HopeForTheHeart.org.

IS THERE A ROOT CAUSE FOR DOMESTIC VIOLENCE?

Some people can't comprehend the whys of abuse. Why does he do it? Why does she accept it? Within the heart of every person are three God-given inner needs—for love, for significance, and for security.[4] At times we attempt to get our needs met illegitimately. The *abuser* abuses his victim in order to *feel significant*. The *abused* stays in the abusive relationship in order to *feel secure*—either because she feels she can't live without him or feels terrified that the violence will escalate if she leaves him. God's solution is that they both need to look to the Lord to meet their deepest inner needs.

> *"The LORD will guide you always; he will satisfy your*
> *needs in a sun-scorched land and will strengthen*
> *your frame. You will be like a well-watered*
> *garden, like a spring whose waters never fail"*
> (ISAIAH 58:11).

Wrong Belief of Abusers Who Abuse in Order to Feel Significant

"She's to blame for what's happening. As head of the home, she belongs to me. If I don't control her, I could lose her, so I'll do whatever it takes to show her who's boss."

Wrong Belief of an Abused Person Who Accepts Abuse in Order to Feel Secure

"I'm to blame for what he's doing to me. If I don't give in to him, I could lose him. He is my security." Or, "If I don't give in to him, he could kill me. Pleasing him is my only security."

Right Belief of the Abuser

"I am the only one responsible for my abusive behavior. She is not to blame. Even if I lose her, I'll never lose God. He is my source of significance and promises to meet my needs."

> *"My God will meet all your needs according*
> *to his glorious riches in Christ Jesus"*
> (PHILIPPIANS 4:19).

Right Belief of the Abused

"I'm not to blame for my husband's abuse. Even if I lose him, I will never lose Jesus, who lives in me. Because the Lord promises to be my provider, I will depend on Him to meet all my needs. The Lord is my source of security."

> *"For your Maker is your husband—*
> *the LORD Almighty is his name"*
> (ISAIAH 54:5).

WHY DOES HE DO IT?[5]

— He grew up watching abuse between his parents.

— He experienced abuse as a child.

— He views her as a possession instead of as a person.

— He thinks using force is his right as a husband.

— He fears losing her.

— He blames her for his low self-esteem.

— He believes his power demonstrates his superiority.

— He wants to feel significant and in control.

— He possesses an unbiblical view of submission.

He has learned that violence works.

WHY DOESN'T SHE LEAVE?[6]

— She is terrified of her husband and what he will do if she leaves.

— She believes abuse is normal and that she must accept it.

— She is afraid he will take her children.

— She has an incorrect understanding of biblical submission.

— She is manipulated by his threats of suicide.

— She blames herself and believes she deserves to be abused.

— She feels that any father for the children is better than no father.

— She fears she can't make it financially without him.

— She has been told she is insane, and she fears that is true.

— She doesn't know there are organizations and services that can help her.

IS IT ALL RIGHT TO LEAVE A VIOLENT OR THREATENING SITUATION?

In the Bible a hierarchy of submission exists, with God being the highest authority. Scripture reveals that godly people sometimes physically separate from their ungodly authorities. Biblically, we are to submit to our governing authorities, yet David fled King Saul with God's blessing. Although David was one of the king's subjects, when Saul's actions became violent, David escaped:

> *"The LORD was with David but had left Saul…*
> *Saul tried to pin him to the wall with his spear, but*
> *David eluded him as Saul drove the spear into the*
> *wall. That night David made good his escape"*
> (1 SAMUEL 18:12; 19:10).

WHY DOES SHE LEAVE?[7]

— She finally realizes he will not change if circumstances remain the same.

— She understands that leaving may be the only way to get her husband to change.

— He is now acting out his threats of abuse.

— His abuse is occurring more frequently.

— He has begun to abuse the children.

— She wants to prevent the children from imitating his behavior.

— She has found help through friends, family, church, or professional organizations.

— She realizes it is not God's will for anyone to be abused.

— She is afraid for her life or for the lives of her children.

— She realizes there is a thin line between threats and homicide.

Is Leaving an Abusive Husband Unbiblical?

The Bible teaches wives are to submit to their husbands. So isn't leaving an abusive husband against the teaching of the Bible? No. The Bible gives specific instruction to the wife of a hot-tempered man. When she is in danger, temporary separation is appropriate:

> *"Do not make friends with a hot-tempered man,*
> *do not associate with one easily angered"*
> (Proverbs 22:24).

How Do You Build Healthy Boundaries?

Today is the day to come out of the ditch of domestic violence...*and stay out*. Allow God to help you build boundaries that will curtail codependant habits and eventually put you on the Road to Transformation, where Christlike maturity protects and takes mastery over all your relationships.

Here are practical steps you can take to nurture healthy B-O-U-N-D-A-R-I-E-S:

B Begin a new way of thinking about yourself, about God, and about abuse (Romans 12:2).

— God did not create you so that you would be abused.

— Abuse is a sin against God's creation.

— You were not created to be abused.

O Overcome fear of the unknown by trusting God with the future (Psalm 34:4). Memorize:

— Deuteronomy 31:8

— Psalm 56:3

— Isaiah 41:10

U Understand the biblical mandate to hold abusers accountable (Psalm 10:15).

— Confrontation is biblical.

— Confrontation can be used by God's Spirit to convict the abuser.

— Lack of confrontation enables abusers to continue abusing others.

N Notify others of your needs (supportive friends, relatives, or others) (Galatians 6:2).

— They must believe you.

— They must be trustworthy.

— If you leave, they must not divulge your new location to your husband.

D Develop God's perspective on biblical submission (Ephesians 5:21).

— Submission never gives a license for abuse.

— Submission is not to be demanded; it should be a voluntary deference to the desire of another.

— Submission is designed by God to be a way of life for everyone.

A Admit your anger and practice forgiveness (Hebrews 12:15).

— Confirm the hurt.

— Confess your anger.

— Choose to forgive.

R Recognize your codependent patterns of relating, and change the way you respond (Galatians 1:10).

— Don't respond fearfully, hiding the truth.

— Don't think you can change him.

— Don't take responsibility for his behavior.

I Identify healthy boundaries for yourself, and commit to maintaining them (Proverbs 19:19).

— Communicate your boundaries.

— State what you will do if he crosses your boundaries.

— Follow through if he crosses your boundaries.

For example: State firmly that the next time he abuses you, you will call the police, or he can no longer live at home, or you will leave with the children. Then follow through with the promised action.

E Ensure your personal safety (and the safety of your children) immediately (Psalm 4:8).

— Have an action plan.

— Know ahead of time where you will go and whom you will call. Have the necessary numbers easily accessible.

— Involve your church. Know, in advance, the person to contact for help.

S See your identity as being a precious child of God through your belief in Jesus Christ, an identity that cannot change, rather than your role as a wife, a role that can change (1 John 3:1).

— God chose you.

— God adopted you.

— God redeemed you.

> Is the "headship" of a husband a license to harm his wife?
> Does your head tell your hand to grab a hammer and hit your eye?
> No, your head protects your body—it matters not the price.
> So the husband as the head should protect his wife with his life.
>
> —JH

============ *Your Scripture Prayer Project* ============

Psalm 11:5

Proverbs 19:19

Romans 13:1

Matthew 18:15-16

Proverbs 27:12

Galatians 1:10

Psalm 4:8

Isaiah 43:18-19

For additional guidance on this topic, see also *Anger, Childhood Sexual Abuse, Codependency, Critical Spirit, Depression, Dysfunctional Family, Fear, Forgiveness, Grief Recovery, Guilt, Hope, Manipulation, Marriage, Parenting, Reconciliation, Rejection, Self-worth, Verbal and Emotional Abuse, Victimization, Worry.*

16

DYSFUNCTIONAL FAMILY

Making Peace with Your Past

S trained relationships…continual tension…a sense of "walking on eggshells" every time you walk in the door…

Dysfunctional families are damaging to individuality and the development of healthy relationships among its members. Sons and daughters, husbands and wives are impaired emotionally, psychologically, and spiritually by at least one person who continually demonstrates improper or immature behavior. Dysfunctional families may gather around the dinner table every night, but their table is in a ditch. Opinions are ridiculed, diversity is disdained, and more, all due to a domineering, emotionally destructive presence. God's design for the family is to be *functional,* a nurturing environment where love and respect are cultivated.

> *"He who brings trouble on his family will inherit only*
> *wind, and the fool will be servant to the wise"*
> (Proverbs 11:29).

WHAT CHARACTERIZES DYSFUNCTIONAL FAMILY ROLES?[1]

Parents

The Problem Parent…
— *engages* in some form of immature, inappropriate, or destructive behavior to the detriment of other family members.

The Passive Parent…
— *allows* the inappropriate behavior to continue, without establishing boundaries, to the detriment of other family members.

Children

The Super-responsible Child
— The *hero* tries to fix family problems and help create a positive family image with noteworthy achievements. This child receives positive attention but often develops perfectionistic, compulsive behaviors.

The Severely Rebellious Child
— The *scapegoat* draws focus away from family problems and onto himself or herself with rebellious, uncontrollable behavior. This child consumes time and energy from family members and often develops self-destructive life patterns.

The Sensitive, Reclusive Child

— The *lost child* hopes that by ignoring family problems, the difficulties will go away. This child avoids attention and is often lonely and withdrawn.

The Saucy, Restless Child
— The *clown* uses humor and antics to direct the focus away from family problems. This child is often hyperactive and usually seeks to be the center of attention.

WHAT ARE THE FOUR TYPES OF DYSFUNCTIONAL FAMILIES?[2]

The Chaotic Family
— Both household and individuals are poorly organized
— Family is plagued by problems
— Parents are inconsistent and indecisive
— Children are emotionally abandoned

Result: Family members are not connected.

Remedy: "A man of understanding and knowledge maintains order" (Proverbs 28:2).

The Controlling Family
— Structure is overly rigid
— Tone is authoritative and dictatorial
— Parents tend to be faultfinding and critical
— Children are task oriented; value is placed on their performance

Result: Family members are fearful and insensitive.

Remedy: "Fathers, do not exasperate your children; instead, bring them up in the training and instruction of the Lord" (Ephesians 6:4).

The Coddling Family
— Parental authority is lacking
— Feelings are overprotected
— Disagreements are avoided
— Children are the center of attention

Result: Family members are undisciplined.

Remedy: "He who spares the rod hates his son, but he who loves him is careful to discipline him" (Proverbs 13:24).

The Codependent Family
— Conformity is strong within the family
— Self-direction is lacking
— Parents are overly possessive
— Children are smothered

Result: Family members are insecure.

Remedy: "Love the LORD your God with all your heart and with all your soul and with all your strength" (Deuteronomy 6:5).

WHAT CHARACTERIZES A FUNCTIONAL FAMILY?

The Cultivating Family
— Structure and discipline are maintained by parents
— Individual responsibility is required
— Love and obedience to God are developed
— Children are secure

Result: Family relationships are balanced.

Remedy: "There, in the presence of the LORD your God, you and your families shall eat and shall rejoice in everything you have put your hand to, because the LORD your God has blessed you" (Deuteronomy 12:7).

WHAT DO I DO IF I RECOGNIZE MYSELF AS THE PROBLEM PARENT?[3]

Put your feet on the path to recovery and pull yourself and your family out of the ditch of dysfunction. Christlike maturity will come as you travel the Road to Transformation and as your family becomes emotionally healthy.

Give yourself time to grieve your past.[4]
— Pray for God to reveal your grief.
— Choose to be honest about your pain.
— Give yourself permission to grieve.

> *"I tell you the truth, you will weep and mourn while the world*
> *rejoices. You will grieve, but your grief will turn to joy"*
> (JOHN 16:20).

Give up your need to be controlling.
— Recognize that God has ultimate control.
— Trust in God's sovereign control.
— Submit to God's control of your personal life.

> *"Cast your cares on the LORD and he will sustain*
> *you; he will never let the righteous fall"*
> (PSALM 55:22).

Give Christ first place in your heart.
— Ask Jesus to be Lord of your life.
— Accept His forgiveness and love.
— Be aware of His constant presence within you.
— Allow Him to lead in all you say and do.

> *"If anyone would come after me, he must deny himself and take*
> *up his cross daily and follow me. For whoever wants to save his*
> *life will lose it, but whoever loses his life for me will save it"*
> (LUKE 9:23-24).

Give God thanks for your past.
— Know that God will be faithful to heal you.
— Recognize that difficult relationships mature you.
— Look for positive ways God can use the pain in your life.

> *"Give thanks in all circumstances,*
> *for this is God's will for you in Christ Jesus"*
> (1 THESSALONIANS 5:18).

Give attention to how you responded to your circumstances as a child. Were you...
— the responsible child?

— the rebellious child?

— the reclusive child?

— the restless child?

> *"The heart of the discerning acquires knowledge;*
> *the ears of the wise seek it out"*
> (PROVERBS 18:15).

Give thought to your present dysfunctional characteristics.
— Pray for God to reveal your weaknesses.

— Pray for wisdom to understand how to change.

— Pray that you will draw on Christ, who is your strength, to help you make changes.

> *"Search me, O God, and know my heart; test me and*
> *know my anxious thoughts. See if there is any offensive*
> *way in me, and lead me in the way everlasting"*
> (PSALM 139:23-24).

Give consideration to your God-given rights.
— You have the right to obey God rather than others.

— You have the right to a clear conscience.

— You have the right to follow the Word of God.

— You have the right to live in your God-appointed role.

> *"We must obey God rather than men!"*
> (ACTS 5:29).

Give yourself boundaries.[5]
— Define who you are: "I am a child of God."

— Define who you are not: "I am not a piece of property."

— Refuse to be manipulated or mistreated.

— Stop playing the victim: "As an adult, I am not powerless."

— Stop blaming others: "I'll take responsibility for my own behavior."

— Learn to say no.

> *"Am I now trying to win the approval of men, or of*
> *God? Or am I trying to please men? If I were still trying*
> *to please men, I would not be a servant of Christ"*
> (GALATIANS 1:10).

Give time to restoring healthy family relationships.

— Be the one to begin rebuilding relationships.

— Be willing to spend quality time to develop healthy relationships.

— Be generous with grace toward others whose attitudes and actions are negative.

— Be a channel of God's unconditional love and acceptance to others.

> *"If you are offering your gift at the altar and there*
> *remember that your brother has something against you,*
> *leave your gift there in front of the altar. First go and be*
> *reconciled to your brother; then come and offer your gift"*
> (MATTHEW 5:23-24).

How Do I Cultivate Healthy Family Relationships?[6]

Emphasize the uniqueness of each family member.

> *"Now the body is not made up of one part but of many. If the foot*
> *should say, 'Because I am not a hand, I do not belong to the body,'*
> *it would not for that reason cease to be part of the body. And if*
> *the ear should say, 'Because I am not an eye, I do not belong to the*
> *body,' it would not for that reason cease to be part of the body. If*
> *the whole body were an eye, where would the sense of hearing be? If*
> *the whole body were an ear, where would the sense of smell be?"*
> (1 CORINTHIANS 12:14-17).

Seek togetherness, but also encourage individuality.[7]

> *"There are different kinds of gifts, but the same Spirit. There are*
> *different kinds of service, but the same Lord. There are different kinds*
> *of working, but the same God works all of them in all men. Now to*
> *each one the manifestation of the Spirit is given for the common good"*
> (1 CORINTHIANS 12:4-7).

Maintain consistency in the messages you communicate.

> *"Out of the same mouth come praise and cursing. My brothers, this*
> *should not be. Can both fresh water and salt water flow from the*

*same spring? My brothers, can a fig tree bear olives, or a grapevine
bear figs? Neither can a salt spring produce fresh water. Who is
wise and understanding among you? Let him show it by his good
life, by deeds done in the humility that comes from wisdom"*
(JAMES 3:10-13).

Allow a generous margin for mistakes.

*"Be kind and compassionate to one another, forgiving
each other, just as in Christ God forgave you"*
(EPHESIANS 4:32).

Encourage the appropriate expression of feelings.

*"The purposes of a man's heart are deep waters, but
a man of understanding draws them out"*
(PROVERBS 20:5).

Promote and develop natural talents and abilities.

*"Train a child in the way he should go, and
when he is old he will not turn from it"*
(PROVERBS 22:6).

Require family members to take responsibility for their attitudes and actions.

*"Each one should test his own actions. Then he can
take pride in himself, without comparing himself to
somebody else, for each one should carry his own load"*
(GALATIANS 6:4-5).

Treat everyone with love and respect.

"Do everything in love"
(1 CORINTHIANS 16:14).

Nurture a dependence on the Lord.

*"Trust in the LORD with all your heart and lean not on
your own understanding; in all your ways acknowledge
him, and he will make your paths straight"*
(PROVERBS 3:5-6).

A poor background is a poor excuse for poor behavior.
With the power of Christ within you,
don't let your past control you.
—JH

Your Scripture Prayer Project

1 Corinthians 13:4-5,11

Proverbs 14:26

Psalm 68:5

Psalm 147:3

Galatians 1:10

Matthew 5:23-24

Colossians 3:13

For additional guidance on this topic, see also *Anger, Codependency, Critical Spirit, Depression, Divorce Recovery, Domestic Violence, Fear, Forgiveness, Grief, Guilt, Hope, Manipulation, Marriage, Parenting, Reconciliation, Rejection, Self-worth, Verbal and Emotional Abuse, Victimization, Worry.*

17

EVIL AND SUFFERING...WHY?

Is God Fair?

At one time or another, we have all thought, *Why? It's just not fair! God, why would You allow...?* Left unanswered or incorrectly answered, these questions often become the basis for rejecting the goodness of God or even denying His existence and can strand people in the ditch of dispair and disbelief. Eventually they become blind to the truth of God's sovereignty over evil and suffering, and His good purposes for them.

Nowhere in Scripture is the fairness of God more poignantly addressed than in the book of Job. In spite of his severe losses, Job posed a profound question—a question for all of us to consider in times of tragedy: "Shall we accept good from God, and not trouble?" (Job 2:10).

Does God Cause Evil?

No, God cannot ever cause evil. God cannot do anything that is contradictory to His character. The Bible clearly teaches that God is good. Because evil is the corruption of good, it is impossible for God to do anything evil.

> *"You are not a God who takes pleasure in evil; with you the wicked cannot dwell...Dear friend, do not imitate what is evil but what is good. Anyone who does what is good is from God. Anyone who does what is evil has not seen God"*
> (PSALM 5:4; 3 JOHN 11).

Why Should You Believe in a God Who Allows Evil?

The often-unspoken question behind this question is, Does God really care that I am hurting? The answer to both questions can be clearly seen in God's actions. God cares about your hurts to the extent that He willingly suffered to identify with you and to save you. The beauty of Christ's crucifixion is that God—on your behalf—voluntarily suffered at the hands of evil people. Although evil and pain are the result of mankind's choices and not God's, God does not subject His creation to something He is unwilling to endure Himself. When you undergo loss, rejection, illness, or pain, remember that God knows how you feel from His own personal experience, and He hurts with you. When God became a man, He entered fully into fallen humanity and thus fully experienced the suffering of humanity, except that He was without sin (see Hebrews 2:10).

Couldn't God Have Made a World Without Evil?[1]

Yes…however, God knew that a world of limited moral freedom would actually be an inferior world because virtues are defined by their opposites. A person can be selfless only if selfishness stands in opposition to it. Being selfless implies the possibility of being selfish. It is in overcoming self-centeredness that character is developed and virtue attained. Although creating a world that became corrupted by evil resulted in God sacrificing His Son in order to defeat that evil, in His omniscience God knew that such a world would be the best world in which to prepare people for the best of all worlds—heaven itself (see Revelation 21:1,3).

Why Hasn't God Destroyed Evil?[2]

Evil is based on moral right and wrong choices; therefore…

— God cannot destroy evil without also destroying the free will of His creatures.

— God determined that free will is for the greater good of humanity or He would not have made people free, especially because He knew sin would occur and result in the death of His Son.

— if God had destroyed or never endowed the creatures He loves with free will—thus making them robots—that action could not be for their greater good.

— God has already initiated a plan to eliminate evil. His solution is not to destroy evil in this life, but to overcome it through Christ (see 2 Peter 1:3).

If God Is All-good and All-powerful, Why Doesn't He Anticipate Evil and Stop It?[3]

God *is* good. He gave people free will, which is good (Psalm 92:15). God *is* all-powerful. He can do anything that is logical, but it is illogical for Him to both grant free will and constrain it (Isaiah 46:10-11). Evil and its effects (sin and suffering) are present in the world because people choose to exert their God-given free will and disobey God (see Romans 3:23).

WHY WOULD A GOOD, ALL-POWERFUL GOD ALLOW SUFFERING?

God sometimes causes suffering in order to bring about a greater good.

Jesus said about the apostle Paul, "I will show him how much he must suffer for my name" (Acts 9:16). Later, when Paul was unjustly jailed and had no ability to leave, he had the opportunity to witness to the prison guards. As a result, many Roman soldiers came to trust in Christ (Philippians 1:12-14).

God sometimes allows evil and suffering through...
 — Free will

   Job's so-called friends badgered him with continual accusations that his sickness must have been caused by his sin (Job 19:1-3).

 — Natural order (earthquakes, death, etc.)

   Job's heartache began when a messenger came to him with reports of a horribly destructive tornado that had killed his sons and daughters (Job 1:18-19).

 — Evil spirit beings

   God declared to Satan that Job was the most blameless man on earth. Afterward, Satan physically attacked Job's possessions, his family, and his physical body (Job 1:13-19; 2:7).

God always has a good purpose for your suffering.

His purposes can vary greatly. Sometimes He allows suffering to...

 — expose your sin
 — build your character
 — produce much good
 — change your perspective
 — bless your future

> *"As you know, we consider blessed those who have persevered. You have heard of Job's perseverance and have seen what the Lord finally brought about. The Lord is full of compassion and mercy"*
> (JAMES 5:11).

IF GOD IS GOOD AND COMPASSIONATE, WHY DOESN'T HE HEAR PLEAS FOR HELP?

God hears all your prayers. In fact, He knows your requests even before you ask. And He answers sometimes with yes, sometimes with no, and sometimes with wait. God the Father even said no to Jesus when He was facing crucifixion and no to the apostle Paul when he was facing a physical malady. The Father's purpose for Jesus' death was your salvation. God's purpose for Paul's physical ailment was to produce humility in Paul. Realize that God always answers your prayers according to His purposes for you (see Psalm 34:17-19).

Do People "Deserve" Their Suffering?

Many times we are not directly responsible for our suffering. In a sinful world, both good and evil people will suffer. The Bible says, "He sends rain on the righteous and unrighteous" (Matthew 5:45). If you are a Christian, you have a promise from God that your suffering here on earth will one day come to an end. Do not become bitter from the pain. Instead, put your faith in God...know that He cares...and wait patiently for His help. God is present. Nothing will happen that He won't equip you to handle.

> *"I waited patiently for the LORD;*
> *he turned to me and heard my cry"*
> (Psalm 40:1).

What Is God's Ultimate Purpose for Suffering?

Although suffering is the result of fallen humanity, God's highest purpose is to use it to conform us to the image of Christ in all we do and say. So what is God's ultimate purpose? He uses suffering for our good to make us like the only One who is truly good!

> *"Those God foreknew he also predestined to be*
> *conformed to the likeness of his Son, that he*
> *might be the firstborn among many brothers"*
> (Romans 8:29).

What Lessons Can You Learn from the Book of Job?

Although Job had been an exemplary man—God called him "blameless"—in a short amount of time, his entire life had become filled to overflowing with physical, mental, and emotional suffering. He certainly could not see "behind the scenes" of his life; neither could he fathom the future. Feeling devastated by his losses, fiercely racked with pain, feeling falsely accused by friends, and completely forsaken by God, Job considered death far more desirable than life.

> *"Why did I not perish at birth,*
> *and die as I came from the womb?"*
> (Job 3:11).

As Job passed through his severe trial, he came to the realization that God was still there, still loved him, and was still providing for all his needs. He saw beyond his circumstances and grasped a new vision and insight into the fairness of God. Instead of questioning the goodness of God by asking, "Why do good people suffer?" he spent the rest of his life humbly trusting God (see Job 46:5-6).

How Does God Use Suffering in Your Life?

Why God Allows Suffering

Understanding that God is not powerless concerning suffering, but *purposeful*, you can leave the ditch of disbelief behind. You will never attain a thorough understanding of the reasons for all the evil and suffering in this world. Yet as a Christian, you do have God's Word (the Bible), which addresses some reasons for His purpose in allowing human pain and suffering. The first clue is revealed in Genesis, where Adam and Eve live in a state of bliss, yet by their own choice defy God's only command. Does their disobedience not demonstrate that when left to its own devices, the human spirit will not surrender self-will to its Creator as long as "all is well"? This being the case, does suffering not then become a "gift" from God that allows you to experience the depth of His love that a life of ease could never conceive? Pain and suffering may take a hardened heart and point it to the inevitable truth that "all is *not* well," thus opening the door to the profound reality that nothing that happens in this life will ever compare to the happiness and joy awaiting those who become children of God.

How God Uses Suffering

To expose your sin
— Suffering *deters you from going astray* and *leads to obedience.*
— Suffering *produces repentance* that *leads you to salvation* from sin.
— Suffering makes you more inclined to *reject sin* and to resist fulfilling *your selfish desires,* and it leads to *living for the will of God.*

To build your character
— Suffering *develops contentment* when you are in need.
— Suffering *produces steadfastness,* which, in turn makes you *emotionally mature* and *morally complete.*
— Suffering *produces endurance,* which is a catalyst to *refine your character* and *renew your hope.*

To produce much good
— Suffering, as well as success and everything else that touches your life, will be *used by God for your good.*
— Suffering gives you the opportunity to *show care* to others who suffer.

— Suffering, because of the compassion it develops, equips you to *comfort others.*

To change your perspective

— Suffering can *reveal* or manifest Jesus, who is living in you.

— Suffering *prepares* great eternal glory for you.

— Suffering *creates* a hunger in you for heaven, where there will be no more death or mourning or crying or pain.

To bless your future

— Suffering for living right in God's sight *secures the blessing* of God.

— Suffering *proves your faith* is genuine.

— Suffering with perseverance results in *being blessed* with the crown of life.

Does God Care About Your Suffering?

God cares deeply about your suffering as demonstrated by the facts that…

— He encamps around you in the midst of trouble.

> *"The angel of the LORD encamps around those*
> *who fear him, and he delivers them"*
> (PSALM 34:7).

— He is near you when you are brokenhearted.

> *"The LORD is close to the brokenhearted and*
> *saves those who are crushed in spirit"*
> (PSALM 34:18).

— He keeps a record of your grief and puts your tears in His bottle.

> *"You have kept count of my tossings; put my tears*
> *in your bottle. Are they not in your book?"*
> (PSALM 56:8 ESV).

No heartache is wasted when put in the Master's hand.
When we enter our home in heaven,
we will see how our sorrows gave us sympathy…
how our tears gave us tenderness…
and our hurts gave us humility.

—JH

Your Scripture Prayer Project

Psalm 25:3

Psalm 9:16

Psalm 18:30

Deuteronomy 10:17

Deuteronomy 32:4

Psalm 145:17

Psalm 10:14

Psalm 1:6

Romans 8:28

Psalm 55:22

For additional guidance on this topic, see also *Depression, Forgiveness, Guilt, Hope, Salvation, Self-worth, Worry.*

18

FEAR

No Longer Afraid

During the Nazi regime, Hitler's minister of propaganda said, "If you want someone to believe something, you have to tell it to him over and over and over." If you are living in a state of fear, it's because you have been brainwashed with false propaganda. You're cowering in a corner, you're in a ditch filled with dread, afraid to turn around, step out, reach out, and *get out.*

Hitler's reign of terror ended years ago, and when the German people learned the truth about Hitler, they were emotionally set free.

Do you want to be set free from fear?

WHAT IS FEAR?

Fear is a strong emotional reaction to imminent danger—real or imagined, rational or irrational, normal or abnormal.

— Fear acts as a protective device placed in us by our Creator to activate all our physical systems when we are faced with real danger. Fear triggers the release of adrenaline in the body, which propels us to action—action often called "fight, flight, or freeze."[1]

— Fear is a natural emotion designed by God. However, living with a fear-based mentality or with a spirit of fear is not from God.[2]

> *"God has not given us a spirit of fear, but of*
> *power and of love and of a sound mind"*
> (2 TIMOTHY 1:7 NKJV).

WHERE DOES YOUR FEAR COME FROM?

Examining your fear, its origin, its legitimacy, and its pattern can help you understand your fear and develop a strategy to resolve it. First, go before God, who is the source of wisdom, and pray this prayer from your heart:

> *"Search me, O God, and know my heart; test me and*
> *know my anxious thoughts. See if there is any offensive*
> *way in me, and lead me in the way everlasting"*
> (PSALM 139:23-24).

Specifically identify your fear—of what exactly are you truly afraid? And then ask yourself these questions:

— Is my fear tied to recent events or did it originate from some specific situation in the past?

— Is the object or occasion of my fear a true threat or merely a perceived threat?

— Is my fear wrongly associated with an event or object that should not be feared?

— Is my fear coming from certain places, people, or things that remind me of possible fearful consequences?

— Is my present fear-based mentality persisting even though the relationship or lifestyle in which it is rooted no longer exists?

— Is the fear I am experiencing a result of faking fear for so long as a means of manipulating people that it has now become real to me?

> *"The wisdom of the prudent is to give thought to*
> *their ways, but the folly of fools is deception"*
> (PROVERBS 14:8).

What Is the Root Cause of Being Controlled by Fear?

Wrong Belief:
"I have no control over my fear. My only recourse is to avoid all fearful situations."

Right Belief:
God asks us to stand in *His strength* when we're afraid. "As I face my fear in His strength, fear will not control me. Christ lives in me, and as I focus on His perfect love, I will feel His perfect peace in the midst of every fear-producing situation."

> *"There is no fear in love. But perfect love drives out*
> *fear, because fear has to do with punishment. The*
> *one who fears is not made perfect in love"*
> (1 JOHN 4:18).

How Do You Overcome a Fear-based Mentality?

If you grew up in a home where fear reigned, you could have easily developed a fear-based mentality as a child and grown into an adult controlled by fear. At times, you find yourself feeling helpless and powerless to confront or to match someone strength for strength. You will remain at the mercy of those who are "master manipulators" with fear tactics unless you recognize the bondage you are in and accept the fact that Christ came to free the oppressed. Yes, Christ came to set you free!

> *"The Spirit of the Lord is on me, because he has anointed*
> *me to preach good news to the poor. He has sent me*
> *to proclaim freedom for the prisoners and recovery*
> *of sight for the blind, to release the oppressed"*
> (Luke 4:18).

Here's what you can do when you feel afraid of a person or a situation:

— Ask yourself if what you fear is actually likely to happen.

— Realize that fixating on your fear guarantees its repetition.

— Understand that most fears have nothing to do with what's happening now.

— Identify the past trauma(s) that first instilled your fear.

— Determine how current the fear is that you are presently feeling. Ask yourself:

  • What past fear am I bringing into the present?

  • When did this fear first begin?

  • How old am I emotionally when I am feeling this fear?

  • Where am I when I am feeling this fear?

  • What is going on when I am feeling this fear?

  • How is this fear affecting my life now? What is it costing me?

— Tell yourself, "I will not let this fear run my life. I will not let past fears control me."

— Repeat this phrase over and over: "That was then, and this is now. That was then, and this is now."

— Determine to get out of the grip of fear.

— Do what it takes to control your fear and to change from being fearful.

— Decide to live in the here and now and act in a way that is not based on fear.

— Share with a trustworthy person your fear and your plan for change.

*"Confess your sins to each other and pray for each
other so that you may be healed. The prayer of
a righteous man is powerful and effective"*
(James 5:16).

THE TRUTH WILL SET YOU FREE

Knowing the truth and then acting on the truth is critical to conquering fear. The source of truth is the One who said He was the Way, the Truth, and the Life. "Jesus answered, 'I am the way and the truth and the life. No one comes to the Father except through me'" (John 14:6). The primary resource we have for finding God's truth is His Word, the Bible. The first step in applying truth is to identify the lies behind the fears you are experiencing and to replace those lies with facts. John 8:32 says, "You will know the truth, and the truth will set you free."

— Fear: "I can't help this feeling of intense fear!"

Fact: "This feeling is a bluff to my mind and body. It is not grounded in truth."

*"Though an army besiege me, my heart
will not fear; though war break out against me,
even then will I be confident"*
(Psalm 27:3).

— Fear: "I have this feeling of doom—a feeling that I am going to die."

Fact: "The time of death is in God's hands. I will choose to trust Him."

*"Man's days are determined; you have decreed the number
of his months and have set limits he cannot exceed"*
(Job 14:5).

— Fear: "I'm afraid of what others are thinking about me."

Fact: "My peace comes from pleasing God, not in pleasing man."

"We make it our goal to please him"
(2 Corinthians 5:9).

— Fear: "I am hopeless and can never change."

Fact: "In Christ, I am a new person. Nothing is hopeless."

*"If anyone is in Christ, he is a new creation;
the old has gone, the new has come!"*
(2 Corinthians 5:17).

— Fear: "I am so nervous, I can't think clearly."

Fact: "God will guard my mind and give me peace."

> *"The peace of God, which transcends all understanding,*
> *will guard your hearts and your minds in Christ Jesus"*
> (PHILIPPIANS 4:7).

— Fear: "To be safe, I have to be in control."

Fact: "God is in control of my life, and He is with me step by step."

> *"The LORD himself goes before you and will be*
> *with you; he will never leave you nor forsake you.*
> *Do not be afraid; do not be discouraged"*
> (DEUTERONOMY 31:8).

— Fear: "I feel trapped with no way of escape."

Fact: "God always makes a way of escape."

> *"No temptation has seized you except what is common to*
> *man. And God is faithful; he will not let you be tempted*
> *beyond what you can bear. But when you are tempted, he will*
> *also provide a way out so that you can stand up under it"*
> (1 CORINTHIANS 10:13).

THE SYMPTOMS OF ABNORMAL FEAR[3]

When abnormal fear exists, the level of fear is out of proportion to the actual situation. In fact, the fear may be totally unrelated to the situation. Abnormal fear can result in a panic attack. A person experiences a panic attack when four or more of the following symptoms occur, reaching a peak within ten minutes or less. (The body cannot sustain the "fight or flight" for any longer.)

— Chest pain or discomfort (feels like you're having a heart attack)

— Chills or hot flashes (feels like you *must* get to the hospital)

— Choking sensation, difficulty swallowing (feels like your throat is closing)

— Cold hands, tingling sensation (feels like you're going numb)

— Detached sensation (feels like you're losing touch with reality)

— Dizziness, lightheaded (feels like you might faint)

— Fear of losing control (feels like you're going crazy)

— Hyperventilating, shortness of breath (feels like you're being smothered)

— Nausea, diarrhea, or abdominal pain and cramping (feels like a life-threatening disease)

— Rapid heart rate, pounding heartbeat (feels like your heart is going to jump out of your chest)

— Sweating, excessive perspiration (feels like you're a huge embarrassment)

— Terror of dying (feels like you're *sure* to die)

— Trembling or shaking (feels like you're doomed)

With abnormal fear you're not as afraid of the object of your fear as the symptoms of that fear.[4] And, indeed, your fear is great. You experience the same feelings Job did: "Terrors overwhelm me; my dignity is driven away as by the wind, my safety vanishes like a cloud" (Job 30:15).

WHAT TRIGGERS FEAR?[5]

Perceived Threat to Security

— Financial security: "If I don't do well on this presentation, I might lose my job."

— Physical safety: "If I drive too far from home, I could have an accident."

— Physical health: "If I'm not careful about what I touch, eat, and drink, I may get sick and lose my job."

— Possessions: "If I lose my home, I'll have nowhere to live."

Your Solution: Learn that your security is in your personal relationship with the Lord.

> *"In God I trust; I will not be afraid.*
> *What can man do to me?"*
> (PSALM 56:11).

Perceived Threat to Significance

— Identity: "If I lose my position at work, I'll lose all I have worked for. Then what reason will I have to live?"

— Self-esteem: "If I embarrass myself in front of the staff, I'll never be able to go back to work."

— Reputation: "If anyone finds out about my compulsive washing, I'll lose face."

— Self-fulfillment: "If I don't complete my education and accomplish all my life goals, I'll be a failure."

Your Solution: Understand you're so significant the Lord chose to save you.

> *"God is my salvation; I will trust and not be*
> *afraid. The LORD, the LORD, is my strength*
> *and my song; he has become my salvation"*
> (ISAIAH 12:2).

Perceived Threat to Love

— Primary relationship: "If I lose my husband, I don't know if I could go on living."

— Talents and abilities: "If I can't perform on stage, I will lose my fans and be all alone."

— Physical attractiveness: "If I start looking older and put on weight, I'll lose the affection of my spouse."

— Position in a relationship: "If I don't perform better than the newcomers, I'll lose my position of respect."

Your Solution: Learn you are loved beyond compare by the Lord.

> *"So do not fear, for I am with you; do not be dismayed,*
> *for I am your God. I will strengthen you and help you;*
> *I will uphold you with my righteous right hand"*
> (ISAIAH 41:10).

HOW DO YOU REPLACE FEAR WITH FAITH?

Know that it is not God's will for you to cower before fear, or to coddle it, but to conquer it—by faith. The path to recovery includes the steps that will move you onto the Road to Transformation.

Begin with a healthy fear (awe) of God by believing...

— God created you because He loves you.

— God has a purpose and plan for your life (Jeremiah 29:11).

— God has the right to have authority over you.

— God wants you to entrust your life to Him.

— God has the power to change you.

— God will keep your mind safe as you trust in Him.

> *"The fear of the LORD is the beginning of knowledge,*
> *but fools despise wisdom and discipline"*
> (PROVERBS 1:7).

Be *aware* living in a state of fear is not part of God's plan for you because fear-based thinking is...

— not trusting God.

— not appropriating the grace of God.

— keeping you in bondage to fear.

— physically, emotionally, and spiritually damaging.

"In God I trust; I will not be afraid.
What can mortal man do to me?"
(PSALM 56:4).

Be *willing* to analyze your fear honestly in order to discover the real source of it.

— Rejection?

— Failure?

— Financial loss?

"Fear of man will prove to be a snare,
but whoever trusts in the LORD is kept safe"
(PROVERBS 29:25).

Be *aware* of the power of God's love for you. It provides you...

— complete acceptance.

— a realization of your value.

— the power to overcome fear.

— true security.

"I have loved you with an everlasting love; I
have drawn you with loving-kindness"
(JEREMIAH 31:3).

Be *committed* to developing your faith in the Lord. Be...

— active in a Bible study.

— in daily prayer, truly talking with God.

— active in a local church that teaches the Word of God.

— committed to memorizing and meditating on God's Word.

— obedient to God's promptings in your spirit.

"His delight is in the law of the LORD,
and on his law he meditates day and night"
(PSALM 1:2).

Be involved with other believers. Be...

— engaged with Christians.

— willing to testify to God's faithfulness in your life.

— focused on serving others.

— aware there is a twofold responsibility (Christ's and yours) in doing anything.

> *"As iron sharpens iron, so one man sharpens another"*
> (PROVERBS 27:17).

Begin using truth from God's Word to rein in your imagination the moment it starts spinning out of control.

—"When I am afraid, I will trust in you" (Psalm 56:3).

—"The LORD is my light and my salvation—whom shall I fear? The LORD is the stronghold of my life—of whom shall I be afraid?" (Psalm 27:1).

> *"God is our refuge and strength,*
> *an ever-present help in trouble"*
> (PSALM 46:1).

Be willing to face the situations you fear through faith in the power of Christ.

— Know Christ is always ready to respond.

— Acknowledge His actual presence and seek His help.

— Give your fear to Him and receive His powerful love.

— Act in love toward others by focusing on their needs.

> *"The one who calls you is faithful and he will do it"*
> (1 THESSALONIANS 5:24).

Become free from your fear and strengthened in your faith. Become more...

— trusting.

— peaceful.

— thankful.

— Christlike.

> *"Just as you received Christ Jesus as Lord, continue to live in*
> *him, rooted and built up in him, strengthened in the faith*
> *as you were taught, and overflowing with thankfulness"*
> (COLOSSIANS 2:6-7).

How Can You Help Others?[6]

Don't become impatient when you don't understand the person's fear. Understand that what fearful people *feel* is *real.*

> *"A patient man has great understanding, but a*
> *quick-tempered man displays folly"*
> (Proverbs 14:29).

Don't think the person is doing this for attention. Realize he or she is embarrassed and wants to change.

> *"I do not understand what I do. For what I want*
> *to do I do not do, but what I hate I do"*
> (Romans 7:15).

Don't be critical or use demeaning statements. Be gentle and supportive. Build up the person's self-confidence.

> *"Encourage one another and build each other up,*
> *just as in fact you are doing"*
> (1 Thessalonians 5:11).

Don't assume you know what is best. Ask how you can help.

> *"We urge you, brothers, warn those who*
> *are idle, encourage the timid, help the*
> *weak, be patient with everyone"*
> (1 Thessalonians 5:14).

Don't make the person face a threatening situation without planning. Give him or her instruction in positive self-talk and relaxation exercises.

> *"Hold on to instruction, do not let it go;*
> *guard it well, for it is your life"*
> (Proverbs 4:13).

Don't make the person face the situation alone. Be there and assure him or her of your support.

> *"Two are better than one, because they have a good return for*
> *their work: If one falls down, his friend can help him up. But*
> *pity the man who falls and has no one to help him up!"*
> (Ecclesiastes 4:9-10).

Don't begin with difficult situations. Help the person face his or her fear in small increments.

> *"Consider it pure joy, my brothers, whenever you*
> *face trials of many kinds, because you know that*
> *the testing of your faith develops perseverance"*
> (JAMES 1:2-3).

Don't constantly ask, "How are you feeling?" Help the person see the value of having other interests.

> *"Each of you should look not only to your own*
> *interests, but also to the interests of others"*
> (PHILIPPIANS 2:4).

Don't show disappointment and displeasure if the person fails. Encourage him or her and compliment his or her efforts to conquer fear.

> *"Do not withhold good from those who deserve it,*
> *when it is in your power to act"*
> (PROVERBS 3:27).

Don't say, "Don't be absurd; there's nothing for you to fear!" Instead, say, "No matter how you feel, tell yourself the truth, 'I will take one step at a time.'"

> *"The wise in heart are called discerning,*
> *and pleasant words promote instruction"*
> (PROVERBS 16:21).

Don't say, "Don't be a coward; you *have* to do this!" Instead, say, "I know this is difficult for you, but it's not dangerous. You have the courage to do this."

> *"A wise man's heart guides his mouth,*
> *and his lips promote instruction"*
> (PROVERBS 16:23).

Don't say, "Quit living in the past; this is not that bad." Instead, say, "Remember to stay in the present and remind yourself, 'That was then and this is now.'"

> *"Pleasant words are a honeycomb,*
> *sweet to the soul and healing to the bones"*
> (PROVERBS 16:24).

> The greater our fear, the less we are controlled by faith.
> The greater our faith, the less we are controlled by fear.
> —JH

Your Scripture Prayer Project

1 Peter 5:6-7

Colossians 3:2-3

Psalm 27:1

1 John 4:18

Philippians 4:7

Deuteronomy 31:8

Psalm 23:4

Psalm 46:1

Isaiah 41:10

For additional guidance on this topic, see also *Anger, Codependency, Critical Spirit, Decision Making, Depression, Forgiveness, Hope, Identity, Manipulation, Phobias, Prejudice, Rejection, Self-worth, Stress Management, Worry.*

19

FINANCIAL FREEDOM

The Dollar Dilemma

Has money mastered you, or are you master over your money? Do you continually find yourself in the red and fear you'll never be in the black? Are you in the deep, deep ditch of debt? You can find freedom through sound biblical principles for wise money management and solve the dollar dilemma.

SOME MYTHS ABOUT FINANCES

Myth About Wealth:
If you live a godly Christian life, you will experience financial gain and prosperity.

Truth:
According to God's Word, godliness is not a means to financial gain. The Bible warns about "false doctrine" taught by false teachers.

> *"Who have been robbed of the truth and who think*
> *that godliness is a means to financial gain"*
> (1 TIMOTHY 6:5).

Myth About Money:
Money is the root of all evil.

Truth:
No, money can be used for great good. It is actually the *love* of money that is wrong.

> *"The love of money is a root of all kinds of evil. Some*
> *people, eager for money, have wandered from the*
> *faith and pierced themselves with many griefs"*
> (1 TIMOTHY 6:10).

Myth About Stewardship:

If I just have enough money, I will be satisfied.

Truth:

Satisfaction with your financial situation does not come from the amount of money you have, but wisely managing what you have.

> *"Whoever loves money never has money enough;*
> *whoever loves wealth is never satisfied with*
> *his income. This too is meaningless"*
> (ECCLESIASTES 5:10).

Myth About Debt:

You must borrow money and pay it back in order to prove financial responsibility and establish good credit references.

Truth:

Borrowing and paying back money is not always necessary to get credit. Most lenders are more than anxious to extend credit in order to collect inflated interest rates over an extended period of time. Why?

> *"The borrower is servant to the lender"*
> (PROVERBS 22:7).

CHECKLIST FOR TRUSTWORTHY SPENDING

How do you know whether you are trustworthy in the way you spend money? You must first desire to please the Lord in every way that you manage the financial resources He has given you. Before you purchase anything, ask yourself:

— Is this purchase a true *need* or just a *desire?*

— Do I have adequate funds to purchase this without using credit?

— Have I compared the cost of competing products?

— Have I prayed about this purchase?

— Have I been patient in waiting on God's provision?

— Do I have God's peace regarding this purchase?

— Does this purchase conform to the purpose God has for me?

— Is there agreement with my spouse about this purchase?

The Bible says,

> *"Now it is required that those who*
> *have been given a trust must prove faithful"*
> (1 CORINTHIANS 4:2).

FIVE PRINCIPLES FOR WISE MONEY MANAGEMENT

Dig yourself out of your ditch of debt by determining to manage money according to the following five biblical principles. They will help put you (and your checkbook) on the road to financial recovery, and guide you on the Road to Transformation so that even your money management is marked by Christlike maturity!

Principle #1: The Law of Contentment

Remind yourself—God owns everything!

> *"The world is mine, and all that is in it"*
> (PSALM 50:12).

Recognize God as the source. He provides all you possess.

> *"You may say to yourself, 'My power and the strength*
> *of my hands have produced this wealth for me.'*
> *But remember the LORD your God, for it is he*
> *who gives you the ability to produce wealth"*
> (DEUTERONOMY 8:17-18).

Realize God wants you to be content with what you have.

> *"I know what it is to be in need, and I know what it*
> *is to have plenty. I have learned the secret of being*
> *content in any and every situation, whether well fed*
> *or hungry, whether living in plenty or in want"*
> (PHILIPPIANS 4:12).

Review what money symbolizes to you.

— Security?
— Significance?
— Self-worth?
— Status?
— Power?
— Independence?
— A means to helping others?
— Other?

Once you discover the needs you expect money to fill, call Philippians 4:19 to mind—especially when you are tempted to spend needlessly:

> *"My God will meet all your needs*
> *according to his glorious riches in Christ Jesus."*

Rest in God's presence no matter what your financial circumstances.

> *"Keep your lives free from the love of money and be*
> *content with what you have, because God has said,*
> *'Never will I leave you; never will I forsake you'"*
> (Hebrews 13:5).

Principle #2: The Law of Self-Control

Start by transferring ownership of everything to God—mentally and emotionally.

> *"'The silver is mine and the gold is mine,'*
> *declares the Lord Almighty"*
> (Haggai 2:8).

Separate yourself from the sin of greed.
— Repent and confess if your trust is in money.
— Remind yourself of the consequences of financial bondage.

> *"Watch out! Be on your guard against all kinds*
> *of greed; a man's life does not consist in the*
> *abundance of his possessions"*
> (Luke 12:15).

Set a new goal for managing your finances.
— Get counsel from someone with financial self-control.
— Commit to staying on course with God's plan for your finances.

> *"We make it our goal to please him, whether we*
> *are at home in the body or away from it"*
> (2 Corinthians 5:9).

Stay away from temptation by controlling your thoughts.
— Avoid thinking you can occasionally indulge yourself.
— Avoid thinking that you can do whatever you want, self-sufficiently.

> *"No temptation has seized you except what is common to man.*
> *And God is faithful; he will not let you be tempted beyond*
> *what you can bear. But when you are tempted, he will*
> *also provide a way out so that you can stand up under it"*
> (1 Corinthians 10:13).

Principle #3: The Law of Stewardship

Recognize your accountability to God for how you spend money.

Accountability means:

— Knowing exactly what comes in.

— Knowing exactly what goes out.

— Knowing exactly where it goes (budgeting).

— Knowing how to save (regardless of your income).

— Knowing how to put your money to work for you (safe investment planning).

— Knowing how to plan for your future (retirement planning).

— Knowing when and where to give money to God and to others.

Return the first tenth of your earnings to God—this must be a commitment!

Many assume that tithing was taught only in the Old Testament. However, Jesus gave full endorsement to the principle of tithing.

> *"Woe to you Pharisees, because you give God a tenth of your mint, rue and all other kinds of garden herbs, but you neglect justice and the love of God. You should have practiced the latter without leaving the former undone"*
> (LUKE 11:42).

Reserve a percentage of your earnings for saving.

A wise steward plans ahead by establishing a habit of saving.

> *"He who gathers money little by little makes it grow"*
> (PROVERBS 13:11).

Respond to the needs of others.

When you allow God's heart to have freedom in your heart, your attitude toward giving will change so that He will use your giving in the lives of others.

> *"He who is kind to the poor lends to the LORD, and he will reward him for what he has done"*
> (PROVERBS 19:17).

Resolve to live by a monthly budget.

Step #1:   Determine your *total monthly income:* add up your salary, dividends, trust income, interest, or any other sources of fixed income.

Step #2:   Determine *spendable income:* subtract your tithes and taxes.

Step #3:   Determine your *fixed monthly expenses* (look at the prior year's expenditures; divide yearly totals by 12 for approximate figures) and your *discretionary expenses* (money spent at your discretion).

Your total expenditures must not exceed net spendable income.

Step #4: Determine if you have a deficit or surplus lifestyle.

— Refuse to live your life deluged by debt.

— Debt is bondage to another.

— Debt dishonors God.

— Debt reveals lack of self-control.

— Debt brings God's judgment.

Financial Categories

Housing	Organizations	Savings
Utilities	Children	Investments
Transportation	Debt	Personal care
Insurance	Food	Entertainment
Education	Clothing	Gifts
Medical expenses	Pets	Miscellaneous

Principle #4: The Law of Giving

Give confidently to God that which He has commanded (Malachi 3:10).

Give regularly to the work of the Lord (1 Corinthians 16:2).

Give sacrificially by giving up some of your own desires (2 Corinthians 8:3).

Give cheerfully, not reluctantly or under pressure (2 Corinthians 9:7).

Give generously to the poor (Deuteronomy 15:11).

Give compassionately to those in need (Romans 12:13).

Give secretly without letting others know (Matthew 6:1).

Principle #5: The Law of Petition—How to Pray for Your Needs

Here are some conditions on which successful prayer depends:

— Is your request within the will of God?

> *"This is the confidence we have in approaching God: that*
> *if we ask anything according to his will, he hears us"*
> (1 John 5:14).

— Have you confessed and repented of any known sin in your life?

> *"If I had cherished sin in my heart, the Lord*
> *would not have listened; but God has surely*
> *listened and heard my voice in prayer"*
> (PSALM 66:18-19).

— Instead of desiring your own will, are you willing to accept God's will with a submissive heart? Pray as Jesus prayed:

> *"Yet not what I will, but what you will"*
> (MARK 14:36).

> *"Do not be anxious about anything, but in everything, by prayer*
> *and petition, with thanksgiving, present your requests to God.*
> *And the peace of God, which transcends all understanding,*
> *will guard your hearts and your minds in Christ Jesus"*
> (PHILIPPIANS 4:6-7).

How to Cancel Debt

> *"Free yourself, like a gazelle from the hand of the*
> *hunter, like a bird from the snare of the fowler"*
> (PROVERBS 6:5).

Identify Your Debt Situation

Make an inventory of your assets:

— What do you own?

— What is the approximate value of the things you own (car, house, property, insurance policy—large items)?

Identify your income:

— How much money do you make?

— How much time per week do you work to obtain this money?

— Do you have any investments?

Describe your debts:

— What do you owe?

— When is it due?

— What interest rates are you paying on each debt?

Approximate your monthly bills:

— What do you pay for utilities, gasoline/transportation, food, phone, clothing, insurance, entertainment?

Consider Your Lifestyle

Be introspective:

— Why do you live the way you do? Is it for career advancement, to impress friends or family, or to live comfortably?

— Were you brought up living this way?

— How do your friends, family, and coworkers live?

Consider what you could do without:

— Do you have expensive items you don't need that, after the initial purchase, have high maintenance costs?

— Do you pay others to do something that you could do yourself?

— Do you eat out when you could eat less expensively at home?

Look for what you can substitute:

— Can you substitute less-expensive items for premium products or services you currently use?

Reconsider gift giving:

— Do you disregard budgets and savings plans during holidays and gift-giving occasions?

— Can you give fewer and less-expensive gifts?

— Does it mean that you love your friends and family any less if you live within your means?

— Would your loved ones want you to go into debt to buy them presents?

Establish Financial Goals

List future expenditures:

— What future expenses do you anticipate?

— Are you looking to buy a home, pay for a daughter's wedding, or replace a vehicle?

Consider future career changes:

— Are you considering going to school or starting your own business?

— How will these plans change your financial situation?

Prepare for family changes:

— Are you expecting a child?

— Are children leaving the home?

— Do you have elderly parents in poor health?

— Prepare for how these changes will affect your finances.

State your future financial goals:

— Financially, where do you want to be five years from now? Ten years from now?

— What are realistic expectations?

Take Action with Your Finances

Pay extra on your debts:

— Which debt has the highest interest rate?

— What amount of money can you pay each month on that debt?

Stop feeding your debt:

— What lifestyle habits contribute to your debt?

— Have you stopped using credit cards and started paying cash?

Change your lifestyle:

— What items can you do without that you really do not need?

— What expensive assets can you sell that would be financially profitable to sell?

Establish a savings plan:

— How much money are you setting aside for the future?

— Are you preparing for retirement and major emergencies so that when they come, you do not find yourself in debt again?

Establish a giving plan:

— How much should you plan to give to God?

— How much money are you setting aside to help those in need?

> *"I walk in the way of righteousness, along the*
> *paths of justice, bestowing wealth on those who*
> *love me and making their treasuries full"*
> (PROVERBS 8:20-21).

> The Bible has predetermined your purpose
> as well as your money's purpose—
> it's all for the glory of God!
> —JH

Your Scripture Prayer Project

Philippians 4:19

Hebrews 13:5

Luke 12:15

Deuteronomy 8:17-18

1 Timothy 6:10

Proverbs 22:7

Luke 16:10-11

Matthew 6:20-21,24

1 Peter 1:7

For additional guidance on this topic, see also *Decision Making, Depression, Fear, Hope, Self-worth, Stress Management, Worry* and other related topics.

20

FORGIVENESS

The Freedom of Letting Go

Forgiving isn't easy...especially when you don't *feel* like it. You have the pain that penetrated too deep, and now resentment has taken root. As you think about your offenders, you choose to live in a "ditch of demand" lined with stones of spite and boulders of bitterness. Yet God commands us to forgive...*just as He forgives us.* Colossians 3:13 says, "Bear with each other and forgive whatever grievances you may have against one another. Forgive as the Lord forgave you."

WHAT IS FORGIVENESS?

— *Forgiveness* is dismissing a debt,[1] dismissing your demand that others owe you something.

— *Forgiveness* is releasing your resentment, releasing your right to hear "I'm sorry" or your right to get even. Forgiveness is as much about you as your offender. It removes from you the weight of resentment, freeing you to live a life of joy and peace.

WHAT IS *NOT* FORGIVENESS?

Misconceptions abound when the word *forgiveness* is mentioned. Some think forgiveness is *excusing* sin and *saying* that what was wrong is now right. Well, that is totally wrong!

— *Forgiveness is not* the same as reconciliation. It takes two for reconciliation, only one for forgiveness.

— *Forgiveness is not* letting the guilty off the hook. It is moving the guilty from your hook to God's hook.

— *Forgiveness is not* being a weak martyr. It is being strong enough to be Christlike.

— *Forgiveness is not* based on what is fair. It was not fair for Jesus to hang on the cross, but He did so that we could be forgiven.

What Is God's Heart on Forgiveness?

— *God commands* that we forgive each other (Ephesians 4:32).

— *God wants* us to forgive others because He forgives us (Colossians 3:13).

— *God wants* us to see unforgiveness as sin (James 4:17).

— *God wants* us to get rid of unforgiveness and have a heart of mercy (Matthew 5:7).

— *God wants* us to do our part to live in peace with everyone (Romans 12:18).

— *God wants* us to overcome evil with good (Romans 12:21).

— *God wants* us to be ministers of reconciliation (2 Corinthians 5:18-19).

What Are Stages of Forgiveness?

Notice the word *forgiveness* has the little word *give* in it. When you choose to forgive, you *give* someone a *gift*—freedom from having to pay the penalty for offending you. Because this can be a difficult gift to give, realize you are also giving yourself a gift—the gift of grudge-free living. That is true freedom!

> *"Do not seek revenge or bear a grudge against one of*
> *your people, but love your neighbor as yourself"*
> (Leviticus 19:18).

Face the Offense

You must face the truth of what actually happened and not hinder true healing with rationalizations and false thinking.

— *Don't minimize the offense:* "No matter how badly he treats me, it's okay." Bad treatment of any kind is never okay (Ephesians 5:11).

— *Don't excuse the offender's behavior:* "He doesn't mean to hurt me. I shouldn't feel upset with him—he's family!" No matter the age of the offender or our relationship, we need to call sin what it is and face the truth instead of trying to change it. There must first be a *guilty* party in order to have someone to forgive (Proverbs 24:24).

— *Don't assume quick forgiveness is full forgiveness:*[2] "As soon as that horrendous ordeal occurred, I forgave him." Many well-intentioned people feel guilty if they don't extend immediate forgiveness, so they "forgive" quickly. They have neither faced the full impact of the offense nor grieved over what happened. Rarely is the full impact of sin felt at the moment it occurs. Rather, its impact is felt at different levels over a period of time. Therefore, forgiveness needs to be extended at each stage (see Psalm 51:6).

Feel the Offense[3]

Anger or even hatred toward an offender needs to be brought up out of the basement of our souls and dealt with. However, not all hatred is wrong.

> *"There is a time for everything, and a season for every*
> *activity under heaven…a time to love and a time to hate"*
> (ECCLESIASTES 3:1,8).

Failing to feel the offense results in…

— *Denying pain:* "I don't blame her for always criticizing me…it didn't really hurt me."

Truth: Being mistreated is painful. Feeling the pain must take place before healing can occur (Psalm 34:18).

— *Carrying false guilt:* "I feel guilty if I hate what was done to me."

Truth: God hates sin; if you are godly you, too, will hate sin (Proverbs 8:13).

Forgive the Offender

You are called by God to forgive. And when you do, genuine forgiveness draws you to the heart of God, and your life takes on the divine character of Christ.

Argument: "I don't feel like forgiving."

Answer: Forgiveness is not a feeling, but an act of will—a choice. Jesus said:

> *"When you stand praying, if you hold anything*
> *against anyone, forgive him, so that your Father*
> *in heaven may forgive you your sins"*
> (MARK 11:25).

Argument: "I can forgive everyone else, but God knows I don't have the power to forgive _____."

Answer: The issue is not your power, but God's power within you.

> *"His divine power has given us everything we need*
> *for life and godliness through our knowledge of him*
> *who called us by his own glory and goodness"*
> (2 PETER 1:3).

Argument: "Forgiveness doesn't seem fair."

Answer: Forgiveness isn't about fairness. God knows how to deal with each person fairly—and He will, in His own time.

> *"Do not take revenge, my friends, but leave*
> *room for God's wrath, for it is written: 'It is*
> *mine to avenge; I will repay,' says the Lord"*
> (ROMANS 12:19).

Argument: "I have forgiven, but he keeps doing the same thing over and over."

Answer: You cannot control what others do, but you can control *how you respond* to what others do. Jesus said you are to respond with forgiveness no matter the number of times you are wronged.

> *"Peter came to Jesus and asked, 'Lord, how many*
> *times shall I forgive my brother when he sins against*
> *me? Up to seven times?' Jesus answered, 'I tell*
> *you, not seven times, but seventy-seven times'"*
> (MATTHEW 18:21-22).

Argument: "I cannot forgive and forget. I keep thinking about being hurt."[4]

Answer: When you choose to forgive, you don't get "holy amnesia." After facing your hurt and confronting the offender, you must willfully close your mind to rehearsing the pain of the past. Refuse to focus on your hurt.

> *"Forgetting what is behind and straining toward what*
> *is ahead, I press on toward the goal to win the prize for*
> *which God has called me heavenward in Christ Jesus"*
> (PHILIPPIANS 3:13-14).

Find Oneness When Appropriate

Relationships filled with resentment ultimately perish, and relationships filled with forgiveness ultimately prevail. However, reconciliation in a relationship—the restoration of oneness—is contingent on several vital factors:

— Has your offender taken responsibility for the wrong? (Proverbs 28:13).

— Is your offender being totally truthful? (Proverbs 11:3).

— Does your offender have worldly or godly sorrow? (2 Corinthians 7:10-11).

When certain conditions are met—with both parties committed to *honesty in the relationship*—there is real hope for oneness of mind and heart.[5] Amos 3:3 says, "Do two walk together unless they have agreed to do so?"

Now, sometimes encouraging reconciliation isn't wise, as with…

— a rapist or the two involved in adultery; 1 Corinthians 15:33 says, "Do not be misled: 'Bad company corrupts good character.'"

— a husband whose anger is out of control. The wife needs to move out of harm's way until he willingly receives counseling with lasting changes clearly evident in his lifestyle. Proverbs 22:24 says, "Do not associate with one easily angered."

How Do I Actually Forgive?

— Make a list of all the offender's offenses—they are your "rocks" of resentment.

— Imagine a meat hook around your neck.

— Imagine a burlap bag filled with those heavy rocks hanging from the hook.

— Imagine carrying the weight from these burdens everywhere.

— Ask, "Do I really want to carry all this pain the rest of my life?" (Obviously not!)

— Now take your offender and the offenses off your emotional hook and put all the pain and this person onto God's hook. The Lord knows how to handle it all, in His time and in His way. Deuteronomy 32:35 says, "It is mine to avenge; I will repay."

═══════════ *Prayer to Forgive Your Offender* ═══════════

Lord Jesus,

Thank You for caring about how much my heart has been hurt.

You know the pain I have felt because of (list every offense). Right now I release all that pain into Your hands. Thank You, Lord, for dying on the cross for me and extending Your forgiveness to me. As an act of my will, I choose to forgive (_name_).

Today, I move (_name_) off my emotional hook to Your hook.

I refuse all thoughts of revenge.

I trust that in Your time and in Your way You will deal with my offender as You see fit. And Lord, thank You for giving me Your power to forgive so I can be set free. In Your precious name I pray. Amen.

> Jesus would never tell you to forgive and love your enemies
> without empowering you to do it.
> —JH

Your Scripture Prayer Project

Proverbs 17:9

Matthew 5:23-24,44

Matthew 6:14-15

Matthew 18:21-22

Luke 6:37

Romans 12:17-19

Hebrews 12:15

Ephesians 4:32

Colossians 3:13

For additional guidance on this topic, see also *Anger, Dysfunctional Family, Evil and Suffering...Why?, Fear, Grief Recovery, Guilt, Hope, Identity, Marriage, Reconciliation, Salvation, Self-worth, Worry.*

21

GRIEF RECOVERY
Living at Peace with Loss

G*rief* is a heart response to hurt, a painful emotion of sorrow caused by the loss or impending loss of someone or something that has deep meaning to us. Grief can dig a "ditch of dependency" with deep ruts of anguish, depression, and isolation—strong emotions very difficult to pull yourself out of. God understands our anguish; even the Lord Jesus is described in the Bible as a "Man of sorrows and acquainted with grief" (Isaiah 53:3 NKJV). But we can also be assured that our pain is always purposeful, and when grief accomplishes its work, a deep well has been carved within us that God, in His time, will fill with joy, peace, and contentment. Lamentations 3:32-33 says, "Though he brings grief, he will show compassion, so great is his unfailing love. For he does not willingly bring affliction or grief to the children of men."

WHAT ARE THE STAGES OF HEALTHY GRIEVING?
"I need to get my act together. I've got to snap out of this."

These thoughts reveal unrealistic expectations about grieving and a failure to understand the grief process and the slow journey of restoration. While stages of grief do exist, they may be experienced with varying degrees of intensity. Some may also be missed, and some stages may be repeated. Give yourself permission to unpredictably experience the stages of grieving as you trust God to bring new life again.

"Though you have made me see troubles, many
and bitter, you will restore my life again; from the
depths of the earth you will again bring me up"
(PSALM 71:20).

Crisis Stage: This can last from two days to two weeks. In this stage of grief, you carry out your daily activities in a mechanical manner. Characteristics include:

Anxiety/fear	Denial
Appetite/sleep loss	Disturbing dreams
Limited concentration	Shock/numbness
Confusion	Uncontrollable crying

Crucible Stage: This can last up to a year or two or more, perhaps even until death if grief is not resolved. Characteristics include:

Anger/resentment	Loneliness/isolation
Anguish	Self-pity
Bargaining with God	Intense yearning
Depression/sadness	Guilt/false guilt

Contentment Stage: This stage accepts the loss, leaving it in the past. This stage not only accepts that the present offers stability, but also accepts that the future offers new and promising hope (Philippians 3:13; 4:11). Characteristics include:

Greater compassion toward others	New ability to leave loss behind
Greater acceptance of others	New patterns for living
Greater humility before others	New hope for the future
Greater dependence on the Lord	New contentment in all circumstances

WHAT ARE UNHEALTHY TYPES OF GRIEF?

Chronic Grief: This is an unresolved, deep sorrow experienced over a long period of time due to not accepting or not experiencing closure over a significant loss.[1] The personal pain is buried so deeply the ability to experience real grief and let go of the loss is blocked. Chronic grief can be resolved by facing the loss and grieving it.

Repressed Grief: This is an unidentified, unexpressed, unresolved grief exhibited in unexplainable negative lifestyle patterns. Repressed grief can be overcome by taking the following "Time Line Test":

— *Draw* a line representing your life.

— *Divide* the line into sections: childhood, adolescence, adulthood.

— *Denote* on the page the major events of each time period.

— *Determine* unresolved hurts and losses that occurred in those stages.

— *Define* the painful events you need to grieve: "I felt abandoned when…"

— *Decide* to genuinely grieve your losses.

— *Defuse* the power of these losses by sharing them.

— *Deepen* your dependence on the Lord to set you emotionally free.

*"In my anguish I cried to the LORD,
and he answered by setting me free"*
(PSALM 118:5).

WHAT ARE THE STAGES OF ACCEPTANCE?

The work of accepting the reality of your unwanted loss may consume all your energy, but your efforts will succeed when you focus on being the person God wants you to be through your season of sorrow (see Colossians 3:23).

Accept the Past as Always Being in the Past
— *Pray* for God's help in embracing your grief (Psalm 34:17-18).
— *Recall* your losses, then write about your losses (Psalm 51:6).
— *Weep* over your losses (Psalm 30:5).
— *Complete* each loss by writing the word *past* beside it and saying, "I will be content to leave this event in the past" (1 Timothy 6:6).
— *Memorize* Psalm 119:28,50,101,156.
— *Give thanks* to God for all He has taught you and how He will use your past in the future (1 Thessalonians 5:18).

Accept the Present as Offering Stability and Significance
— *Choose* to live one day at a time (Matthew 6:34).
— *Put* the Lord at the center of your life (Matthew 16:24).
— *Go* to God with your specific questions; make a list (James 1:5).
— *Thank* God for providing everything you need for life (2 Peter 1:3).
— *Praise* God that though your situation has changed, He will never leave you (Hebrews 13:5).
— *Focus* on the joy and satisfaction of helping others; make a list (Galatians 6:2).

Accept the Future as Affording New Opportunities
— *Hope* in the plans that God has for your future (Jeremiah 29:11).
— *Know* that your sorrow and grief will not be wasted (Psalm 119:71).
— *Put* all of your hope in God (Psalm 62:5).
— *Have* faith in God, whom you cannot see (2 Corinthians 4:18).
— *Know* that God will fill the void in your life (Isaiah 43:18-19).

GUIDELINES FOR HEALTHY GRIEVING

> *"The prudent see danger and take refuge, but*
> *the simple keep going and suffer for it"*
> (PROVERBS 27:12).

The path for recovery requires ministering to *body, soul, and spirit* to diminish painful emotions and find your way out of the ditch of despondency. A new path can be charted on which renewed peace is possible and Christlike maturity is manifested even in the most grievous circumstances.

Emotional Guidelines

Cultivate a strong, sensitive support system.

Having people around who genuinely care about you is essential—people who accept you wherever you are in the grieving process and encourage you to share your feelings.

> *"As iron sharpens iron, so one man sharpens another"*
> (PROVERBS 27:17).

Cultivate the freedom to cry.

Expressing emotions honestly, openly, and as frequently as needed is vital to walking through grief in a healthy, productive way.

> *"Those who sow in tears will reap with songs of joy"*
> (PSALM 126:5).

Cultivate a plan for socializing regularly.

One way to feel good about life, even while mourning, is attending social activities and interacting with others on a regular basis.

> *"Let us not give up meeting together...*
> *but let us encourage one another"*
> (HEBREWS 10:25).

Cultivate a trustworthy, honest confidante.

Being able to be yourself with someone and share your struggles, troubled thoughts, and swinging emotions—and still be accepted and affirmed—is healing to the soul.

> *"Two are better than one, because they have a good return for*
> *their work: If one falls down, his friend can help him up. But*
> *pity the man who falls and has no one to help him up!"*
> (ECCLESIASTES 4:9-10).

Cultivate the release of resentment.

If you have unresolved issues, anger, or hostile feelings regarding your loss, take the time to list your resentments along with their causes. Journaling can bring buried emotions to the surface. Release into the hands of God each offender and the pain of each offense. Pray, "Lord, You know the pain I have felt over (<u>situations</u>). I release all that pain into Your hands and, as an act of my will, I choose to forgive (or release) (<u>person's name</u>). Thank You, Lord Jesus, for setting me free."

> *"Be kind and compassionate to one another, forgiving*
> *each other, just as in Christ God forgave you"*
> (Ephesians 4:32).

Physical Guidelines

Get a sufficient amount of rest.

Grieving often disturbs regular sleep patterns and disrupts prolonged periods of sleeping, so getting sufficient rest during the grieving process is often a challenge—but doing so is critically important to the body.

> *"The LORD replied, 'My Presence will go with you,*
> *and I will give you rest'"*
> (Exodus 33:14).

Get a generous intake of fluid and eat a balanced nutritional diet.

Because the sense of thirst frequently goes unnoticed during the grieving process, drinking nonalcoholic and caffeine-free fluids is important. Eat daily portions of food from each of the four basic food groups and avoid skipping meals. Don't become dependent on eating junk foods, smoking, or drinking alcohol.

> *"The angel of the LORD came back a second time and*
> *touched him and said, 'Get up and eat, for the journey*
> *is too much for you.' So he got up and ate and drank.*
> *Strengthened by that food, he traveled forty days and forty*
> *nights until he reached Horeb, the mountain of God"*
> (1 Kings 19:7-8).

Get daily exercise.

Regular exercise is a natural deterrent to feeling depressed and contributes to feeling a sense of well-being. Exercise carries oxygen to the blood and promotes overall good health.

> *"Physical training is of some value, but godliness*
> *has value for all things, holding promise for*
> *both the present life and the life to come"*
> (1 Timothy 4:8).

Get big doses of sunshine.

Taking a walk in the sunlight is another natural way to fight depression. Light coming in through the eyes stimulates the brain to send a message to the body to release antidepressant endorphins.

> *"Light is sweet, and it pleases the eyes to see the sun"*
> (Ecclesiastes 11:7).

Spiritual Guidelines

Develop a purposeful prayer life.

The grieving process provides a strong impetus for "getting down to business" with God. Have candid conversations with Him about your thoughts and feelings. Listen to Him and lean on Him for comfort and reassurance.

> *"I recounted my ways and you answered me;*
> *teach me your decrees"*
> (Psalm 119:26).

Develop a positive, practical perspective.

Maintaining a positive mental attitude based on the practical application of spiritual truths during the grieving process carries you to victory even through the darkest valley and the deepest loss.

> *"Whatever is true, whatever is noble, whatever is right, whatever*
> *is pure, whatever is lovely, whatever is admirable—if anything*
> *is excellent or praiseworthy—think about such things"*
> (Philippians 4:8).

Develop a sense of peace about the past.

Resolve any unfinished business regarding the past by asking forgiveness of God for any failures on your part and by extending forgiveness for any failures on the part of others. Then let go of the past and embrace the present and the future God has planned for you.

> *"If we confess our sins, he is faithful and just and will*
> *forgive us our sins and purify us from all unrighteousness"*
> (1 John 1:9).

Develop a Scripture-memorization method.

God spoke the world into existence, and His written Word, the Bible, is powerful enough to create new life and to restore joy to your heart, peace to your mind, and hope for your future.

"All Scripture is God-breathed and is useful for
teaching, rebuking, correcting and training in
righteousness, so that the man of God may be
thoroughly equipped for every good work"
(2 Timothy 3:16-17).

Develop a yearning for eternity.
One of the most helpful, hopeful, and healing truths is realizing that this present life is lived in a temporal body, and a permanent body is waiting for you. In that body you will live throughout all eternity. Grasp God's promise of living eternally!

"We fix our eyes not on what is seen, but on what is unseen.
For what is seen is temporary, but what is unseen is eternal"
(2 Corinthians 4:18).

How Can I Help Those Who Are Grieving?

Extend a compassionate hand to those weighed down in the ditch of grief, and lend a listening ear and encourage a broken heart.

— Acknowledge their loss immediately.

— Accept all emotional or verbal responses without judgment.

— Hug with tender affection.

— Expect tears and emotional extremes.

— Find helpful things to do without being asked.

— Give the one grieving many opportunities to talk about the loss.

"A word aptly spoken is like apples of gold
in settings of silver"
(Proverbs 25:11).

"A generous man will prosper; he who refreshes
others will himself be refreshed"
(Proverbs 11:25).

"Encourage one another and build each other up"
(1 Thessalonians 5:11).

The farther you are from a flower, the smaller it seems to the eye—
so the farther your distance from grief, the smaller your sadness in sorrow.
—JH

======= *Your Scripture Prayer Project* =======

Psalm 10:14

Psalm 62:5

Psalm 147:3

Psalm 30:5

Psalm 42:11

2 Corinthians 1:3-4

John 16:20

Job 6:10

Isaiah 43:18-19

For additional guidance on this topic, see also *Alcohol and Drug Abuse, Anger, Decision Making, Depression, Forgiveness, Guilt, Hope, Identity, Overeating, Rejection, Salvation, Self-worth, Singleness, Stress Management, Suicide Prevention, Worry.*

22

GUILT

Getting Rid of Guilt for Good

It can be a farsighted friend or a formidable foe. Guilt can goad you down the path of righteousness or it can stop you in your tracks as you become fixated on failure and unmet expectations.

True guilt can lead to freedom, while false guilt leads to emotional bondage, leaving people polarized and immobilized in their ditch as the walls silently close in around them. God always uses guilt for the *good*—to convict, correct, and conform your character to Christ's, *and never to condemn.* The Bible says, "Godly sorrow brings repentance that leads to salvation and leaves no regret, but worldly sorrow brings death" (2 Corinthians 7:10).

WHAT IS TRUE GUILT?

From earliest childhood, no one has escaped guilt. You experienced guilt when you stole a cookie or told a lie. The Old Testament Hebrew word *asham,* with its many derivatives, paints a three-dimensional picture of true guilt.[1]

— *True guilt* refers to the facts of being at fault, deserving punishment, and requiring a sacrificial offering.[2]

— *True guilt* is the result of any wrong attitude or action that is contrary to the perfect will of God.

— *True guilt* is the result of sin for which a penalty must be paid for your sin so fellowship with God can be restored.[3]

WHAT IS FALSE GUILT?

— *False guilt* is based on self-condemning *feelings* that you have not lived up to your own expectations or those of someone else.[4]

— *False guilt* arises when you blame yourself, even though you've committed no wrong, or even though you've confessed and turned from your sin.

— *False guilt* keeps you in bondage to three destructive weapons—shame, fear, and anger.[5]

— *False guilt,* ironically, is not resolved by confession. Revelation 12:10 says Satan is the "accuser of our brothers."[6] He loves to burden believers with false guilt and condemnation. Some of his favorite strategies are bringing up the past, reminding you of failures, and making you feel unforgiven and unaccepted by God.

*"The accuser of our brothers, who accuses them before
our God day and night, has been hurled down"*
(REVELATION 12:10).

WHAT CHARACTERIZES TRUE AND FALSE GUILT?

True Guilt	False Guilt
"When he, the Spirit of truth, comes, he will guide you into all truth" (JOHN 16:13).	"Then he showed me Joshua the high priest standing before the angel of the LORD, and Satan standing at his right side to accuse him. The LORD said to Satan, 'The LORD rebuke you, Satan!…Is not this man a burning stick snatched from the fire?'" (ZECHARIAH 3:1-2).
Based on Fact	**Based on Feelings**
"I was wrong to take paper and other office supplies home for my personal use. This is actually stealing."	"I feel horrible because I am horrible for wanting something that isn't mine, much less thinking about taking it."
Results in a Godly Sorrow over Sin	**Results in a Worldly Fear of Consequences**
"My failure to be honest makes me aware of how much I don't reflect the character of Christ. Dear God, I want to change. I am heartsick over bringing shame to my Savior."	"I should have worked all weekend to make up for slacking off all week. Now my employer may decide to fire me. If only I'd accomplished more, I wouldn't be in this predicament. What am I going to tell my wife if I lose my job? How am I going to pay my bills?"

Brings Conviction from the Holy Spirit	Brings Condemnation from Satan
"I now see my attitude was wrong in assuming the company owed me what I took."	"I am a terrible person for feeling anger at my employer."
Results in Repentance	**Results in Depression**
"I want to be a person of integrity. I will make restitution at work and pray for the Lord's strength to change my dishonest habits."	"I might as well give up! I'll never be the kind of person I should be. I'm just no good, and nothing will change that. I'm truly hopeless."
Accepts Forgiveness	**Abides in Self-pity**
"I am thankful I have a heavenly Father who will always forgive me, no matter what I have done."	"I'm always trying to do my best, but I just don't have all the advantages others have. If I had a better-paying job, I wouldn't have to resort to taking things."
Appropriates Christ's Finished Work	**Achieves Many Personal Good Works**[7]
"Only by relying on Jesus Christ to meet my needs and His redeeming work within me will I be able to become the person I was created to be."	"The more I do for the church and others, the better I feel about myself and the more others will respect me."
Brings Reconciliation with God and Others	**Brings Alienation from God and Others**
"Knowing God always loves me allows me to be more loving and forgiving of others."	"God could never love me. If I let others get too close and see what I am really like, they will reject me. I can't count on anyone except myself."

*"Then you will know the truth,
and the truth will set you free"*
(John 8:32).

How Do I Differentiate God's Conviction from Satan's Condemnation?

The Bible says Satan loves to disguise himself by masquerading as a spokesman for God. Brutally accusing and condemning those with a sensitive conscience, he uses undeserved guilt as his most powerful weapon. Satan tenaciously incriminates committed Christians, using guilt and fear to generate severe spiritual discouragement. That's why it is important to learn to discern the lies of Satan. He often communicates with a subtle use of unreasonable "shoulds."

— "You *should* be smarter and more capable."

— "You *should* be able to get over your loss much more quickly."

— "You *should* be more careful and conscientious."

— "You *should* do more for the poor people around you."

— "You *should* endure hardship and pain with dignity."

— "You *should* never display anger or disappointment."

— "You *should* never let anyone know your real feelings."

— "You *should* never cry or show weakness."

— "You *should* never tell your pastor no."

— "You *should* be the perfect friend, mate, parent, or employee."

> *"The accuser of our brothers, who accuses them before*
> *our God day and night, has been hurled down"*
> (REVELATION 12:10).

How Do I Find Forgiveness and Freedom from Guilt?

Do you remember falling down and scraping your knee as a child? Did you run to your mother for her to pick you up and kiss the hurt away? Miraculously, it always worked! You felt good again and ran back out to play. The same is true when we take our bruised and broken lives to God: He forgives and forgets, and it always works! And when we trust Him, He takes away all the guilt. [8]

> *"When Jesus saw their faith, he said,*
> *'Friend, your sins are forgiven'"*
> (LUKE 5:20).

Don't stay stuck in the ditch of guilt. Take the following eight steps toward the Road to Transformation, where Christlike maturity will help you bring all your guilt to a forgiving God.

Here is what we need to know about being F-O-R-G-I-V-E-N:

F Find the source of your guilt.

— Examine why you feel guilty.

— Determine if your guilt is true or false.

— Use Scripture as the only standard for determining true guilt.

"You desire truth in the inner parts;
you teach me wisdom in the inmost place"
(PSALM 51:6).

O Own responsibility for your sin.

— Agree with God you are guilty of sinning.

— Ask God to reveal your personal sin patterns.

— Make restitution to those against whom you have sinned.

"If we confess our sins, he is faithful and just and will
forgive us our sins and purify us from all unrighteousness"
(1 JOHN 1:9).

R Realize God means what He says.

— Thank God for the gift of His Son, who paid for your forgiveness.

— Thank God for His unending forgiveness, even if you don't feel forgiven.

— Choose to believe what God says.

"In him we have redemption through his blood,
the forgiveness of sins"
(EPHESIANS 1:7).

G Give up dwelling on the past.

— Give up holding on to past pain.

— Give up self-condemnation.

— Give up refusing to forgive others.

"Forget the former things; do not dwell on the past"
(ISAIAH 43:18).

I Invest time in renewing your mind.

— Memorize scriptures that reinforce God's forgiveness.

— Remember that in Christ, you are "a new creation" (2 Corinthians 5:17).

— Learn to see yourself as a valuable child of God.

"You were taught, with regard to your former way of
life…to be made new in the attitude of your minds"
(EPHESIANS 4:22-23).

V Verify truth when Satan accuses.

— Learn to discern the difference between the Holy Spirit's voice and that of Satan.

— Answer Satan's accusations with truth from Scripture.

— Verbalize a personal prayer receiving God's forgiveness.

> "'No weapon forged against you will prevail, and
> you will refute every tongue that accuses you. This
> is the heritage of the servants of the LORD, and this
> is their vindication from me,' declares the LORD"
> (ISAIAH 54:17).

E Exchange your life for the life of Christ.

— Understand you cannot live the Christian life in your own strength.

— Allow Christ to transform you and live out His character through you.

— Continue to nurture the Holy Spirit's presence through personal prayer and Bible study.

> "I have been crucified with Christ and I no longer live, but
> Christ lives in me. The life I live in the body, I live by faith
> in the Son of God, who loved me and gave himself for me"
> (GALATIANS 2:20).

N Notice God brings your feelings in line with the facts when you obey Him.

— Know that God is a God of second chances!

— Know that your feelings won't change immediately.

— Know that feelings usually follow thinking.

> "Blessed is he whose transgressions are forgiven, whose sins
> are covered. Blessed is the man whose sin the LORD does
> not count against him and in whose spirit is no deceit"
> (PSALM 32:1-2).

========= *Prayer About Your Guilt* =========

Dear heavenly Father,

Please give me the discernment to know when I'm feeling false guilt instead of true guilt.

I ask that Your Spirit convict me when I'm headed the wrong way so that I will get on the right path. I also pray that I will always be sensitive to the convicting touch of the Holy Spirit's hand. Thank You that I'm forgiven and set free.

In Your holy name I pray. Amen.

> Guilt covertly constructs a self-imposed prison
> when granted residence in your life.
> —JH

========= *Your Scripture Prayer Project* =========

Proverbs 20:9

Ezra 9:13

Isaiah 64:6; 53:6

Proverbs 28:13

Psalm 32:5

Isaiah 6:7

Acts 24:16

Hebrews 10:22

Romans 8:1

For additional guidance on this topic, see also *Depression, Fear, Forgiveness, Hope, Identity, Reconciliation, Salvation, Self-worth, Suicide Prevention, Worry.*

23

HABITS

Success in Self-Control

Interestingly, in most dictionaries, the first definition for the word *habit* reveals it to be "a type of clothing characteristic of a certain calling." Eventually a habit came to be "a pattern of behavior acquired by frequent repetition that reflects the prevailing character of a person."[1] The Bible is interwoven with the same concept: Your habits characterize your character. If you are a Christian, you are called to be clothed in the *habit* of Christ so that your character actually reflects His character—pure and unblemished.

> *"Clothe yourselves with the Lord Jesus Christ, and do not think about how to gratify the desires of the sinful nature"*
> (Romans 13:14).

What Do All Habits—Good or Bad—Have in Common?

All habits...

— occur with regularity.

— happen without thinking.

— reflect inner morals.

— tend to grow stronger and more ingrained over time.

— persist and become hard to change.

— provide some degree of pleasure.

> *"No servant can serve two masters. Either he will hate the one and love the other, or he will be devoted to the one and despise the other. You cannot serve both God and money"*
> (Luke 16:13).

What Are the Signs of an Unhealthy Habit?

If any of the following statements are true, your habit has mastery over you:

— My thoughts are consumed with it.

— My time is scheduled around it.

— My health could be harmed by it.

— My guilt increases following it.

— My finances are affected by it.

— I am defensive when asked about it.

— My relationships are hurt by it.

— I am upset when I can't do it.

> *"Search me, O God, and know my heart…See if there is any*
> *offensive way in me, and lead me in the way everlasting"*
> (Psalm 139:23-24).

What Three Factors Fuel Negative Habits?

Misguided choices—Choosing to escape from painful emotions and circumstances in an attempt to avoid the harsh realities of life.

Misplaced dependencies—Attempting to meet your God-given emotional needs for love, significance, and security through unhealthy dependencies on people, things, or activities.[2]

Misaligned beliefs—Telling yourself, "This makes me feel better and, besides, I deserve it."[3] Or, "It's useless to try to change or quit."

A healthy godly approach involves…

Choosing to meet the harsh realities of life head-on by processing painful emotions and circumstances.

Depending on the Lord to meet your needs for love, significance, and security.

Believing you can take responsibility for your behavior because you have the Spirit of Christ living in you to help you.

How Can Faith Help Overcome Bad Habits?

Much of a habit's power rests in your belief that you are "on your own" during times of temptation. However, if you are a Christian, you are *never* alone. You have "Christ in you" (Colossians 1:27) to win the victory through you.[4] The Bible says you are "united" with Christ, that you are "one with him." This means if you yield to temptation to be pulled down by a negative habit, you pull down Christ with you! Likewise, if you yield to Christ, He will pull you up above the temptation and be glorified within you. This understanding can be a life-changing motivator for you to reconsider your choices!

How Do You Improve Self-control?

The essential quality of self-control is restraining desires that may pull you down so that you may achieve your goals.[5] It is saying no to a negative habit so you can say yes to a positive goal. Self-control is a gift from God that empowers you to fulfill the will of God.

Steps to self-control:

Start with a commitment to God.[6]

— Believe that God is good and just.[7]

— Believe that God has the desire and power to help you.

Separate yourself from sin.[8]

— Repent and confess that your habit is sin.

— Review in your mind, on a regular basis, the negative consequences of your habit.

Set a new goal.[9]

— Make it your goal to know God.

— Make it your goal to depend on God.

Stand on the truth.[10]

— Know that in Christ you are set free from the penalty and power of sin.

— Know that you no longer have to be a slave to sin.

Substitute God's thoughts for your thoughts.[11]

— When you think you are powerless over a habit, say, "I can do everything through him who gives me strength" (Philippians 4:13).

— When you think no one will know about the habit, understand that "nothing in all creation is hidden from God's sight. Everything is uncovered and laid bare before the eyes of him to whom we must give account" (Hebrews 4:13).

Surrender your will.[12]

— Acknowledge that God has authority over all your thoughts, words, desires, time, money, and possessions.

— Acknowledge that the decision to change is yours. *You* are making a choice!

Stay on track.[13]

— Avoid thinking it will be okay to occasionally indulge the habit.

— Avoid moving out from under God's grace into self-sufficiency.

How Do You Replace Bad Habits with Good Habits?

Stop trudging around in your muddy ditch and move up to higher ground to the Road to Transformation and the opportunity to "clean up" by clothing yourself in good habits. Habits reflect the underlying character of a person, so good habits become the apparel you wear to reflect the character of Christ (see Romans 8:29). Begin today! Take off the tattered rags of sin and replace them with the beautiful robes of Christ. Here are the steps to doing that:

Put On the Habit of Faith

Faith is developed through hearing God's Word.

> *"Faith comes from hearing the message, and the message is heard through the word of Christ"*
> (Romans 10:17).

Faith is strengthened by believing the promises of God.

> *"[Abraham] did not waver through unbelief regarding the promise of God, but was strengthened in his faith and gave glory to God"*
> (Romans 4:20).

Put On the Habit of Goodness

Goodness is developed by storing up what is good in your heart.

> *"Out of the overflow of the heart the mouth speaks. The good man brings good things out of the good stored up in him, and the evil man brings evil things out of the evil stored up in him"*
> (Matthew 12:34-35).

Goodness is displayed by acts of kindness and generosity to others.

> *"Command them to do good, to be rich in good deeds, and to be generous and willing to share"*
> (1 Timothy 6:18).

Put On the Habit of Knowledge

Knowledge is developed by studying God's Word.

> *"Do your best to present yourself to God as one approved, a workman who does not need to be ashamed and who correctly handles the word of truth"*
> (2 Timothy 2:15).

Knowledge is displayed by a willingness to accept discipline.

> *"Whoever loves discipline loves knowledge,*
> *but he who hates correction is stupid"*
> (PROVERBS 12:1).

Put On the Habit of Perseverance

Perseverance is developed through trials and testing.

> *"Consider it pure joy, my brothers, whenever you*
> *face trials of many kinds, because you know that*
> *the testing of your faith develops perseverance"*
> (JAMES 1:2-3).

Perseverance produces maturity.

> *"Perseverance must finish its work so that you may*
> *be mature and complete, not lacking anything"*
> (JAMES 1:4).

Put On the Habit of Godliness

Godliness is developed by turning away from the pursuit of evil and worldly gain.

> *"The love of money is a root of all kinds of evil. Some*
> *people, eager for money, have wandered from the faith*
> *and pierced themselves with many griefs. But you, man*
> *of God, flee from all this, and pursue righteousness,*
> *godliness, faith, love, endurance and gentleness"*
> (1 TIMOTHY 6:10-11).

Godliness is displayed through the power of Jesus living His life through you.

> *"His divine power has given us everything we need*
> *for life and godliness through our knowledge of him*
> *who called us by his own glory and goodness"*
> (2 PETER 1:3).

Put On the Habit of Brotherly Kindness

Brotherly kindness is strengthened by honoring others above yourself.

> *"Be devoted to one another in brotherly love.*
> *Honor one another above yourselves"*
> (ROMANS 12:10).

Brotherly kindness is displayed by showing hospitality and sharing with others in need.

> *"Share with God's people who are in need.*
> *Practice hospitality"*
> (ROMANS 12:13).

Put On the Habit of Love

Love is developed by recognizing that God first loved you.

> *"This is love: not that we loved God, but that he loved*
> *us and sent his Son as an atoning sacrifice for our sins"*
> (1 JOHN 4:10).

Love is strengthened by obeying God's commands.

> *"If you love me, you will obey what I command"*
> (JOHN 14:15).

HOW IS IT POSSIBLE TO CHANGE HABITS REFLECTING A NEGATIVE CHILDHOOD MIND-SET?

Many habits are the result of childhood experiences. But, no longer a child, you do not have to be controlled by the attitudes and actions of others. You can choose to plant, cultivate, and harvest good habits that are desirable and pleasing to God. As His precious child, you are called to:

Sow the Seeds of Moral Sensitivity

— Study the Scriptures daily so you can know God's standards.

— Consider what it means to "have no other gods before me" (Psalm 119:11).

Sow the Seeds of Accountability

— Be open to the truth when others criticize you.

— Think about your negative attitudes and review their consequences.

— Confess your failures to God, and ask forgiveness from those whom you have offended.

— Read Proverbs 28:13.

Sow the Seeds of Gratefulness

— Acknowledge the gifts of God for which you can be grateful.

— Thank God for what He is teaching you through each trial.

— Read 1 Thessalonians 5:18.

Sow the Seeds of Forgiveness
— Choose to forgive others even when you feel justified in your anger.

— Remind yourself of the many times God forgives you.

— Read Colossians 3:13.

Sow the Seeds of Selflessness
— Set a high standard for yourself, expect less from others.

— Perform an act of kindness toward someone each day.

— Read Philippians 2:3.

Sow the Seeds of Communion with God
— Seek out time every day to be alone with God.

— Be quiet in your spirit, and wait on God to reveal Himself to you.

— Read Psalm 104:34.

You are not born with bad habits…
you weave them and wear them.
Your habits can be the rags of destructive addictions
or the royal robes of Christlike character.

—JH

Your Scripture Prayer Project

Luke 16:13

1 Corinthians 6:19-20

Romans 6:1-2

Galatians 5:16

Psalm 139:23-24

1 Peter 1:13

Philippians 4:13

Psalm 116:16

1 Thessalonians 5:24

For additional guidance on this topic, see also *Alcohol and Drug Abuse, Co-dependency, Crisis Intervention, Depression, Dysfunctional Family, Fear, Forgiveness, Guilt, Hope, Identity, Lying, Overeating, Prejudice, Rejection, Salvation, Self-worth, Sexual Addiction, Stress Management, Victimization, Worry.*

24

HOMOSEXUALITY

A Case of Mistaken Identity

When someone is sexually attracted to a person of the same gender, confusion can abound and sexual identity can be questioned. And when God's truth about homosexuality either is not known or rejected, people can find themselves in a ditch of sinking sand, with serious consequensces and deep sorrow.

Same-sex attraction does not reflect the individual's *true identity* as created by God. Rather, it can result in a *mistaken identity.* This creates a desperate need for truth—God's truth. Jesus said, "You will know the truth, and the truth will set you free" (John 8:32).

WHAT DOES THE BIBLE SAY ABOUT HOMOSEXUALITY?

Discerning what is right in God's sight requires knowing the truths of Scripture and understanding the character of God. Emphasizing only one aspect of God's character to the exclusion of others does not give an accurate assessment. Do you view God as loving, but with no holy standard for living? Or do you see Him as a holy judge, but with no compassion for human frailty? First John 4:16 says, "God is love," and Psalm 99:9 says, "God is holy." And He calls us all to live a holy life, set apart and free from all sexual immorality.

> *"Be holy because I, the LORD your God, am holy"*
> (LEVITICUS 19:2).

Is homosexual behavior a sin?

Yes, according to numerous passages in the Bible.

> *"Do not lie with a man as one lies with*
> *a woman; that is detestable"*
> (Leviticus 18:22; see also
> Genesis 19:4-7; Leviticus 20:13).

Is homosexual temptation a sin?

No, Jesus was tempted "in every way," yet He did not sin (Hebrews 4:15).

Is a person born a homosexual?

No. Homosexuality is a *behavior,* not an *identity.*[1] Scientific studies have never supported a "gay gene" that makes people homosexual. The two primary factors that influence someone toward homosexual behavior are the *environment* in which a child is raised, and the child's *responses* to that environment.

Is homosexuality "natural" for some people?

While unnatural behavior can feel natural to those with unnatural desires, the Bible unequivocally states that sexual relations between members of the same sex are *unnatural, indecent,* and a *perversion* of His creation.

> *"God gave [those who suppress the truth] over in the sinful*
> *desires of their hearts to sexual impurity for the degrading*
> *of their bodies with one another. They exchanged the*
> *truth of God for a lie…Because of this, God gave them*
> *over to shameful lusts. Even their women exchanged*
> *natural relations for* unnatural *ones. In the same way*
> *the men also abandoned natural relations with women*
> *and were inflamed with lust for one another. Men*
> *committed* indecent *acts with other men, and received*
> *in themselves the due penalty for their* perversion*"*
> (Romans 1:24-27).

Is homosexual behavior risky?

Yes. Relating to health issues in the United States alone, objective facts show that homosexuality is painfully risky and negative. While 9 percent of homosexual men have AIDS,[2] only .03 percent of heterosexual men have AIDS. According to generally accepted estimates, approximately 2 to 4 percent of the population is homosexual,[3] yet…

They account for…

— 17 percent of gonorrhea cases[4]

— 85 percent of the syphilis cases in some regions[5]

— 42 percent of new HIV infections[6]

— 55 percent of AIDS cases[7] (only 5 percent through heterosexual contact; another 22 percent through injected drug use)

They are...

- five times more likely to be infected with an *incurable* sexually transmitted disease (STD) linked to cancer[8] (one in three gay men have an incurable STD).[9]
- 50,000 times more likely to be the victim of physical abuse by a homosexual partner than "hate crimes"[10] (battering occurs in 39 percent of gay male couples: 22 percent are physically abused by a partner, and 5 percent are sexually abused by a partner[11]).

They are at a significantly higher risk for...[12]
- eating disorders,[13] anxiety, and psychiatric disorders[14]
- substance abuse, depression, suicide[15]
- death by anal, prostate, testicular, or colon cancer
- premature death by 8 to 20 years[16]

Statistics represent only a snapshot in time, but they reveal the devastating impact of homosexuality. And though these statistics are tragic, they should not be surprising because God's Word clearly communicates the negative impact of sexual sin on the physical body (1 Corinthians 6:18).

What Does God Offer?

An Offer of Hope

Most homosexuals feel condemned by the church. Many Christians are unloving toward homosexuals, although Christians are called by God to love everyone...including homosexuals. At the same time, Christians are also called to declare God's truth about sin so people can turn to Him to experience His forgiveness of their sin and His power to forsake their sin. This is not unloving condemnation, but rather an *offer of hope*. God offers forgiveness along with the power to live a changed life. David, an adulterer, learned the secret of how to be *set free*—and more importantly, how to *stay free*.

> *"How can a young man keep his way pure?*
> *By living according to your word. I seek you with*
> *all my heart...I have hidden your word in my heart*
> *that I might not sin against you"*
> (Psalm 119:9-11).

David's words and life show us that a life of compromise never brings contentment, but staying true to God's principles brings peace. The Bible repeatedly presents God's scriptural standard regarding homosexuality in both the Old and New Testaments.

The Scriptural Standard

*"All the men from every part of the city of Sodom…called
to Lot, 'Where are the men who came to you tonight?
Bring them out to us so that we can have sex with
them'…'No, my friends. Don't do this **wicked** thing'"*
(GENESIS 19:4-5,7).

*"If a man lies with a man as one lies with a woman,
both of them have done what is detestable"*
(LEVITICUS 20:13).

*"'Bring out the man who came to your house so we
can have sex with him.'…'No, my friends, don't
be so vile…don't do this disgraceful thing'"*
(JUDGES 19:22-23).

*"Neither the sexually immoral…nor male prostitutes nor
homosexual offenders…will inherit the kingdom of God"*
(1 CORINTHIANS 6:9-10).

Argument:

Biblical morality is no longer the mandate today. The mandate against homosexuality has changed, just as the mandate for a woman covering her head has changed (see 1 Corinthians 11:6).

Answer:

Cultures change, but biblical morality has never changed. New Testament truth is consistent with Old Testament truth. Saying that God's standard has changed would imply that God has changed. God Himself said, "I the LORD do not change" (Malachi 3:6).

WHAT FACTORS LEAD MEN INTO HOMOSEXUALITY?

A variety of factors draw men to homosexual relationships. The following three causes are the most common bases for a man getting involved in gay relationships with other men.[17]

1. He doesn't identify with his weak or absent father and views women as undesirable

— Considers his father weak and powerless, and his mother overpowering

— Condemns his father for allowing his mother to rule the family

— Recoils from women because of his domineering, controlling mother

— Fantasizes about sex with his mother to get back at his weak father
— Despises being taken as a surrogate "husband" by his lonely mother
— Retreats from women due to an emotionally detached, absent, or alcoholic mother

Result:

He unconsciously concludes, *Women are not safe. I'm going to look to men for love.* Because of the emotional void in his life, he is drawn to men perceived as strong; thus, he plunges into homosexuality. These sons feel emotionally wounded:

> *"There are those who curse their fathers*
> *and do not bless their mothers"*
> (Proverbs 30:11).

2. He doesn't bond with his nonaffirming father

— Feels he can never measure up to his father's standards of manliness
— Knows his artistic, feminine traits are a disappointment to his athletic father
— Envies his athletic brothers, whose maleness is affirmed, while his own maleness is denied
— Resents being given money or gifts instead of love and affirmation
— Perceives himself a failure as a male both at home and among peers
— Leans on the acceptance of his nurturing mother and sisters because he is rejected by the males in his life

Result:

He unconsciously concludes, *I need to look for a new home.* He longs for a male father figure who will affirm him and give him a sense of significance. The Bible cautions fathers to be careful about their attitudes and actions toward their children (Ephesians 6:4).

3. He is not emotionally attached to a positive, healthy male because of mistreatment by a significant male

— Resents his father, whom he views as harsh and rejecting
— Rejects his father for having an affair and abandoning the family
— Rebels against a hypocritical father who espouses religious beliefs but fails to live them

— Reacts with sexual identity confusion to sexual abuse by another male before the age of 12

— Refuses to have a relationship with his abusive, alcoholic father

— Retreats from his own maleness because of hurt and rejection by males in early years

Result:

He unconsciously concludes, *If this is what being a man is like, I'd rather be like a woman.* Thus, in his warped thinking, he despises his own male gender and seeks security within the female gender.

What Factors Lead Females into Lesbianism?

There is a variety of factors that influence girls to seek solace in homosexual relationships. Here are three of the more common ones:[18]

1. She doesn't identify with her weak mother

— Views her mother as weak and powerless; lives with a victim mentality

— Condemns her mother and competes with her

— Excels in athletics and becomes a tomboy, thus hindering the development of her femininity

— Competes with males and tries to be more masculine in order to be better accepted

— Rejects her mother and parents herself, thus creating a craving for a mother figure

— Distrusts men because of her adulterous father, thus leaving her with no acceptable male role model

— Assumes the role of emotional mate to her mother after the loss of her father

Result:

She unconsciously concludes, *If this is what being a woman is like, I'm going to be like a man.* Thus she rejects her female gender and identifies with the male gender.

Because of heartache, she looks for love within a lesbian relationship.

2. She doesn't bond with her nonnurturing mother

— Views her mother as harsh and overly critical; feels she can never please her mother

— Sees her mother as nonnurturing, and feels she can never be accepted
— Knows she is a disappointment to her parents because they wanted a son
— Blames her mother for breaking up the family
— Despises her overachieving mother in contrast to her weak, passive father
— Resents being treated as though what she thinks, says, and does doesn't matter
— Perceives herself as an "invisible" child deprived of being mothered

Result:

She unconsciously concludes, *I need to look for a new home.* She detaches her mind from her emotions and searches for security from a surrogate mother, and she attaches herself to a mother figure who sexualizes their relationship. The mother who fails to nurture her children is unwise and emotionally destructive (Proverbs 14:1).

3. She is not drawn to males because of her abusive father or mistreatment from other men

— Refuses to trust men as a result of having an emotionally detached, absent, or alcoholic father
— Recoils from men as a result of sexual or physical abuse by a male
— Retreats from men as a result of hurt and rejection by males in childhood
— Resents male children who are favored by family members
— Reacts to men in leadership and feels she is more capable
— Rebels against a hypocritical father who espouses religious beliefs but fails to live them
— Rejects her father for his denigration of women

Result:

She unconsciously concludes, *Men are not safe. I want relationships only with women.* She plunges into homosexuality. A nurturing father has a vital role in helping establish a daughter's feminine identity. If male nurture is lacking, a daughter can become embittered and lack the courage to trust males (Colossians 3:21).

DOES GOD OFFER HOPE?

If you choose to submit control of your life into the hands of the heavenly Father and trust Jesus as your Lord and Savior—giving Him control of your life—He will forgive all your sins and provide the power you need to overcome the sexual desires tearing at your heart.

If you have engaged in homosexual behavior, but have yielded your life to Christ, you need to know you are not a hardened homosexual. You may have bought into the lie that you cannot change. But the Bible never lies, and the Bible states that many homosexuals *have* changed (1 Corinthians 6:11). Your righteous Judge declares the charges against you "a case of mistaken identity." Now live in the light of your new identity and walk in the light of your newfound freedom!

> *"It is for freedom that Christ has set us free.*
> *Stand firm, then, and do not let yourselves be*
> *burdened again by a yoke of slavery"*
> (GALATIANS 5:1).

What Is the Way to Freedom?

Climb out of your sandy ditch and stand firm on the solid truths of God's Word. You'll find yourself on the path toward recovery as you understand and accept His perfect plan for your sexuality.

The way to begin changing your behavior is to accentuate the positive.

Focus on God's everlasting love for you.
— Respect how wonderfully God has made you.
— Respond to God's call on your life.

> *"I have loved you with an everlasting love;*
> *I have drawn you with loving-kindness"*
> (JEREMIAH 31:3).

Own all your negative emotions and recognize which ones are connected to past pain.
— Choose to reject the control your emotions have had over you.
— Pray for God to break the bondage to your childhood feelings.

> *"He who conceals his sins does not prosper, but*
> *whoever confesses and renounces them finds mercy"*
> (PROVERBS 28:13).

Refuse to act on your irrational emotions.
— Tell yourself the truth when negative emotions push you toward inappropriate behavior.

— Put the truth into your heart by memorizing Psalm 4:4; Proverbs 29:11; Ecclesiastes 7:9; Romans 6:11; Philippians 4:19; James 1:19-20.

> *"I have hidden your word in my heart*
> *that I might not sin against you"*
> (Psalm 119:11).

Make forgiveness your priority.[19]

— Confess your unforgiveness as sin.

— Choose to forgive those who hurt you in the past—even if you don't feel like doing that.

> *"Do not condemn, and you will not be condemned.*
> *Forgive, and you will be forgiven"*
> (Luke 6:37).

Understand and identify your triggers to sexual temptation.[20]

— Take responsibility for your past failures.

— Avoid anything that stimulates sexual temptations.

> *"Each one is tempted when, by his own evil desire,*
> *he is dragged away and enticed"*
> (James 1:14).

Embrace your true identity as a dearly loved "child of God" and concentrate on pleasing Him.

— Choose to be the person and gender God created you to be.

— Hide God's truth in your heart by memorizing Isaiah 43:1; Ezekiel 36:26-27; Romans 6:4; Philippians 1:6; 1 John 3:1.

> *"I have been crucified with Christ and I no longer live, but*
> *Christ lives in me. The life I live in the body, I live by faith*
> *in the Son of God, who loved me and gave himself for me"*
> (Galatians 2:20).

For Christians who struggle with same-sex attraction:
You will experience the power of victory
as you walk daily in your new identity in Christ.

—JH

Your Scripture Prayer Project

1 Corinthians 6:18-20

1 Corinthians 10:13

2 Corinthians 5:17

Hebrews 4:15

Romans 6:11-12

2 Peter 1:3

Leviticus 19:2

Philippians 4:13

Luke 1:37

For additional guidance on this topic, see also *Adultery, Anger, Childhood Sexual Abuse, Codependency, Crisis Intervention, Critical Spirit, Depression, Domestic Violence, Dysfunctional Family, Fear, Forgiveness, Grief Recovery, Guilt, Hope, Identity, Prejudice, Rape Recovery, Reconciliation, Rejection, Salvation, Self-worth, Sexual Addiction, Sexual Integrity, Singleness, Suicide Prevention, Verbal and Emotional Abuse, Victimization, Worry.*

25

HOPE
The Anchor for Your Soul

What an anchor provides for a ship, hope provides for the soul. Both provide necessary stability amidst the storms of life, something to hold on to should you find yourself floundering in the ditch of despair. Although the *popular* understanding of hope is an optimistic wish that something good will happen, *Christian hope* is based on God's unchanging word in the Bible. By patiently relying on what God says, you will have all the hope necessary—with all the certainty you will ever need—because...

> *"...everything that was written in the past was written*
> *to teach us, so that through endurance and the*
> *encouragement of the Scriptures we might have hope"*
> (ROMANS 15:4).

WHAT IS GOD'S HEART ON HOPE?

The Bible says that when your hope is anchored in God, He will teach you His truth and lead you in the way you should go. Christian hope is an optimistic assurance from God that something will be fulfilled. This hope is a *guaranteed* hope not subject to change because it is anchored in our unchangeable Savior and Lord.[1]

Although the Bible uses the word *hope* in both the secular and the spiritual sense, the focus of our Christian hope is always based on the *guaranteed promises* of God. Thus, this hope will never be a disappointment. As Christians, we are promised peace with God:

> *"We also rejoice in our sufferings, because we know that suffering*
> *produces perseverance; perseverance, character; and character, hope.*
> *And hope does not disappoint us, because God has poured out his*
> *love into our hearts by the Holy Spirit, whom he has given us"*
> (ROMANS 5:3-5).

WHAT HAPPENS WHEN PEOPLE LOSE HOPE?

Hopelessness is characterized by absolute despair with no expectation of good.[2]

Hopeless thinking can result in a desire to die. Those who feel hopeless are unable to envision any viable option for their problems—death seems the only solution (see "Suicide Prevention" on page 395).

In the midst of our personal storms, rather than drowning in a sea of hopelessness, we are called by God to put our hope in Him, allowing Him to be our Anchor and relying on His promises.

WHAT IS THE DIFFERENCE BETWEEN FAITH AND HOPE?

Hope is an assured promise, whereas faith is acting on that promise. In other words, *faith is hope put into action*. Acting in faith is necessary so that our hope is not merely a mental concept, but rather a truly living hope—a guaranteed hope that becomes a reality when we experience an anchored life.

> *"Find rest, O my soul, in God alone; my hope comes*
> *from him. He alone is my rock and my salvation; he is*
> *my fortress, I will not be shaken. My salvation and my*
> *honor depend on God; he is my mighty rock, my refuge"*
> (PSALM 62:5-7).

WHAT IS THE UPWARD SPIRAL OF HOPE?

If your life is anchored in Christian hope, you will never drown in despair. Swirling currents and pounding waves will offer you no cause for alarm. You are held secure in the hope of Christ, the Master over both the storms and the seas. When you have Christ, you have...

— *Contentment:* You are able to be patient because of God's hope within you.

> *"If we hope for what we do not yet have,*
> *we wait for it patiently"*
> (ROMANS 8:25).

— *Courage:* You are able to be bold because of God's hope within you.

> *"Since we have such a hope, we are very bold"*
> (2 CORINTHIANS 3:12).

— *Confidence:* You experience assurance because of God's hope within you.

> *"You have been my hope, O Sovereign LORD,*
> *my confidence since my youth"*
> (PSALM 71:5).

— *Cheerfulness:* You experience joy because of God's hope within you.

> *"Be joyful in hope, patient in affliction,*
> *faithful in prayer"*
> (ROMANS 12:12).

— *Comfort:* You experience encouragement because of God's unfailing love for you.

> *"May your unfailing love rest upon us, O LORD,*
> *even as we put our hope in you"*
> (PSALM 33:22).

— *Conviction:* You are anchored in hope because of God's Word within you.

> *"May those who fear you rejoice when they see*
> *me, for I have put my hope in your word"*
> (PSALM 119:74).

— *Christlikeness:* You are conformed to the character of Christ because of God's hope for you.

> *"I eagerly expect and hope that I will in no way be ashamed,*
> *but will have sufficient courage so that now as always Christ*
> *will be exalted in my body, whether by life or by death"*
> (PHILIPPIANS 1:20).

WHAT CAUSES HOPE TO FAIL?

We all have placed our confidence in something or someone that did not hold, or that broke under pressure. To avoid this, you must cultivate Christian hope. Christian hope is…

— *Not* dependent on another person or a group of people.

Rather, it is dependent on the Lord alone.

— *Not* wishful thinking, vague longing, or trying to fulfill a dream.

Rather, it is assured, unchangeable, and absolute.

— *Not* determined by circumstances, events, or abilities.

Rather, it is determined by what is already secure and promised.

— *Not* merely a desire.

Rather, it is delayed fulfillment of reality.

— *Not* dependent on the stars, luck, chance, or timing.

Rather, it is predestined and settled in the heart and mind of God.

> *"In him we were also chosen, having been predestined*
> *according to the plan of him who works out everything*
> *in conformity with the purpose of his will"*
> (Ephesians 1:11).

After Losing Hope, How Do We Regain It?

To regain a hopeful outlook on life is not difficult or complicated. All it requires is a shift in focus. As hope is restored and anchors you, you'll grow toward Christlike maturity. Then, no matter how strongly the winds bluster and blow, you won't get knocked off course. The challenge comes in focusing not on the storm or the ditch you're in, but on the hope God has for you—His path of recovery for you. Because of God's faithfulness, *hope anchored in His character* will hold. That is why meditating on God's unfailing promises, which are found in His unchanging Word, will supply all the stability you will ever need.

Key Verse to Memorize

> *"'I know the plans I have for you,' declares the Lord, 'plans to prosper*
> *you and not to harm you, plans to give you hope and a future'"*
> (Jeremiah 29:11).

Key Passage to Read and Reread—Lamentations 3:19-25

Even the deepest failures in your life cannot thwart God's faithfulness to you. Do you know the genuine goodness of God in your life—His immense mercy, His constant compassion, His everlasting love? (see Salvation, pp. 349-55). God will be faithful to you forever. The Bible says to put your *hope* in Him. Repeatedly say to yourself when you are in the midst of the storm, "I will hope in him" (Lamentations 3:24 esv).

How to Put Your Hope in Him

— *Look* at the situation accurately.

> *"I remember my affliction and my wandering,*
> *the bitterness and the gall. I well remember them,*
> *and my soul is downcast within me"*
> (Lamentations 3:19-20).

— *Line* up your thinking with what gives you hope.

> *"This I call to mind and therefore I have hope"*
> (verse 21).

— *Learn* what gives hope in the midst of this situation.

> *"Because of the LORD's great love we are not*
> *consumed, for his compassions never fail"*
> (VERSE 22).

— *Linger* on this fact: Every day God will be faithful to you.

> *"They are new every morning; great is your faithfulness"*
> (VERSE 23).

— *Let* the Lord fulfill you totally—not just partially.

> *"The LORD is my portion; therefore I will wait for him"*
> (VERSE 24).

— *Lean* on this truth to receive hope for your heart.

> *"The LORD is good to those whose hope is in him,*
> *to the one who seeks him"*
> (VERSE 25).

How Do I Overcome Grief with Hope?

All of us experience deep grief and mourning. And if you stay locked in the prison of emotional pain, your heart will become deadened to hope. Realize that you have a Savior who experienced the most severe grief—the One who agonized in the garden of Gethsemane with the anguish of His soul—Jesus, who said, "My soul is overwhelmed with sorrow to the point of death" (Matthew 26:38).

To weather the storm gales of grief...

— *Remember* that some grief and suffering is natural and must be endured for a time.

> *"We do not lose heart. Though outwardly we are wasting*
> *away, yet inwardly we are being renewed day by day.*
> *For our light and momentary troubles are achieving*
> *for us an eternal glory that far outweighs them all"*
> (2 CORINTHIANS 4:16-17).

— *Reach* out to God in your grief and sorrow.

> *"The LORD is close to the brokenhearted and*
> *saves those who are crushed in spirit"*
> (PSALM 34:18).

— *Reflect* on fond memories of the past and allow yourself to grieve over specific events.

> *"There is a time for everything...a time to weep and a*
> *time to laugh, a time to mourn and a time to dance"*
> (ECCLESIASTES 3:1,4).

— *Reach* out to a friend and share your pain.

> *"Carry each other's burdens, and in this way you*
> *will fulfill the law of Christ"*
> (GALATIANS 6:2).

— *Remain* hopeful, knowing that this feeling of deep grief will pass.

> *"I tell you the truth, you will weep and mourn while the*
> *world rejoices. You will grieve, but your grief will turn to joy"*
> (JOHN 16:20).

— *Reinforce* your faith by giving hope to others.

> *"Praise be to the God and Father of our Lord Jesus Christ, the*
> *Father of compassion and the God of all comfort, who comforts*
> *us in all our troubles, so that we can comfort those in any*
> *trouble with the comfort we ourselves have received from God"*
> (2 CORINTHIANS 1:3-4).

HOW DO I OVERCOME BITTERNESS WITH HOPE?

Bitterness can be like a winter storm blowing in from the north, pushing you back to the ditch of despair. At first the signs are subtle, but soon bitterness swirls into a blizzard of complaints, unforgiveness, depression, sustained grief, hopelessness, and rage against God. Most people have great difficulty admitting that they are bitter. They say, "I'm not bitter, but I just can't forgive him!" or, "I'm not angry, but it's just not fair." Bitterness is buried anger that has become frozen in resentment. Unresolved anger is like a chain that ties us to the past.

> *"See to it that no one misses the grace of God and that no*
> *bitter root grows up to cause trouble and defile many"*
> (HEBREWS 12:15).

If you are struggling to overcome bitterness...

— Believe that it is possible, with God's help, to get rid of all of your resentment.

— Know that you are not a helpless victim of other people, circumstances, or events.

— Take personal responsibility for your attitude of bitterness.

— Confess before God that you are harboring anger. Express your true desire to overcome the bondage of bitterness.

— Search your heart for the past events or people that embitter your heart, then release your right for revenge.

— Understand that only a close relationship with Jesus can give you the love and confidence to let go. Leave your vengeance to the judgment of God.

— Cultivate a heart of forgiveness toward others that allows you to experience God's total forgiveness of you.

WHAT ARE THE BENEFITS OF LIVING A HOPE-FILLED LIFE?

Putting your hope in Christ will keep you from being wrecked by the crushing events of life. Although your anchor is unseen, you will feel its pull and know it is holding you. No matter what storm you might be presently enduring or might soon be encountering, if your anchor is Jesus Christ, your anchor will hold! Extraordinary benefits await the one who holds on to the hope He offers—benefits based on the promises of God, benefits both in this present life and in the life to come. You cannot earn or deserve the benefits of hope—they are a gift of grace to you based on the Lord's great love for you. What are these benefits?

His blessed hope...

— *Generates* faith and love in you

> *"We have heard of your faith in Christ Jesus and of the love*
> *you have for all the saints—the faith and love that spring*
> *from the hope that is stored up for you in heaven and that you*
> *have already heard about in the word of truth, the gospel"*
> (COLOSSIANS 1:4-5).

— *Causes* you to live a pure life

> *"Everyone who has this hope in him purifies*
> *himself, just as he is pure"*
> (1 JOHN 3:3).

— *Inspires* you to persevere with endurance

> *"We continually remember before our God and Father your*
> *work produced by faith, your labor prompted by love, and*
> *your endurance inspired by hope in our Lord Jesus Christ"*
> (1 THESSALONIANS 1:3).

— *Uplifts* your downcast soul

> *"Why are you downcast, O my soul? Why so*
> *disturbed within me? Put your hope in God, for I*
> *will yet praise him, my Savior and my God"*
> (Psalm 42:5).

— *Causes* you to praise God

> *"As for me, I will always have hope;*
> *I will praise you more and more"*
> (Psalm 71:14).

— *Anchors* your soul

> *"We have this hope as an anchor for the soul, firm and*
> *secure. It enters the inner sanctuary behind the curtain"*
> (Hebrews 6:19).

— *Gives* you reason to rejoice

> *"Through whom we have gained access by faith into this grace in*
> *which we now stand. And we rejoice in the hope of the glory of God"*
> (Romans 5:2).

— *Establishes* your security and safety

> *"You will be secure, because there is hope; you will*
> *look about you and take your rest in safety"*
> (Job 11:18).

— *Guarantees* your eternal life

> *"He saved us, not because of righteous things we had*
> *done, but because of his mercy. He saved us through the*
> *washing of rebirth and renewal by the Holy Spirit, whom*
> *he poured out on us generously through Jesus Christ our*
> *Savior, so that, having been justified by his grace, we*
> *might become heirs having the hope of eternal life"*
> (Titus 3:5-7).

> *"We have put our hope in the living God, who is the*
> *Savior of all men, and especially of those who believe"*
> (1 Timothy 4:10).

> In Christ, we have
> an Anchor securing us through our storms.
>
> His holding power is without question—
> He holds us secure in His arms.
>
> —JH

Your Scripture Prayer Project

Psalm 42:5-6

1 Timothy 6:17

Hebrews 6:17,19

Psalm 39:7

Lamentations 3:25

Psalm 25:3

Romans 5:3-5

1 Peter 1:3

Jeremiah 29:11

For additional guidance on this topic, see also *Crisis Intervention, Decision Making, Depression, Evil and Suffering...Why?, Fear, Forgiveness, Grief Recovery, Guilt, Identity, Reconciliation, Salvation, Self-worth, Stress Management, Suicide Prevention, Victimization, Worry.*

26

IDENTITY
Do You Know Who You Really Are?

Who are you…*really?* Do you identify yourself with your occupation, "I'm a teacher" or with your nationality, "I'm a German" or with your struggles, "I'm an alcoholic"?

All of these labels do help identify us by distinguishing us one from another, but they are not our *primary* identity. Based on the Bible, everyone on earth is identified with one of two persons, either Adam or Jesus. And the implications of whose family line you belong to are a matter of life and death—*for eternity.*

When Adam, the first man, disobeyed God in the Garden of Eden, sin entered the world and was passed down to every one of us. And along with sin came death. "For as in Adam all die." But Jesus died on the cross for our sins and rose again, providing forgiveness and the free gift of eternal life. "In Christ all will be made alive" (1 Corinthians 15:22).

And that's not all. By trusting in Jesus as our Lord and Savior, a *transfer* takes place—from one family to the next. We are adopted into the family of God and are given a glorious new identity—a new nature reflective of Jesus Christ Himself! "Therefore, if anyone is in Christ, he is a new creation; the old has gone, the new has come!" (2 Corinthians 5:17).

WHAT IS YOUR IDENTITY?

— *The identity* of a person is based on the distinguishing characteristics of that person.

— *Your identity* involves both inner character and outer conduct, which distinguish you from everyone else. Your visible conduct should consistently reflect your inner character. This forms your identity.

> *"As water reflects a face, so a man's heart reflects the man"*
> (PROVERBS 27:19).

The Visible You

— How you are known by *others:* your personality, actions, masks, pretenses, outer appearance

> *"Even a child is known by his actions,*
> *by whether his conduct is pure and right"*
> (PROVERBS 20:11).

The Real You

— How you are known by *God:* your basic nature, your character, your value system

> *"All a man's ways seem right to him,*
> *but the LORD weighs the heart"*
> (PROVERBS 21:2).

CLAIMING YOUR IDENTITY IN CHRIST

In order for us as Christians to walk in victory, we need to identify the lies we believe about ourselves and find the path to recovery, where we discover who we really are in Christ.[1] Consider the following seven lies we tell ourselves contrasted with seven truths from God's Word. For lasting change to occur, we must bypass the lies and constantly rely on the truth of Scripture, which steers us onto the Road to Transformation and charts a course toward Christlike maturity, where it's the Savior, and not our sins, that characterizes us and our true identities.

> *"Do not conform any longer to the pattern of this world,*
> *but be transformed by the renewing of your mind"*
> (ROMANS 12:2).

Look at one of the lies each day. Ask yourself, *Am I believing this lie, or something similar?* Then look up scriptures for that day and write them down in your own words. Read them aloud, and thank God that His Word confirms the truth about you—*whether you feel like it or not.* If you repeat this practice for three weeks, you will begin to *see yourself in the way God sees you!*

Day One—Your New Family

Lie: "I can't feel valuable unless I'm loved and accepted by the significant people in my life."

At times, do you feel as though you'll never measure up? No matter how hard you try, it's never good enough—*you're never good enough*—to earn the love and acceptance of those around you. When your shortcomings always overshadow your successes, your heart says, *I can't do anything right!*

If this is so, you need to know…

Truth: You have God-given value because you have been placed into a *new family* where you are unconditionally loved and accepted by God.

— You are chosen by God (Ephesians 1:4).

— You are adopted by God (Ephesians 1:4-5).

— You are a child of God (John 1:12).

— You are born again (1 Peter 1:23).

— You have been adopted into the family of God (Romans 8:15-16).

Day Two—Your New Characteristics

Lie: "I'll never feel valuable because this is just the way I am. I cannot change."

At times, do you feel there's just no hope? You are hooked by a habit you just can't shake…and it's shattering your sense of self-worth. You've struggled, you've prayed, you've renounced the deplorable practice, only to return to it again.

Sometimes a wrong attitude of unforgiveness will weigh you down with guilt. Every time you contemplate getting out of the ditch, the gut-wrenching pain won't let you let go. You fear you'll always be the same.

If this is so, you need to know…

Truth: You have God-given value because God has changed you on the inside and has given you *new characteristics.*

— You are a new creation (2 Corinthians 5:17).

— You have a new nature (Colossians 2:11).

— You have a new heart (Ezekiel 36:26).

— You have a new Spirit (Ezekiel 36:27).

— You have a new mind (1 Corinthians 2:16).

Day Three—Your New Clothing

Lie: "I can't feel I have value unless I live in the right neighborhood, drive the right car, and wear the right clothes."

At times, do you feel you must "keep striving"? You have to work more to earn more, to do more, to get more. *This* must be bigger…*that* must be better!

Anything else would be second-rate, second-best, second-class—and therefore would punch a sizeable hole in your self-image. Slowing down, settling for a little less, would somehow soil your starched and pressed identity.

If this is so, you need to know...

Truth: You have God-given value because you have a new residence in God's kingdom and the *new clothing* of Christ.

— You are clothed with Christ (Galatians 3:27).

— You are baptized into Christ (Romans 6:4).

— You are hidden in Christ (Colossians 3:3).

— You are sealed with the Spirit of Christ (Ephesians 1:13-14).

— You are given the full armor of God (Ephesians 6:13-17).

Day Four—Your New Life

Lie: "My life has no value since I've done so many things wrong—my life is ruined."

At times, do you feel like the "sorriest of sinners"? You think no one's stack of wrongs could tower as high as yours.

God forgives...but you're sure His grace has run out where you're concerned. His arms are always open, but surely this time He's turned His back. After all, you've confessed these same sins time and time and time again.

If this is so, you need to know...

Truth: You have God-given value, for you've been given a *new life* in Jesus Christ.

— You are redeemed (Ephesians 1:7).

— You are washed (1 Corinthians 6:11).

— You are purified (1 John 1:7).

— You are justified (Romans 5:1).

— You are sanctified (1 Corinthians 6:11).

Day Five—Your New Image

Lie: "My life has value as long as I can look good to others."

At times, do you hope and pray that no one finds "this" out? Even if it happened long ago, if people knew what you did, any respect would be erased.

Do you have "pockets of perfectionism" because of the pressure? People mustn't find out about your struggles, faults, or shame. What other people think means everything to you.

If this is so, you need to know...

Truth: You have God-given value even though you have fallen in the past and may stumble in the future. He has given you a *new image.*

— You are totally accepted by Christ (Romans 15:7).

— You are totally blameless before Christ (Colossians 1:22).

— You are totally righteous in Christ (2 Corinthians 5:21).

— You are totally complete in Christ (Colossians 2:9-10).

— You are totally perfect (meaning "mature" in the original Greek text— not flawless) because of Christ (Hebrews 10:14).

Day Six—Your New Freedom

Lie: "My life has no value because I have failed and deserve to be punished."

At times, do you feel you don't deserve forgiveness? Mercy is for other people, not for you. You've failed so many times...*you are a failure.*

Punishment, a penalized life, and a painful future all await you. God can bring good out of a lot of things, but not this miserable mess. Furthermore, why would He care? Surely His love has been lost.

If this is so, you need to know...

Truth: You have God-given value based not on your past performance but on Christ, who lives in you and who gives you *freedom* from condemnation.

— You are free from accusation (Colossians 1:22).

— You are free from condemnation (Romans 8:1).

— You are free from the law (Romans 7:4).

— You are free from sin (Romans 6:11).

— You are free from God's wrath (Romans 5:9).

Day Seven—Your New Inheritance

Lie: "My life has no value if I do not succeed financially and leave a comfortable inheritance."

At times, do you feel that success is measured only in dollars and cents? When the bank account heads south, does your self-image trail behind? You work...work... work...seven days a week, providing what is needed, but needing to protect your self-image.

You're driven to provide, driven to bear all the burdens alone.

If this is so, you need to know...

Truth: You have God-given value because you've been given a *new inheritance* that provides the only true and lasting significance and security possible.

— You have been made an heir of God (Galatians 4:7).

— You have inherited everything needed to be godly (1 Peter 1:3).

— You are a partner of the divine nature (2 Peter 1:4).

— You have inherited every spiritual blessing (Ephesians 1:3).

— You have inherited eternal life (John 3:16).

> **What is your true identity?**
> If the *real you* has "*Christ in you,*"
> the *visible you*
> reflects Christ *through* you.
> —JH

Your Scripture Prayer Project

1 John 3:1

Ephesians 1:5

Psalm 27:10

1 Peter 1:3

1 Corinthians 6:11

2 Corinthians 5:17

Colossians 1:22

1 Corinthians 6:19-20

2 Corinthians 5:20

Matthew 5:14-16

For additional guidance on this topic, see also *Alcohol and Drug Abuse, Childhood Sexual Abuse, Codependency, Critical Spirit, Cults, Depression, Dysfunctional Family, Evil and Suffering...Why?, Fear, Forgiveness, Guilt, Homosexuality, Hope, Prejudice, Rejection, Salvation, Self-worth, Stress Management, Suicide Prevention, Victimization, Worry.*

27

ILLNESS—CHRONIC AND TERMINAL

God's Peace in the Midst of Pain

*C*hronic and *terminal* are two words no one wants to hear in association with illness. A person with chronic illness suffers physically and can face a lifetime of persistent pain. Terminal illness is a physical sickness with the prognosis that life expectancy will be less than a year, although patients can live longer. Both can be debilitating ditches physically and emotionally, with constrained activities and strained relationships. Spiritual vitality too can diminish, with plaintive cries of "Why me?" In the midst of suffering God longs to bring peace, with the promise of His presence now, *and for eternity.*

> *"All men are like grass, and all their glory is like the*
> *flowers of the field; the grass withers and the flowers fall"*
> (1 PETER 1:24).

WHAT ARE GOD'S TRUTHS CONCERNING SUFFERING?

> *"My soul is weary with sorrow; strengthen*
> *me according to your word"*
> (PSALM 119:28).

Troubles are temporary, glory is eternal.

> *"Therefore we do not lose heart. Though outwardly we are*
> *wasting away, yet inwardly we are being renewed day by*
> *day. For our light and momentary troubles are achieving*
> *for us an eternal glory that far outweighs them all. So we*
> *fix our eyes not on what is seen, but on what is unseen. For*
> *what is seen is temporary, but what is unseen is eternal"*
> (2 CORINTHIANS 4:16-18).

Your physical body is designed to decay.

> *"Dust you are and to dust you will return"*
> (GENESIS 3:19).

Afflictions are allowed by God to teach you.

> *"It was good for me to be afflicted so that*
> *I might learn your decrees"*
> (PSALM 119:71).

Suffering opens your eyes to see God.

> *"My ears had heard of you but now my eyes have seen you"*
> (JOB 42:5)

Lives are conformed to the image of Christ through suffering.

> *"We know that in all things God works for the good*
> *of those who love him...those God foreknew he also*
> *predestined to be conformed to the likeness of his Son"*
> (ROMANS 8:28-29).

WHAT ARE THE FIVE STAGES OF SORROW?[1]

Denial—avoiding painful reality
— "The test results are clearly wrong."
— "I'm feeling much better...I'm sure I am improving."

Anger—opening up honest emotions
— "Why has this happened to me?"
— "God is not fair!"

Bargaining[2]—attempting to change reality
— "I have not been a good person. I'll change, and God will forgive me."
— "If I have enough faith, God will miraculously heal me."

Depression—feeling despair over the situation
— "I hate being so dependent on others."
— "My life is over. I am useless to everyone."

Acceptance—gaining a positive outlook
— "Lord, I choose to embrace Your grace on a daily basis, and to move

from being a 'victim' of illness to being a victorious, shining testimony to Your sufficiency."

— "I accept this circumstance as allowed by You for my good and Your glory" (see Ephesians 3:20-21).

DOES TAKING MEDICATION DEMONSTRATE A LACK OF FAITH?

God placed medicinal qualities within nature. You can certainly exercise faith in God and at the same time take medicine as prescribed. Ezekiel 47:12 states that God made "leaves for healing."

> **Q:** I prayed with faith expecting God to heal me, but nothing happened. What went wrong?
>
> **A:** God can heal anyone at any time in any way. However, many godly people of genuine faith do not receive physical healing. Pray for God's will for your life as you seek emotional, psychological, and spiritual healing.[3] Honestly and openly experience each stage of sorrow, and know that in His time, God *will* heal your *heart.*[4]
>
> *"He [God] heals the brokenhearted*
> *and binds up their wounds"*
> (PSALM 147:3).

WHAT SHOULD BE SAID TO A TERMINALLY ILL PERSON?

Typically it is best to tell the truth. While medical science is never the last word, and miracles *do* happen at times, most terminally ill patients instinctively know they are not getting well. Dishonesty and deception robs them of dignity and the motivation to get relationships and affairs in order before they die.

"Do not lie. Do not deceive one another"
(LEVITICUS 19:11).

WHAT DO YOU NEED TO UNDERSTAND ABOUT DEATH?

Death Is Designed

Embracing God's gift of life means accepting death as part of life's package. The moment you are born, you take the first step toward death. Spiritual maturity recognizes death as a natural part of God's design following the Fall.

The path to recovery leads to a sound understanding of God's perfect plan for your life, which will accelerate your progress on the Road to Transformation—such that your maturity in Christ will one day silence the cries, "Why me?"

> *"There is a time for everything...a time to*
> *be born and a time to die"*
> (ECCLESIASTES 3:1-2).

Death Is a Doorway

Death can be a doorway to a more abundant (eternal) life, or it can be the gateway to eternal misery. Death is not an end to life, but the beginning of a different kind of life. We are born with a heart's desire to live forever, and only through faith in Christ can we reach out and embrace God's promise of eternal life.

> *"Small is the gate and narrow the road that leads to*
> *life, and only a few find it"*
> (MATTHEW 7:14).

Death Is Divine

The reality for all Christians is that *you have already died!* God's desire for you as His child is *death to self* and submission to the divine life of Christ living within you, expressing His life through you. Eternal life began the moment you accepted Christ.

> *"I have been crucified with Christ and I no longer live, but*
> *Christ lives in me. The life I live in the body, I live by faith*
> *in the Son of God, who loved me and gave himself for me"*
> (GALATIANS 2:20).

WHAT IS HEAVEN LIKE?

> *"It [heaven] shone with the glory of God, and its brilliance was*
> *like that of a very precious jewel, like a jasper, clear as crystal"*
> (REVELATION 21:11).

Heaven is the place where God dwells (1 Kings 8:30) and it is the place where there is no...

— hunger or thirst

> *"Never again will they hunger; never again will they thirst"*
> (REVELATION 7:16).

— crying or pain

> *"He will wipe every tear from their eyes.*
> *There will be no more...crying or pain"*
> (REVELATION 21:4).

— death or mourning

> *"There will be no more death or mourning"*
> (Revelation 21:4).

— impurity or evil

> *"Nothing impure will ever enter it, nor will anyone
> who does what is shameful or deceitful"*
> (Revelation 21:27).

Helping Your Family Prepare for Your Impending Death

If you yourself are terminally ill, the best way to allay concerns for your family is to put your house in order. You can make many decisions that will help lighten the load of your loved ones.[5]

> *"This is what the Lord says: Put your house in order,
> because you are going to die; you will not recover"*
> (2 Kings 20:1)

When facing the *reality* of death, here is how you can help your family:

Prepare Your Will
— Prepare a legally binding will.
— Make a list of specific items for special family members and friends.
— Consider a bequest to your church and trustworthy ministries.
— Pray about becoming an organ donor.
— Consider a "living will" declaring your preferences in medical decisions.
— Read Hebrews 9:17.

Express Your Desires
— Choose whom you want to conduct the service.
— Select meaningful poems, music, and scriptures.
— Designate pallbearers and favorite musicians.
— Name organizations you want to receive memorials.
— Communicate choices about your funeral and burial.
— Read Hebrews 11:22.

Arrange Your Affairs
— Vest someone with power of attorney to act as your agent or attorney-in-fact to make property, financial, and other legal decisions.

— Gather important documents in one place (insurance, investments, key to safety deposit box).

— Secure legal guardianship for any dependents.

— Write out names of persons to be contacted (lawyers, family, friends).

— Communicate decisions to dependents.

— Read 1 Chronicles 28:11,19.

Leave a Legacy of Love

— Share the significance of your Christian faith with others.

— Communicate love, appreciation, and words you've always wanted to say.

— Write, phone, or visit special people.

— Mend broken relationships with "I'm sorry," or "Please forgive me."

— Read 2 Timothy 1:3-4.

Identify Your Fears

— *Fear of death*	Examine your life to be sure you have a personal relationship with Jesus Christ.
— *Fear of pain*	Physical pain can be controlled through properly administered medication.
— *Fear of loneliness*	God promises to never leave you nor forsake you.
— *Fear of losing control*	It is good that God is in control. He manages better than we can.
— *Fear of abandonment*	The Lord will be the Provider for your loved ones; they need to lean on Christ.

> *"God is our refuge and strength, an ever-present help in trouble. Therefore we will not fear"*
> (Psalm 46:1-2).

Trust Your God

— God has a purpose for everything that happens to you (Proverbs 19:21).

— God's thoughts and ways are not your thoughts and ways (Isaiah 55:8).

— God promises a silver lining behind your darkest cloud (Romans 8:28).

— God holds on to you even if you let go of Him (2 Timothy 2:13).

Yield Your Heart

— Submit your will to God's will and be at peace with Him (Matthew 26:39).

Choose to reflect Christ's spirit in hope and humility (Philippians 2:8).

— Allow Christ to strengthen your heart (Ephesians 3:16).

— Respond to your circumstances with the strength of Christ (Philippians 4:13).

— Anticipate God's promise of hope for the future (1 Corinthians 2:9).

How Do I Lead Someone Who Is Terminally Ill to Christ?

For guidance on this, see "Salvation" on pages 349-56.

As you face illness, and eventually death, adopt Paul's mind-set:

> *"I eagerly expect and hope that I will in no way be ashamed, but will have sufficient courage so that now as always Christ will be exalted in my body, whether by life or by death. For to me, to live is Christ and to die is gain"*
> (Philippians 1:20-21).

> Any illness which can be a burden can also be a blessing. When we allow difficulty to draw us closer to the Lord, the gift tag simply reads, "Grace from God included."
> —JH

═══════════════ *Your Scripture Prayer Project* ═══════════════

Psalm 10:17

Psalm 22:24

Psalm 119:50,71

Psalm 23:4

Psalm 56:3

Psalm 73:26

Mark 14:36

2 Corinthians 12:9

1 Peter 1:6-7

Romans 8:18

Philippians 1:21

For additional guidance on this topic, see also *Alcohol and Drug Abuse, Decision Making, Depression, Evil and Suffering...Why?, Fear, Financial Freedom, Grief Recovery, Hope, Rejection, Salvation, Self-worth, Stress Management, Suicide Prevention, Victimization, Worry.*

28

LYING

Stopping Truth Decay

If your nose grew every time you told a lie, would you stop telling lies? Pinocchio was a wooden marionette given the opportunity to be transformed into a real boy, but on one condition: He had to follow his conscience. Every time he told a lie, his nose would grow.

Pinocchio faced one roadblock after another—tell a lie or be embarrassed, tell a lie or miss out on some fun. Each time, telling a lie seemed a better choice than telling the truth. Over time he deadened his conscience by repeatedly telling lies, leading him to a ditch of desperation lined with deceit. Before long, his nose measured more than a foot long and he was buried under a muddy pile of myths.

ARE SOME LIES HARMLESS?

No. Over time, repeated lying deadens the conscience. Then it becomes easier and easier to lie and be deceptive.

— *Lies* are untrue statements made with the intent to deceive (Proverbs 27:3-4).

— *Half-truths* are partially true statements made with the deliberate intent to deceive (Genesis 12:13).

— *Perjury* is false testimony given under oath (Deuteronomy 19:16-20).

— *Deception* is intentionally giving a false impression through a statement or by omission (Psalm 12:2).

— *Duplicity* is a form of deception in which a person gives two different and opposing impressions (Proverbs 11:3).

— *White lies* are untrue statements that appear harmless and unimportant (Hebrews 3:13).

Many people tell white lies because they are quick, easy, and seem to be the simplest way out of an uncomfortable situation.

— I can't say, "I'm too tired to come over."
 I'll say, "I have other plans."

— I can't say, "I am really angry."
 I'll say, "Anything you want is okay with me."

— I can't say, "I am depressed."
 I'll say, "I have a headache."

— I can't say, "I really don't want to date you."
 I'll say, "I'm going out of town."

— I can't say, "I forgot to read the book you gave me."
 I'll say, "I haven't finished reading it yet."

— I can't say, "I haven't sent the check yet."
 I'll say, "The check's in the mail."

— I can't say, "Dad passed out from drinking."
 I'll say, "He's home today because he has the flu."

> *"Nothing in all creation is hidden from God's*
> *sight. Everything is uncovered and laid bare before*
> *the eyes of him to whom we must give account"*
> (HEBREWS 4:13).

WHAT ARE THE ROOT CAUSES FOR LYING?

Typically, liars don't see themselves as liars. They are just trying to get their needs met. When our God-given inner needs for significance and security are not met—especially in childhood—the tendency is to try to meet those needs illegitimately. Therefore, the two primary causes for lying are:

— *feeling insignificant* and lying to appear more important, and

— *feeling insecure* and lying to keep from looking bad, stupid, or inadequate.

Wrong Beliefs:

— *Insignificance:* "I need to change the truth because the real truth doesn't sound important enough."

— *Insecurity:* "I need to change the truth because if I speak the truth, I'm afraid of what others will think of me or do to me."

Right Belief:

"The Lord promises to meet all my inner needs. As a Christian, I need to tell the truth all the time because Jesus lives within me, and He is Truth! He will empower me to overcome lying so that I can reflect His character."

> *"My God will meet all your needs according*
> *to his glorious riches in Christ Jesus"*
> (Philippians 4:19).

How Can You Encourage Truth-Telling in Difficult Situations?[1]

Know that you cannot please everyone.

> *"Am I now trying to win the approval of men, or of*
> *God? Or am I trying to please men? If I were still trying*
> *to please men, I would not be a servant of Christ"*
> (Galatians 1:10).

Know that you are not responsible for everyone's feelings.

> *"Whoever corrects a mocker invites insult; whoever rebukes*
> *a wicked man incurs abuse. Do not rebuke a mocker*
> *or he will hate you; rebuke a wise man and he will*
> *love you. Instruct a wise man and he will be wiser still;*
> *teach a righteous man and he will add to his learning"*
> (Proverbs 9:7-9).

Know that you can speak the truth in a loving way.

> *"Speaking the truth in love, we will in all things grow*
> *up into him who is the Head, that is, Christ"*
> (Ephesians 4:15).

Know that you are not a perfect person—no one is perfect.

> *"We all, like sheep, have gone astray,*
> *each of us has turned to his own way"*
> (Isaiah 53:6).

Know that you are not accountable for how others respond to the truth. You are accountable to God to tell the truth.

> *"So then, each of us will give an account of himself to God"*
> (Romans 14:12).

What Are Truthful, Diplomatic Ways to Say No?

When pressured to buy an item:

Don't say, "I don't have the money right now" if you have some.

Do say, "Thank you, I'm not interested at this time."

When a person tells you to say he's not in when he is:

Don't say, "I'm sorry. He's not here."

Do say, "I'm sorry; as a Christian, I cannot do that. But I'll be happy to tell him you're not available at this time."

When asked for a date and you don't want to go:

Don't say, "I'm too busy to go."

Do say, "I appreciate your invitation. I feel it would be best for you to ask someone else, but please know I'm honored that you would invite me."

When asked to spend time on a project:

Don't say yes when you don't sense the Lord's leading.

Do say, "I appreciate the effective work you are doing; however, I am so heavily committed I cannot in good conscience undertake another project."

When asked to serve in a church-related capacity you are not at peace about:

Don't say yes because you fear letting God or someone else down.

Do say, "I am not led by the Spirit of God to do this, but I will pray that God will lead you to the person of His choice."

> *"A word aptly spoken is like apples*
> *of gold in settings of silver"*
> (Proverbs 25:11).

How Can You Find Deliverance from the Ditch of Deceit?[2]

Even white lies dirty the conscience and darken the prospect for transparent relationships. Follow these six steps on the path to recovery and exchange half-truths for honesty. Then watch truth trample down your muddy pile of myths!

Discover God's consequences for lying and His hatred for deceit.

> *"You destroy those who tell lies; bloodthirsty and*
> *deceitful men the Lord abhors"*
> (Psalm 5:6).

Determine to be totally honest with God and admit your failures.

> *"If we claim to be without sin, we deceive*
> *ourselves and the truth is not in us"*
> (1 John 1:8).

Discern your areas of personal temptation. Stop and think before you answer.

> *"Set a guard over my mouth, O LORD; keep*
> *watch over the door of my lips"*
> (PSALM 141:3).

Decide you want your life to reflect Christ, who lives in you.

> *"Those God foreknew he also predestined to be*
> *conformed to the likeness of his Son, that he*
> *might be the firstborn among many brothers"*
> (ROMANS 8:29).

Depend on the strength of Christ within you to enable you to change.

> *"I can do everything through him who gives me strength"*
> (PHILIPPIANS 4:13).

Delight in speaking the truth, which is more rewarding than telling lies.

> *"He who conceals his sins does not prosper, but*
> *whoever confesses and renounces them finds mercy"*
> (PROVERBS 28:13).

Tell a lie, you'll look better—at least you hope you do.
Tell the truth, you'll feel better—reflecting *Christ in you.*
—JH

============= *Your Scripture Prayer Project* =============

Proverbs 11:3

Proverbs 12:19,22

Proverbs 19:5

Proverbs 26:18-19

Proverbs 28:13

Hebrews 4:13

Ephesians 4:25

Psalm 119:30

Psalm 141:3

For additional guidance on this topic, see also *Dysfunctional Family, Fear, Forgiveness, Guilt, Habits, Hope, Identity, Manipulation, Rejection, Self-worth, Stress Management, Verbal and Emotional Abuse, Worry.*

29

MANIPULATION
Severing the Strings of Control

M anipulators are skillful strategists. They map out their art of subtly steering and controlling people or circumstances by using indirect, unfair, or deceptive tactics.[1] People-pleasing is at the root of being manipulated. Those who are manipulated allow others the control that God alone should have. Exodus 20:3 says, "You shall have no other gods before me."

How Do Manipulators Control Others?

Aggressive Manipulation

1. Scheming "Shoulds"[2]
— "You should show me respect...should meet my needs...should make me happy...should give me security."
— "You owe me...ought to...have to...need to..."
— *Manipulators imply:* "If you don't meet my expectations, you're guilty of neglect."
— In contrast, the Bible says, "[Love] is not self-seeking" (1 Corinthians 13:5).

2. Strident Screaming
— Yelling as a pressure tactic to unnerve, publicly humiliate, or personally intimidate
— *Manipulators imply:* "If you don't do what I want, I'll make you wish you had."

— Psalm 64:3 says, "They sharpen their tongues like swords and aim their words like deadly arrows."

3. Sarcastic Swords

— Stabbing with cutting humor, jabbing words, painful put-downs, or malicious mocking

— *Manipulators imply:* "If you aren't what I want you to be, I'll wound you with words."

— Those who crucified Jesus "mocked him. 'Hail, king of the Jews!'" (Matthew 27:29).

4. Sexy Seduction

— Seductive talk, suggestive clothing, sensual advertising, sexual body movements

— *Manipulators imply:* "If you don't buy what I'm selling, you're not macho."

— Proverbs warns about the manipulative, seductive woman: "She seduced him with her smooth talk" (Proverbs 7:21-22).

5. Showering Sentiments[3]

— Excessive praise—to flatter for control

— Excessive gifts—to create a sense of obligation

— Excessive affection—to gain a sexual or emotional advantage

— Excessive money—to buy power

— *Manipulators imply:* "If you don't respond to my generosity by doing what I want you to do, you are ungrateful."

— In contrast, Proverbs 26:28 says, "A flattering mouth works ruin."

6. Sly Suggestions

— *Guilt Game #1:* Wife says, "John bought Sara a new car. It must be nice to be so loved."

— *Guilt Game #2:* Husband says, "Mary encourages her husband to go out with the guys any time he wants, for as long as he wants. He's lucky to have such a wife."

— *Guilt Game #3:* "Friend" says, "Chris has a fabulous friend who will give him any amount of money—no questions asked. Now that's a true friend."

— *Guilt Game #4:* Teenager says, "None of my friends have a curfew. It must be nice to have such great parents."

— In contrast, Proverbs 26:24 says, "A malicious man disguises himself with his lips, but in his heart he harbors deceit."

— *Manipulators imply:* "You ought to meet my every need, and if you don't, I'll make you feel guilty."

7. Sympathy Seekers[4]

— Speaking and acting intentionally needy…with "pity parties"…helpless and childlike…hopeless unless a rescuer arrives

— *Manipulators imply:* "You should take care of my heart, and if you don't, you're callous and cruel."

— In contrast, Galatians 6:5 says, "Each one should carry his own load."

Passive-Aggressive Manipulation

1. Silent Treatment

— Pouting, brooding, and ignoring; coldly turning their back; not answering the phone or door as punishment; refusing to speak

— *Manipulators imply:* "If you don't do what I want, you don't get my approval, my communication, or me."

— In contrast, Psalm 39:2 says, "When I was silent and still, not even saying anything good, my anguish increased."

2. Slam/Bam Slamming

— Slamming drawers, doors, phones, books

— *Manipulators imply:* "If you don't meet my expectations, you don't deserve any dialogue with me, but I'll make my point in other ways."

— In contrast, Ephesians 4:26 says, "In your anger do not sin: Do not let the sun go down while you are still angry."

3. Scornful Sneers

— Curling the lip, rolling eyes, raising eyebrows, squinting eyes

— *Manipulators imply:* "If you don't do what I want you to do, you don't deserve my respect."

— In contrast, Isaiah 57:4 says, "Whom are you mocking? At whom do you sneer and stick out your tongue? Are you not a brood of rebels, the offspring of liars?"

4. Sizeable Sigh

— Audible sighs, deep grunts, long groans, smacked lips

— *Manipulators imply:* "If you don't meet my expectations, I will let you know how perturbed I am with you."

— Job 3:24 says, "Sighing comes to me instead of food; my groans pour out like water."

5. Suppressed Support

— Withholding compliments, gifts, affection, withdrawing presence

— *Manipulators imply:* "If you don't meet my standards, you will not get any attention whatsoever from me."

— In contrast, the apostle Paul said to the Corinthians, "We are not withholding our affection from you, but you are withholding yours from us" (2 Corinthians 6:11-13).

6. Strategic Stalling

— Intentionally slow, late, not hearing, forgetful

— *Manipulators imply:* "If you don't give me control, I'll take control in other ways."

— In contrast, 1 Corinthians 13:5 says, "[Love] is not rude."

7. Sniveling Sobbers[5]

— Timed tears, subtle sniffles, tearful stories, extended crying

— *Manipulators imply:* "If you don't meet my emotional needs, I'll get your attention and make you feel guilty by falling apart."

— In contrast, Hosea 7:14 says, "They do not cry out to me from their hearts but wail upon their beds."

WHY DO PEOPLE MANIPULATE?

Manipulators attempt to:

— Make others feel guilty.

— Get others to believe what they want them to believe.

— Keep others "hooked" into a relationship—even when the relationship is unhealthy and one-sided.

— Avoid meeting their obligations and responsibilities.

— Appear positive when they feel negative toward others.

— Set up "fixers," "caretakers," "rescuers" to take care of them.

— Intentionally confuse others.

— Get others to do for them what they would not normally choose to do.

— Get others to feel responsible for them or for their welfare.

— Control the emotions and reasoning of others.

— Use religious words for personal gain, causing harm to another's walk with God.

— Win the battle for control.[6]

Proverbs 26:24 describes the manipulator: "A malicious man disguises himself with his lips, but in his heart he harbors deceit."

WHY DO PEOPLE ALLOW THEMSELVES TO BE MANIPULATED?

"You even put up with anyone who enslaves you or exploits you or takes advantage of you or pushes himself forward or slaps you in the face"
(2 CORINTHIANS 11:20).

Typically those who are manipulated don't understand why they are so easily led to the ditch of pleasing. However, the reasons reveal much insight:

Identity Misplaced in the Manipulator
— "I must have you in my life."

"You give meaning and purpose to my life."

— "I need your approval in order to feel significant."

Solution: Isaiah 2:22

Misplaced Priorities[7]
— "What others think is more important than anything else."

— "The judgment and opinion of others takes precedence over my own."

— "The end justifies the means even if it involves violating my conscience."

Solution: Acts 24:16

Scared of Disapproval
— "I can't say no for fear of making someone angry at me."

— "I'm afraid of being rejected."

— "I can't take a stand against someone whose approval I need."

Solution: Psalm 3:5-6

Performance-based Acceptance
— "I am accepted only because of what I do."

— "I have value only if my work is acceptable."

— "I have worth only if I please others."

Solution: Luke 12:7

Controlled by Personality or Power

— "I am controlled by what the manipulator…

…does or does not do."

…wants and desires."

…threatens to do."

Solution: Galatians 5:1

Defensiveness About the Relationship

— "I can't see why the relationship is unhealthy."

— "I don't understand the need for change."

— "I'm not willing to do anything about changing the relationship."

Solution: Proverbs 29:25

Excuses the Manipulator

— "He doesn't mean to act this way."

— "He can't help being this way."

— "He is not really bothering me."

Solution: Proverbs 27:5

What Is the Root Cause of Being Manipulated?

Wrong Belief:

"I must have the approval of others in order to feel good about myself."

Right Belief:

"I must not live for the approval of others, but instead I realize that God will meet all my inner needs because He accepts me totally and loves me unconditionally."

> *"This is what the LORD says: 'Cursed is the one who trusts*
> *in man, who depends on flesh for his strength and whose*
> *heart turns away from the LORD…But blessed is the man*
> *who trusts in the LORD, whose confidence is in him'"*
> (JEREMIAH 17:5,7).

How Do You Stop Being Manipulated?

Stop allowing your manipulator to maneuver you into gullies of guilt. The path to recovery begins with putting your relationship with Christ first, and growing in Christlike maturity on the Road to Transformation.

Decide not to be dependent on the manipulator.

Decide you...[8]

— have an unhealthy dependent relationship and confess that to God.

— want only a healthy relationship that glorifies God.

— will be dependent on the Lord to meet your deepest needs.

(Philippians 4:19)

Expect exasperation.

Don't expect your manipulator to...[9]

— understand or agree with your decisions.

— acknowledge being manipulative.

— be willing to give up control to set you free.

(Psalm 31:3-4)

Prepare yourself for pain.

Accept...[10]

— change as painful; however, in time you will have peace.

— if you don't change, you will stay in pain and peace will elude you.

(Job 3:26)

Examine the methods of the manipulator.

— Ask God to open your eyes to ways you have been manipulated.

— Ask yourself, "How am I being manipulated?" Write out your tactics for change.

— Ask a trusted friend to help you see blind spots and develop a plan of action.

(Proverbs 22:3)

Notify the manipulator of the necessity for change.[11]

— Admit you have been wrong.

"I've come to realize I am wrong in the way I relate to you. At times I don't speak up because I'm afraid. This is not healthy for either of us."

— Give your commitment.

"I really do care about you. I want you to know I am committed to change. I believe we can ultimately have a much healthier relationship."

— State your resolve if it is not appropriate to continue the relationship.

"We cannot continue in a relationship as it is and still be the persons we need to be before God."

(Hebrews 12:1)

Don't defend yourself.

Even if you are accused of being unkind and unloving, you can choose to...[12]

— be silent, but don't use silence as a weapon.
— state the truth only once or twice: "I'm sorry you feel that way." "What you've said is not true." "It does not reflect my heart."
— say, "I understand you think I am being heartless, but my intent is to become healthy."

(Ecclesiastes 3:7)

Expect the manipulator to try new strategies.

The manipulator...[13]

— may resort to using other methods to regain control.
— needs to know you are aware of these new methods.
— needs to see that the new methods will not succeed.

(Proverbs 14:24)

Nullify your need to meet all the manipulator's needs.

Realize...

— God didn't design anyone to meet *all* the needs of another person.
— if you meet all the manipulator's needs, then the manipulator won't need the Lord.
— you need to redirect the manipulator's focus to the Lord as the only true need-meeter.

(Psalm 37:4-5)

Commit to memory Galatians 1:10.

Continue to ask, "Am I now trying to win the approval of men, or of God? Or am I trying to please men? If I were still trying to please men, I would not be a servant of Christ."

— Realize, you are "transformed by the renewing of your mind" (Romans 12:2).

— Recognize you are given the mind of Christ to direct your thoughts (1 Corinthians 2:16).

Yield to pleasing the Lord first.

— You must not be a peace-at-any-price person.

— Jesus was not a peace-at-any-price person.

— Keep your trust in God and fear no one.

> *"The LORD is my light and my salvation—whom*
> *shall I fear? The LORD is the stronghold of my life—*
> *of whom shall I be afraid?"*
> (PSALM 27:1).

Sometimes you must say *no*
to people so you can say *yes* to God.
—JH

=========== *Your Scripture Prayer Project* ===========

Exodus 20:3

Proverbs 29:25

Proverbs 12:18

1 John 4:18

2 Timothy 1:7

Jeremiah 17:5,7

Galatians 6:4

Galatians 1:10

Psalm 31:3

For additional guidance on this topic, see also *Anger, Childhood Sexual Abuse, Codependency, Critical Spirit, Domestic Violence, Evil and Suffering…Why?, Fear, Forgiveness, Guilt, Habits, Hope, Lying, Marriage, Rejection, Self-worth, Stress Management, Verbal and Emotional Abuse, Worry.*

30

MARRIAGE

To Have and to Hold

Why do some marriages endure and others not? Why do some couples struggle and others not? What one factor makes the greatest difference and prevents so many marriages from failing? It's the word *covenant*. The concept of covenant is a long, winding path that ends when "death do us part."

The marriage covenant is a couple's lifetime commitment—a lifetime journey of love and loyalty. Jesus states it well: "They are no longer two, but one. Therefore what God has joined together, let man not separate" (Matthew 19:6).

WHAT IS GOD'S PATTERN FOR MARRIAGE?

Marriage is a covenant agreement in which a man and a woman are legally and spiritually joined together as husband and wife. And Genesis 2:24-25 establishes the four elements in God's perfect order for marriage.

Separation—"a man will leave his father and mother"

> Both the husband and wife leave the authority of their parents and become a separate family unit. In marriage the loyalty to your parents should never be stronger than the loyalty to your spouse.

Bonding—"and be united to his wife"

> By an act of your will, bonding is a mental commitment to have a faithful, permanent marriage relationship with your spouse regardless of difficulties.

Oneness—"they will become one flesh"

> Physical oneness is the ultimate consummation of sexual closeness. For this sexual oneness to be continually mutually satisfying, look for ways to express

unselfish love to each other. Openly ask, "What best communicates love to you?" and then take the time to enjoy one another.

Intimacy—"they felt no shame"

Emotional intimacy is encouraged when you seek to be vulnerable and transparent, honestly sharing with one another your feelings of frustration and failure, your deepest disappointments and desires.

Spiritual intimacy is achieved when you continue to reveal to one another your unmet needs, praying together, praying for each other and sharing what God is doing in your lives.[1]

WHAT ARE GOD'S PURPOSES FOR MARRIAGE?

God has a unique purpose for marriage. In the same way that Christ sacrificially gave Himself to the church, you and your mate should be willing to sacrifice your individual desires for the sake of your marriage covenant.

Partnership

God has given you each other as partners for life—true companionship grows when there is emotional, spiritual and physical unity. Malachi 2:14 emphasizes, "She is your partner, the wife of your marriage covenant."

Parenting

God's first scriptural command was for Adam and Eve to be fruitful and multiply, filling the earth with godly offspring. "God blessed them and said to them, 'Be fruitful and increase in number; fill the earth and subdue it'" (Genesis 1:28).

Pleasure

The marriage relationship and your mate are God's special gifts to you…true enjoyment will grow out of self-control and a servant's heart. Proverbs 5:18 says, "May your fountain be blessed, and may you rejoice in the wife of your youth" (Proverbs 5:18).

WHAT ARE THE CHARACTERISTICS OF FIVE KINDS OF TROUBLED MARRIAGES?

God uses marriage as a chisel to chip away your character flaws. He intends both partners to move from selfish to sacrificial behavior, reflecting the sacrificial love of Christ.

The Make-believe Marriage—*lacking honest and intimate communication by...*

— not working through problems (stubbornness)

— not accepting responsibility (defensiveness)

— not acknowledging your mate's feelings (rejection)

— not concerned about your mate's needs (self-centeredness)

— not displaying affection (apathy)

Make-believe marriages are marriages in name only. To enjoy intimate communication is to be as concerned about your partner's needs as about your own. Philippians 2:3 says, "Do nothing out of selfish ambition or vain conceit, but in humility consider others better than yourselves."

The Maladjusted Marriage—*experiencing sexual difficulties because of...*

— frigidity (fearfulness)—from false guilt, sexual abuse, psychological problems

— impatience (insensitivity)—being demanding, coercive

— infidelity (selfishness)—indulging in adultery, pornography

— fatigue (exhaustion)—caused by excessive busyness or overcommitment

— anger (bitterness)—unforgiveness, manipulation

Maladjusted marriages fail to experience the unique expression of physical oneness. As an act of love, God's design is that both partners yield their bodies to one another. True sexual fulfillment comes through seeking to provide pleasure to the other. The Bible says, "The husband should fulfill his marital duty to his wife, and likewise the wife to her husband. The wife's body does not belong to her alone but also to her husband. In the same way, the husband's body does not belong to him alone but also to his wife" (1 Corinthians 7:3-4).

The Mixed-up Marriage—*having conflicting values over...*

— opposing religious beliefs

— opposing parental responsibilities

— opposing marital commitments

— opposing friendship choices

— opposing moral principles

Mixed-up marriages produce power struggles, tension, and criticism. With basic values in conflict, the couple has great difficulty developing oneness of mind, heart, and will. However, Philippians 2:2 says, "Make my joy complete by being like-minded, having the same love, being one in spirit and purpose."

The Money-troubled Marriage—*experiencing financial disagreements over...*

— how family income will be earned...and spent
— how credit cards will be used
— how credit card *misuse* will be handled
— how the budget will be followed
— how the lack of money for essentials will be handled

Conflicting answers to these questions and other financial difficulties can result in an unhealthy focus on money and material needs. However Hebrews 13:5 says, "Keep your lives free from the love of money and be content with what you have."

The Misaligned Marriage—*failing to recognize/respond to God-given roles*

Failure of the husband...

— to be a spiritual leader
— to be financially responsible
— to make wise decisions
— to seek to solve problems
— to be attentive to his wife

Failure of the wife...

— by not having a gentle spirit
— by trying to control her husband
— by becoming involved in power struggles
— by withdrawing emotionally
— by being bitter and sarcastic

God's design is for the husband to feel *significant* through providing for his family and receiving the respectful love of his wife.[2] He fulfills her need to feel *secure* through his love, acceptance, and sensitivity to her desires. Ephesians 5 paints the picture:

> *"Wives, submit to your husbands as to the Lord. For*
> *the husband is the head of the wife as Christ is the*
> *head of the church, his body, of which he is the*
> *Savior...Husbands, love your wives, just as Christ*
> *loved the church and gave himself up for her"*
> (Ephesians 5:22-23,25).

What Are Common Causes of Broken Marriages?

Many enter marriage expecting "personal payoffs." Eventually, these *unrealistic expectations* become lost hopes and dreams that grow a root of bitterness. Hebrews 12:15 states, "See to it…that no bitter root grows up to cause trouble and defile many."

Couples *expect* marriage will always provide…

— love and acceptance

— affection and sexual intimacy

— a loving family

— rescue from present circumstances

— financial security

— social acceptance

— protection from loneliness

— time to change a mate's behavior

When these *unrealistic expectations* are unfulfilled, many spouses say,

— "Life is too short to live like this. We'll both be happier apart."

— "This was *not* a marriage made in heaven. We should *never* have married."

— "I've tried everything—our situation is hopeless."

— "You're wrong. You'll never change!"

— "Everybody's getting divorced—marriage doesn't matter anymore."

— "It's better for the children if I leave, to protect them from the arguing."

— "I'll never be happy here, but I'll try to stay until the children are grown."

Instead of living with unrealistic expectations regarding what you *don't have,* be grateful to God for what you *do have.* First Thessalonians 5:18 says, "Give thanks in all circumstances, for this is God's will for you in Christ Jesus."

What Is the Key Verse to Memorize?

Submission is based on your love for the Lord and your desire to do His will. Because of your love for God, you both must learn to defer to the desires of each other. Ephesians 5:21 says, "Submit to one another out of reverence for Christ."

What Unique Longings Do Husbands and Wives Have?

Although everyone has three God-given inner needs—for love, significance, and security[3]—God designed the husband to have a greater need for *significance*, while the wife is uniquely created with a deeper need for *security*. A crucial element in the marriage relationship is becoming aware of your partner's desires and learning to meet them creatively.[4] Philippians 2:4 says, "Each of you should look not only to your own interests, but also to the interests of others."

How *Wives* Fulfill Their Husbands' Desires

Admiration (Proverbs 31:23)
— Praise his positive character traits.
— Respect his burden of responsibility.

Domestic Support (Proverbs 31:27)
— Provide a peaceful home atmosphere.
— Manage the home efficiently.

Companionship (Mark 10:8)
— Develop mutual interests together.
— Learn to talk knowledgeably about your husband's occupation.

Attractiveness (Proverbs 31:25)
— Develop inner beauty that earns respect.
— Display inner strength regardless of outward circumstances.

Sexual Fulfillment (1 Corinthians 7:4-5)
— Communicate your sexual desires.
— Give assurance that your husband is sexually adequate.

How *Husbands* Fulfill Their Wives' Desires

Affection (Song of Solomon 1:2; 2:6)
— Give hugs, kisses, cards, flowers, and gifts.
— Tell her how much you care for her.

Communication (Ephesians 4:29)
— Listen with concern and interest.
— Encourage and praise her positive character traits.

Honesty (Proverbs 24:26)
— Commit to total truthfulness.
— Share your true thoughts, feelings, and desires.

Financial Security (1 Timothy 5:8)
— Shoulder the financial responsibility.
— Prepare a budget together to plan for the future.

Commitment (Hebrews 13:4)

— Schedule quality and quantity time alone with her.

— Make your wife and family your highest earthly priority.

MAKING A GOOD MARRIAGE GREAT!

A husband and wife must never lose their commitment to each other. This commitment to both your mate and your marriage goes deeper than romantic love. It empowers you to keep an unbreakable covenant with your marriage partner regardless of unexpected circumstances. Our covenant God says to us, "I will betroth you to me forever; I will betroth you in righteousness and justice, in love and compassion" (Hosea 2:19).

My Covenant Commitment
(Note the acrostic for C-O-V-E-N-A-N-T)

C Commit to working through problems and not walking away (1 Corinthians 7:27).

— Decide together that divorce is not an option.

— Agree to communicate feelings honestly and lovingly.

O Offer love to your mate even when you don't feel like it (1 Corinthians 13:4-8).

— Evaluate how your love compares to that described in 1 Corinthians 13. Substitute your name in the place of the word "love" in verses 4-8.

— Pray daily for those who have hurt you—forgive and forgive again—refusing to keep a record of wrongs.

V View your marriage as God's setting for spiritual growth (Proverbs 15:13).

— Realize that God did not create any one person to meet all your needs.

— While God is your ultimate need-meeter, see your mate as God's gift to meet some of those needs.

E Eliminate any emphasis on your rights (1 Corinthians 6:19-20).

— Identify what makes you angry.

— Sensitively express your honest desires—"It would mean a lot to me if you would take out the trash."

N Nurture your identity in Christ (Philippians 4:13).

— Evaluate if your sense of self-worth is based on how your mate treats you.

— Acknowledge that your true identity is in Christ, not in your mate.

A Ask God to change you (Psalm 51:10).

— Evaluate what areas in your life need changing.

— Ask your mate, "Would you name one area in my life where you feel I need the most change?"

N Nourish your extended family relationships (Exodus 20:12).

— Evaluate the tangible and emotional needs of your in-laws.

— Consistently look for the positive in your mate's family.

T Turn your expectations over to God (Psalm 62:1).

— Evaluate the unrealistic expectations you've had of marriage and your mate.

— Realize God can bring complete fulfillment to you regardless of your marriage partner.

"My soul finds rest in God alone"
(Psalm 62:1).

To make the most of your marriage,
the key to success is *commitment*.
While fortunes change from good to bad
and feelings move from glad to sad,
commitment is the highest goal...
commitment is the glue that holds.

—JH

Your Scripture Prayer Project

Ephesians 5:21

1 Corinthians 7:3-4

1 Corinthians 13:4-5

1 Corinthians 13:6-7

Philippians 2:2-4

1 Peter 3:7

Ephesians 5:25

Mark 10:9

For additional guidance on this topic, see also *Adultery, Alcohol and Drug Abuse, Anger, Codependency, Counseling, Crisis Intervention, Critical Spirit, Decision Making, Domestic Violence, Dysfunctional Family, Financial Freedom, Forgiveness, Grief Recovery, Guilt, Habits, Lying, Manipulation, Parenting, Pregnancy...Unplanned, Reconciliation, Rejection, Self-Worth, Sexual Addiction, Stress Management, Verbal and Emotional Abuse, Victimization, Worry.*

31

THE OCCULT

Demystifying the Deeds of Darkness

If someone were to ask, "What exactly is wrong with the occult?" most people wouldn't know how to answer. How would you answer? The word *occult* describes any practice used in an attempt to gain supernatural power or knowledge apart from the God of the Bible.[1] Generally the occult is broken down into five categories: superstition, fortune-telling, spiritism, black and white magic, and parapsychology.[2] The word *occult* comes from the Latin *occultus*, which means "hidden, covered up, concealed."[3] The occult is not just a ditch of deceit, but a pit cloaked in despair and darkness. In Leviticus 20:6-7 God says, "I will set my face against the person who turns to mediums and spiritists to prostitute himself by following them, and I will cut him off from his people. Consecrate yourselves and be holy, because I am the LORD your God."

WHAT OPENS THE DOOR TO OCCULT INVOLVEMENT?

Superstition

Occult involvement often begins with unfounded beliefs—based on *tradition*—regarding items or practices assumed to have supernatural power. Colossians 2:8 says, "See to it that no one takes you captive through hollow and deceptive philosophy...which depends on human tradition and the basic principles of this world." Examples of traditions include:

— *Bad luck*—assigning supernatural power to black cats, breaking a mirror, walking under ladders, the number 13, evil eye

— *Good luck*—assigning supernatural power to rabbits' feet, four-leaf clovers, horseshoes, knocking on wood, crystals, amulets, talismans, religious items

Divination

Divination is an attempt to "divine" or foretell the future. Jeremiah 29:8 warns against this, saying, "Yes, this is what the Lord Almighty, the God of Israel, says: 'Do not let the prophets and diviners among you deceive you. Do not listen to the dreams you encourage them to have.'" Here are some different forms of divination:

— *Astrology*—the study of the positions of the stars and planets to reveal their supposed influence on people and events

— *Cartomancy*—the reading of tarot cards or a deck of 52 cards

— *Horoscopes*—the forecasting of the future based on dividing the year into 12 sections according to the signs of the zodiac and determining supernatural influences by time, date of birth, alignment of the stars

— *Numerology*—the assigning of power to numbers such as the date of your birth

— *Palmistry*—or chiromancy, the reading of lines in the palm of a hand

— *Psychic games*—the use of games such as the *Ouija* board and the magic eight ball for answers

— *Rod and pendulum*—the use of which is alleged to locate lost objects, persons, or diagnose diseases

— *Scrying*—gazing into a crystal ball, water, or mirrors

— *Sortilege*—the casting of lots

— *Tasseography*—the reading of loose tea leaves on the sides or base of a cup

— *Water witching/dowsing*—the use of a divining rod to locate water, minerals, or oil

> *"Do not let the prophets and diviners*
> *among you deceive you"*
> (Jeremiah 29:8).

With regard to astrology, there is proof that such readings are not valid. More specifically, astrology has three major problems.[4] *The scientific problem:* Astrology is based on the ancient belief that the sun circles the earth; however, science has proven that the earth circles the sun.[5] *The sociological problem:* Since astrological readings are based on a person's exact date and place of birth, identical twins should have identical futures—but they don't. One might be a college professor and the other a high school dropout! Then there is *the biblical problem:* Astrology violates the Word of God.

"Let your astrologers come forward, those stargazers
who make predictions month by month...Surely
they are like stubble; the fire will burn them up"
(ISAIAH 47:13-14).

Spiritism

Spiritism is an attempt to communicate with the unseen world through various practices. Leviticus 19:31 says, "Do not turn to mediums or seek out spiritists, for you will be defiled by them. I am the LORD your God." Here are the major forms of spiritism:

— *Channeling*—a spirit guide or medium channels information from the spirit world of the dead person to the living person seeking communication. This channeler is in the middle position between both worlds.

— *Familiar spirits*—a "familiar" companion spirit is usually embodied in a small animal and is held to serve and protect a person.

— *Halloween*—a day on which the spirits of the dead are believed to roam the earth and commit violent acts and when occult practices are used for power and protection.

— *Materialization*—the physical manifestation of spirits, ghosts, or apparitions

— *Necromancy*—communication with spirits of the dead

— *Psychometry*—knowledge gained through contact with personal possessions

— *Reincarnation*—the belief a person's soul migrates from one body into another through numerous death and rebirth cycles. This belief is prevalent in Hinduism and Buddhism.

— *Séances*—meetings designed to receive spirit communications

— *Sexual spirits*—sexual contact with unseen spirits

— *Shamanism*—ancestral spirits

— *Spirit writing*—automatic writing under the influence of spirits

— *Spirit guides*—a demonic spirit that appears to befriend and protect a person

"When men tell you to consult mediums and spiritists, who
whisper and mutter, should not a people inquire of their
God? Why consult the dead on behalf of the living?"
(ISAIAH 8:19).

Can dead ancestors bring either help or harm to the living? No. The dead know nothing. According to the Bible, the dead have no knowledge or feelings about the events on earth, and they have no ability to be involved in this life. A demonic spirit, however, could be a counterfeit of a deceased person.

> *"The living know that they will die, but the dead know*
> *nothing; they have no further reward, and even the*
> *memory of them is forgotten. Their love, their hate and*
> *their jealousy have long since vanished; never again will*
> *they have a part in anything that happens under the sun"*
> (Ecclesiastes 9:5-6).

Is channeling mentioned in the Bible? While it is not mentioned by name, channeling makes a dramatic entrance in the Garden of Eden immediately following the creation of Adam and Eve. The serpent channeled a message to Eve from Satan himself. But true to Satan's character, this message was a lie.

> *"Now the serpent was more crafty than any of the wild animals*
> *the LORD God had made. He said to the woman, 'Did God*
> *really say, "You must not eat from any tree in the garden"?'…*
> *'You will not surely die,' the serpent said to the woman"*
> (Genesis 3:1,4).

> *"The great dragon was hurled down…that ancient serpent*
> *called the devil, or Satan, who leads the whole world astray.*
> *He was hurled to the earth, and his angels with him"*
> (Revelation 12:9).

Magic/Sorcery

Magic and sorcery involve attempts to control the natural world by invoking supernatural power from the spirit world through various practices. Ezekiel 13:20 says, "This is what the Sovereign LORD says: I am against your magic charms with which you ensnare people like birds and I will tear them from your arms; I will set free the people that you ensnare like birds."

Channels of Magic

Objects such as voodoo dolls, talismans, amulets, potions, locks of hair, chicken bones, clothing, shells

Sayings such as chants, charms, spells, curses, incantations, calling up of spirits

Forms of Magic

Black magic is intended for evil and uses spiritual powers "for evil ends, such as selfish gain or to harm rivals and enemies."[6]

White magic is intended for "good" and uses rituals to bring about healing, fertility, and divining information.[7]

Modern magic includes books, videos, and computer games with characters that possess magical powers, and those who use or play with these players or leaders call upon these same powers.

Modern magic is rooted in the "Old Religion" sometimes called the "craft" of witchcraft.[8] Many engage in modern magic without realizing they are drawing from the same power source as witchcraft.

Satanism is the worship of Satan. It is marked by the mockery of Christianity or exaltation of the powers of evil and baseness. Satanism is practiced by a broad range of individuals. Some declare allegiance to a personal Satan and practice black magic, vengeance, and ritual sacrifice. Others deny Satan as a personal being yet practice Satanism as a way to live out their desire for personal power, as well as an outlet for an indulgent and hedonistic lifestyle.[9] Satanic practices include black magic, dismemberment, sexual sacrifices, the killing of animals and humans, eating human flesh, and drinking blood.

> *"Do not paractice divination or sorcery"*
> (Leviticus 18:19-26).

Witchcraft
What is the truth about witchcraft?

— Witchcraft is forbidden by God.

> *"Let no one be found among you who sacrifices his son*
> *or daughter in the fire, who practices divination or*
> *sorcery, interprets omens, engages in witchcraft"*
> (Deuteronomy 18:10).

— Witchcraft angers God.

> *"He sacrificed his sons in the fire in the Valley of Ben*
> *Hinnom, practiced sorcery, divination and witchcraft,*
> *and consulted mediums and spiritists. He did much*
> *evil in the eyes of the LORD, provoking him to anger"*
> (2 Chronicles 33:6).

— Witchcraft will be destroyed by God.

> *"I will destroy your witchcraft*
> *and you will no longer cast spells"*
> (Micah 5:12).

— Witchcraft destroys peace.

> *"'How can there be peace,' Jehu replied, 'as long as all the*
> *idolatry and witchcraft of your mother Jezebel abound?'"*
> (2 KINGS 9:22).

— Witchcraft enslaves people.

> *"The wanton lust of a harlot, alluring, the*
> *mistress of sorceries…enslaved nations by her*
> *prostitution and peoples by her witchcraft"*
> (NAHUM 3:4).

— Witchcraft is a barrier to entering the kingdom of God.

> *"The acts of the sinful nature are obvious: sexual*
> *immorality, impurity and debauchery; idolatry and*
> *witchcraft; hatred, discord, jealousy, fits of rage, selfish*
> *ambition, dissensions, factions and envy; drunkenness,*
> *orgies, and the like. I warn you, as I did before, that those*
> *who live like this will not inherit the kingdom of God"*
> (GALATIANS 5:19-21).

Supernatural Phenomena

These are the appearances or manifestations of things beyond the natural realm. Parapsychology is a field of study investigating appearances of *paranormal psychological phenomena*, or supernatural mental manifestations.[10]

Paranormal means "beyond the norm, or supernatural."[11] Below are some different types of allegedly supernatural phenomena:

— *Apports*—the supernatural power to transfer objects through closed rooms and sealed containers

— *Clairaudience*—the supernatural power to hear something beyond the senses

— *Clairvoyance*—the supernatural power to see something not present

— *ESP/extrasensory perception*—the supernatural power to perceive something beyond the senses

— *Kirlian effect*—the supernatural power to see colored auras revealing information about the people they surround

— *Levitation*—the supernatural power to lift objects or people so they appear to float

— *Mental telepathy*—the supernatural power to communicate from one mind to another without the use of senses

— *Precognition*—the supernatural power to know something before it occurs

— *Psychic surgery*—the supernatural power to perform surgery using only the mind

— *Psychometry*—the supernatural power to identify facts about an object or a person through contact with personal items

— *Telekinesis*—the supernatural power to move physical objects using the mind, such as playing a musical instrument without using the hands

> *"Since no man knows the future, who can tell him what is to come? No man has power over the wind to contain it; so no one has power over the day of his death"*
> (ECCLESIASTES 8:7-8).

COMMON QUESTIONS CONCERNING THE OCCULT

Q: Many psychics say their power comes from God. If a prophecy comes true, doesn't that prove the fortune-teller possesses God's power?

A: The true test of genuine prophets from God is that their predictions must be 100 percent accurate. If *any* of their prophecies do not come true, neither the so-called "prophet" nor the power is from God (Deuteronomy 18:20-22).

Q: Can a person be possessed by Satan?

A: Yes. Judas was possessed and used by Satan to betray Jesus. Satan literally entered into Judas. John 13:27 says, "As soon as Judas took the bread, Satan entered into him. 'What you are about to do, do quickly,' Jesus told him."

Q: Can Christians be demon possessed?

A: No. The Bible never presents even one believer as being possessed by a demon. Christians can be oppressed, but not possessed. They have been bought by the blood of the Lamb; therefore, their bodies are not their own—they belong to Christ. First Corinthians 6:19-20 says, "Do you not know that your body is a temple of the Holy Spirit, who is in you, whom you have received from God? You are not your own; you were bought at a price. Therefore honor God with your body."

Q: Does Satan have the power to affect a person's actions?

A: Yes. Satan can influence a person's heart to do evil. Satan prompted Judas to betray Jesus. John 13:2 says, "The evening meal was being served, and the devil had already prompted Judas Iscariot, son of Simon, to betray Jesus."

Q: Should I be afraid of the occult?

A: No. There is no reason to fear the occult as long as you avoid involvement and rely on the indwelling power of Jesus Christ to overcome evil. Remember, 2 Timothy 1:7 says, "God did not give us a spirit of timidity, but a spirit of power, of love and of self-discipline."

What Can I Do If I Recognize I'm Involved in the Occult?

God's powerful truth can light your way out of the pit of darkness and deception and put you on the path to recovery, where answers are found in God alone. The Road to Transformation will bring you to Christlike maturity, and God may then use you to pull others up from the pit.

— *Renounce* any involvement with the occult (Acts 19:18).

— *Remove* all objects related to the occult (Acts 19:19).

— *Recognize* your enemy as Satan (1 Peter 5:8).

— *Rely* on your authority in Christ over evil (1 John 4:4).

— *Refuse* fascination with the occult (Deuteronomy 18:10-14).

— *Reside* in close fellowship with believers (2 Corinthians 6:14).

— *Reap* the benefit of earnest prayer (James 5:16).

— *Realize* the truth of Scripture (2 Timothy 3:16).

— *Read* Scripture for wisdom and knowledge (Proverbs 2:1-6).

— *Remain* clothed in the armor of God (Ephesians 6:10-18).

=== *A Prayer of Deliverance* ===

Lord God,

Right now I bow only to Your power and authority. I confess that I have submitted to ungodly powers and practices. Jesus, thank You for shedding Your blood on the cross to purchase my forgiveness. Thank You for enabling me to become a child of God. Through Your supernatural power I totally renounce (name occult influences). Thank You that in Christ, I am forgiven and free. In His powerful name I pray. Amen.

> The person drawn into the occult is like the addict drawn into drugs:
> Both are dependent on a destructive, potentially deadly mirage.
>
> —JH

Your Scripture Prayer Project

Deuteronomy 18:10-12

Jeremiah 10:2

Leviticus 19:31

Exodus 20:4-5

Ezekiel 13:20

Micah 5:12

Isaiah 8:19

1 Timothy 4:1

1 Corinthians 10:20-21

Revelation 21:8

For additional guidance on this topic, see also *Anger, Codependency, Crisis Intervention, Critical Spirit, Cults, Depression, Evil and Suffering...Why?, Fear, Forgiveness, Guilt, Hope, Identity, Lying, Manipulation, Rejection, Salvation, Self-worth, Suicide Prevention, Verbal and Emotional Abuse, Victimization.*

32

OVEREATING
Freedom from Food Fixation

I f a little bit is good, then a lot must be better! In truth, that's not always the case—especially when overeating results in negative consequences, such as the ditch of overindulgence or compulsive eating. Reasons may vary, but oftentimes an emotional or spiritual void is trying to be satisfied with temporary filler instead of permanent fulfillment.

"A man is a slave to whatever has mastered him"
(2 PETER 2:19).

WHAT IS COMPULSIVE OVEREATING?
— Compulsive eating is a seemingly irresistible impulse to eat.[1]

— Compulsive eating is uncontrolled eating based on satisfying emotional hunger rather than physical hunger.

— This repeated act is an addiction that can result in physical disorders.

*"Like a city whose walls are broken down is
a man who lacks self-control"*
(PROVERBS 25:28).

What Is Gluttony?
— Gluttony is excessive eating and drinking.[2]

— Gluttony typically results in obesity, a condition characterized by excessive body fat that is 20 percent or more above recommended weight.[3]

— In Scripture, *gluttony* refers to a loss of control and a yielding to fleshly desires instead of yielding to God.

> *"Do not join those who drink too much wine or gorge
> themselves on meat, for drunkards and gluttons
> become poor, and drowsiness clothes them in rags"*
> (Proverbs 23:20-21).

What Is a Binge?

— *Bingeing* is a period of unrestrained indulgence to eating, drinking, shopping.[4]

— Repeated bingeing can become an addictive behavioral pattern. Proverbs 25:16 says, "If you find honey, eat just enough—too much of it, and you will vomit."

Some people have been motivated to "get serious" by thinking of their overeating as a lack of submission to God. They admit that their primary focus has been letting food be their god, and not letting God be their God.

> *"Their destiny is destruction, their god is their stomach, and
> their glory is in their shame. Their mind is on earthly things"*
> (Philippians 3:19).

Symptoms Resulting from Compulsive Overeating

Physical Symptoms

— cycles of excessive eating and severe dieting

— chronic neck and joint pain

— high blood pressure

— diabetes

— kidney disorder

— heart disease

— limited range of motion and activity

— shortness of breath after mild exertion

— anorexia/bulimia

— gall bladder problems

Note: If you are experiencing any of these physical problems, consult your health care professional.

Emotional Symptoms

— low self-esteem

— anxiety

— shame

— irritability

— depression

— passivity

— guilt

— powerlessness

— anger

— hopelessness

> *"Don't you know that you yourselves are God's temple and that*
> *God's Spirit lives in you? If anyone destroys God's temple, God will*
> *destroy him; for God's temple is sacred, and you are that temple"*
> (1 Corinthians 3:16-17).

What Indicates an Overeating Problem?

We are wise to ask the Lord to help us see ourselves accurately. Then if the Lord impresses upon our hearts the need to change, we will see and recognize the need.

> *"The prudent see danger and take refuge, but the*
> *simple keep going and suffer for it"*
> (Proverbs 27:12).

The Compulsive Eater Checklist

☐ Do you spend a lot of time thinking about food?

☐ Do you look forward to an event because of the food that will be there?

☐ Do you eat when you are sad, angry, or depressed?

☐ Do you eat when you are bored or under stress?

☐ Do you eat certain foods as a personal reward?

☐ Do you eat even when you are not hungry?

☐ Do you ever feel ashamed of how much you eat?

☐ Do you fear not being able to stop eating once you start?

☐ Do you ever feel embarrassed about your personal appearance?

☐ Do you ever eat secretly to avoid someone's knowing what you eat?

☐ Do you lose weight on diets, then gain the weight (and more) back again?

☐ Do you feel you have to eat everything on your plate or you're being wasteful?

☐ Do you think you could control your weight if you *really* wanted to?

☐ Do you resent it when family or friends express concern over your weight?

If you answered yes to three or more, you could be a compulsive eater.

If at times you feel frustrated over your eating extremes, let this scripture motivate you:

"The man who fears God will avoid all extremes"
(ECCLESIASTES 7:18).

WHAT ARE SITUATIONAL SETUPS FOR OVEREATING?

In reality, no snack food can create an obsession. The causes of compulsive overeating are much more complex and deep-rooted. For many people, compulsive eating is based not on physical hunger, but emotional hunger—a craving for the love and gratification they missed when they were growing up. As you search for the truth about your past, honest answers can be the first step toward healing.

"Surely you desire truth in the inner parts; you teach
me wisdom in the inmost place"
(PSALM 51:6).

Here are some situational setups for overeating:

— Overweight parents who establish poor eating patterns in childhood

— Overcoming other habits by self-will, substituting one bad habit for another, compensating for a loss by replacing smoking with eating

— Childbirth—gaining weight during pregnancy

— Mild depression—eating for emotional comfort

— Change to a less physically active lifestyle, change jobs, retire

— Specific drugs—antidepressants, steroids, hormones

— Underactive thyroid gland, which decreases production of fat-burning hormones

— Hormonal—changing metabolism affects the rate the body burns fat

— High-caloric eating patterns—preferring fried foods, sweets, starches

— Protection from sexual attraction, fearing attention, fearing being attractive

WHAT IS THE ROOT CAUSE OF OVEREATING?

The root cause of overeating is attempting to meet one or more inner needs through food.

— *Unconditional love—eating to feel nurtured*

— *Significance—*eating to feel a sense of *control*

— *Security—*eating and hoarding food in fear of *deprivation*

The problem with using food to meet any of these inner needs is simple—it can't be done! Only God can meet your needs and satisfy the longings of your heart. When you allow Him to fill you and submit your life to Him, He gives you His power for victory out of the ditch of overindulgence. Getting habits under control may take time, but you can take the first step by embracing the hope, the joy, and the freedom God offers.

Wrong Belief:

"I can't sustain enough willpower to resist the foods that give me pleasure."

Right Belief:

"The issue is not the power of your *will,* but the power of your *God.* Christ's Spirit within you is able to change your focus from food to a faith that He will fulfill your deepest needs."

The moment you choose to believe in Him—entrusting your life to Christ—He gives you His Spirit to live inside you. The Spirit of Christ gives you His power to live the fulfilled life God has planned for you. God will work in your life!

> *"Those who live according to the sinful nature [flesh]*
> *have their minds set on what that nature desires;*
> *but those who live in accordance with the Spirit*
> *have their minds set on what the Spirit desires"*
> (Romans 8:5).

FACTS ABOUT EATING AND HEALTH

Obedience to God Brings Physical and Spiritual Strength

— Daniel made a commitment to obey God (Daniel 1:8).

— God backed up Daniel's resolve with supernatural support (verse 9).

— Daniel requested only vegetables and water for his meals (verse 12).

— Daniel became noticeably healthier and better nourished (verse 15).

— God blessed Daniel with great knowledge and understanding (verse 17).

Fakes and Fads That Don't Bring Lasting Results[5]

Among the methods to be wary of are acupuncture, hypnotism, diet pills, fad diets, fasting, laxatives, reducing machines, special clothing to melt fat calories, shots, surgery, starvation, and vomiting.

> *"Do not conform any longer to the pattern of this*
> *world, but be transformed by the renewing of your*
> *mind. Then you will be able to test and approve what*
> *God's will is—his good, pleasing and perfect will"*
> (ROMANS 12:2).

Do's and Don'ts of Dieting

On the path to recovery, follow the "do" signs and avoid the "don'ts." Soon you will find yourself on the Road to Transformation, where lasting sustenance is found in Christ Himself.

— *Don't* say you are dieting. *Do* say you are learning to eat healthy foods.

— *Don't* keep unhealthy food around you. *Do* keep healthy food prepared for snacks.

— *Don't* weigh yourself every day. *Do* record your weight once a week.

— *Don't* eat fast. *Do* chew slowly!

— *Don't* reward yourself with food. *Do* enjoy the rewards and blessings of the Lord.

— *Don't* eat at restaurants without planning. *Do* predetermine which foods to order.

— *Don't* keep your new plan a secret. *Do* share with a friend or support group.

— *Don't* shop for groceries on impulse or when you are hungry. *Do* shop with a prepared list.

— *Don't* get caught off guard by temptation. *Do* have an alternate plan— for example, read Scripture and take God at His Word, call a friend, read a book.

— *Don't* fail to set goals. *Do* set a target weight and realistic short-term goals.

— *Don't* start a new eating plan during a crisis, illness, holiday, or high stress situations. *Do* consult a doctor before beginning any new eating plan.

— *Don't* adopt a plan just because it worked for someone else. *Do* adopt a personalized plan that will work for your individual lifestyle.

> *"A prudent man sees danger and takes refuge, but*
> *the simple keep going and suffer for it"*
> (PROVERBS 22:3).

Think Thin!

Think of yourself as the person God created you to be.

— God has given you a new nature in Jesus Christ.

— God has given you all you need to live a self-controlled life.

> *"His divine power has given us everything we need for life
> and godliness through our knowledge of him who called
> us by his own glory and goodness. Through these he has
> given us his very great and precious promises, so that
> through them you may participate in the divine nature and
> escape the corruption in the world caused by evil desires"*
> (2 PETER 1:3-4).

Have the correct motive for losing weight.

— Taking good care of your physical body, the temple of the Holy Spirit.

— Wanting to be free from the bondage of self-indulgence.

— Being healthy and living the life God planned for you.

> *"So we make it our goal to please him, whether
> we are at home in the body or away from it"*
> (2 CORINTHIANS 5:9).

Identify the real reasons for overeating. Are you...

— responding to a lack of *love?*

— responding to feelings of *insignificance?*

— fearful and *insecure?*

> *"Search me, O God, and know my heart; test
> me and know my anxious thoughts"*
> (PSALM 139:23).

Nail down a personal commitment to obey God. Acknowledge...

— your need for change.

— you are powerless to change.

— God's power in you to change.

— His constant presence within you.

> *"Those who obey his commands live in him,
> and he in them. And this is how we know that he lives
> in us: We know it by the Spirit he gave us"*
> (1 JOHN 3:24).

Learn to **listen** *to the Lord.*
— Listen to God through His written Word.

— Listen for His leading through the Holy Spirit.

— Listen and recognize Satan's lies so you can replace them with God's truths.

> *"I will instruct you and teach you in the way you*
> *should go; I will counsel you and watch over you"*
> (PSALM 32:8).

Turn your focus to things you should eat.
— Develop a knowledge of good nutrition.

— Choose to eat healthy foods.

— Don't give up if you blow it.

> *"Do not destroy the work of God for the sake of*
> *food. All food is clean, but it is wrong for a man to*
> *eat anything that causes someone else to stumble"*
> (ROMANS 14:20).

Have an exercise plan that will increase your metabolism, and vary the plan.
— Walk or ride a bicycle 30 minutes a day four or five times weekly.

— Do aerobics for 30 minutes three days a week. Start using the stairs!

— Make a commitment to join athletic activities with friends.

> *"He who ignores discipline despises himself, but*
> *whoever heeds correction gains understanding"*
> (PROVERBS 15:32).

Initiate a daily journal, keeping a small notebook with you.
— Choose a scripture to memorize daily or weekly.

— Write down when and what you eat, recording caloric or fat value.

— Record your thoughts and feelings.

> *"A wicked man puts up a bold front, but an*
> *upright man gives thought to his ways"*
> (PROVERBS 21:29).

Nurture your relationship with God.
— Pray throughout the day meditating on Scripture, reflecting the self-control of Christ.

— Ask God to remind you of His protection and power over temptation, thanking Him for His faithfulness.

— Know that God will never give up on you. If you blow it, start again— God is faithful!

> *"Being confident of this, that he who began a good work in you*
> *will carry it on to completion until the day of Christ Jesus"*
> (PHILIPPIANS 1:6).

Success Is Just a Choice Away

Although you may have failed in the past, with God's help, you don't have to fail in the future!

Choose to...

— give control of your life to the Lord Jesus Christ

— change your eating through the power of Christ within you

— live to please God, not to please your appetite

— make wise choices when tempted to eat unwisely

— make right choices when tempted to eat excessively

— glorify God and reflect Him through your body

— focus not on food but on faithfulness to the Lord in your life

— let God be your God—don't let food be your God

There is only one true God.
If food is your god,
then God is not your God.
—JH

"So whether you eat or drink or whatever
you do, do it all for the glory of God"
(1 CORINTHIANS 10:31).

======== *Your Scripture Prayer Project* ========

Proverbs 25:28

Proverbs 15:32

Romans 8:5

Romans 12:1

Romans 14:20

Matthew 6:25

1 Corinthians 6:12

1 Corinthians 10:31

Philippians 4:13

2 Peter 1:3

For additional guidance on this topic, see also *Alcohol and Drug Abuse, Critical Spirit, Depression, Domestic Violence, Dysfunctional Family, Fear, Grief Recovery, Guilt, Habits, Hope, Identity, Marriage, Rejection, Self-worth, Stress Management, Victimization, Worry.*

33

PARENTING

Steps for Successful Parenting

The painted lines on a road form boundaries that help ensure the safety of all drivers. At times we see solid lines that indicate no passing is allowed. At other times the lines are not solid, which allows drivers to pass, but with caution. Beyond the solid lines along the edges of a highway we find additional boundaries, such as rough pavement, guardrails, and medians that shield us from embankments, cliffs, or travelers going the opposite direction. Likewise, in life, parents are to delineate the boundary lines for their children, helping to map out a safe route as the children journey from infancy to independence, and steering them clear of the ditches of rebellion and regret. Though no job is more difficult, no reward is more fulfilling than to see your child grow "in wisdom and stature, and in favor with God and men" (Luke 2:52).

WHAT IS YOUR PARENTING STYLE?[1]

People parent their children differently, and your method of parenting greatly affects the development of your children, as well as their behavior. There are five main parenting styles: domineering, doting, dependent, detached, and developing. The first four approaches are problematic. The fifth style reflects God's heart on healthy, constructive parenting.

Domineering parents seek to control a child's behavior. These parents tend to think in black-and-white terms and may be controlling, inflexible, critical, and performance-oriented (versus people-oriented). Consequently, their children may become rebellious, fearful of failure, overly sensitive to criticism, bitter, and underachievers or overachievers.

(Colossians 3:21)

Doting parents seek to control a child's feelings. These parents yield easily to pressure in their desperation to achieve family harmony. They tend to be too helpful, "rescuing," and overprotective. Consequently, their children often become spoiled, manipulative, disrespectful, irresponsible, and helpless.

(Proverbs 13:24)

Dependent parents seek to control a child's behavior and feelings. These parents tend to be possessive, manipulative, suspicious, inconsistent, and controlling. Consequently, their children may become fearful, deceitful, jealous, indecisive, and passive.

(Jeremiah 17:5)

Detached parents seek to avoid responsibility for a child's failures. These parents lack boundaries and follow-through and tend to be apathetic, ambivalent, and uninvolved. Consequently, their children tend to be self-sufficient, emotionally hardened, rebellious, insecure, and underachievers.

(1 Timothy 3:4)

Developing parents seek to teach a child and develop his or her character. These parents are loving, encouraging, comforting, and sincere. As a result, their children grow up secure, confident, compassionate, honest, and wise.

(Luke 2:40)

How Will Your Parental Role Change As Your Child Grows?

A basic understanding of child development, along with the art of positive disciplining, will help you to become the parent God wants you to be.

Infants (Bonding Stage): Infants' needs are met by forming an attachment to their parents. Help your child feel secure with tender caressing and cuddling. Infants cannot understand spiritual concepts, but can be influenced by the overall spiritual atmosphere within the home. Pray over your child and fill your home with Christian music.

Toddlers (Exploration Stage): Toddlers are intensely curious, unaware of danger, and eager to explore their world. Encourage your child's curiosity in a protected environment. Toddlers begin to separate from parents by being independent and saying no. To support your child's separation, do not overreact or squelch his or her spirit.

Preschoolers (Testing Stage): Preschoolers push against your rules to test the limits. To establish structure, set limits clearly and hold the line with love. Preschoolers may begin to be deceitful as they realize that their parents cannot read their minds. Correct your child while reflecting the compassion of God.

Elementary School Children (Acceptance Stage): At this age, children seek acceptance from different groups through performing various activities and roles. To affirm your acceptance, help your child understand his or her God-given worth. School-age children want to please their parents and teachers, and they adopt their parents' morals, whether good or bad. Help your child memorize meaningful Bible passages that show God's holy standards and His plan for eternal life. For example: "Anyone, then, who knows the good he ought to do and doesn't do it, sins" (James 4:17).

Teenagers (Identity Stage): Teens seek to define their own set of values. Increase your teens' exposure to godly role models. Teens are idealistic and often ask questions about their purpose and role in life. Explain that God's purpose is that you both become more and more like Christ.

WHAT ARE SOME DO's AND DON'TS OF PROPER DISCIPLINE?

Discipline is training that corrects, molds, and improves your child's character. Discipline is an expression of love and acceptance and builds a sense of security in your child.

(Proverbs 22:15)

The Don'ts of Discipline

— *Don't* feel guilty when you discipline your child. You show love to your child when you set limits and enforce them.

— *Don't* be afraid of losing your child's love. By doing God's will, you will earn your child's respect.

— *Don't* view structure and limits as punishment. You are establishing beneficial boundaries.

— *Don't* embarrass your child in front of others. Remember to praise in public and correct in private.

— *Don't* belittle your child with sarcasm. Speak the truth in love, and discipline with compassion.

— *Don't* discipline your child in anger. Wait for immediate anger to pass as you pray for wisdom in order to discipline appropriately.

— *Don't* try to manipulate your child with fear or guilt. Base your appeals on the need to have a clear conscience before God.

— *Don't* compare your child with others. See your child as a unique creation of God.

(Proverbs 13:24)

The Do's of Discipline

— *Do* mold the will without breaking the spirit, treating your child with kindness and respect. A child's spirit can be broken in an atmosphere of too many rules, overreacting, criticizing, teasing, false accusations, inflexibility, impatience, or harsh punishment.

(Colossians 3:21)

— *Do* communicate your expectations clearly by getting on your child's eye level, describing what you expect of your child in terms of structure and limits, and giving one gentle reminder when needed. For example: "We agreed that your bedtime is 8:30. It's now 8:20, so what do you need to be doing?"

(1 Thessalonians 4:1)

— *Do* establish and enforce negative consequences for misbehavior— consequences that are related to the behavior and clearly communicated and agreed to by your child.

(Proverbs 19:18)

— *Do* encourage and develop responsibility, allowing your child to make choices and to experience the benefits and consequences of those choices.

(Proverbs 17:25)

— *Do* assign and enforce beneficial chores to everyone in the family based on individual capabilities, with assigned times for completion. Post these responsibilities in the kitchen.

(Proverbs 14:23)

— *Do* reinforce positive behavior, offering smiles and physical affection, praise regarding character traits, recognition in front of others, saying, "thank you," giving focused attention, and respecting physical, spiritual, and emotional needs.

(1 Thessalonians 5:11)

— *Do* maintain consistency, evaluating and modifying rules as your child grows, presenting a united front in public and resolving disagreements in private.

(Proverbs 24:3-4)

How Can You Nurture Godly Character in Your Child?[2]

When parents structure their home according to God's Word, children learn to turn negative or destructive impulses into constructive problem solving. The following are wise parenting strategies that can help your child become compassionate, loving, and self-confident.

— *Love and listen attentively with your ears and your heart.* Get to really know the heart of each child. Ask about their dreams and desires, their feelings and fears, their likes and dislikes. Listen without judging them, with the goal of understanding them (James 1:19).

— *Organize your family God's way.* When the home is controlled by godly parents, many of the dynamics that create negativity and anger in children are removed (Proverbs 1:8).

— *Love your spouse openly and unconditionally.* How parents relate to each other is often reflected in how their children relate to others. The best way to give security to your children is to love your spouse (Ephesians 5:33).

— *Validate each child by refusing to show favoritism.* Be fair and do not show more love to one child than to another. "Don't show favoritism" (James 2:1).

— *Encourage and affirm each child daily.* Offer praise regularly for little things as well as big things. Let your children know they do not have to seek your approval, but that you love them unconditionally and are grateful to God for them (Psalm 127:3).

— *Model repentance and forgiveness.* When you sin *in the presence* of your children, ask forgiveness in front of them. Then demonstrate your change of behavior. When you sin *against* your children, ask their forgiveness, and then change your behavior toward them, "I was wrong when I _____. Will you forgive me?" (Matthew 5:23-24).

— *Establish reasonable age-appropriate boundaries with rewards and repercussions.*[3] Determine *rewards* for your children when they stay within the boundaries, (such as increased time with friends) and *repercussions* when they cross the boundaries (such as decreased time with friends). Tell them you want them to be with their friends, but they will determine whether they receive a reward or a repercussion (1 Thessalonians 4:1).

— *Enforce boundaries consistently.* Be true to your word. If you are not able to discipline at the time of disobedience, enforce the repercussion at a later time (Proverbs 19:18).

— *Learn to deal appropriately with your strong emotions, including anger and sadness.* You are your children's role model for emotional well-being and healthy relationships. Children of angry parents generally perceive God as harsh and filled with anger (Colossians 3:8).

— *Base your discipline on love, never anger.* Discipline because your children need it, not because they have hurt or angered you. Make it clear that you reject the behavior, not the child (Revelation 3:19).

HELPING CHILDREN DEVELOP INDEPENDENCE AND CONFIDENCE

Remember that your child is a temporary gift from God.[4] Just as arrows are made to be thrust from a bow, children are created to soar on their own. The more you pray and trust in God's personal involvement in your child's life, the less possessive and reluctant you will be to release your child into His hands.

— *Let go* of seeing your child as an extension of yourself.

— *Let go* of your desire to possess your child.

— *Let go* of your expectations for your child.

— *Let go* of jumping in to save your child from failure.

— *Let go* of seeking harmony at all times.

— *Let go* of your need to be appreciated.

— *Let go* of parenthood as your primary identity.

> *"Sons are a heritage from the LORD, children a*
> *reward from him. Like arrows in the hands*
> *of a warrior are sons born in one's youth"*
> (PSALM 127:3-4).

Kids are like kites—struggling to become airborne,
yet needing stability from the string.
God designed your role as a parent
to prepare your kite for flight.[5]

—JH

Your Scripture Prayer Project

Ephesians 6:4

Proverbs 29:17

Deuteronomy 6:6-7

1 Timothy 3:4

Proverbs 22:6

Proverbs 19:18

Proverbs 13:24

Proverbs 17:6

Titus 2:4-5

1 Thessalonians 2:11-12

For additional guidance on this topic, see also *Anger, Childhood Sexual Abuse, Dating, Decision Making, Domestic Violence, Dysfunctional Family, Fear, Financial Freedom, Forgiveness, Grief Recovery, Guilt, Hope, Lying, Manipulation, Marriage, Reconciliation, Rejection, Self-worth, Sexual Integrity, Stress Management, Suicide Prevention, Worry.*

34

PHOBIAS
No Longer Terribly Afraid

Misunderstood...criticized...ridiculed? Do you have a persistent, irrational fear that just won't go away? It's excessive, out of proportion to the actual degree of threat, and it's affecting every area of your life—curtailing activities and suffocating joy. People in this ditch are deathly afraid, huddled in a corner, fearful that no matter how high the ditch walls, they won't escape the threat. Whether it's a formidable fear of elevators, spiders, or something else, one thing is certain: God wants to empower you to move from the pandemonium of panic to peace. He says,

> *"Do not fear, for I am with you; do not be dismayed, for*
> *I am your God. I will strengthen you and help you;*
> *I will uphold you with my righteous right hand"*
> (Isaiah 41:10).

WHAT ARE SOME EXAMPLES OF PHOBIAS?[1]

Specific Phobias (Simple Phobias)—the Fear of a Specific Object or Situation

This type of phobia is a persistent excessive fear when in the presence of, or in the anticipated presence of, a specific object or situation.

> *Examples of feared objects:* elevators, spiders, knives, snakes, cats, fire, insects
>
> — Zoophobia is the *fear of animals* characterized by a sense of danger even in the presence of nonthreatening animals.
>
> *Examples of situations:* flying, heights, darkness, driving over bridges or through tunnels
>
> — Acrophobia is the *fear of heights* characterized by feelings of extreme insecurity and of falling even when there is no danger of doing so.

— Claustrophobia is the *fear of closed spaces* characterized by a sense of being smothered in a confined environment.

Social Phobias (Social Anxiety Disorder)—a Fear of Embarrassment

This is fear of embarrassment. This type of phobia is characterized by the paralyzing fear of appearing stupid or being judged as shameful in a social situation.

Examples: A persistent fear of initiating and maintaining a conversation, eating in public, attending a party; also, a persistent fear of performance situations such as stage fright and fear of public speaking.

Agoraphobia—Literally Fear of Open Spaces, Fear of Fear

This phobia is the fear of having a panic attack in a place where escape could be difficult or embarrassing. It comes as a result of repeated panic attacks and is the fear of having yet another panic attack. Therefore, any situation that could cause a sense of panic is avoided.

Example: Being so afraid of having a panic attack in a public place or in a strange place that a person becomes homebound or even room bound.

*"I so feared the crowd and so dreaded the contempt of
the clans that I kept silent and would not go outside"*
(Job 31:34).

What Can You Do at the Onset of an Anxiety/Panic Attack?

*"Fear and trembling have beset me;
horror has overwhelmed me"*
(Psalm 55:5).

Hyperventilation goes hand in hand with those suffering from anxiety. Hyperventilation is shallow, rapid breathing that reduces carbon dioxide in the blood, which then produces light-headedness, dizziness, tingling of the extremities, palpitations of the heart, and feelings of faintness and respiratory distress. At the onset of rapid breathing, which serves as a warning signal, these symptoms can be stopped by any of the following techniques:

— Take slow, deep breaths and hold the air in your lungs for several seconds...then slowly release the air.
— Place the open end of a paper bag around your nose and mouth. Breathe normally into the bag, being sure to breathe in the same air being expelled.

— Place a blanket or sheet totally over your head, increasing the amount of carbon dioxide being taken into your lungs and warding off the frightening symptoms produced by too little carbon dioxide in your blood.

Those experiencing a panic attack feel as though they will die. Therefore, knowing what to do at the onset will greatly minister to the hearts of those who are suffering. Proverbs 23:12 says, "Apply your heart to instruction and your ears to words of knowledge."

WHAT ARE KEY CONTRIBUTORS TO IRRATIONAL FEAR?[2]

Phobias do not appear in a vacuum. Something set you up to be controlled by fear, and something serves to trigger that fear. The setup occurred in the past, while the trigger occurs in the present. Here are the key contributors to F-E-A-R:

F Former Experiences Are Typically...

— *Traumatic experiences:*

Childhood sexual abuse or rape

Car accident or death of a loved one

— *Scare tactics used on you by others:*

Threats of violence by a parent, sibling or others

Fear-producing pranks, stories, movies

— *Caused by an underdeveloped sense of self-worth:*

Neglect, criticism, ridicule

Poor school performance

— *Parents or family members displaying excessive fear:*

A father who was a constant worrier

A mother who was fearful and overprotective

Analyze the reason for your fear...then tell yourself the truth about the past and the present.

> *"Surely you desire truth in the inner parts;*
> *you teach me wisdom in the inmost place"*
> (PSALM 51:6).

E Emotional Overload

— *Denying feelings:*

"I must not show my pain."

"I must not have any anger."

— *People-pleaser mentality:*

"I must keep everyone from getting angry."

"I must keep everyone happy."

— *Internalizing stress:*

"I have a lot of hidden anxiety."

"I have no outlet for venting my emotions."

— *Strict or perfectionist authority figures:*

"I never pleased my parents."

"I received harsh punishments."

Analyze the reason for your fear, and let the Lord help you heal from your hurts.

> *"Humble yourselves, therefore, under God's mighty hand, that he may lift you up in due time. Cast all your anxiety on him because he cares for you"*
> (1 PETER 5:6-7).

A Avoidance of Threatening Situations

— *Refusing to face fears:*

"I think it will go away in time."

"I believe I can avoid fearful situations."

— *Giving no opportunity for change:*

"I don't seek help or talk to anyone."

"I don't try to figure out why I am fearful."

— *Continuing to reinforce fears:*

"Everything I do is contingent on my fearfulness."

"I don't go anywhere that might raise my anxiety level."

— *Reinforcing negative thought patterns:*

"Fear dominates all my decisions."

"I evaluate everything through the filter of fear."

Analyze the reason for your fear, and let the Lord help you face your fears.

"I am the LORD, your God, who takes hold of your right
hand and says to you, Do not fear; I will help you"
(ISAIAH 41:13).

R   Runaway Imagination
— *Expecting life to be threatening:*
   "I always expect resistance and roadblocks."
   "I always expect danger and disaster."

— *Anticipating the worst will happen:*
   "I expect rejection and ridicule."
   "I expect hurt and heartache."

— *Believing you can never change:*
   "I think I will always be controlled by fear forever."
   "I think God can't help me."

— *Thinking you have no control over the situation:*
   "I feel overwhelmed when I have fear."
   "I feel powerless when I have fear."

Analyze the reason for your fear, and change your thought life.

"Whatever is true...noble...right...pure...lovely... admirable...
excellent...praiseworthy—think about such things"
(PHILIPPIANS 4:8).

Memorize Isaiah 41:10:

"Do not fear, for I am with you; do not be dismayed, for
I am your God. I will strengthen you and help you; I
will uphold you with my righteous right hand."

How Can You Decrease Phobic Fear with "Desensitization"?[3]

If you are overly sensitive to an object or situation, "desensitization" can be the key that opens the door to freedom. Systematically repeat each of the following steps one at a time. Repeat the same step day after day for a week or two, or until you no longer have a strong emotional reaction, then move on to the next step. Anxiety should be expected when moving to the next step, but it will dissipate as the step is done with increased repetition.

Gradually increase your exposure to the fear
Example of a specific phobia: fear of elevators

— Stand near an elevator and watch people get on and off.

— Push the button, *as if* getting ready to step inside.

— Step inside when others are not around. Hold the "Door Open" button, count to five, and step out.

— Step inside again (when others aren't around). Hold the "Door Open" button, count to ten, then step out.

— Step inside, ride to only one floor, then exit.

— Ride to two floors, then three...eventually all the way up and down for ten minutes.

A supportive person can be present for each step, initially also doing the activity—then later not participate, but remain present to encourage and praise.

Practice facing your fear
Example of a social phobia: fear of initiating conversation

— Practice asking a salesperson questions.

— Initiate saying hello with a smile.

— Listen carefully to what is said by others.

— Ask simple questions of others about themselves.

— Make brief comments about yourself.

— Develop a genuine interest in others.

Repeat each step over again until it evokes little reaction
Example of agoraphobia: fear of a panic attack (fear in open spaces)

— Open the front door and leave it open.

— Stand at the open doorway for as long as possible.

— Go out the door and stand on the porch—breathe deeply.

— Walk down the sidewalk to the edge of your property.

— Walk around the outside of your house.

— Sit in the car while it is in the driveway.

— Have someone drive you around the block.

— Drive yourself around the block.

— Go to the mall and sit in your car in the parking lot.

— Go to the mall when it is not too crowded and walk around.

— Go into a store and greet a sales clerk.

— Make a small purchase.

Each step of the way, say, "The LORD is with me; I will not be afraid" (Psalm 118:6). Personalize Deuteronomy 31:6 with "I, my, me":

> *"Be strong and courageous. [I will be strong.] Do
> not be afraid or terrified because of them, [I will
> not be afraid] for the LORD your God goes with
> you [goes with me]; he will never leave you nor
> forsake you [never leave me nor forsake me]."*

EXCHANGE PANIC FOR PEACE—FOCUS ON PSALM 23

The Lord wants to lead you out of fear and into faith, trusting in His strong, protective hand rather than the flimsy refuge of your fear-lined ditch walls. The path to recovery begins with focusing on the Lord rather than the object of your fear. Then peace, not panic, will rule your life.

Verse 1: "The LORD is my shepherd, I shall not be in want."
Imagine a grassy pasture in which the Lord is with you. Slowly say five times, "The Lord is my Shepherd." Each time you say that, emphasize a different word:

The Lord is my Shepherd.

The **Lord** is my Shepherd.

The Lord **is** my Shepherd.

The Lord is **my** Shepherd.

The Lord is my **Shepherd**.

Verse 2: "He makes me lie down in green pastures, he leads me beside quiet waters."
Imagine yourself lying down beside a calm pool of water.

Verse 3: "He restores my soul. He guides me in paths of righteousness for his name's sake."
Take several deep breaths and slowly say five times, "My Shepherd restores my soul." Each time you say that, emphasize a different word:

My Shepherd restores my soul.

My **Shepherd** restores my soul.

My Shepherd **restores** my soul.

My Shepherd restores **my** soul.

My Shepherd restores my **soul**.

Verse 4: "Even though I walk through the valley of the shadow of death, I will fear no evil, for you are with me; your rod and your staff, they comfort me."

Realize that you are not trapped. Slowly say, "I will fear no evil...the Lord is with me." Repeat five times.

Verse 5: "You prepare a table before me in the presence of my enemies. You anoint my head with oil; my cup overflows."

Each time emphasize a different word:

> **The** Lord is my Protector.
>
> The **Lord** is my Protector.
>
> The Lord **is** my Protector.
>
> The Lord is **my** Protector.
>
> The Lord is my **Protector**.

Verse 6: "Surely goodness and love will follow me all the days of my life, and I will dwell in the house of the LORD forever."

Thank the Lord for the way He will use each fearful situation for *good* in your life.

My Prayer for Peace

Dear God,

I thank You that You are my Shepherd. You guide me, You protect me, and You give me Your peace. You are the One who restores my soul. You know my weaknesses and the times I've caved in to fear. Now, in my weakness, I will choose to rely on Your strength. You are my Shepherd. I am choosing to rely on Your power to move from fear to faith. As I turn my fear over to You, use it for good in my life to remind me of my continual need for You. In Your holy name I pray. Amen.

Note: For serious phobic reactions, the process of desensitization is almost always used in combination with medical help.

> If you focus on your fear, your panic will increase.
> If you focus on your faith, your heart will be at peace.
>
> —JH

Your Scripture Prayer Project

Psalm 34:4

1 Peter 5:6-7

Psalm 27:1

Deuteronomy 31:8

Isaiah 41:10

Psalm 91:5

Romans 13:3

1 John 4:18

Psalm 23:1-4

Philippians 4:7

For additional guidance on this topic, see also *Childhood Sexual Abuse, Cults, Depression, Domestic Violence, Fear, Guilt, Hope, Identity, Rejection, Self-worth, Stress Management, Suicide Prevention, Victimization, Worry.*

35

PREGNANCY...UNPLANNED

I'm Pregnant?

You're pregnant. Those two words can thrill...signaling a time for celebration, or they can chill...sending a wave of panic throughout the ditch of dire desperation. The mind of a woman faced with an unplanned pregnancy can start spinning with options—adoption, parenting, or abortion—and out of desperation and loneliness, a choice can be made that will bring tragic consequences. This woman needs to be affirmed of God's unconditional love, His constant presence, *and His plan for the one who was unplanned:*

> *"Before I formed you in the womb I knew you,*
> *before you were born I set you apart"*
> (JEREMIAH 1:5).

WHAT IS GOD'S HEART FOR YOUR UNBORN CHILD?

Even if you made a mistake, *your child is not a mistake!* God is not surprised by the creation of this new life—He is the Creator. And those whom He creates, He loves. Therefore, nothing will ever separate you or your baby from the love of God (Romans 8:39).

God is the author of life.

> *"I bring to life"*
> (DEUTERONOMY 32:39).

God opens and closes the womb.

> *"The LORD...opened her womb"*
> (GENESIS 29:31).

"The LORD...closed her womb"
(1 SAMUEL 1:5).

God ordains all pregnancies, regardless of the circumstances.

"This is what the LORD says—your Redeemer, who formed
you in the womb: I am the LORD, who has made all things"
(ISAIAH 44:24).

God creates every life.

"Is he not your Father, your Creator,
who made you and formed you?"
(DEUTERONOMY 32:6).

God never forms a life without having plans for that life.

"'For I know the plans I have for you,' declares
the LORD, 'plans to prosper you and not to harm
you, plans to give you hope and a future'"
(JEREMIAH 29:11).

From God's perspective, all pregnancies are from Him and therefore are wanted by Him.

WHAT ARE PREDICTABLE REACTIONS TO UNPLANNED, UNWANTED PREGNANCIES?[1]

From God's perspective, life doesn't begin at the point of delivery when a baby takes a first breath. Rather, it begins at conception. Even though you may not feel pregnant or look different, within three weeks of conception, that little life within you has developed a brain, a beating heart, and tiny limbs that begin to "sprout" and move about. During this time, your unborn will grow from zygote to embryo to fetus—and after birth, from child to adolescent to adult.

Denial
"This isn't true...It's a mistake."
"This couldn't happen to me."
"This is not my fault."
"There are many reasons for missing a period."
When it's difficult to face the truth, acknowledge the truth of God (John 8:32).

Distress
"Who should I tell about this?"
"What will people think of me?"

"My life is ruined."

"How could I have been so stupid?"

When drowning in the sea of distress, cry out to God (Psalm 102:2).

Depression

"I feel so alone and helpless."

"I hate myself."

"I can't face the shame."

"I would rather die than face the future."

When all hope seems gone, place your hope in God (Psalm 25:3).

Dread

"I can't bear to tell my parents."

"Will my boyfriend leave me?"

"What will I do about school or a job?"

"No one will ever want to marry me."

When overcome with fear of the future, turn to God (Psalm 119:39).

Dilemma

"I can't keep this baby—but I can't let my baby go."

"Should I marry the baby's father even if I don't love him?"

"Should I consider abortion even if I know it's wrong?"

"Should I raise my baby or consider adoption?"

When dealing with a difficult dilemma, seek godly wisdom (James 1:5).

WHAT ARE YOUR OPTIONS?[2]

Abortion

If you're considering an abortion, carefully consider the following questions and accompanying truths.

Are you afraid that the response of others will be ridicule or rejection?

— *Realize* it is wiser to fear the response of God than the response of people.

Are you being pressured, especially by parents, the baby's father, or abortion counselors?

— *Realize* there is no easy way out, and doing what God says is more important than doing what people say.

Are you concerned about problems in your relationship with the baby's father?

— *Realize* if the father truly loves you, he will support you emotionally.

Are you wanting to escape the reminder that you made a major mistake?

— *Realize* God wants your child to be a reminder of His sovereignty and His purposes, not of your mistake.

Are you afraid of the financial responsibility and care of your baby?

— *Realize* God will provide for you and your baby.

Are you reluctant to bring an unwanted child into the world?

— *Realize* every child is wanted by God, and you can choose to want to have your child.

Are you concerned about the baby's possible health problems?

— *Realize* the value of life is not related to the health of the baby but to the God-given value placed on this baby by the Creator of life.

Are you unaware that life begins at conception?

— *Realize* a separate life begins when a woman's egg and a man's sperm are joined.

Are you viewing abortion as a form of birth control?

— *Realize* abortion kills a life, which is different from preventing the conception of a life.

Are you wanting to get rid of a baby who is a result of a wrongful act such as rape or incest?

— *Realize* your baby is innocent of any wrongful act and is undeserving of the death penalty.

Terminating an innocent life will not end your grief but will rather compound your grief with guilt.

> *"There is a way that seems right to a man,*
> *but in the end it leads to death"*
> (Proverbs 14:12).

Parenting

Single Parenting

Parenting requires emotional maturity. It means obligating yourself to physically raise, emotionally nurture, and spiritually train a son or daughter—at great sacrifice to your independence (Proverbs 31:15).

— Do you have a network of family or friends who can support you in your decision?

— Can you raise your child while living with your parents?

— How do your parents feel about helping with your child?

— What financial resources or assistance do you have available to help take care of your baby?

— Can you handle caring for a child plus your work/school responsibilities?

— Are you able to give the time and attention that your child needs?

— Can you provide an adequate and safe home for your baby where you are now living?

— What goals would you have to delay or give up to raise your child?

(Philippians 2:4)

Marrying

If you are considering marrying the father—or someone else—pregnancy must not be the primary reason to marry. You need to have similar commitments, goals, and values. Amos 3:3 says, "Do two walk together unless they have agreed to do so?"

— Would an immediate marriage be wise in the long-term?

— Are you in a good place to consider marriage?

— Would your husband love your child and be a good role model?

— Can he financially support the baby and you?

— Does he like and want children?

— Is he someone with whom you would like to spend the rest of your life?

— Do you feel led by the Lord to marry him?

— Do you share core spiritual values?

If you *are* considering marriage, first obtain premarital counseling. Be aware that 75 percent of teenage marriages end in divorce. In order to consider marrying, you both need to have the same spiritual foundation, or your marriage may fall apart.

(2 Corinthians 6:14-15)

Raising a Child Within a Marriage

If you are married and contemplating keeping your child, realize that God's best is that both mother and father be actively involved in the parenting of children (Proverbs 1:8).

To determine your biblical accountability as parents, ask yourselves: Will we...

— unconditionally accept, love, and nurture our child regardless of any physical problems?

— approach parenting with common goals and purposes?

— take every opportunity to teach our child spiritual truth?

— clearly instruct our child by doing what is ethically right and just?

— plan ahead to protect our child from danger?

— provide for our child's material needs?

— lovingly and effectively discipline our child?

— regard our child as a blessing?

Although you may not see it now, the baby in your womb is a gift from God and will be a blessing in your life.

(Psalm 127:3)

Adoption

Are you aware that...

— while birth mothers experience the grief of loss, they can have more peace by knowing that their child will be raised in a loving and stable environment?

— adoption often provides the best environment for the baby?

— adoption can be an answer to prayer for the many childless couples who are eagerly seeking to love and care for a child?

— there are more couples wanting to adopt a baby than there are babies available for adoption?

— birth mothers who prepare an adoption plan are more likely to get an education, get a job, and get married?

— when a baby is placed for adoption, all birth expenses are paid?

— you can choose your child's family and get to know them personally?

— you can stay in contact with the couple who adopts your child through letters and pictures?

— you can visit with your adopted child at specific, agreed upon times?

— adoption can be the highest expression of spiritual love? Adoption reflects the loving relationship of God with all who accept Jesus as their Lord and Savior. Those who accept Christ are "adopted" into the family of God.

"He predestined us to be adopted as his sons through
Jesus Christ, in accordance with his pleasure and will"
(EPHESIANS 1:5).

Note: Your adoption facilitator can help you decide what is best for you.

> **Q:** How can a mother who loves her unborn baby give up the baby when the child is born?
>
> **A:** God the Father gave up His Son, Jesus, based on His sacrificial love (1 John 3:16). In a similar way, a birth mother allows her baby to be placed in another home based on her sacrificial love. She desires the child's very best, and she has come to understand that she cannot provide what is best. Just as God's actions were based on love, her actions are also based on love.

What Is Required to Make a Decision?

The pressure surrounding an unplanned pregnancy can seem overwhelming. But peace can govern your decision and disintegrate the ditch walls around you by your knowing God has a purpose and plan for your child. You may feel you must make a quick decision to resolve a difficult dilemma, but a bad quick decision will produce long-term grief. Making the best decision for both you and your unborn baby requires time, wisdom, and foresight (see Ecclesiastes 7:12). Here are some steps you can take to act with W-I-S-D-O-M:

W Write down your thoughts and feelings, admitting your anxiety, confessing any guilt, and casting your cares on the Lord (1 Peter 5:6-7).

I Imagine what life would be like for you and your baby in the short-term (next year) and in the long-term (ten years from now) if you followed each option (abortion, parenting, adoption) (Proverbs 14:8).

S Sort through your options in terms of what God has revealed about your baby's life and what is best for your child (Psalm 32:8).

D Develop a support structure of family and friends (Proverbs 17:17).

O Obtain counsel that lines up with what God says in His Word (Psalm 37:30).

M Make a decision to entrust your future and your baby's future into the hands of the Lord.

> *"Trust in the LORD with all your heart and lean not on*
> *your own understanding; in all your ways acknowledge*
> *him, and he will make your paths straight"*
> (PROVERBS 3:5-6).

> If your unborn baby was unplanned,
> soon you will see the precious plan of God...
> beyond what your mind can conceive.
>
> —JH

Your Scripture Prayer Project

Jeremiah 29:11

Isaiah 41:10

Psalm 103:10-12

Psalm 10:14

Psalm 138:8

Isaiah 43:18-19

Isaiah 54:5-6

2 Timothy 2:22

Ecclesiastes 3:11

2 Corinthians 5:17

For additional guidance on this topic, see also *Abortion Recovery, Adultery, Anger, Childhood Sexual Abuse, Dating, Decision Making, Depression, Dysfunctional Family, Fear, Guilt, Hope, Marriage, Parenting, Premarital Counseling, Rape Recovery, Self-worth, Sexual Addiction, Sexual Integrity, Stress Management, Worry.*

36

PREJUDICE

Pulling Up the Roots of Pride

Those who look at others through the lens of prejudice have a mental blind spot that prevents them from seeing others accurately. Prejudiced people delve into a ditch that serves as a psychological fence, keeping them from seeing the God-given value in other relationships and confining them to their own "backyard" of bigotry. Isaiah 5:21 says, "Woe to those who are wise in their own eyes."

WHAT IS PREJUDICE?

Prejudice is a preconceived opinion, usually unfavorable, formed without sufficient knowledge or just grounds.[1] The word *prejudice* comes from the Latin word *praejudicium,* which means to "prejudge" (*prae,* "before"; *judicium,* "judgment").[2]

Prejudice is an irrational *attitude* based on an overgeneralized belief that is directed toward an individual, group, or race.[3]

If you struggle with prejudice, pray to see others through God's eyes so you will not be prideful or haughty. Proverbs 30:13 cautions against "those whose eyes are ever so haughty, whose glances are so disdainful."

WHAT ARE THE CATEGORIES OF PREJUDICE?

We tend to characterize people on the basis of the differences we observe—differences that place them in certain classes or groups. These characterizations tend to produce unfounded, negative attitudes toward others based on:[4]

age	gender	marital status	race
appearance	group membership	nationality	region
disability	income	occupation	religion
education	intelligence	personal habits	social class

The Bible speaks against any kind of prejudice. James 2:9 says, "If you show favoritism, you sin and are convicted by the law as lawbreakers."

CAN PERCEPTION LEAD TO PREJUDICE?

Look honestly at your life and evaluate:

— Has a bad experience with one person led you to be prejudiced against an entire group of people?

— Have stereotypes of a certain group led you to prejudices against the entire group?

— Have negative images in the media of a particular group of people influenced your opinion against them?

— Has peer pressure persuaded you to adopt an intolerant attitude against a certain person or group?

— Has a misunderstanding of cultural values led to prejudice toward a particular group?

— Has belief in evolution—believing all humanity evolved—led you to believe one race is superior to another?

Those who are prejudiced have a mental slant. Although they see their position as right, they are wrong. Proverbs 26:12 gives this pointed warning: "Do you see a man wise in his own eyes? There is more hope for a fool than for him."

WHAT IS THE ROOT CAUSE OF PREJUDICE?

The primary problem with prejudice is that it goes against everything Jesus stands for. He poses a question: "Do you have eyes, but fail to see?" (Mark 8:18).

Wrong Belief:

"Some people are created better than others, and so it is natural for me to see myself as superior."

Right Belief:

"Because God does not show favoritism toward anyone, when I have a heart of prejudice toward others, I am placing myself as a judge higher than God Himself. My needs for significance and security are met through a personal relationship and reliance on Christ, who loves me, died for me, and accepts me. I do not have the need or the right to feel superior to anyone or be prejudiced toward anyone."

"Accept one another, then, just as Christ accepted
you, in order to bring praise to God"
(ROMANS 15:7).

WHAT ARE THE DO'S AND DON'TS OF ACCEPTING OTHERS?

How do you begin accepting others who are different from you? Examine your heart, examine your thoughts, examine your motives:

— *Don't* judge the heart of another (Matthew 7:1).

> Ask God to search your heart (Psalm 139:23-24).

— *Don't* judge by outward appearances (1 Samuel 16:7).

> See and seek to meet the needs of others (Philippians 2:4).

— *Don't* assume you can't change your attitudes (2 Corinthians 5:17).

> Assume responsibility for changing your thinking (Romans 12:2).

— *Don't* use derogatory names or terms (Titus 3:1-2).

> Ask God to season your speech with His love (Ephesians 4:29).

— *Don't* discriminate just because "everybody does it" (Proverbs 14:12).

> Treat others the way you want to be treated (Matthew 7:12).

— *Don't* laugh at the differences in others (Proverbs 11:12).

> Instead, learn to value the differences that create the rich tapestry of God's creation (Malachi 2:10).

— *Don't* react when others are prejudiced against you (1 Peter 3:8-9).

> Be prepared to suffer the painful effects of prejudice for the cause of Christ (Matthew 5:11-12).

HOW CAN YOU TREAT EVERYONE EQUALLY?

What would happen if you saw yourself from God's perspective? Initially, you would be ashamed and wouldn't want to have even a hint of prejudice. Then you would want your heart to be "godly"—therefore, you would *insist* on changing because Romans 2:11 says, "God does not show favoritism."

E-Q-U-A-L-I-T-Y in Your Heart

E Express to others God's perspective on the equality of all people.

— Ask God to express His love equally to others through you.

— Reach out with compassion equally to others.

> *"There is neither Jew nor Greek, slave nor free, male*
> *nor female, for you are all one in Christ Jesus"*
> (GALATIANS 3:28).

Q Quit the tendency to stereotype any persons different from yourself.[5]

— Be willing to set aside your preconceived notions.

— Learn to appreciate and enjoy cultural differences.

> *"Believers in our glorious Lord Jesus Christ,*
> *don't show favoritism"*
> (James 2:1).

U Understand the God-given worth of all human beings.

— Look at every person as being created in God's image.

— Realize that every person God created was designed with His plan and purpose.

> *"God created man in his own image, in the image of*
> *God he created him; male and female he created them"*
> (Genesis 1:27).

A Acknowledge your need to be forgiven as well as your need to forgive.

— Acceptance of God's grace enables you to give grace to others.

— Acceptance of God's forgiveness enables you to give forgiveness to others.

> *"Bear with each other and forgive whatever grievances you may*
> *have against one another. Forgive as the Lord forgave you"*
> (Colossians 3:13).

L Learn that prejudice is a result of irrational, emotional stereotypes—not rational reasoning.

— Be willing to admit you may not know all the facts.

— Study Scripture to develop discernment between good and evil.

> *"Anyone who claims to be in the light but hates his brother is*
> *still in the darkness...But whoever hates his brother is in the*
> *darkness and walks around in the darkness; he does not know*
> *where he is going, because the darkness has blinded him"*
> (1 John 2:9,11).

I Invest in others by having a servant's heart toward everyone.[6]

— Get involved in helping people you would not normally help.

— Get to know someone well who is the object of your prejudice.

> *"Even the Son of Man did not come to be served, but*
> *to serve, and to give his life as a ransom for many"*
> (MARK 10:45).

T Turn from judging others to self-examination.

— Pray for God to reveal your blind spots.

— When tempted to judge others, focus on your own sin.

> *"How can you say to your brother, 'Let me*
> *take the speck out of your eye,' when all the*
> *time there is a plank in your own eye?"*
> (MATTHEW 7:4).

Y Yield in obedience to the nature of Christ living within you.

— With Christ in you, you can choose to respond to everyone with His love.

— With Christ in you, you can choose to live a godly life.

> *"His divine power has given us everything we need for life*
> *and godliness through our knowledge of him who called*
> *us by his own glory and goodness. Through these he has*
> *given us his very great and precious promises, so that*
> *through them you may participate in the divine nature and*
> *escape the corruption in the world caused by evil desires"*
> (2 PETER 1:3-4).

The problem of prejudice is ultimately
the sin of superiority.
The solution for prejudice is undeniably
living with Christlike humility.
—JH

=== *Your Scripture Prayer Project* ===

Romans 2:11

Titus 3:2

Acts 10:34-35

1 John 2:9-10

James 2:9

1 Peter 3:9

Galatians 5:14

Ephesians 2:14

2 Corinthians 5:19

1 Peter 3:8

For additional guidance on this topic, see also *Anger, Critical Spirit, Depression, Dysfunctional Family, Evil and Suffering...Why?, Fear, Forgiveness, Habits, Hope, Identity, Reconciliation, Self-worth, Verbal and Emotional Abuse, Victimization.*

37

PREMARITAL COUNSELING
Are You Fit to Be Tied?

The statistics are staggering concerning the number of marriages that end in the ditch of divorce, where heartache, despair, and confusion abound. We need to be wise about our expectations for marriage and wise about whom we let into our hearts. *Premarital counseling* is a path of practical advice given to a couple in preparation for marriage, covering essential issues. It is a preventative tool to help preserve what is designed to be a lifelong commitment. In order to build a strong foundation for marriage, learn as much as possible about yourself, your future mate, and God's will for marriage...*before you tie the knot.*

"Above all else, guard your heart,
for it is the wellspring of life"
(Proverbs 4:23).

What Is Preparation for Partnership?

A couple needs to have an accurate understanding of each other's expectations and desires. *Preparation for Partnership* is an excellent exercise for opening the door to meaningful communication. Both parties should complete each of the following sentences in writing and then talk through each point.

— My definition of love is...

— My reason for marriage is...

— My way of handling conflict is...

— My way of dealing with anger is...

— My views on sex within marriage are...

— My preference for spending free time is...

— My concept of the role and responsibilities of a wife is…

— My concept of the role and responsibilities of a husband is…

— My expectation after marriage regarding time with friends is…

— My debt history and my commitment regarding debt are…

— My commitment to be active in a church fellowship is…

— My commitments to my extended family are…

— My commitments to my future in-laws are…

— My priorities for spending money are…

— My priorities for saving money are…

— My experience with illegal drugs is…

— My position on the use of alcohol is…

— My desires regarding children are…

— My spiritual goals and desires are…

— My goals for marriage are…

> *"How much better to get wisdom than gold, to*
> *choose understanding rather than silver!"*
> (PROVERBS 16:16).

WHAT SHOULD YOU CONSIDER WHEN CONTEMPLATING MARRIAGE?

— *Don't* live in your past.

Look for the positive in the present (Isaiah 43:18-19).

— *Don't* focus on your future mate's past mistakes.

Focus on your future mate's choice to marry you (Proverbs 10:12).

— *Don't* expect to change your future mate.

Accept your future mate the way he/she is (Romans 15:7).

— *Don't* expect your future mate to meet all your needs.

Expect God to be your primary need-meeter (Philippians 4:19).

— *Don't* expect oneness to be equivalent to sameness.

Aim for unity while accepting that no two people always think the same (Romans 15:5-6).

— *Don't* criticize your future mate's parents.

> Speak about them with kindness and understanding (Ephesians 4:29).

— *Don't* nag your future mate.

> Make your position clear; then commit the matter to prayer (Proverbs 19:13).

— *Don't* joke about sexual promiscuity.

> See sexual intimacy as a picture of the holy union between Christ and His bride, the church (Ephesians 5:3-4).

— *Don't* joke about divorce as an option.

> Eliminate the word *divorce* from your vocabulary. *God hates divorce!* (Malachi 2:16).

— *Don't* rationalize, "It's okay to have sex—we're engaged, and we'll be married soon."

> Realize that sexual responsibility before marriage demonstrates that you will be sexually responsible after marriage. And statistically, sexual impurity prior to marriage increases the odds of divorce after marriage. God calls us to sexual purity (1 Thessalonians 4:7).

— *Don't* disregard a feeling of uneasiness in your spirit.

> Talk with someone who knows your future mate well in order to discern the cause of your uneasiness. Then wait for God's confirmation (Psalm 32:8).

■ OUR NEGOTIATION CONTRACT

> *"Do two walk together unless they have agreed to do so?"*
> (AMOS 3:3).

We agree to go first to God with our problem.

— Seek guidance from God's Word, asking, "Has God spoken about this anywhere in His Word?"

— Seek discernment from God in order to come to a mutual agreement on the problem.

— Seek God's will through prayer, asking for His peace if the decision is correct.

> *"Do not be anxious about anything, but in everything, by prayer*
> *and petition, with thanksgiving, present your requests to God.*
> *And the peace of God, which transcends all understanding,*
> *will guard your hearts and your minds in Christ Jesus"*
> (PHILIPPIANS 4:6-7).

We agree to negotiate a solution.

— Make a joint list of all options.

— Individually mark each option as…
(P) Possible   (I) Impossible

— Evaluate all the *P*'s and jointly choose the best option.

We agree, if all options cancel out, to delay making a decision until there is unity or until a decision must be made.

— Trust in the sovereignty of God.

> *"We know that in all things God works for the good of those*
> *who love him, who have been called according to his purpose"*
> (ROMANS 8:28).

OUR COMMITMENT TO GROW TOGETHER SPIRITUALLY[1]

We commit…

— our lives to Jesus Christ and submit to His control (Luke 9:23).

— our home to God and pledge to make it Christ-centered (Joshua 24:15).

— our bodies to each other and vow to be sexually faithful (Hebrews 13:4).

— our finances to God and will honor Him with our tithe (Malachi 3:10).

— to reading the Bible and praying with each other daily (Psalm 119:105-106).

— to not going to bed while still angry with one another (Ephesians 4:26).

— to nurturing each other through loving encouragement (Hebrews 10:24).

— to admitting our weaknesses and seeking prayer support in order to change (James 5:16).

— to growing with each other into a deeper relationship with the Lord (Hebrews 10:22-23).

Q: Is there really a problem with marrying an unbeliever whom I love? I believe our love will overcome all our problems.

A: Although your non-Christian fiancé may have many positive qualities, you need to be realistic about the long-term ramifications of marrying a nonbeliever. Assuming you become yoked to him in marriage…

— if he is headed toward darkness, where are you pulled?

— if he is headed toward death, where are you pulled?

— if he is headed toward destruction, where are you pulled?

"Do not be yoked together with unbelievers…what fellowship can light have with darkness?…What does a believer have in common with an unbeliever?… Therefore come out from them and be separate"
(2 Corinthians 6:14-15,17).

Q: I agreed to marry someone I really don't want to marry. Won't God stop the marriage if it's not His will?

A: No. God doesn't stop you from exercising your free will when you know a decision is against His will. To communicate His will, God either gives you His peace or withholds it. If God has not given you His peace, it's up to you to obey by not marrying this person.

"The peace of God, which transcends all understanding, will guard your hearts and your minds in Christ Jesus"
(Philippians 4:7).

Checklist for Choosing a Mate

Because no one is perfect, selecting a perfect marriage partner is impossible. But certain questions can help you determine whether a person would be a *great* mate or not. For example, an excellent predictor of the future is wrapped up in the question, How does he treat his mother? or How does she treat her father? The following checklist is composed of other questions that, when answered, will help in the selection of a great mate.

Is this a person...

— about whom God has given me peace as a marriage partner?

— who is growing spiritually?

— whose values I greatly respect?

— with whom I can communicate honestly?

— who refuses to become bitter?

— who is responsible?

— who desires sexual purity?

— who has a joyful heart and not a critical spirit?

— capable of a lifelong commitment?

— who loves God first and then loves me?

— who does not depend solely on me for happiness?

— who values the life God has given each of us?

— who honors and shows respect to both of our parents?

— who is flexible and willing to make adjustments?

— who "fights fairly"?

— with whom I can laugh and cry?

— who reads God's Word and prays with me now?

— with whom I strongly desire to share the rest of my life?

A couple who wants to experience the maximum out of their marriage needs to look at God's original design for the marital relationship. The Bible tells us that marriage is to reflect the sacrificial love that Christ has for His bride, the church. Although the backgrounds of a husband and wife may be different and expectations may differ, they can develop unity of heart through mutual submission and godly respect for one another.

> *"Submit one to another out of reverence for Christ...*
> *Each one of you [husbands] also must love his wife as he*
> *loves himself, and the wife must respect her husband"*
> (Ephesians 5:21,33).

> The best marriage bond is this:
> two people committed to Christ
> and, together, committed to each other.
> —JH

Your Scripture Prayer Project

Genesis 2:24

Exodus 20:12

Proverbs 11:3

Hebrews 13:4

2 Corinthians 6:14-15

1 John 4:18

Proverbs 27:5-6

Ephesians 5:15

Psalm 86:11

Ephesians 5:21

For additional guidance on this topic, see also *Adultery, Dating, Decision Making, Domestic Violence, Dysfunctional Family, Financial Freedom, Forgiveness, Hope, Identity, Marriage, Parenting, Self-worth, Sexual Integrity, Singleness.*

38

RAPE RECOVERY
Rescued and Restored

That which was designed by God to be an expression of love can be twisted into a horrendous and hateful act. Rape is a vile act of violence that humiliates and degrades like no other, assaulting body, soul, and spirit and sending the victim into a ditch of shock and shame. In the midst of a victim's suffering, the Lord sees and grieves, and is willing to bring emotional help and spiritual hope for true inner healing.

*"The LORD is close to the brokenhearted and saves those
who are crushed in spirit"*
(PSALM 34:18).

WHAT IS RAPE?

Rape is sexual intercourse by threat, force, or deception, victimizing males as well as females.[1] It is grossly misunderstood:

Myth: Women secretly want to be raped.

Truth: No one wants to be a victim of a violent criminal act. No one wants to be violated either sexually or emotionally by another person. Ezekiel 45:9 says, "Give up your violence and oppression and do what is just and right."

Myth: Rape fulfills sexual needs.

Truth: Rape is *not* about sex. Within God's heart, sex is an act of love. Within a rapist's heart, sex is an act of violence. In fact, rape and sex are opposites. By definition, sex requires consent. But sex without consent is rape. Genesis 19:7 calls rape "wicked." When men from Sodom and Gomorrah were intent on rape, they were told, "Don't do this wicked thing."

What Are Different Categories of Rape?

Statutory rape is sexual intercourse with a female or male under the legal age of consent, with or without force and when the victimizer is more than two years older than the victim.

— *Consent* is not an issue, and the legal age of consent varies from state to state or region.[2]

— *Aggravated sexual assault* is a legal term used in the prosecution of a statutory rape offense.

Stranger rape is forced sexual intercourse by one who is unknown to the victim.

Myth: Provocative women cause rape.

Truth: No one causes one person to rape another. The most probable victim is someone who appears vulnerable. Regardless of how a person dresses or behaves, no one deserves to be raped. The responsibility lies with the rapist, not the victim (Psalm 36:2-4).

Date/acquaintance rape is nonconsensual sexual intercourse by people socially acquainted.

— The vast majority of rapes are committed by someone known to the victim (boyfriend, relative, coworker, neighbor, friend, spouse). These rapes are the most difficult to convince a victim to report. Yet Ecclesiastes 8:11 warns, "When the sentence for a crime is not quickly carried out, the hearts of the people are filled with schemes to do wrong."

— The Jewish law clearly communicates the severe consequences of rape in ancient Israel (Deuteronomy 22:25-26).

Mate rape is forced sexual relations by a husband.

— Unfortunately, many states exempt a husband from prosecution for the rape of his wife.

Myth: A wife must be subject to sexual relations at *any time* with her husband. The Bible says wives are never to deprive their husbands sexually" (1 Corinthians 7:4).

Truth: A wife is not a piece of property. Sexual expression was designed by God to be an act of love, not violence. Forced sex is not love, but is the opposite. The Bible is clear: "Husbands, love your wives and do not be harsh with them" (Colossians 3:19).

Gang/group/pack rape is sexual assault by two or more people and is one of the most cruel and brutal crimes imaginable (Judges 19:25).

WHAT ARE THE THREE STAGES TO RECOVERY?[3]

The T-R-A-U-M-A Stage

For approximately two days to two weeks, the victim is traumatized:

T Terror—Extreme fear, causing flashbacks, nightmares

R Refusal—Denial, causing memory loss or minimizing

A Anger—Rage, causing an inability to eat or sleep

U Uncontrollable actions—Feeling overwhelmed, causing hysteria, sobbing

M Misplaced guilt—Self-blame, causing nausea, diarrhea

A Anxiety—Apprehension, causing severe muscle tension, fatigue

The rape victim has the same reactions recorded by the writer of Psalm 55:4-7:

> *"My heart is in anguish within me; the terrors of*
> *death assail me. Fear and trembling have beset me;*
> *horror has overwhelmed me…Oh, that I had the*
> *wings of a dove! I would fly away and be at rest."*

The Teetering Stage

For up to a year or longer, perhaps until death, the victim will teeter up and down, sometimes suppressing emotions and sometimes surfacing emotions.

Fears of the Victim

being alone	the inability to judge character
being followed	pregnancy
strange places	venereal disease, AIDS
the dark	intimacy
the rape site	the rejection of loved ones

The rape survivor will feel increased calm by repeating over and over, in prayer, "When I am afraid, I will trust in you" (Psalm 56:3).

The Trusting Stage

Some survivors never make it to this stage. Those who do will experience peace.

> *"I will lie down and sleep in peace, for you alone,*
> *O LORD, make me dwell in safety"*
> (PSALM 4:8).

The survivor views the incident with a balanced perspective...

— not trusting everyone, but selecting trustworthy friends.

> *"Jesus would not entrust himself to them,*
> *for he knew all men"*
> (JOHN 2:24).

— not trusting circumstances, but trusting God, who is over all circumstances (Proverbs 3:5-6).

WHAT ARE THE ABC'S OF IMMEDIATE RESPONSE TO RAPE?[4]

A Assure your own safety (read Psalm 23)

— Move to a secure place of safety and wrap yourself in a warm blanket.

— Breathe very deeply to get more oxygen to the brain, so as not to become lightheaded or faint.

— Repeat positive affirmations, prayers, scripture—such as...

> *"The LORD is my shepherd...I will fear no evil"*
> (PSALM 23:1,4).

B Begin a support system (Proverbs 23:12)

— Report incident to the police (don't wash or shower—this will help preserve physical evidence).

— Ask a friend to take you to a medical care facility to check for injuries and STDs (sexually transmitted diseases).[5]

— Seek legal advice to learn the rights of rape victims.

C Call on others for emotional support (Proverbs 18:24)

— Call someone you trust.

— Call a rape crisis center.

— Seek professional counseling.

HOW DO YOU WALK THROUGH THIS SEASON OF S-U-F-F-E-R-I-N-G?

The path to recovery is long and steep, with deliberate steps needed to leave the ditch. But don't languish in shame over something that wasn't your fault. Gain emotional wholeness on the Road to Transformation, where hope and healing abound!

S Seek God's supernatural help to overcome the negative consequences of rape (1 John 5:14-15).

U Understand that no one is protected from tragedy (Matthew 5:45).

F Forgive the offender, and leave the revenge to God. Ask God for the power of Christ to do this in you—you cannot do it yourself (Romans 12:19).

F Forgive others—family members and friends who have let you down (Colossians 3:13).

E Exchange your old identity for your new identity in the person of Christ (Galatians 2:20).

R Remember, the Lord is your Shepherd (Psalm 23:1-2).

I Incorporate reading and meditating on Scripture along with listening to praise music as a daily habit (Psalm 119:50).

N Notice and encourage others around you who are hurting. Your sensitivity and compassion for others will be a blessing to them and healing to you (2 Corinthians 1:3-4).

G Glorify Christ by allowing His splendor to be displayed through you (Isaiah 49:1-2).

How to Replace Fear with Faith

Perhaps more than any other group of people, rape victims experience frequent defeat because of lies they believe in their ongoing battle with fear about themselves, the future, and God. The best way to combat lies is to replace fear with faith. Assess the lies believed, then every single day commit to believing God's truth because "the truth will set you free" (John 8:32).

> **Fear**: "I can't get through this."
>
> **Faith**: The Lord your God will walk with you all the way through to the end.
>
> (Isaiah 43:2)

> **Fear**: "I'll never stop crying."
>
> **Faith**: In time, weeping will wane, and joy will return to your heart.
>
> (Psalm 30:5)

> **Fear**: "I will always feel dirty."

Faith: A dirty-minded person did something despicable to you, but you are not dirty! Every day, claim your true identity in Christ—you are holy in His sight.

(Colossians 1:22)

Fear: "No good could ever come out of this."

Faith: God promises that what others do for evil, He will use for good. In time, you will see this promise fulfilled in your life.

(Romans 8:28)

Fear: "No one will want to marry me."

Faith: Until the Lord brings a husband into your life, He promises to be your husband, provider, and protector.

(Isaiah 54:5)

Fear: "I will never want sexual intimacy. My memories are too painful."

Faith: The Lord is able to heal all emotional hurt, no matter how severe the memories.

(Jeremiah 17:14)

Fear: "I don't have the strength to go on."

Faith: When you don't have strength to live from day to day, the Lord Jesus will give you His strength (read Isaiah 40:28-31).

(Philippians 4:13)

Fear: "I will always be consumed by fear."

Faith: All people experience fear when their lives are truly in danger—that is normal. But the Lord will deliver you from excessive fear because of His presence within you.

(Deuteronomy 31:8)

Fear: "I have no hope for the future."

Faith: Because God is a God of hope, your future is safe in His hands.

(Jeremiah 29:11)

What Are Practical Do's and Don'ts for Others?

How you speak with a survivor makes a significant difference in the recovery process. Realize the healing power of your words. Proverbs 12:18 says, "Reckless words pierce like a sword, but the tongue of the wise brings healing."

— *Don't* react with shock or horror.

> Respond with compassion.

— *Don't* suggest the victim could have avoided it.

> Affirm that the victim is not at fault in any way.

— *Don't* ask for details of the incident.

> Suggest the victim write down details for authorities.

— *Don't* offer quick and simplistic answers.

> Encourage the victim with God's unfailing love.

— *Don't* press the victim to initiate immediate forgiveness.

> Refer the victim to professional counseling.

— *Don't* criticize choices or decisions made by the victim.

> Strongly suggest the victim report the crime.

— *Don't* infer that this was God's chastisement for sin.

> Encourage medical treatment.

— *Don't* change the subject.

> Urge the victim to write down her feelings.

— *Don't* speak at all if you don't know what to say.

> Comfort with your presence.

In all that you say and do, "carry each other's burdens, and in this way you will fulfill the law of Christ" (Galatians 6:2).

> Realize, regardless of your suffering,
> there are no hopeless situations,
> only those who have grown hopeless.
>
> Ecclesiastes 9:4 says,
> "Anyone who is among the living has hope."
> Therefore, never, never, never give up hope!
>
> —JH

Your Scripture Prayer Project

Psalm 34:18

2 Corinthians 4:8-9

Psalm 119:28

Ecclesiastes 9:4

Romans 12:19

Proverbs 3:5-6

Psalm 37:7

Psalm 119:50

Isaiah 43:19

2 Corinthians 1:3-4

For additional guidance on this topic, see also *Abortion Recovery, Adultery, Anger, Childhood Sexual Abuse, Crisis Intervention, Dating, Decision Making, Depression, Domestic Violence, Evil and Suffering...Why?, Fear, Forgiveness, Grief Recovery, Homosexuality, Hope, Identity, Phobias, Pregnancy...Unplanned, Self-worth, Sexual Integrity, Stress Management, Suicide Prevention, Victimization, Worry.*

39

RECONCILIATION
Restoring Broken Relationships

O h, the pain of a relationship ripped apart—hurting hearts, needless loss. Rocky relationships can relegate us to a ditch riddled with disagreements and disputes. Reconciliation leads to the Road to Transformation, where peace and harmony are restored.

WHAT ARE RECONCILIATION AND MEDIATION?

— *Reconciliation* is the act of settling or restoring differences.[1] While a relationship will not always be salvaged, the spirit of reconciliation will always reflect the heart of God. That's why Romans 12:18 says, "If it is possible, as far as it depends on you, live at peace with everyone."

— *Mediation* is the intervention between conflicting parties to promote reconciliation.[2] A mediator is an outside agent brought in to produce a change or compromise between opposing individuals.

WHEN SHOULD WE INITIATE RECONCILIATION?

Most people don't know the *when*. But the Bible states two specific times, much like two sides of a coin:

— When you have wronged another

> *"If you are offering your gift at the altar and there*
> *remember that your brother has something against you,*
> *leave your gift there in front of the altar. First go and be*
> *reconciled to your brother; then come and offer your gift"*
> (MATTHEW 5:23-24).

— When you have been wronged

> *"If your brother sins against you, go and show him his*
> *fault, just between the two of you. If he listens to you, you*
> *have won your brother over. But if he will not listen, take*
> *one or two others along, so that 'every matter may be*
> *established by the testimony of two or three witnesses'"*
> (MATTHEW 18:15-16).

WHAT PAVES THE ROAD FOR RECONCILIATION?

When you've been hurt, you first need to bury the hatchet in your dispute-filled ditch before you can climb out. Early in America's history the tomahawk, or war hatchet, was used as a war club and hunting weapon. But when peace was forged with an enemy, a ceremonial tomahawk was buried in the ground. From this old Indian custom comes the expression "burying the hatchet"—a phrase that speaks of a sincere commitment to forgive and be reconciled. Unfortunately, many people who bury the hatchet still leave the handle exposed! First Peter 3:9 says, "Do not repay evil with evil or insult with insult, but with blessing, because to this you were called so that you may inherit a blessing."

How to Bury the Hatchet

Prepare your heart for seeking reconciliation. Be willing to...

— view the conflict as an opportunity for growth.[3]
— learn what God wants you to learn.[4]
— discover that you are partly at fault.[5]
— expose your weaknesses.
— be open with your feelings.
— risk the relationship.
— accept a negative outcome.
— pray for God's will to be done.

> *"Let the peace of Christ rule in your hearts,*
> *since as members of one body you were*
> *called to peace. And be thankful"*
> (COLOSSIANS 3:15).

Know that refusal to seek reconciliation affects the intimacy of your relationship with God. Humble your heart and pray,

— "Lord, I don't want to be prideful and unbending."

— "Lord, I want Your favor on my life—not Your disfavor."

— "Lord, I want to reflect Your character and be open to reconciliation."

"Blessed are the peacemakers,
for they will be called sons of God"
(MATTHEW 5:9).

Seek forgiveness and apologize for words that have hurt the other person.

— "I have tried to see our relationship from your point of view."

— "I realize I've been wrong in my attitude of _____."

— "Will you forgive me?"

"If you have been trapped by what you said, ensnared by
the words of your mouth, then do this...to free yourself,
since you have fallen into your neighbor's hands: Go and
humble yourself; press your plea with your neighbor!"
(PROVERBS 6:2-3).

Recognize the ground rules of communication.[6]

— Offer unconditional acceptance.

— Confront the problem, not the person.

— Listen without interrupting.

— Verbalize your feelings.

— Use words that build self-worth.

— Aim for mutual understanding.

— Give more than you take.

"Be completely humble and gentle; be patient,
bearing with one another in love"
(EPHESIANS 4:2).

Be kind and gentle, trusting God to work in the heart of the other person.[7]

— Don't harbor resentment.

— Don't make excuses for yourself.

— Don't get drawn into arguments.

— Don't fail to pray.

— Don't have expectations of immediate acceptance.

> *"The Lord's servant must not quarrel; instead, he must be kind*
> *to everyone, able to teach, not resentful. Those who oppose*
> *him he must gently instruct, in the hope that God will grant*
> *them repentance leading them to a knowledge of the truth"*
> (2 Timothy 2:24-25).

Reflect the character of Christ in all you do. In order to prepare your heart to reflect the character of Christ, pray,

— "Lord, I die to my personal rights."

> *"I have been crucified with Christ and I no longer live, but*
> *Christ lives in me. The life I live in the body, I live by faith*
> *in the Son of God, who loved me and gave himself for me"*
> (Galatians 2:20).

— "Lord, I die to defending myself."

> *"The LORD is my strength and my shield;*
> *my heart trusts in him, and I am helped"*
> (Psalm 28:7).

— "Lord, I die to relying on my own abilities."

> *"He who trusts in himself is a fool,*
> *but he who walks in wisdom is kept safe"*
> (Proverbs 28:26).

Enlist a mediator if necessary.[8]

— Pray for God to prepare the heart of your opposer for mediation.

— Seek a person whom your opposer can respect.

— Say, "At times an outside person can have a different perspective that is more objective. Would you consider having a mediator help us think through our problems with the hope of reaching a successful end?"

> *"If he will not listen [to you], take one or two others*
> *along, so that 'every matter may be established by the*
> *testimony of two or three witnesses'"*
> (Matthew 18:16).

Do not hold yourself responsible for the outcome.[9]

— When reconciliation is refused, don't live with false guilt.

— You cannot force reconciliation to occur.

— Everyone is individually responsible to God.

> *"Each of us will give an account of himself to God"*
> (ROMANS 14:12).

Rest in the knowledge you have done all you can to seek peace.

— Continue to show love and treat the other person with forgiveness.

— Thank God for giving you the desire to be at peace with everyone.

— Praise God for His commitment to orchestrate your own spiritual growth.

> *"If it is possible, as far as it depends on you,*
> *live at peace with everyone"*
> (ROMANS 12:18).

WHAT IF YOUR EFFORTS ARE REFUSED?[10]

> *"Let us not become weary in doing good, for at the proper*
> *time we will reap a harvest if we do not give up"*
> (GALATIANS 6:9).

Remember:

— If your heart has been repentant, you have God's total forgiveness.

> *"If we claim to be without sin, we deceive ourselves and the truth*
> *is not in us. If we confess our sins, he is faithful and just and*
> *will forgive us our sins and purify us from all unrighteousness"*
> (1 JOHN 1:8-9).

— Pray for those who refuse reconciliation—for their unmet need.

> *"Love your enemies and pray for those who persecute you"*
> (MATTHEW 5:44).

— God never leaves you when you suffer the loss of a close relationship.

> *"The LORD is close to the brokenhearted and*
> *saves those who are crushed in spirit"*
> (PSALM 34:18).

— Control what you say about those who refuse reconciliation.

> *"Bless those who persecute you; bless and do not curse"*
> (ROMANS 12:14).

— Don't be vengeful—in time, God deals with those who do wrong.

> *"Do not take revenge, my friends, but leave room for God's wrath,*
> *for it is written: 'It is mine to avenge; I will repay,' says the Lord"*
> (ROMANS 12:19).

— God will bring something good out of the pain.

> *"Forget the former things; do not dwell on the past.*
> *See, I am doing a new thing!"*
> (ISAIAH 43:18-19).

Reconciliation is restoring a relationship based on restored trust.
It requires repentance and is to be extended only when earned.
—JH

Your Scripture Prayer Project

2 Corinthians 5:17-18

Proverbs 6:2-3

Proverbs 28:14

Matthew 5:23-24

Matthew 5:44

Matthew 6:14-15

Matthew 18:15-16

Ephesians 4:29

Romans 12:17-18

Romans 12:20-21

For additional guidance on this topic, see also *Adultery, Alcohol and Drug Abuse, Anger, Childhood Sexual Abuse, Crisis Intervention, Decision Making, Domestic Violence, Dysfunctional Family, Forgiveness, Hope, Marriage, Rejection, Self-worth.*

40

REJECTION

Healing a Wounded Heart

Nothing ravages a heart like rejection. Has someone dear to you walked out of your life, leaving you in the ditch of despair, feeling devalued? Were you told, "You should *never* have been born. You were never wanted. You will never amount to anything"? When you feel painfully rejected by a special person, take comfort in these tender words:

> *"The LORD is close to the brokenhearted and*
> *saves those who are crushed in spirit"*
> (PSALM 34:18).

At times you will be rejected, but that doesn't make you a reject. You have a God-given purpose.

WHAT IS REJECTION?

— Rejection is refusing to accept or consider someone.

— To be rejected is to be cast aside, cast off, cast away—to be thrown away as having no value.[1]

DO YOU FEEL REJECTED EVEN BY GOD?

Did you grow up in a home where you never measured up, where you were mistreated, where you were maligned and, as a result, you're convinced God could never approve of you? Have you committed some hidden sin or harbored hatred in your heart such that you feel beyond the reach of God's forgiveness? If you are thoroughly persuaded that God has rejected you, then claim this promise from God's unchanging Word:

"The LORD will not reject his people;
he will never forsake his inheritance"
(PSALM 94:14).

WHAT DO YOU NEED TO KNOW ABOUT GOD?

Know God's Character

First John 4:8 says, "God is love." And He Himself says to you, "I have loved you with an everlasting love" (Jeremiah 31:3).

Know God's Heart

God wants to adopt you into His family. First John 3:1 says, "How great is the love the Father has lavished on us, that we should be called children of God!"

Know God's Plan

God offers salvation to you (John 3:17).

Know God's Purposes

God uses your suffering to hone your character and increase your hope (Romans 5:3-5).

"He extends compassion and comfort to you,
which, in turn, you can give to others"
(2 CORINTHIANS 1:3-4).

HOW DOES REJECTION BREED REJECTION?[2]

When rejected, a chain reaction can occur that leads to more rejection. Through conscious choices, a cycle becomes a pattern that eventually becomes a way of life. Unless truth is embraced, the cycle broken, and the pattern replaced, rejection will continue to breed rejection.

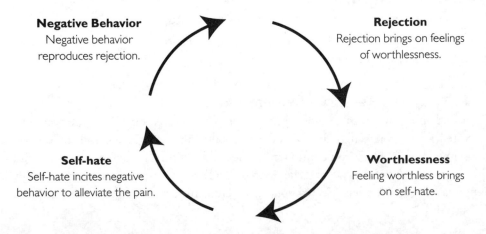

Negative Behavior
Negative behavior reproduces rejection.

Rejection
Rejection brings on feelings of worthlessness.

Worthlessness
Feeling worthless brings on self-hate.

Self-hate
Self-hate incites negative behavior to alleviate the pain.

When you are rejected, be aware of a tendency to overgeneralize, assuming that others will reject you, too. Fearing the worst, you may inadvertently push away your remaining friends to prevent further hurt. When they respond negatively, you will interpret their reaction as confirmation of your deepest fears. This vicious cycle will lead to a self-fulfilling prophecy and explains the saying, "Rejection breeds rejection."

To stop feeling like a reject:

— don't assume that one person's opinion reflects everyone's opinion.

— don't let one person's negative attitude toward you define you.

— realize because Jesus calls you "friend" (Luke 7:34), you can trust that His love will be with you always.

— nurture several friendships, focusing on God's description of how true friends treat one another. A true friend will never reject you.

"A friend loves at all times"
(Proverbs 17:17).

Truths for Meditation and Memorization

Rejection

Just because someone withholds love from you doesn't mean everyone will withhold love from you. God always listens and never withholds His love from you.

"Praise be to God, who has not rejected
my prayer or withheld his love from me!"
(Psalm 66:20).

Worthlessness

Just because someone doesn't value you doesn't mean that no one values you. God valued you enough to send Jesus to die for you so you can spend eternity with Him.

"God so loved the world that he gave his one and only Son, that
whoever believes in him shall not perish but have eternal life"
(John 3:16).

Self-hate

Just because someone has rejected you doesn't mean you should condemn yourself. God will never condemn you because you are in Christ's family.

"There is now no condemnation for
those who are in Christ Jesus"
(Romans 8:1).

Negative behavior

Just because someone has rejected you doesn't give you license to do what is wrong. God has given you the power to do what is right. Sin will not be your master!

> *"If you do what is right, will you not be accepted? But*
> *if you do not do what is right, sin is crouching at your*
> *door; it desires to have you, but you must master it"*
> (GENESIS 4:7).

WHAT IS THE ROOT CAUSE OF REJECTION?

All of us are created with three God-given inner needs—for love, significance, and security. We experience rejection from our earliest years when we are deprived of having someone who loves us unconditionally, someone who regards us as highly significant, or someone who welcomes us as part of a family. Because people fail people, it is essential not to let other people define who you are. Realize that rejection can quickly skew your view! Even though you may not see the path you should take, the Lord promises never to leave you.

> *"The LORD himself goes before you and will be*
> *with you; he will never leave you nor forsake*
> *you. Do not be afraid; do not be discouraged"*
> (DEUTERONOMY 31:8).

Wrong Belief:

"Because of being rejected, I feel so unloved, so insignificant, so unwanted. My life isn't worth anything!"

Right Belief:

"I do not like being rejected, but I know my worth isn't based on whether or not others reject me but on the fact that the Lord accepts me. Jesus not only loved me enough to die for my sins, but He also lives inside me and will never leave me nor forsake me."

> *"I trust in your unfailing love;*
> *my heart rejoices in your salvation"*
> (PSALM 13:5).

HOW DO YOU ACCEPT YOURSELF WHEN OTHERS REJECT YOU?[3]

Those in the ditch of rejection can rejoice because they are of utmost value to God and completely accepted by Him. Praise God as you walk triumphantly on the Road to Transformation in full recognition of the truth that you've been purchased with the priceless blood of Christ.

*"I will turn the darkness into light before them and make the rough
places smooth. These are the things I will do; I will not forsake them"*
(ISAIAH 42:16).

Focus on Facts, Not Feelings

Admit the rejection of the past and acknowledge its pain.

*"I remember my affliction and my wandering,
the bitterness and the gall"*
(LAMENTATIONS 3:19).

— *Ask* God to bring to mind every rejection from your childhood to the
present, and then consider the circumstances of each situation.

— *Acknowledge* the gamut of feelings of rejection you experienced with
each past event. Release to God the pain and the person(s) involved.

— *Ask* God to heal the physical, emotional, and spiritual damage caused by
each of these painful experiences of rejection.

Claim God's acceptance and unconditional love.

— *Confess* God's love for you and the various ways He has shown you His
love (for example, Christ dying for you).

— *Cite* Psalm 139:1-18 and praise God for orchestrating your conception,
forming you in your mother's womb, and planning each day of your life.

— *Convey* your appreciation to God for His love of you by loving Him
with all your heart, soul, mind, and strength. And love others as He
loves you.

Choose to forgive those who rejected you.

*"Bear with each other and forgive whatever
grievances you may have against one another.
Forgive as the Lord forgave you"*
(COLOSSIANS 3:13).

— *Consider* all the hurt and anger you feel over your rejection.

— *Count* the cost of withholding forgiveness: a bitter spirit building up
inside you, which will cause trouble and spread to those around you.

— *Commit* to forgiving those who rejected you just as Christ forgave those
who rejected Him (including you). Write down their names, their
offenses, and the pain caused you. Then release each person, offense,
and pain into the loving hands of God.

Expect future rejection as natural in a fallen world.

> *"Do not be surprised at the painful trial you are suffering,*
> *as though something strange were happening to you"*
> (1 Peter 4:12).

— *Empty* yourself of the pride that drives your desire to be accepted by everyone. Since gaining everyone's approval is impossible, commit yourself to pleasing God.

— *Empathize* with others who feel rejected by friends, family, employers, business associates, or anyone else important to them.

— *Embrace,* if you are a believer, the truth that according to the Bible sharing in the sufferings of Christ is a privilege. As a believer you *will* experience rejection, just as Jesus did. You are not exempt from being rejected in daily life. Jesus is rejected daily by those who refuse to turn to Him for salvation.

Plant Scripture in your mind to produce new thought patterns.

> *"Do not conform any longer to the pattern of this*
> *world, but be transformed by the renewing of your*
> *mind. Then you will be able to test and approve what*
> *God's will is—his good, pleasing and perfect will"*
> (Romans 12:2).

— *Purpose* to renew your mind by selecting meaningful scriptures to read, meditate on, and commit to memory. These will help you deal with any past, present, or possible future rejection.

— *Plan* a specific time each day to read God's Word and pray.

— *Partner* with someone who will hold you accountable for applying God's truth to your heart.

Thank God for what you've learned through your rejection.

> *"It was good for me to be afflicted*
> *so that I might learn your decrees"*
> (Psalm 119:71).

— "Thank You, Lord, for using my pain to make me more dependent on You."

— "Thank You, Lord, for using my pain to make me less dependent on people."

— "Thank You, Lord, for using my pain to make me more dependent on Your Word."

Encourage others as an expression of Christ's love.

> *"Encourage one another daily"*
> (HEBREWS 3:13).

— *Extend* compassion to those who are hurting as someone who has also been hurt.
— *Enfold* them in prayer, faithfully praying for them and with them.
— *Ease* emotional wounds by embracing those in pain and encouraging them to talk.

Draw on the power of Christ's life within you.

> *"I can do everything through him who gives me strength"*
> (PHILIPPIANS 4:13).

— "I will see Christ as my security whenever I feel insecure."
— "I know that I have all I need, for Jesus will meet all my needs."
— "I will daily set aside my selfish desires in favor of His desires, saying, 'Not my will, but Yours, be done.'"

Following in Jesus' footsteps...

Though I've been hurt, I will not harbor hate;
Though betrayed, I will still live with love;
Though my heart aches, I will hold onto hope;
Though I'm afraid, I will face life with faith.

—JH

=== *Your Scripture Prayer Project* ===

Psalm 34:18

Psalm 27:10

Lamentations 3:22

1 John 3:1

Psalm 66:20

Romans 8:38-39

1 Samuel 12:22

Isaiah 41:10

Psalm 13:5

Deuteronomy 31:8

For additional guidance on this topic, see also *Anger, Critical Spirit, Depression, Dysfunctional Family, Evil and Suffering...Why?, Fear, Forgiveness, Grief Recovery, Hope, Identity, Recovery, Prejudice, Self-worth, Singleness, Suicide Prevention, Verbal and Emotional Abuse, Victimization.*

41

SALVATION

The Cornerstone of Counseling

T he Bible refers over and over again to our need to be saved—to be rescued from an impending threat, to be delivered from a disastrous destiny. What is this desperate ditch of doom—this formidable future—faced by every single person who has ever lived? It is separation from God and all that is good (Luke 19:10).

WHAT DO WE NEED TO BE SAVED FROM?

1. We need to be saved from the *penalty of sin*. This is *justification*—meaning "declared righteous, vindicated, acquitted"[1]—a completed action.

   > *"For God did not appoint us to suffer wrath but to*
   > *receive salvation through our Lord Jesus Christ"*
   > (1 THESSALONIANS 5:9).

2. We need to be saved from the *power of sin*. This is *sanctification*—meaning "set apart to God, set apart from sin"[2]—a current process.

   > *"Continue to work out your salvation with fear*
   > *and trembling, for it is God who works in you to*
   > *will and to act according to his good purpose"*
   > (PHILIPPIANS 2:12-13).

3. We need to be saved from the *presence of sin*. This is *glorification*—meaning the final state of all believers who, with transformed, imperishable bodies, will live in the presence of God—a future condition.[3] The Bible refers to "the redemption of our bodies," and says that "in this hope we were saved" (Romans 8:23-24).

How Do You Know If You Are Saved?

God wants you to know if you are an authentic Christian or not. In fact, He has devoted one whole book of the Bible to letting you know whether or not you have eternal life (1 John 5:13). Read the letter of 1 John and notice how the word "know" is repeated seven times throughout this short book to make this point clear. Then evaluate your life in light of this insightful book of the Bible.

Take the following Salvation Test (mark *yes* or *no* by each statement to indicate if it is true of you or not).

☐ *"We know that we have come to know him if we obey his commands"* (1 John 2:3).

☐ *"If anyone obeys his word, God's love is truly made complete in him. This is how we know we are in him: Whoever claims to live in him must walk as Jesus did"* (1 John 2:5-6).

☐ *"You know that everyone who does what is right has been born of him"* (1 John 2:29).

☐ *"No one who lives in him keeps on sinning. No one who continues to sin has either seen him or known him"* (1 John 3:6).

☐ *"No one who is born of God will continue to sin, because God's seed remains in him; he cannot go on sinning, because he has been born of God. This is how we know who the children of God are...Anyone who does not do what is right is not a child of God"* (1 John 3:9-10).

☐ *"Those who obey his commands live in him, and he in them. And this is how we know that he lives in us"* (1 John 3:24).

☐ *"We know that anyone born of God does not continue to sin"* (1 John 5:18).

What Are Common Questions About Salvation?

Q: Can I continue to live a sinful lifestyle after I am saved?

A: You cannot belong to Christ and stay in a sinful lifestyle for very long. Many people intellectually understand salvation, yet they have never yielded their will to God's will and allowed Him to take ownership of their lives. That is why Jesus said,

> *"Not everyone who says to me, 'Lord, Lord,' will enter the kingdom of heaven, but only he who does the will of my Father who is in heaven"*
> (Matthew 7:21-23).

Q: If we are not saved by our works, but by faith, why does the book of James say that faith without works is dead? Does Scripture contradict Scripture?

A: No! Scripture never contradicts itself. The primary purpose of the book of James is to communicate not *how* to be saved, but rather *what* your life will be like after you are saved. James lets us know that true faith in Christ transforms your character and your conduct. If there is the root of faith, there will be the fruit of faith. You do good works not to *become* saved, but rather because you *are* saved. Ultimately, if there are no good works in your life, then there is no authentic salvation. That is why James says:

> *"In the same way, faith by itself, if it is*
> *not accompanied by action, is dead"*
> (JAMES 2:17).

WHAT ARE COMMON CONCERNS OF THOSE WHO ARE NOT SAVED?

Some people have confusion and real concerns about whether salvation is even possible for them. They have an acute awareness of their shortcomings and feel burdened because of their failures and personal sin. Fortunately, these real concerns have encouraging answers.

Concern: "God would never accept me. You don't know what I've done."

Correction: The issue is not what you've done, but what Christ has done for you.

> *"Here is a trustworthy saying that deserves full*
> *acceptance: Christ Jesus came into the world*
> *to save sinners—of whom I am the worst"*
> (1 TIMOTHY 1:15).

Concern: "God could never forgive all my sins."

Correction: God not only forgives your sins, but He also "forgets" your sins. He says:

> *"I, even I, am he who blots out your transgressions, for*
> *my own sake, and remembers your sins no more"*
> (ISAIAH 43:25).

Concern: "I can't give up my sins."

Correction: The power of Christ in you is bigger than the power of sin over you.

> *"His divine power has given us everything*
> *we need for life and godliness"*
> (2 PETER 1:3).

Concern: "I think I've committed the unpardonable sin."

Correction: Blasphemy against the Holy Spirit—the only unpardonable sin—is a complete and total hardening of the heart that results in an unwillingness to yield to the convicting work of the Holy Spirit and in repeatedly rejecting the need for forgiveness and reconciliation to God[4] (Mark 3:29).

Concern: "I want to become a Christian, but I don't want to make a decision now."

Correction: Not making a decision is still a decision—it's a decision against Christ.

> *"He who is not with me is against me"*
> (MATTHEW 12:30).

Concern: "I might be harassed or hated."

Correction: Every authentic Christian will be opposed and oppressed, but not overcome by trouble:

> *"If the world hates you, keep in mind that it hated*
> *me first...If they persecuted me, they will persecute*
> *you also...In this world you will have trouble.*
> *But take heart! I have overcome the world"*
> (JOHN 15:18,20; 16:33).

Concern: "It's too late for me."

Correction: It's never too late for a heart to be humbled before God.

> *"Now is the day of salvation...He [God] is*
> *patient with you, not wanting anyone to*
> *perish, but everyone to come to repentance"*
> (2 CORINTHIANS 6:2; 2 PETER 3:9).

WHAT MUST YOU DO TO BE SAVED?

The ditch of doom doesn't have to be your destiny. Your home can be heaven, and your future bright in the presence of a God who dearly loves you and has rescued you through His Son, Jesus.

1. God's Purpose for You Is *Salvation*

What was God's motive in sending Christ to earth? To condemn you? No—His motive was to express His love for you by saving you!

> *"God so loved the world that he gave his one and only Son,*
> *that whoever believes in him shall not perish but have*
> *eternal life. For God did not send his Son into the world*
> *to condemn the world, but to save the world through him"*
> (JOHN 3:16-17).

What was Jesus' purpose in coming to earth? To make everything perfect and to remove all sin? No—His purpose was to forgive your sins, empower you to have victory over sin, and enable you to live a fulfilled life!

> *"I [Jesus] have come that they may have life,*
> *and have it to the full"*
> (JOHN 10:10).

2. Your Problem Is *Sin*

What exactly is sin? Sin is living *independently* of God's standard—knowing what is right, but choosing wrong.

> *"Anyone, then, who knows the good he*
> *ought to do and doesn't do it, sins"*
> (JAMES 4:17).

What is the major consequence of sin? Spiritual death and spiritual separation from God.

> *"The wages of sin is death, but the gift of God is*
> *eternal life in Christ Jesus our Lord"*
> (ROMANS 6:23).

3. God's Provision Is the *Savior*

Can anything remove the penalty for sin? Yes. Jesus died on the cross to personally pay the penalty for your sins.

> *"God demonstrates his own love for us in this:*
> *While we were still sinners, Christ died for us"*
> (ROMANS 5:8).

What is the solution to separation from God? Belief in Jesus Christ as the *only* way to God the Father.

> *"Jesus answered, 'I am the way and the truth and the
> life. No one comes to the Father except through me'"*
> (JOHN 14:6).

4. Your Part Is *Surrender*

Place your faith in (rely on) Jesus Christ as your personal Lord and Savior, rejecting your good works as a means of gaining God's approval.

> *"It is by grace you have been saved, through faith—and
> this not from yourselves, it is the gift of God"*
> (EPHESIANS 2:8).

Give Christ control of your life, entrusting yourself to Him.

> *"Jesus said to his disciples, 'If anyone would come after me,
> he must deny himself and take up his cross and follow
> me. For whoever wants to save his life will lose it, but
> whoever loses his life for me will find it. What good will
> it be for a man if he gains the whole world, yet forfeits his
> soul? Or what can a man give in exchange for his soul?'"*
> (MATTHEW 16:24-26).

Perhaps today you realize that you have never received Jesus into your life. If you desire to be fully forgiven by God and become the person He created you to be, you can tell Him in a simple, heartfelt prayer such as this:

===== *Prayer of Salvation* =====

God,

I want a real relationship with You. I admit that many times I've chosen to go my own way instead of Your way. Please forgive me for my sins. Jesus, thank You for dying on the cross to pay the penalty for my sins. Come into my life to be my Lord and my Savior. I give You control of my life.

Make me the person You created me to be.

In Your holy name I pray. Amen.

If you, with utmost sincerity, prayed that prayer, look at what Jesus says about you!

> *"I tell you the truth, whoever hears my word and*
> *believes him who sent me has eternal life and will not*
> *be condemned; he has crossed over from death to life"*
> (JOHN 5:24).

While at a restaurant, a friend announces, "This gift is for you!"
If you don't take it, is the gift really yours? No, if you leave the gift on
the table, it hasn't become yours yet. Likewise, salvation is a gift—
it is yours for the taking, but it's not yours until you receive it.
—JH

Your Scripture Prayer Project

Matthew 7:21

John 3:16

Romans 5:8

Romans 10:13

John 14:6

Acts 4:12

Romans 6:23

Ephesians 2:8-9

1 John 5:13

Matthew 16:24

For additional guidance on this topic, see also *Forgiveness, Hope, Identity, Self-worth.*

42

SELF-WORTH

Discovering Your God-given Worth

Repeated rejection can send self-worth sinking into ditches of dejection and desolation. When people are continually told they don't measure up, or they're consistently passed up for the smarter, prettier, or stronger, the collective message is that their lives have little or no value or significance. But nothing could be further from the truth. God dearly loves each person He creates and has a unique plan and purpose for each life. True self-worth always starts and ends with Him, and never depends on the perceptions of others. God forever established your worth (over 2,000 years ago) by one act: He gave His Son for you.

> *"The Lord does not look at the things man looks at. Man looks*
> *at the outward appearance, but the Lord looks at the heart"*
> (1 Samuel 16:7).

What Are the Differences/Similarities Between Self-worth and Self-esteem?

To have self-worth is to believe your life has value and significance.

The term *self-esteem* actually has two different meanings that stand in opposition to each other:

— The first is an *objective regard of your value,* and is rooted in the recognition of your sin and your need for the Savior. It is also based on the fact that Christ established your worth by dying for you. The Bible refers to this self-esteem as humility. God says, "This is the one I esteem: he who is humble and contrite in spirit, and trembles at my word" (Isaiah 66:2).

— The second is an *exaggerated regard of your value,* and is rooted in the idea that you are good enough and sufficient enough within yourself that you do not need to live dependently on the Savior. The Bible refers to this self-esteem as pride. Philippians 2:3 says, "Do nothing out of selfish ambition or vain conceit, but in humility consider others better than yourselves."

First Peter 5:5 presents God's view of these two kinds of self-esteem in sharp contrast to one another: "God opposes the proud but gives grace to the humble."

WHAT ARE STEPS TO SELF-ACCEPTANCE?

I accept God's Word that I was created in His image.

> "God created man in his own image, in the image of
> God he created him; male and female he created them"
> (GENESIS 1:27).

I accept myself as acceptable to Christ.

> "Accept one another, then, just as Christ accepted you,
> in order to bring praise to God"
> (ROMANS 15:7).

I accept what I cannot change about myself.

> "Who are you, O man, to talk back to God? 'Shall
> what is formed say to him who formed it, "Why did
> you make me like this?"' Does not the potter have
> the right to make out of the same lump of clay some
> pottery for noble purposes and some for common use?"
> (ROMANS 9:20-21).

I accept the fact that I will make mistakes.

> "Not that I have...already been made
> perfect, but I press on to take hold of that
> for which Christ Jesus took hold of me"
> (PHILIPPIANS 3:12).

I accept criticism and the responsibility for failure.

> "I acknowledged my sin to you and did not cover up
> my iniquity. I said, 'I will confess my transgressions
> to the LORD'—and you forgave the guilt of my sin"
> (PSALM 32:5).

I accept the fact that I will not be liked or loved by everyone.

> *"If the world hates you, keep in mind that it hated me*
> *first…If they persecuted me, they will persecute you also"*
> (JOHN 15:18,20).

I accept the unchangeable circumstances in my life.

> *"I have learned to be content whatever the circumstances"*
> (PHILIPPIANS 4:11).

DOES YOUR SELF-IMAGE LINE UP WITH GOD'S IMAGE OF YOU?

Your self-image has been greatly shaped by the messages you've received and internalized from others, from your experiences, and from your self-talk. When you were a child, you did not have control over who influenced you, but that is no longer the case. You are now able to choose those with whom you associate, and you can certainly control your self-talk. Therefore, by pursuing these new paths, you can take an active part in changing the distorted view you have of yourself. The following will help you begin seeing yourself as God sees you—a perspective that will accelerate your journey along the Road to Transformation.

Accept Yourself

— Stop striving for perfection or trying to be like someone else.

— Realize that the Lord made you for a purpose, and He designed your personality and gave you the gifts and abilities you needed in order to accomplish His purpose for you.

> *"Many are the plans in a man's heart,*
> *but it is the LORD's purpose that prevails"*
> (PROVERBS 19:21).

Thank God for Encouraging You

— Acknowledge and praise God for the abilities He has given you and the things He has accomplished through you.

— Engage in biblically based, encouraging self-talk and mute the condemning critic inside your head.

> *"May our Lord Jesus Christ himself and God our*
> *Father, who loved us and by his grace gave us eternal*
> *encouragement and good hope, encourage your hearts*
> *and strengthen you in every good deed and word"*
> (2 THESSALONIANS 2:16-17).

Accept the Compliments of Others

— To discount the positive comments of those who have heartfelt appreciation for you is to discount their opinions and their desire to express their gratitude to you.

— Practice graciously accepting compliments and turning them into praise to God for the affirmation that He is at work in you and producing good fruit through you.

> *"This is to my Father's glory, that you bear much*
> *fruit, showing yourselves to be my disciples"*
> (JOHN 15:8).

Release Past Negative Experiences and Focus on a Positive Future

— Refuse to dwell on negative things said or done to you in the past and release them to God.

— Embrace the work God is doing in your life now and cooperate with Him by focusing on Him and on His character. Trust in His promise to fulfill His purposes in you.

> *"It is God who works in you to will and to*
> *act according to his good purpose"*
> (PHILIPPIANS 2:13).

Live in God's Forgiveness

— God has extended forgiveness to you for all your sins (past, present, and future). Confess and repent of anything offensive to God. Do not set yourself up as a higher judge than God by refusing to forgive yourself.

— Lay harsh judgment of yourself aside and accept that you will not be made fully perfect and totally without sin until you stand in the presence of Christ and are fully conformed to His image.

> *"We are children of God, and what we will be has not yet*
> *been made known. But we know that when he appears, we*
> *shall be like him, for we shall see him as he is. Everyone*
> *who has this hope in him purifies himself, just as he is pure"*
> (1 JOHN 3:2-3).

Benefit from Mistakes

— Realize that you can learn from your mistakes, as well as from the mistakes of others, and decide to view mistakes as opportunities to learn needed lessons.

— Ask God what He wants to teach you from your mistakes. Listen to Him and learn from Him. Then move forward with a positive attitude and put into practice the insights you have gained.

> *"We know that in all things God works for the good of those who love him, who have been called according to his purpose"*
> (ROMANS 8:28).

Form Supportive, Positive Relationships

— Realize that critical people are hurt people who project their own feelings of inadequacy onto others in an attempt to ease their own emotional pain.

— Minimize the time you spend with negative, critical people—whether family, friends, or coworkers—and seek out those who encourage and support you emotionally and spiritually.

> *"He who walks with the wise grows wise, but a companion of fools suffers harm"*
> (PROVERBS 13:20).

Formulate Realistic Goals and Plans

— Elicit the help of others to identify your strengths/weaknesses and the gifts God has given you, as well as the things you are persuaded God has called you to do.

— Prayerfully set some achievable goals that capitalize on your strengths and make a plan for how you will accomplish those goals.

> *"Do you not know that in a race all the runners run, but only one gets the prize? Run in such a way as to get the prize"*
> (1 CORINTHIANS 9:24).

Identify Your Heart's Desires

— Make a list of the things you have dreamed of doing but have never attempted for fear of failure or because you lack self-assurance.

— Share each desire with the Lord, asking Him to confirm which ones are from Him, and then lay out the steps you need to take in order to accomplish them.

> *"Delight yourself in the LORD and he will give you the desires of your heart"*
> (PSALM 37:4).

Plan for Success

— Anticipate any obstacles to accomplishing your goals and desires and plan strategies for overcoming them.

— Think of yourself achieving each of your goals and doing the things God has put on your heart to do.

"May he give you the desire of your heart
and make all your plans succeed"
(PSALM 20:4).

Celebrate Each Accomplishment

— Your feeling of self-worth and self-confidence will grow with the acknowledgment of each accomplishment.

— Rejoice with the Lord and the significant people in your life over the things God and you have done together. Affirm and celebrate your success.

"In the presence of the LORD your God, you
and your families shall eat and shall rejoice in
everything you have put your hand to, because
the LORD your God has blessed you"
(DEUTERONOMY 12:7).

WHAT ARE ANSWERS TO SELF-DEFEATING STATEMENTS?

At times do you feel inadequate, fearful, or insecure even when you know you shouldn't feel that way? If so, you're not alone. When God first spoke to Moses, he was a man filled with insecurity and fear. When the Lord instructed Moses to confront Pharaoh, Moses argued with God. He felt inadequate for the job; he thought he couldn't speak well enough. But God wouldn't hear that excuse. He told Moses,

"Who gave man his mouth? Who makes him deaf or mute?
Who gives him sight or makes him blind? Is it not I, the LORD?
Now go; I will help you speak and will teach you what to say"
(EXODUS 4:11-12).

— **If you say,** "I just can't do anything right."

   The Lord says, "I'll give you My strength to do what is right."

"I can do everything through him who gives me strength"
(PHILIPPIANS 4:13).

— **If you say,** "I feel that I'm too weak."

The Lord says, "My power is perfect when you are weak."

> *"My grace is sufficient for you,*
> *for my power is made perfect in weakness"*
> (2 CORINTHIANS 12:9).

— **If you say,** "I feel I'm not able to measure up."
The Lord says, "Rely on Me. I am able."

> *"God is able to make all grace abound to you, so*
> *that in all things at all times, having all that you*
> *need, you will abound in every good work"*
> (2 CORINTHIANS 9:8).

— **If you say,** "I don't feel that anyone loves me."
The Lord says, "I love you."

> *"I have loved you with an everlasting love;*
> *I have drawn you with loving-kindness"*
> (JEREMIAH 31:3).

— **If you say,** "I can't forgive myself."
The Lord says, "I can forgive you."

> *"I, even I, am he who blots out your transgressions, for*
> *my own sake, and remembers your sins no more"*
> (ISAIAH 43:25).

— **If you say,** "I wish I'd never been born."
The Lord says, "Since before you were born, I've had plans for you."

> *"Before I formed you in the womb I knew you,*
> *before you were born I set you apart"*
> (JEREMIAH 1:5).

— **If you say,** "I feel my future is hopeless."
The Lord says, "I know the future I have for you."

> *"'For I know the plans I have for you,' declares*
> *the LORD, 'plans to prosper you and not to harm*
> *you, plans to give you hope and a future'"*
> (JEREMIAH 29:11).

At an auction, how is an item's worth determined? Only by the highest price paid. Jesus paid the highest price possible—He gave His life to give you life. This priceless sacrifice established your worth...forever!

—JH

Your Scripture Prayer Project

1 John 1:9

1 John 3:1

Romans 5:8

Romans 8:1

Jeremiah 31:3

2 Corinthians 3:5

2 Corinthians 10:12

Ephesians 2:10

Psalm 139:15-16

Matthew 6:26

For additional guidance on this topic, see also *Childhood Sexual Abuse, Codependency, Critical Spirit, Depression, Domestic Violence, Dysfunctional Family, Evil and Suffering...Why?, Fear, Hope, Identity, Rejection, Singleness, Suicide Prevention, Verbal and Emotional Abuse, Victimization.*

43

SEXUAL ADDICTION
The Way Out of the Web

D o you continually find yourself entangled in a web of sexual addiction? Is there any hope for breaking free from the ditch of this debilitating lifestyle? The Bible assures us that with God, all things are possible, including the transformation of an immoral life into one marked by purity (Colossians 3:5).

WHAT IS A SEXUAL ADDICTION?

— *Sexual addiction* is a compulsive, enslaving dependence on erotic excitement, resulting in detrimental patterns of thinking and behavior.

— *Sexual addiction* involves a wide array of outlets and items (magazines, movies, Internet, adult bookstores).

HOW DO YOU KNOW IF YOU HAVE A SEXUAL ADDICTION?
Is your sexual activity...

Secretive, and not within godly boundaries?
— If so, then you are living a double life.

Hollow, and not a passionate relationship with your spouse, but empty sex?
— If so, then you are prioritizing sexual passion over people.

Abusive, and not uplifting to yourself or others, but degrading to both?
— If so, you are exploiting others and debasing yourself.

Mood-altering, and not facing difficult feelings, but seeking an emotional quick fix?
— If so, you are using sexual passion for comfort or to avoid working through your pain.

Essential, and not an option, suggesting you cannot live without sexual passion?
— If so, you are convincing yourself sex is the most important thing in life.

> *"For a man is a slave to whatever has mastered him"*
> (2 PETER 2:19).

WHAT IS THE SPIRAL OF SEXUAL ADDICTION?

— *Curiosity:* A seemingly harmless temptation to look at sexual objects (James 1:14).

— *Addiction:* A recurring stimulus in the brain. When a person experiences significant stimulation, the hormone epinephrine is secreted into the bloodstream by the adrenal gland. Epinephrine stamps emotional memories into the brain. These memories continue to surface regardless of the person's desire to forget.

> *"A man reaps what he sows"*
> (GALATIANS 6:7).

— *Compulsive Masturbation:* A response of sexual self-comfort to relieve emotional discomfort. This act becomes part of a sexual ritual.

> *"I will not be mastered by anything"*
> (1 CORINTHIANS 6:12).

— *Escalation:* The need for more shocking and explicit sexuality to be stimulated (Ephesians 4:19).

— *Desensitization:* The shocking becomes acceptable and unstimulating (Jeremiah 6:15).

— *Acting Out:* A compulsion to act out what has been seen and imagined because the visual experience is no longer satisfying in itself (Galatians 5:19).

— *Despair:* Utter disgust over the behavior and utter hopelessness to change (Romans 7:15).

WHAT IS THE STRUGGLE?

No one lives with more shame, isolation, and fear of alienation than the sex addict. Addicts believe they can't help the way they are. Each time they surrender to sexual temptation, sin's tenacious grip gets a stronger hold on their hearts. Sexual addicts believe the only solution to getting their love needs met and relieving their emotional pain is through sexual stimulation. Their minds and bodies are held captive to sexual passion.

(Romans 7:19)

Worthless Feelings:	"I can't control my sexual urges." "I feel like a failure." "I'm not a good person."
Withdrawal:	"I can't trust people." "If they knew what I've done, they would be disgusted." "If they knew the real me, they would reject me."
Wrong Assumptions:	"Sex is my greatest need in life." "Sex is the solution to my need for love." "Sex is the solace for all my pain."

WHAT IS THE SEQUENCE?[1]

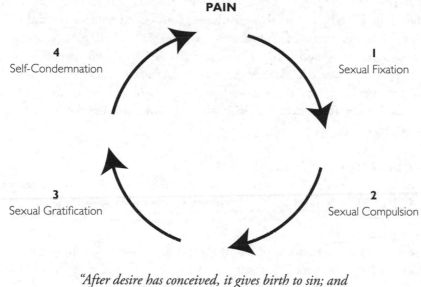

PAIN

4
Self-Condemnation

I
Sexual Fixation

3
Sexual Gratification

2
Sexual Compulsion

*"After desire has conceived, it gives birth to sin; and
sin, when it is full-grown, gives birth to death"*
(JAMES 1:15).

1. Sexual Fixation
An erotic, trancelike state in which obsessing on sex becomes a sedative for the addict's emotional pain.

2. Sexual Compulsion
Compulsive, ritualistic routines heighten the excitement and intensify the addict's sexual arousal (cruising, pornography, stalking).

3. Sexual Gratification
Feeling a total loss of self-control, the addict commits the actual sex act.

4. Self-Condemnation

Following on the heels of this intoxicating sexual experience comes shame, condemnation, and hopelessness. Left with self-contempt and self-loathing, the addict looks for relief, and the sexual cycle perpetuates itself by escaping into the mood-altering fixation on sex.

WHAT IS THE CAUSE?

Our beliefs birth our behaviors. The messages we received in childhood—especially those regarding our worth, relationships, and sexuality—formed our beliefs. These beliefs are powerful, and from them come all our priorities, choices, habits, and our addictions.

Everyone has three inner needs: love, significance, and security.[2] If in your childhood these God-given needs were unmet, your beliefs reflect a painful lack of nurturing, and you attempt to fill the void. The sex addict believes that sexual passion is comforting and nurturing and that a sexual experience will meet those needs. Because people are not dependable, the addict does not risk a relationship with *a person,* but enters into a relationship with *passion.* People and things are merely the stimuli used. Because the desire of those who are addicted is passion, their relationship is with passion.

WHAT IS THE SOLUTION?

In every addict's mind a sexual time bomb threatens to destroy both the body and soul. With the right combination, you can save yourself if you break the code.

Cracking the Code

The mind of every addict is locked by faulty beliefs: what you think about your value, your relationships, and your sexuality. If your thinking is faulty, your findings are faulty, and then the way you function becomes faulty.

You must reprogram your mind with the right code. Every day for twelve weeks, read these life-changing truths, and pray for God to open your heart.

"The truth will set you free"
(JOHN 8:32).

Your Need for Love

False Belief: "I am unlovable. Sex gives me the feeling of being loved."

True Belief: You are loved; God loves you.

— Jesus loved you enough to die on the cross for you (John 3:16).
— Your heavenly Father loved you enough to adopt you into His family (1 John 3:1).

Conclusion:

Sex is not love, love is not sex—sex is sex. Love is a commitment seeking the highest and best for another person. Because God loves you in this way, He will give you the ability to develop other loving relationships in which sex is not a substitute for love (1 Corinthians 13:5).

Your Need for Significance

False belief: "I am unworthy. Sex makes me feel significant."

True belief: You already have worth; God has established your worth.

— God created you. Therefore, you have worth (Psalm 139:13).

— If you are a Christian, you have worth because Christ lives in you (Colossians 1:27).

Conclusion:

Sex does not give you significance. You are significant because Jesus Himself is in you and imparts His power to you. He is your source of power and significance (2 Peter 1:3).

Your Need for Security

False belief: "I am unwanted. Sex numbs the pain of my insecurity."

True belief: You are wanted; the Lord wants you.

— The Lord wants to be your Shepherd throughout your life (Psalm 23:1).

— The Lord wants to walk with you throughout your life (Isaiah 43:2).

Conclusion:

Sex does not give you security. True security is found only in a love relationship with the Lord. This security can never be taken away from you (Deuteronomy 31:8).

The Freedom Formula

Don't focus on the negative.

Every time you focus on quitting an obsession, you want it all the more. Living under moral law never changes you. If you focus only on what you shouldn't do, you will be pulled more powerfully to do it.

— "I need to quit thinking about sex."

— "I won't rent X-rated movies."

— "I shouldn't call the sex line."

(1 Corinthians 15:56)

Focus on the positive.

— A New Purpose

> *"I want to reflect the character of Christ through*
> *what I see and do"*
> (Romans 8:29).

— A New Priority

> *"I will do whatever it takes to have a*
> *pure heart and a transformed life"*
> (Romans 12:2).

— A New Plan

> *"I will rely on Christ's strength, and not on my own"*
> (Philippians 4:13).

What Is the Doorway Out of Addiction?

When you trust Jesus Christ as your Lord and Savior, you receive a new identity. You are not just a creation of God, but a child of God. You are "set apart," you are in His family, you receive His nature, and you are to reflect His character. Your path is diverted from death to life. Because sexual sin doesn't reflect Christ accurately, you can be assured He has already provided a way out for you. The following steps will help lift you from the self-destructive ditch of addiction and place you on the Road of Transformation, where *real* fulfillment and freedom await you.

Decide you really want to be set free.

— "Am I ready to take responsibility for my addiction?"

— "Am I sick and tired of being in this bondage?"

— "Am I willing to go to war in order to win?"

> (1 Peter 1:13)

Dispel the myth you don't need help.

— "I admit I'm out of control."

— "I admit my sexual addiction is sin."

— "I admit I can't change myself."

> (Psalm 51:10)

Deal with the secret of child abuse (some say over 80 percent of addicts were sexually abused, over 90 percent were emotionally abused).

— Talk with a friend and let go of the secret.

— Talk to a counselor to understand abuse issues.

— Talk to the perpetrator in a safe place—confrontation is biblical.

(Matthew 18:15-16)

Discern the inner need you have tried to satisfy through sexual passion.

— Your need for sacrificial love

— Your need for significance

— Your need for security

(Psalm 51:6)

Determine to let Jesus meet your needs.

— Ask Him to forgive you for your willful sin.

— Ask Him to come into your life as your personal Lord and Savior.

— Ask Him to meet your deepest inner needs.

(Philippians 4:19)

Dedicate your life to the Lord Jesus.

— Let His will be your will.

— Let the Lord be Lord of your life.

— Let Christ have absolute control.

(Luke 9:23-24)

WHAT IS THE PATHWAY TO PURITY?

Whatever God calls you to do, He will equip you to do. When God calls you to avoid sexual immorality, He enables you to do it. You don't have to live as a prisoner of past defeat. Claim your high calling on the pathway to P-U-R-I-T-Y:

P Participate in an accountability group dealing with sex addictions.

— Meet regularly and talk specifically each week.

— Set realistic guidelines and goals.

— Admit each time you slip.

(Ecclesiastes 4:9-10)

U Uphold boundary lines that must be off-limits.

— With the help of an accountability partner, make a list of times in your daily routine—places in your home, in the community, or on the Internet—during which you are tempted.

— With your accountability partner, establish ways of breaking routines and setting boundaries (such as installing monitoring software on your computer or changing schedules) to avoid tempting situations.

— Establish a regular pattern of accountability by giving your partner permission to ask you about your behavior, and when necessary, make further changes in your routine to avoid temptation.

(Proverbs 27:12)

R Rid yourself, your home, and your workplace of all sexually addictive items.

— Throw away all pornography.

— Clear away all erotic paraphernalia.

— Discard addresses and calling cards of all sexual contacts.

(Isaiah 1:16-17)

I Incorporate the power of Christ daily when temptation overwhelms you.

—"Lord, I'm relying on You to be my Redeemer."

—"Lord, I'm depending on You to be my Deliverer."

—"Lord, in my weakness I need Your strength."

(2 Corinthians 12:9)

T Take on positive habits of discipline, such as exercise, sports, regular sleep, new hobbies.

— Make a to-do list of healthy activities you enjoy.

— When you are tempted, choose to do one item that's on the list.

— Write a letter, call a friend, or help someone in need.

(Proverbs 10:17)

Y Yield your mind to meditating on and memorizing Scripture.

— Read a chapter from the New Testament each day.

— Read Romans chapter 6 once a week.

— Read Colossians 3:1-5 each day, and memorize Philippians 4:8-9.

(James 1:21)

The Lord would never tell you to stop lusting without giving you the power to stop. The starting point for victory is realizing that when a sexual thought flashes into your mind, you must redirect that thought or replace it. You are the only one who controls how long you entertain a thought. Make a covenant to not allow an immoral thought to reside in your heart.

(Job 31:1)

> Make a commitment to Christ
> not to dwell on an impure thought.
> Make a covenant with Christ
> to live with purity in your heart.
> —JH

Your Scripture Prayer Project

1 Thessalonians 4:3,7

Matthew 5:28

Job 31:1

Colossians 3:5

Psalm 25:15

Galatians 6:7-8

1 Corinthians 10:13

Romans 12:2

Philippians 4:8

For additional guidance on this topic, see also *Adultery, Childhood Sexual Abuse, Dating, Forgiveness, Guilt, Habits, Homosexuality, Hope, Identity, Lying, Manipulation, Marriage, Premarital Counseling, Rape Recovery, Rejection, Self-worth, Sexual Integrity, Singleness, Victimization.*

44

SEXUAL INTEGRITY

Balancing Passion with Purity

We love our heroes. We need heroes in every generation and in every culture—heroes who possess what they profess, reflect what they represent, walk their talk, and survive close scrutiny. True heroes have integrity and are worthy of imitation. We find hope in heroes who sidestep the seductive ditches of immorality, and are willing to stand alone regardless of stress—who hold to principle no matter the pressure, who will not compromise their convictions. Though not perfect, true heroes are committed to following a path of spiritual, emotional, and physical purity, including sexual integrity.

WHAT IS SEXUAL INTEGRITY?

— *Sexual integrity* is consistently living according to the highest moral sexual standards—consistently guarding your mind, will, and emotions from sexual impurity (Proverbs 10:9).

— *Integrity* means whole, undivided, and void of hypocrisy[1] (Proverbs 11:3).

— *Sexual integrity* is to be the same in the dark as you are in the light—not double-minded with contradictory thoughts, words, or deeds. The person without integrity "is a double-minded man, unstable in all he does" (James 1:8).

WHAT IS GOD'S HEART ON SEXUAL INTIMACY?

You don't have to go far in the Bible to learn God's heart on healthy sexual relationships. We find four points of His plan mentioned in the second chapter of Genesis, and this blueprint, repeated in the New Testament, demonstrates God's desire for us to *get it right!* (Matthew 19:4-5).

— The man and the woman will establish a separate family unit from their parents.

> *"For this reason a man will leave his father and mother"*
> (GENESIS 2:24).

— The married couple will cleave, unite, bond to each other as the priority relationship.

> *"...and be united to his wife..."*
> (GENESIS 2:24).

— The "one flesh" sexual relationship will begin *after* the God-ordained marriage between husband and wife.

> *"...and they will become one flesh"*
> (GENESIS 2:24).

— The sexual and emotional intimacy in marriage will be open and vulnerable, with moral purity between husband and wife.

> *"The man and his wife were both naked,*
> *and they felt no shame"*
> (GENESIS 2:25).

WHAT IS THE DIFFERENCE BETWEEN LUST AND LOVE?

When infatuation turns to feverish passion, innocence is lost. Then what you think is love turns out to be lust...an *illusion* of true intimacy...a *counterfeit* of the lasting love that sustains a relationship. Too late, you may learn there are great differences between lust and love. Matthew 5:28 says, "Anyone who looks at a woman lustfully has already committed adultery with her in his heart."

Lust is:	Love is:
temporary	enduring
sudden	gradual
selfish	unselfish
untrustworthy	trustworthy
impatient	patient
uncontrolled desire	controlled desire
emotionally shallow	emotionally deep

based on fantasy	based on reality
full of emotion	full of devotion
driven by one's passion	chosen by one's will
focused on external looks	focused on internal character
established on faulty reasoning	established on solid reasoning
set on getting happiness	set on giving happiness
eager to get	eager to give
(Colossians 3:5)	(1 Corinthians 13:4-8)

HOW FAR IS TOO FAR?

God intended the sexual relationship for pleasure within the protected confines of marriage. With pleasure as a goal, the number one question asked about sex (outside of marriage) is, How far is too far? When holding hands or casual kissing no longer arouses the flame of passion, "the law of diminishing returns" kicks in. If passion is the goal, then more intimate sexual activity is needed to reach the same level of pleasure experienced before. This progression is built into us by God and is intended to lead to the culmination of sexual oneness in marriage. Apart from a marriage relationship between a man and a woman, God never approves of sexual oneness—nor does He condone attempts at sexual arousal (1 Thessalonians 4:3).

In the progression of touch (from hugging to holding hands to kissing to the ultimate sex act), where do you draw the line? Never underestimate the power of sexual passion!

Consider the following:

— The best approach is a mutual commitment: Never touch any part of another person's body that is covered by a bathing suit.

— The best imagery is, "Can a man scoop fire into his lap without his clothes being burned?" (Proverbs 6:27).

— The best question to ask is, Which steps can you take and still glorify God? Don't start down a progression that could ignite a fire—*a fire that cannot be legitimately put out!* **Note:** Because French kissing simulates the sex act, many conscientious yet-to-be-married couples have declared this act off-limits.

— The best scripture is Ephesians 5:3: "Among you there must not be even a hint of sexual immorality, or of any kind of impurity."

Practical Steps for Sexual Purity[2]

Many decisions need to be made *prior* to needing them. This involves knowing the end result you desire and then, *ahead of time,* committing yourself to a plan to achieve it. Otherwise, in the heat of the moment, you will react and later realize, with regret, you made the wrong decision. The following path will help you avoid the alluring ditch of sexual immorality and pursue a purity of spirit, soul, and body that will help you enjoy a life of true satisfaction that God Himself has prepared for you.

Write out—and consider framing—your vow to be sexually pure from this day on.

— Share your pledge with someone you trust who knows the Lord (Ecclesiastes 5:4).

Find friends who hold the same commitment.

— Abstaining from sex is easier alongside close friends who honor the same vow (Philippians 2:2).

Pray for the right accountability partner.

— Ask someone who cares about you—someone whom you deeply respect—to hold you accountable sexually. Ideally, this person should be older—someone who will ask candid questions and speak the truth in love (Ephesians 4:15). Meet with this person regularly (Proverbs 27:6).

Develop a proactive strategy for countering sexual triggers.

— Don't be alone in your date's home. Don't go into your date's bedroom. If your sexual challenge is the Internet, use an Internet filter; if your challenge is sex on TV, use a blocking service. Ask God to help keep you on His path (Proverbs 4:14).

Make a list of goals you have for life.

— Develop both short-term and long-term goals. Pray for God to stir your heart with work He has planned for you to do (Ephesians 2:10).

Wear a purity or chastity ring, bracelet, or necklace as a reminder of your commitment.

— A physical item can be a spiritual reminder of your pledge to sexual purity (Psalm 61:8).

Write a love letter to your future mate.

— Tell him or her why you choose to save yourself and what purity means to you. Sign, date, then read your letter once a month (Hebrews 13:4).

Rely on the teachings of your church.

— Almost all churches, and even many world religions, teach the value of maintaining sexual purity. Spiritual faith is a strong motivation to do what is right (1 Corinthians 16:13).

What If It's Too Late?

If you are single and no longer a virgin, God still desires you to live a life of sexual integrity. You can choose "secondary virginity." God can, if you permit Him, empower you to have victory over the past. From this point on, save yourself for the one whom God has saved for you.

> *"Create in me a pure heart, O God"*
> (Psalm 51:10).

No matter what your past, now is the time to commit yourself to sexual I-N-T-E-G-R-I-T-Y:

I Invite others to walk the road of sexual integrity with you (Ecclesiastes 4:9-10).

N Never put yourself or your loved one in a tempting situation (Romans 6:13).

T Trust God to meet your need for love in the future (Psalm 143:8).

E Enjoy others instead of using others (Romans 12:9-10).

G Give yourself only to sexually pure relationships (1 Peter 1:22).

R Refuse to justify any sexual impurity (Matthew 26:41).

I Isolate yourself from tempting people (1 Corinthians 15:33).

T Transform your mind through the written Word of God (Psalm 119:11).

Y Yield to Christ, who lives in you, trusting Him to produce in you a life of purity (John 15:5).

You can't be fulfilled in the way God intended unless you are connected to Him, living dependently on Him. If you allow Christ living in you to find expression through you, He will empower you to have sexual purity.

Make a Promise List

I promise I will...

— practice sexual abstinence.

— date only those who are committed to sexual integrity.

— set sexual boundaries and stay within those boundaries.

— not be alone with a date in a bedroom, a parked car, or any other compromising place.

— guard my eyes, my mind, and my heart against sexual impurity.

— not take any drink or drug that would weaken my defenses.

— not look at pornography or visit Internet sex chat rooms.

Personalize this list and read it at least once a week, renewing your vows to the Lord.

> *"Since we have these promises, dear friends, let us purify*
> *ourselves from everything that contaminates body and*
> *spirit, perfecting holiness out of reverence for God"*
> (2 CORINTHIANS 7:1).

When you have sexual integrity—no matter what others do or don't do, no matter the pressure or pull—you will do what is right in God's sight... you will stay sexually pure.
—JH

Your Scripture Prayer Project

1 Thessalonians 4:3-5,7

1 Corinthians 6:9-10

1 Corinthians 6:18-20

Proverbs 6:27,32

Hebrews 13:4

Ephesians 5:3

Galatians 6:7-8

For additional guidance on this topic, see also *Abortion Recovery, Adultery, Childhood Sexual Abuse, Dating, Guilt, Homosexuality, Hope, Identity, Lying, Manipulation, Marriage, Parenting, Pregnancy...Unplanned, Premarital Counseling, Rape Recovery, Self-worth, Singleness.*

45

SINGLENESS

How to Be Single and Satisfied

He goes to weddings—always as *guest* and never as *groom* because he has not been gifted with a bride of his own. He is regarded by some in his community as different—a misfit who doesn't conform to society's norm. However, he is intelligent, verbally gifted, and can more than hold his own in community debates. He is a content, confident man who knows who he is and what he wants. While he experiences times of intense loneliness and longing, he doesn't detour into the ditch of dissatisfaction. Who is he? This single man is Jesus.

WHAT DOES IT MEAN TO BE SINGLE?

The single life offers special opportunities. Contrary to the negative stereotypes about singleness, countless singles live happy, fulfilled, and productive lives.

Singleness is the state of any man or woman of marriageable age who is not married. There are three categories of single people:

Single for All Seasons

— Adults who never marry

Single for a Season

— Adults who will marry sometime in the future

Single Again

— The widowed, whose mates have died

— The divorced, whose marriage contracts have been terminated

— The separated, who are still married but not living with their mates due to desertion, imprisonment, employment, or military duty

What Are the Myths About Singleness?

Myth of the Never Married: "God's best is marriage. Singleness is second best."

Truth: According to Scripture, marriage is best for those whom God calls to marry, and singleness is best for those whom God calls to be single. Singleness is referred to as the best state for having undivided devotion to the Lord.

Myth of the Separated: "Living in limbo is terrible—any decision is better than no decision."

Truth: God wants us to learn to be content in any state and to patiently wait on His timing.

> *"I have learned to be content whatever the circumstances"*
> (Philippians 4:11).

Myth of the Divorced: "All you need is another mate. Then you will find fulfillment again."

Truth: If you are a Christian, the Lord is already your mate, and only He can give you true fulfillment.

> *"I will betroth you to me forever; I will betroth*
> *you in righteousness and justice, in love and*
> *compassion. I will betroth you in faithfulness,*
> *and you will acknowledge the Lord"*
> (Hosea 2:19-20).

Myth of the Widowed: "After your mate dies, you are left incomplete and unfulfilled."

Truth: You will deeply grieve the loss of your spouse, but as a Christian, you are given complete fullness in Christ, whether married or single.

> *"For in Christ all the fullness of the Deity lives in bodily*
> *form, and you have been given fullness in Christ"*
> (Colossians 2:9-10).

Myth of the State of Singleness: "Since God uses the family to build character, you will never become mature if you remain unmarried."[1]

Truth: Your marital state does not determine the degree of your maturity. When you become a believer, God does the work of bringing you to maturity.

"He who began a good work in you
will carry it on to completion"
(PHILIPPIANS 1:6).

WHAT IS GOD'S HEART ON SINGLENESS?

According to 1 Corinthians chapter 7:

Singleness is...
— a good state in which to be (verse 1)
— a gift from God (verse 7)
— a good state for widows (verse 8)
— the state in which to remain if separation occurs and reconciliation is impossible (verse 11)

Single people...
— can face crises and worldly difficulties with fewer concerns (verse 26)
— should not search for mates, but seek a deeper relationship with God (verse 27)
— face fewer troubles in life (verse 28)
— can more single-mindedly focus on pleasing the Lord (verses 32-34)
— can have undivided devotion to the Lord (verse 35)
— have the right and the freedom to marry (verse 36)
— who are widowed are usually happier staying unmarried (verse 40)

HOW TO BE CONTENT WITH YOUR SINGLENESS

Finding the path of contentment is the most important and sometimes the greatest challenge for a person who is single. When you allow God to fulfill His purpose for your life instead of pursuing your own, you've begun the exciting journey on the Road to Transformation—a trip on which God Himself is your faithful companion.

"Godliness with contentment is great gain"
(1 TIMOTHY 6:6).

Here are some key thoughts about remaining C-O-N-T-E-N-T:

C Confess the difficulty. Admit...

...if you are discontented, angry, frustrated, lonely

...if you desire to marry

...God's right to order your life

(Jeremiah 10:23)

O Overcome the "greener grass" mentality. Marriage does not...

...cure loneliness

...provide self-worth

...cure depression

...provide security

(Philippians 4:19)

N Nourish a heart of gratefulness. Be thankful for the freedom...

...to attain your own aspirations

...to take risks

...to use your time as you need

...to be mobile

...to have greater control over financial planning

...to nurture several deep relationships

...to lean completely on the Lord

...to serve the Lord in any way

...to be spontaneous

...to be yourself

(1 Thessalonians 5:16-18)

T Treasure your identity in Christ. Remember that...

...you belong to God (Romans 8:16)

...you are never alone (Deuteronomy 31:8)

...you have all the confidence you need (Proverbs 3:26)

...you have the mind of Christ (1 Corinthians 2:16)

...you have a purpose in life (Psalm 138:8)

E Expect God to give you a ministry. You can...

...learn your spiritual gift

...love others with agape love (seeking other people's highest good)

...learn the art of encouraging others

…look for ways to meet the needs of others

(Romans 12:4-17)

N Nurture a family of friends. You can…

…be open to several significant relationships

…be free in sharing your true thoughts and feelings

…be interested in your friends' interests

…be compassionate about your friends' concerns

> *"He who walks with the wise grows wise, but a*
> *companion of fools suffers harm…A friend loves*
> *at all times, and a brother is born for adversity"*
> (PROVERBS 13:20; 17:17).

T Trust your future to God. As you do so…

…lay down your emotions—feelings follow thinking, so learn to think the way God thinks through studying and memorizing Scripture.

…lay down your will—give up having to have things your way. Instead, seek God's will.

…lay down your expectations—allow the Holy Spirit to direct your aspirations.

> *"This is how we know what love is: Jesus Christ laid down his*
> *life for us. And we ought to lay down our lives for our brothers"*
> (1 JOHN 3:16).

> *"Seek first his kingdom and his righteousness,*
> *and all these things will be given to you as well"*
> (MATTHEW 6:33).

If you are single—for whatever length of time—
God plans to use this time significantly in your life.
Bloom where you are planted…now!

—JH

============ *Your Scripture Prayer Project* ============

Psalm 138:8

Philippians 4:11

Colossians 2:9-10

James 4:8

Matthew 28:20

1 Corinthians 7:35

Philippians 4:13

Jeremiah 10:23

Isaiah 54:5

Philippians 4:6

For additional guidance on this topic, see also *Adultery, Anger, Codependency, Critical Spirit, Dating, Decision Making, Depression, Dysfunctional Family, Fear, Financial Freedom, Forgiveness, Grief Recovery, Guilt, Homosexuality, Hope, Identity, Manipulation, Marriage, Overeating, Parenting, Pregnancy... Unplanned, Prejudice, Premarital Counseling, Rape Recovery, Reconciliation, Rejection, Self-worth, Sexual Addiction, Sexual Integrity, Stress Management, Victimization, Worry.*

46

STRESS MANAGEMENT
Beating Burnout Before It Beats You

Are you at the breaking point? Feel like you're simmering just under the surface and ready to crack? While stress can serve as *positive* pressure that results in motivation and movement, it oftentimes is *negative* pressure that derails you into ditches of distress, danger, or destruction.[1] Be encouraged that with God you can discover both peace and rest…no matter what the stressful circumstance.

> *"Come to me, all you who are weary and burdened, and I will give you rest. Take my yoke upon you and learn from me, for I am gentle and humble in heart, and you will find rest for your souls. For my yoke is easy and my burden is light"*
> (MATTHEW 11:28-30).

WHAT ARE THE FOUR STAGES OF STRESS?

Stage 1: No Light
When there is "negative" demoralizing stress, a person…

— avoids responsibility

— has poor relationships

— is not productive

— has no energy

— experiences depression

— has no purpose

— lacks perspective on life

Stage 2: Green Light

When there is "positive" motivating stress, a person...

— faces responsibility

— has responsible relationships

— is productive

— is energetic

— is enthusiastic

— has fulfillment of purpose

— has a positive perspective

Stage 3: Yellow Light

When there is continual stress over a period of time, it will manifest itself in physical warning signs. Such warning signs are like amber lights on a traffic signal, which caution you to be alert, slow down, and be prepared for upcoming change. Physical warning signs of stress can include...

— tension headaches

— muscle aches

— heavy sighing

— high blood pressure

— ulcers

— hyper-alertness

— loss of sleep/excessive sleep

— lack of concentration

— indecisiveness

— irritability

Stage 4: Red Light

When stress is not processed, burnout occurs, which is not God's will for us. When a person has not processed the stresses of life in a godly way, that person lives at Stage 2, experiences burnout, and becomes...

— overwhelmed by responsibility

— withdrawn from relationships

— minimally productive

— depressed (lack of enthusiasm)

— purposeless

— without perspective

— easily fatigued

— lacking in ability to concentrate

— indecisive

— irritable

> *"A man may be chastened on a bed of pain*
> *with constant distress in his bones"*
> (JOB 33:19).

A CHECKLIST FOR BURNOUT[2]

Here are some of the many signs of burnout:

☐ I have difficulty relaxing.

☐ I have a tightness in my neck and shoulders.

☐ I have lower-back pain.

☐ I feel tired and lifeless most of the time.

☐ I have frequent severe headaches.

☐ I get indigestion often.

☐ I have diarrhea or constipation often.

☐ I could be getting an ulcer.

☐ I have trouble sleeping at night.

☐ I grind my teeth at night.

☐ I am more susceptible than usual to colds and viruses.

☐ I have allergies or asthma.

☐ I eat and snack excessively.

☐ I have lost a lot of weight.

☐ I often have cold hands or sweaty palms.

☐ I have shortness of breath.

☐ I have a rapid pulse.

☐ I generally feel nervous and unsettled.

No one will experience all these symptoms, but if you checked four or more, you may need to evaluate how you are responding to the pressures in your life. Are you releasing your heavy load to the Lord and allowing His peace to permeate your heart?

"A heart at peace gives life to the body"
(Proverbs 14:30).

How Do You Get Out of the Overload Ditch?

Adopting healthy stress management skills will enable you to slow down, stop, yield, and resume speed at appropriate intervals on the path of life—thus regulating your pace and lifting you out of the ditch of overload and burnout. Soon you'll begin walking the Road to Transformation in peaceful assurance that God will never call you to do more than He gives you time and ability to do (1 Thessalonians 5:24).

Slow

Slow down and make the necessary changes for good physical health.

— Do you eat a balanced and healthy diet?

— Do you exercise at least three times a week?

— Do you take at least one day of rest each week?

— Do you get adequate restful sleep most nights?

> *"In vain you rise early and stay up late, toiling for*
> *food to eat—for he grants sleep to those he loves"*
> (Psalm 127:2).

Slow down and evaluate your priorities.

— Make a list of everything you do.

— Consider other priorities that should be on the list.

— Number the items on your list in order of importance.

— Choose your commitments carefully.

— Eliminate unnecessary stressful obligations.

— Don't accept impossible deadlines.

— Don't give in to the pressure of urgency.

— Tackle only one problem at a time.

> *"Better one handful with tranquility than two*
> *handfuls with toil and chasing after the wind"*
> (Ecclesiastes 4:6).

Slow down and nourish your spiritual life.

— Remind yourself daily to "be still, and know that [He is] God" (Psalm 46:10).

— Open lines of honest communication with God about your concerns, needs, and fears.

— Set aside time daily for personal prayer and Scripture meditation.

— Memorize Scripture that builds assurance of God's love (Psalm 36:7; Jeremiah 31:3; John 14:21; Romans 8:39).

> *"It was good for me to be afflicted so that*
> *I might learn your decrees"*
> (PSALM 119:71).

Stop

Stop and look at the real reason you are experiencing stress.

— Do you try to meet your own needs instead of waiting on the Lord?

— Do you think God cannot accomplish His purposes without your over-achieving?

— Do you seek self-worth through proving your adequacy and effectiveness?

— Are you Spirit-led or people-pressured?

> *"Am I now trying to win the approval of men, or of*
> *God? Or am I trying to please men? If I were still trying*
> *to please men, I would not be a servant of Christ"*
> (GALATIANS 1:10).

Stop, confess, and turn away from any known sin in your life.

— Do you manipulate or control others?

— Do you feel envious or jealous of others?

— Do you express your feelings inappropriately?

— Do you overreact to criticism?

— Do you have impure motives?

> *"He who conceals his sins does not prosper, but*
> *whoever confesses and renounces them finds mercy"*
> (PROVERBS 28:13).

Yield

Yield to God's sovereign control over your circumstances.

— What is God doing in your circumstances?

— In what way does God want you to change?

— How does God want you to respond?

— Do you have impure motives?

> *"The king's heart is in the hand of the LORD; he*
> *directs it like a watercourse wherever he pleases"*
> (PROVERBS 21:1).

Yield to God your rights and expectations.

Dear God,

— "I yield my right to control my circumstances."

— "I yield my right to be accepted by others."

— "I yield my right to be successful."

— "I yield my right to be heard and understood."

— "I yield my right to be right."

> *"Trust in the LORD with all your heart and lean*
> *not on your own understanding"*
> (PROVERBS 3:5).

Resume Speed

Resume speed, living in the presence of God.

Dear Lord God,

— "I choose to let Christ live His life through me."

— "I choose to live in the present, not worrying about tomorrow."

— "I choose to refocus my thoughts away from my pressures to Your purposes for allowing these pressures."

— "I choose to have a thankful heart regardless of the pressure I feel."

— "I will choose to call on You, Lord, for wisdom and peace."

— "I will choose to commit to talking less and listening more."

> *"My soul finds rest in God alone;*
> *my salvation comes from him"*
> (PSALM 62:1).

On your journey through life, don't miss the SIGNS God has for you. When stress is signaling possible burnout...
>   SLOW DOWN and turn from danger...
>   STOP and ask for directions—God's...
>   YIELD the driver's seat to Christ...
>   RESUME SPEED, trusting in the Lord.

—JH

Your Scripture Prayer Project

Ecclesiastes 4:6

Matthew 11:28-30

Galatians 3:3

Romans 12:2

Galatians 1:10

Proverbs 14:30

Psalm 18:6

2 Corinthians 12:9

Philippians 4:6-9

For additional guidance on this topic, see also *Alcohol and Drug Abuse, Anger, Critical Spirit, Decision Making, Fear, Financial Freedom, Hope, Identity, Overeating, Salvation, Self-worth, Suicide Prevention, Worry.*

47

SUICIDE PREVENTION
Hope When Life Seems Hopeless

Despair has overtaken you. Trapped and terrified, darkness descends…and then you see it: the ditch of self-inflicted death. This gaping pit looms large, presenting a perilous path to the absence of pain and to much-desired peace. You feel like no one understands, no one really cares. *But God does!* He is grieved by your suffering and longs to come alongside you to help you, to restore hope, and to bring healing. Suicide is *never* God's will for your life—He has a unique purpose and plan for you that validates your value and significance. *You* matter to Him.

> *"'I know the plans I have for you,' declares the*
> *LORD, 'plans to prosper you and not to harm*
> *you, plans to give you hope and a future'"*
> (JEREMIAH 29:11).

WHAT ARE THE SUCCESSIVE SIGNS SOMEONE IS CONTEMPLATING SUICIDE?

Downcast: Early Stage

Dejection	Change in eating and sleeping habits
Avoidance of family	Decline in work or school performance
Anxiety	Inability to concentrate or make decisions
Boredom	Lack of interest in the future

> *"Why are you downcast, O my soul? Why so*
> *disturbed within me? Put your hope in God, for I*
> *will yet praise him, my Savior and my God"*
> (PSALM 43:5).

Distressed: Advanced Stage

Depression	Withdrawal from family and friends
Rapid mood swings	Physical problems, self injury, anorexia
Self-pity	Excessive absences from work or school
Apathy	Neglect of personal appearance

*"Surely no one lays a hand on a broken man
when he cries for help in his distress"*
(JOB 30:24).

Despairing: Danger Stage

Hopelessness	Abusing alcohol/drugs
Deep remorse	Isolation or morose behavior
Previous suicide attempts or threats of suicide	Giving away personal possessions
Organizing personal affairs; making a will	Sudden change from depression to cheerfulness (indicating being at peace with the decision to commit suicide)

*"Why, O LORD, do you reject me and hide your face from
me? From my youth I have been afflicted and close to
death; I have suffered your terrors and am in despair"*
(PSALM 88:14-15).

We are each born from the seed of Adam and doomed to continue in sin and destined for death. But we no longer have to be slaves to this self-destructive tendency. In Christ we have a new inheritance and a legacy that provides power over sin and the gift of eternal life. (See **Biblical Counseling Keys** on *Identity* and the book *Seeing Yourself Through God's Eyes* by June Hunt—for more information, see page 448.)

*"There is now no condemnation for those who are in
Christ Jesus, because through Christ Jesus the law of the
Spirit of life set me free from the law of sin and death"*
(ROMANS 8:1-2).

WHAT SHOULD YOU DO IF YOU'RE IN CRISIS?

When suicidal thoughts overtake you, it's important to have a plan. Determine, in advance, to take the following steps. They will protect you from the dark ditch of suicide—Satan's counterfeit solution to your pain—and point you toward the Road to Transformation. Step by step you will discover God's peace, and a life that is well worth living.

Pray

> *"In you, O LORD, I have taken refuge; let me never be put to shame; deliver me in your righteousness. Turn your ear to me, come quickly to my rescue; be my rock of refuge, a strong fortress to save me. Since you are my rock and my fortress, for the sake of your name lead and guide me"*
> (PSALM 31:1-3; PRAY VERSES 1-9,14-24).

Recite Scriptures Aloud

> *"Have mercy on me, O God, have mercy on me, for in you my soul takes refuge. I will take refuge in the shadow of your wings until the disaster has passed"*
> (PSALM 57:1; ALSO READ PSALM 27 AND 28).

Claim God's Promises

> *"My comfort in my suffering is this: your promise preserves my life"*
> (PSALM 119:50).

Listen to Christian Praise Music and Scripture Songs

> *"Sing to the LORD, you saints of his; praise his holy name...Weeping may remain for a night, but rejoicing comes in the morning"*
> (PSALM 30:4-5).

Consider How Special It Is to Be a Child of God

> *"How great is the love the Father has lavished on us, that we should be called children of God! And that is what we are!"*
> (1 JOHN 3:1).

Question Yourself

— "Why do I feel the need to hurt myself?"

— "What do I think I will accomplish through this?"

— "According to God, is this the truth or a lie?"

— "Are my actions and desires reflecting my true identity in Christ, or are they coming out of my past experiences?"

— "What effect would harming myself have on those who care about me?"

"Surely you desire truth in the inner parts; you
teach me wisdom in the inmost place"
(Psalm 51:6).

Make Positive Affirmations

— "I'm worth being treated with goodness and kindness—I am a child of God."

— "God loves me and has a purpose for my life. I am also loved by others."

— "Because God has a plan for me, I will show kindness and respect to the body He gave me."

— "Even though I can't see the future, I will walk by faith, not by sight."

"The LORD himself goes before you and will be
with you; he will never leave you nor forsake
you. Do not be afraid; do not be discouraged"
(Deuteronomy 31:8).

Review Encouraging Words

— Read aloud positive letters and notes from friends and family.

— Review positive thoughts about why it's worth it to heal.

— Recall those who believe in you and your growth.

— Remember what others have said about why there is hope for you.

— Rehearse God's promise.

Avoid Impulse Behavior

Do not...

— act on impulse.

— take any action that is harmful or even potentially harmful to yourself, others, or property.

— drive your automobile if there is a possibility you will drive recklessly.

— act rashly.

"A word aptly spoken is like apples
of gold in settings of silver"
(Proverbs 25:11).

Ask Yourself

— Would God approve of this?

— Would the people I love approve of this?

— Would the people who care about me approve of this?

If the answer is no, then you must not do it. If you would hurt innocent people whom you care about, then you must not do it. No rationalizations or excuses—just *do not do it.*

> *"You need to persevere so that when you have done the*
> *will of God, you will receive what he has promised"*
> (Hebrews 10:36).

Call for Help

After going through the steps above, if you are still in a crisis, reach out and call others who will be helpful and truthful. They can help you regain perspective. Continue to go down your list of phone numbers until you have reached someone and state directly, "I am calling because I am in an emotional crisis." Then honestly discuss the feelings and events that led to the crisis and possible solutions. Continue making phone calls, repeatedly, if necessary, until the crisis is resolved, no matter what time of day or night.

Numbers to Call for Help

Friend _____

Relative _____

Friend _____

Relative _____

Friend _____

Therapist _____

Doctor _____

Church _____

Pastor _____

Crisis hotline _____

Suicide prevention   1-800-SUICIDE (784-2433)

> *"If one falls down, his friend can help him up. But pity*
> *the man who falls and has no one to help him up!"*
> (Ecclesiastes 4:10).

If you are still in crisis after completing these steps, take action to ensure your physical and emotional safety by getting yourself to a safe environment in which you are not alone.

— Make arrangements to get together with a friend or supportive person.

— Go to a public place where harming yourself is difficult.

— If all else fails, go to a hospital emergency room and tell the staff you are at risk of harming yourself. Make it clear that you do not want to check in, but that you simply want to sit in the waiting room for a little while so you will not act upon your impulses. Have hospital staff sit with you, or speak with the chaplain.

— If you have honestly worked through these steps and are still in trouble, then you are truly in a crisis situation that may require hospitalization for your protection.

Are You Willing to Be Willing?

Even if you do not want to live, all you need is the willingness to be made willing. God can use the tiniest thread of hope as your lifeline out of the ditch of despair.

> *"Restore to me the joy of your salvation*
> *and grant me a willing spirit, to sustain me"*
> (Psalm 51:12).

Lord, make me willing to be...

Broken

"O God, I'm at the end of all my resources. My heart feels overwhelmed with despair."

God's Response

> *"Unless the Lord had given me help, I would*
> *soon have dwelt in the silence of death. When I*
> *said, 'My foot is slipping,' your love, O Lord,*
> *supported me. When anxiety was great within*
> *me, your consolation brought joy to my soul"*
> (Psalm 94:17-19).

Prayer

"Thank You, God, that I have reached the end of my self-effort."

Yielded

"I see no hope and have no one to help me. My mind is made up that death is the only answer."

God's Promise

> *"Submit yourselves, then, to God. Resist the devil,*
> *and he will flee from you. Come near to God*
> *and he will come near to you"*
> (JAMES 4:7-8).

Prayer

"Thank You, God, that evil has no power in Your presence, and that I am safe when I focus on You."

Willing

"I am not even willing to try. I have no desire to go on living."

God's Promise

> *"So do not fear, for I am with you; do not be dismayed,*
> *for I am your God. I will strengthen you and help*
> *you; I will uphold you with my righteous right hand"*
> (ISAIAH 41:10).

Prayer

"Thank You, God, for Your supernatural power that can touch and change my heart."

Assured

"God, I feel so completely alone. Can anything relieve this terrible loneliness?"

God's Promise

> *"When you pass through the waters, I will be with you;*
> *and when you pass through the rivers, they will not*
> *sweep over you. When you walk through the fire, you*
> *will not be burned; the flames will not set you ablaze"*
> (ISAIAH 43:2).

Prayer

"Thank You, God, that I am never alone. Thank You for being with me even when I don't feel that You are walking with me."

Guilt-free

"I have even passed the point of tears. My heart seems to have no room for forgiveness—for myself, for others, or even for You."

God's Promise

> *"He who conceals his sins does not prosper, but*
> *whoever confesses and renounces them finds mercy"*
> (PROVERBS 28:13).

Prayer

"Thank You, God, that as I confess my anger and bitterness, I receive cleansing from You. Then I'm able to forgive those who have hurt me deeply."

Accepting

"Even if I could forgive, I cannot accept these miserable circumstances that will never change."

God's Promise

> *"I can do everything through him who gives me strength"*
> (PHILIPPIANS 4:13).

Prayer

"Thank You, God, for giving me the desire and power to accept life as it now is and let go of the things I do not understand."

Grateful

"How can I be grateful? I could never feel gratitude for my life or what I endure."

God's Promise

> *"Give thanks in all circumstances, for this is*
> *God's will for you in Christ Jesus"*
> (1 THESSALONIANS 5:18).

Prayer

"Thank You, God, for reminding me to give thanks in all circumstances. Help me to trust You with Your plans for my life."

Hopeful

"Secretly, I am afraid to have hope. What if I begin to hope, then nothing really changes?"

God's Promise

> *"We rejoice in the hope of the glory of God. Not only*
> *so, but we also rejoice in our sufferings, because we*

know that suffering produces perseverance; perseverance,
character; and character, hope. And hope does not
disappoint us, because God has poured out his love into
our hearts by the Holy Spirit, whom he has given us"
(ROMANS 5:2-5).

Prayer
"Thank You, God. I will choose to trust You and put my hope in You. I will not trust in things as they seem to be, but will hope in the unseen power of Your love."

How can I Extend Hope to the Hopeless?

Honestly Confront

— Take all talk of death and suicide seriously.

— Ask the direct question, "Are you thinking about suicide?"

— Express your concern.

— Seek to find out what problem is causing the pain.

— Ask, "How have you been coping with the pain?"

"The purposes of a man's heart are deep waters, but
a man of understanding draws them out"
(PROVERBS 20:5).

Offer Options

— Acknowledge the fact that life is hard.

— Point out that choices in life often consist of unpleasant possibilities.

— List possible options on a sheet of paper.

— Rank the options in order of preference.

— Communicate God's purposes for suffering. One purpose, for example, is compassion: "Many people are hurting in the same way you are. They feel desperately alone and assume that no one understands their pain. You know what it is like to experience such hurt. Your personal pain enables you to have a ministry of compassion. You are being prepared right now to be a lifeline of hope for someone else who feels hopeless."

"No temptation has seized you except what is
common to man. And God is faithful; he will not
let you be tempted beyond what you can bear. But
when you are tempted, he will also provide a
way out so that you can stand up under it"
(1 CORINTHIANS 10:13).

Present a Contract[1]

— Build a relationship by showing your care and willingness to help.

— Ask if the person would be willing to make a contract with you: "Will you promise that if you are considering harming yourself, you will talk with me before doing anything?"

— Be sure to obtain a signature.

— Make a commitment to stay in contact.

> *"Carry each other's burdens, and in this way*
> *you will fulfill the law of Christ"*
> (GALATIANS 6:2).

Enlist Help[2]

— Encourage the person to have a physical checkup.

— Seek a trained counselor or therapist.

— Call a minister.

— Contact the Suicide Crisis Center.

— Help make arrangements for hospitalization.

> *"Plans fail for lack of counsel,*
> *but with many advisers they succeed"*
> (PROVERBS 15:22).

My Contract of HOPE

The following is a solemn binding contract. This contract cannot be declared null and void without the written agreement of both parties.

I promise that if I should consider harming myself, I will talk with you before I do anything destructive.

I sign my name as a pledge of my integrity.

Signature_____ Date _____

Signature_____ Date _____

> *"We have this hope as an anchor*
> *for the soul, firm and secure"*
> (HEBREWS 6:19).

The true goal of suicide is not the absence of life,
but the absence of pain. The true goal of Christ is salvation—
to save you not from your pain, but for life…His life in you,
His joy filling you, His hope securing you.

—JH

Your Scripture Prayer Project

Psalm 43:5

Psalm 34:18

Psalm 147:3

Psalm 27:13-14

Proverbs 3:5-6

Proverbs 23:18

Isaiah 41:10

1 Corinthians 6:19-20

2 Corinthians 4:8-9

Philippians 4:13

Jeremiah 29:11

For additional guidance on this topic, see also *Anger, Childhood Sexual Abuse, Crisis Intervention, Decision Making, Depression, Evil and Suffering…Why?, Fear, Financial Freedom, Grief Recovery, Guilt, Hope, Identity, Phobias, Rejection, Salvation, Self-worth, Stress Management, Victimization, Worry.*

VERBAL AND EMOTIONAL ABUSE

Victory over Abuse

Y ou're worthless!" "You'll never amount to anything!" "I wish you had never been born!" Words like these can wound, tripping you into a ditch of doubt and defeat for a lifetime.

Maybe control is the name of the game. Threats such as, "If you leave me, I'll hurt the children!" or "I'll take the keys away from you!" are both emotionally and verbally abusive and are ways of maintaining control in relationships.

Abuse also can be perpetrated without a word—with degrading looks, obscene gestures, or threatening behaviors. Such abuse can make you feel worthless until you look to the truth in Jesus' words from Luke 12:6-7:

> *"Are not five sparrows sold for two pennies? Yet not*
> *one of them is forgotten by God. Indeed, the very*
> *hairs of your head are all numbered. Don't be*
> *afraid; you are worth more than many sparrows."*

WHAT DISTINGUISHES HARMFUL WORDS FROM HELPFUL WORDS?

> *"Do not let any unwholesome talk come out of your mouths,*
> *but only what is helpful for building others up according*
> *to their needs, that it may benefit those who listen"*
> (EPHESIANS 4:29).

WORDS THAT HURT	WORDS THAT HEAL
Attacking a Person's Identity	**Addressing a Person's Action**
You are inherently wrong.	You did something wrong.
You are intrinsically bad.	You did something bad.

Yelling	**Discussing**
"Shut up!"	"Please listen to me."
Name-calling	**Casting a Vision**
"You stupid idiot!"	"You are good at (_____)."
"You crazy fool!"	"You have positive qualities."

Abuse can be subtle or blatant, quiet or loud, smooth or abrasive. Whether verbal or nonverbal in delivery, abuse always deeply impacts an individual's personal and social life.

What Victims of Abuse May Experience

> *"The tongue that brings healing is a tree of life,*
> *but a deceitful tongue crushes the spirit"*
> (Proverbs 15:4).

Loss of...

— self-worth, increased self-doubt

— self-confidence, increased self-consciousness

— self-perception, increased self-criticism

— happiness, increased emotional flatness

— freedom, increased vigilance

— inner peace, increased peace-at-all-cost behavior

— self-assurance, increased anxiety

— security, increased desire to escape

— trust, increased distrust

— sexual identity, increased sexual confusion

— a clear conscience, increased guilt or shame

— friendship, increased isolation

— faith, increased fear

— safety, increased insecurity

— self-respect, increased self-destruction

— optimism, increased pessimism

— pride, increased self-hatred

— hope, increased despair

What Self-demeaning Statements Result from Being Abused?
Place a check (√) by any that apply to you.

☐ "I feel defective."

☐ "I am bad if I feel angry."

☐ "I am bad for having needs."

☐ "I will be loved only if I am perfect."

☐ "I am worthless and unlovable."

☐ "Mistakes confirm my worthlessness."

☐ "If people I care about reject me, I must be unlovable."

☐ "I need the approval of people to be happy."

☐ "I am responsible for the behavior and feelings of others."

☐ "I am responsible for bringing change in others when I see that it's needed."

☐ "I must be dependent on others who are wiser and stronger than me."

☐ "I need to be self-sufficient because others are untrustworthy."

☐ "I will never let anyone get close enough to hurt me again."

☐ "The feelings of others are more important than my own."

☐ "Everything I do is wrong."

☐ "Nothing matters anymore. Life is hopeless."

☐ "Whatever you want makes me happy."

☐ "Bad love is better than no love."

☐ "I don't see any way out."

☐ "I'll never measure up."

How Do You Confront an Abusive Person?[1]

"Better is open rebuke than hidden love"
(Proverbs 27:5).

Educate Yourself
— Emotional abuse can go on for years before victims realize the difficult dynamics in relationships.

— Abusers are calculating, and their behavior is deliberate and designed to keep them in control.

— Once your eyes are opened to the tactical behavior of the abuser, much of your discouragement will begin to dissipate.

"Let the wise listen and add to their learning,
and let the discerning get guidance"
(Proverbs 1:5).

Set Boundaries[2]

— Communicate you will not be treated disrespectfully.
— Be specific about what behavior is unacceptable.
— Refuse to accept excuses and reasons for inconsiderate behavior.

"Reckless words pierce like a sword,
but the tongue of the wise brings healing"
(Proverbs 12:18).

Seize the Moment

— Speak up as soon as the abuser begins to change the subject or twist your words to mean something different than you intended.
— When abusers say something absurd, repeat it back.
— Remain calm. Your abuser wants a strong reaction from you.

"The quiet words of the wise are more to
be heeded than the shouts of a ruler of fools"
(Ecclesiastes 9:17).

Seek to Surface the Other Person's Hostility

— Acknowledge that you sense the anger in the other person.
— Confirm that being angry is permissible. (Never attempt to humor an abuser out of anger.)
— An abuser may need help recognizing the cause of the anger, but don't try to psychoanalyze the person.

"The purposes of a man's heart are deep waters,
but a man of understanding draws them out"
(Proverbs 20:5).

Soften the Confrontation Process

— Confront the behavior, not the person.
— Avoid threats, sarcasm, hostility, put-downs, or judgment of the abuser's intentions.

— If you don't get a clear answer, ask again (respectfully).

> *"Live a life worthy of the calling you have received. Be*
> *completely humble and gentle; be patient, bearing*
> *with one another in love. Make every effort to keep*
> *the unity of the Spirit through the bond of peace"*
> (EPHESIANS 4:1-3).

Stay in the Present

— Focus on the issue.

— Don't bring up past issues.

— Don't get off track.

> *"Let your eyes look straight ahead, fix your gaze*
> *directly before you. Make level paths for your feet*
> *and take only ways that are firm. Do not swerve*
> *to the right or the left; keep your foot from evil"*
> (PROVERBS 4:25-27).

Squelch Unrealistic Expectations

— Don't hope that an abuser will change. Rather, put your confidence in God and in His sufficiency.

— Be aware you cannot make the abuser change no matter how much you try or how good you are.

— Know that change will occur only after the abuser admits to the problem and begins to receive help.

> *"If we claim to be without sin, we deceive ourselves*
> *and the truth is not in us. If we confess our sins,*
> *he is faithful and just and will forgive us our*
> *sins and purify us from all unrighteousness"*
> (1 JOHN 1:8-9).

Strengthen Your Relationship with the Lord

— Look first to the Lord for discernment. Ask Him for wisdom, insight, and direction in all your relationships.

— Read Scripture and take God at His word, renewing your mind so you won't continue living as a victim. Get involved in a Bible study. Memorize scriptures that emphasize your worth and authority as one who is a temple of the Holy Spirit.

— Live dependent on Christ, who lives within you. Don't live out of your own resources. Throughout the day, acknowledge your total dependence on the Lord.

> *"His divine power has given us everything we need for life*
> *and godliness through our knowledge of him who called*
> *us by his own glory and goodness. Through these he has*
> *given us his very great and precious promises, so that*
> *through them you may participate in the divine nature and*
> *escape the corruption in the world caused by evil desires"*
> (2 Peter 1:3-4).

How to Change the Course of an Abusive Relationship

Curtail verbal and emotional abuse by planning to prevent being controlled. You cannot change someone else, but you can change yourself so abusive tactics previously used are no longer effective. Determine appropriate boundaries that will help protect your heart. Proverbs 4:23 says, "Above all else, guard your heart, for it is the wellspring of life."

After you determine the ways you will protect yourself and the boundaries you will establish, then do the following:

1. In a conversation or letter, state what you are willing to accept and not accept from the abuser.[3]

— Communicate your position in a positive way.

— Do not justify or be apologetic. Say that you want the relationship to continue, then state your boundaries:

"I won't listen to name-calling."

"I won't hear accusations concerning (_____) any longer."

"I won't accept the silent treatment."

— Keep what you say short and succinct.

> *"A man of knowledge uses words with restraint, and*
> *a man of understanding is even-tempered"*
> (Proverbs 17:27).

2. Announce the consequences for violating your requests.

— Disengage from the abuser.

— Remove yourself from exposure to unacceptable behavior. Say you are willing to talk, with these stipulations:

"If you call me a name again, I will leave for a period of time."

"If you persist in making accusations, I will end our conversation."

"If you give me the silent treatment, I'll find someone else to talk with."

— Consequences are part of God's divine plan.

"A man reaps what he sows"
(GALATIANS 6:7).

3. *Enforce the consequence every single time abuse occurs.*
   — Do not bluff! The abuser needs to know you are firm and will be consistent.
   — Plan on being tested several times.
   — In your mind and heart, say no to…

   manipulation

   pressure

   control

   — Eventually your abuser will stop an abusive tactic—but only after it proves ineffective.

"Let your 'Yes' be yes, and your 'No,' no"
(JAMES 5:12).

4. *Never negotiate.*
   — Verbal abusers do not use words fairly; negotiation will not work.
   — Instead of "talking out" the problem, abusers will seek to wear you out.
   — Simply state that when the behavior stops, you look forward to a renewed relationship.

   "I am not willing to discuss this any longer."

   "I have stated clearly what I won't accept."

   "When you're ready to respect my requests, let me know. I look forward to being together at that time."

   — Keep your words brief and to the point.

"When words are many, sin is not absent, but
he who holds his tongue is wise"
(PROVERBS 10:19).

5. Never react when boundaries are violated—only respond.
- — Reacting puts you back under the control of the abuser.
- — Respond by detaching yourself from the abuser and enforcing your consequences.
- — Do not...

    cry because of feeling hurt.

    beg because of feeling fearful.

    explode because of feeling frustrated.

- — Protect your boundaries so they can protect you.

> *"The end of a matter is better than its beginning, and*
> *patience is better than pride. Do not be quickly provoked*
> *in your spirit, for anger resides in the lap of fools"*
> (ECCLESIASTES 7:8-9).

6. Solicit support from wise, objective people.
Include supporters (friend, mentor, counselor) as you...

- — analyze and identify the problem.
- — determine how to articulate your plan.
- — enforce the consequences.
- — move through this critical period. Discuss the situation, the tactics, and the plan of action.

> *"Listen to advice and accept instruction,*
> *and in the end you will be wise"*
> (PROVERBS 19:20).

The time necessary to disassemble and disable an abusive relationship is limited. But during that limited time, expect manipulative maneuvers and emotional ups and downs. Assume your actions will make the abuser angry. Allow him or her to react without reacting yourself. Don't seek to placate this person; it won't work. Think of this time as comparable to surgery—it's a painful experience, yet it provides the only hope for healing and having a healthy relationship.

> *"The tongue of the wise brings healing"*
> (PROVERBS 12:18).

HOW CAN YOU KNOW IF YOU ARE AN ABUSER?[4]
Many abusers have no idea they are abusive.

> *"A truthful witness gives honest testimony,*
> *but a false witness tells lies"*
> (PROVERBS 12:17).

Take the Honesty Test

— Has a loved one ever said you are emotionally insensitive or uncaring?

— Has a loved one ever said your behavior is abusive or unreasonable?

— Has a loved one said you act nicer when you are with others than when you are alone with that person?

— Has a loved one ever said you tend to overreact?

— Do you avoid responding to questions you don't like?

— Do you get angry when asked questions you don't like?

— Do you refuse to acknowledge your past negative behaviors?

— Do you have a short fuse that ignites anger?

— Do you think your personal interactions with others could be destructive?

— Do you have multiple failed, unresolved relationships?

If you answered yes to at least three of the above, chances are good that you are an abuser.

> *"Honest scales and balances are from the LORD;*
> *all the weights in the bag are of his making"*
> (PROVERBS 16:11).

If you find that you are an abuser, desiring to change is your greatest need.

> *"Search me, O God, and know my heart; test me and*
> *know my anxious thoughts. See if there is any offensive*
> *way in me, and lead me in the way everlasting"*
> (PSALM 139:23-24).

Take Responsibility

— *Don't* vent pent-up anger on another person.
   Realize that feeling angry is not a sin.

— *Don't* say, "You're the reason I am so angry."
   Recognize and admit you may not know how to handle your anger.

— *Don't* say, "I can never please you!"
   Realize you may be using your anger to get your own way.

— *Don't* say, "After all I do for you, it's still never enough."
   Begin to see things from the other person's point of view.

— *Don't* utter harsh, belittling, or sarcastic statements.

Recognize courageous people are willing to admit their weaknesses.

— *Don't* withdraw emotionally.

Realize you can change. It's never too late.

Be willing to enlist friends and family members who can hold you accountable.

Sticks and stones do break bones,
and words can wound a tender heart.
But God shatters prisons of pain
to set captives free.
—JH

Your Scripture Prayer Project

Proverbs 18:21

Proverbs 12:18

Jeremiah 17:14

Proverbs 28:23

Proverbs 29:25

Philippians 2:3-4

Romans 12:17-18

Matthew 6:14-15

1 Thessalonians 5:17-18

Jeremiah 29:11

For additional guidance on this topic, see also *Anger, Childhood Sexual Abuse, Codependency, Critical Spirit, Cults, Dating, Depression, Domestic Violence, Dysfunctional Family, Fear, Forgiveness, Grief Recovery, Guilt, Habits, Hope, Identity, Lying, Manipulation, Marriage, Parenting, Prejudice, Reconciliation, Rejection, Salvation, Self-worth, Stress Management, Suicide Prevention, Victimization, Worry.*

49

VICTIMIZATION

Victory over the Victim Mentality

I f you are living with a crippling trauma from your past, hoping to somehow get beyond it, take hope. God wants to help you overcome your painful past and conquer the destructive patterns that have resulted from your victimization. By facing your past and taking responsibility for your healing, you can trade the ditch of victimization for the pathway to victory!

> *"It is for freedom that Christ has set us free.*
> *Stand firm, then, and do not let yourselves be*
> *burdened again by a yoke of slavery"*
> (Galatians 5:1).

What Is a Victim?

— *A victim*[1] is a person who is adversely treated.

   Examples: a victim of alcoholic, neglectful, or workaholic parents; of infidelity, spiritual abuse, elder abuse, stalking, or sexual harassment

— *A victim* is a person who is tricked or duped.

   Examples: a victim of robbery, identity theft, fraud, kidnapping, or cult entrapment

— *A victim* is a person who is injured, destroyed, or sacrificed.

   Examples: a victim of incest, domestic violence, rape, satanic ritual abuse, or a natural disaster

— *A victim* is a person who is subjected to oppression, hardship, or mistreatment.

   Examples: a victim of any verbal, emotional, sexual, physical, racial, or economic abuse

What Is the Victim Mentality?[2]

The victim mentality is a mind-set in which a person who was once a victim continues in old thought patterns of feeling powerless, even when the victimization has ended. This mind-set leads those who were once genuinely powerless to stop abuse to needlessly assume the same powerless state in the present. The victim mentality can consciously or subconsciously be used to deny responsibility for the former victim's present actions. The individual continues to manifest self-destructive attitudes and actions, and blames others for the undesirable results. You can overcome a victim mentality by changing the way you see God and the way you see yourself in relationship to Him.

> *"In all these things we are more than conquerors*
> *through him who loved us"*
> (Romans 8:37).

God's Heart for the Victim

— God hears the cry of the battered and abused.

> *"You hear, O Lord, the desire of the afflicted; you*
> *encourage them, and you listen to their cry"*
> (Psalm 10:17).

— God holds the victim of abuse in the palm of His hand.

> *"Do not fear, for I am with you; do not be dismayed, for*
> *I am your God. I will strengthen you and help you;*
> *I will uphold you with my righteous right hand"*
> (Isaiah 41:10).

— God confirms the victim's value and worth.

> *"Are not five sparrows sold for two pennies? Yet not*
> *one of them is forgotten by God. Indeed, the very*
> *hairs of your head are all numbered. Don't be*
> *afraid; you are worth more than many sparrows"*
> (Luke 12:6-7).

— God brings good out of the evil deeds of others.

> *"The Lord works out everything for his own*
> *ends—even the wicked for a day of disaster"*
> (Proverbs 16:4).

What Are the Emotional Effects of Victimization?

At the heart of the victim's wounded emotions is the feeling of powerlessness—feeling unable to make healthy choices in circumstances and relationships. Left with a damaged sense of self-worth, unhealed victims of abuse develop unhealthy beliefs and behaviors. Because of a past lack of control, victims often have a hidden fear of being controlled and therefore become overcontrolling. Those who have been extensively victimized generally struggle with severe emotional side effects:

Low Self-worth[3]

— Accepting abuse, blame, condemnation, and injustice

— Being critical of self and others

— Being desperate for approval

— Being unable to set boundaries

— Being unable to accept compliments

— Being a people-pleaser

— Being defensive

Those who have a warped view of themselves often have a warped view of God. When people feel unworthy of love, respect, and approval from others, often they feel even more unworthy of God's love, respect, and approval. Their faulty beliefs lead them to draw faulty conclusions about God. These wrong beliefs about God serve only to sabotage their relationship with God and kill their hope that they could be valued and used by God.

Fear[4]

— Of abandonment

— Of rejection

— Of failure

— Of affection

— Of intimacy

— Of authority figures

— Of God

Fear is a natural emotion designed by God. However, *fearfulness* is not designed by God, for fearfulness means living in a *state of fear*.

> *"God has not given us a spirit of fear, but of power*
> *and of love and of a sound mind"*
> (2 Timothy 1:7 nkjv).

Obsessiveness
— In control
— In work
— In organization

Dependency[5]
— On food
— On drugs/alcohol
— On people
— On religion

Compulsion
— Addictions
— Perfectionism
— Irresponsibility
— Repeated victimization
— Cleanliness

WHAT IS THE PROFILE OF AN ABUSED PERSON?

Abusers leave their innocent victims with abiding feelings of rejection and personal defectiveness. Constant fear that their "stains" will be exposed causes the abused to develop destructive ways of relating to others. These self-protective patterns of behavior are pitfalls to healthy adult relationships and decrease the ability to know God intimately.

An A-B-U-S-E-D person typically has several of these characteristics:

A	Ambivalent	Conflicted emotions about the pain and pleasures of sexual feelings give mixed signals to others on an emotional level
B	Betrayed	Unable to trust or have faith in God or others
U	Unexcitable	Lacks passion for both good and evil, and merely seeks to be free of conflict with others
S	Self-absorbed	Consumed with self-protection; unable to be sensitive to others
E	Emotionally Controlled	Disengages from true feelings and becomes blind to the feelings of others
D	Dependent on Self	Seeks to always be in control due to an inability to depend on God or others

WHAT ARE THE PHYSICAL SIDE EFFECTS OF VICTIMIZATION? [6]

Sexual difficulties
— Frigidity/impotence
— Promiscuity
— Sexual identity confusion

Sleeping disruptions
— Nightmares
— Insomnia
— Restlessness

Eating disorders
— Anorexia
— Bulimia
— Overeating

Memory disturbances
— Memory blocks
— Flashbacks
— Memory loss

WHAT ARE THE SPIRITUAL SIDE EFFECTS OF VICTIMIZATION?

Those who are repeatedly victimized often struggle with obstacles to their spiritual growth. They have...

Warped negative perceptions of God
— Perceive God as being distant and disinterested
— Perceive God as being indifferent to their pain

Anger at God for not stopping the abuse
— Think God is responsible for bad things that happen
— Think God is unfair, cruel, and unloving

Distrust of God for allowing the abuse
— Consider God to be unrestricted in the use of His power
— Consider God to be undependable

Feelings of rejection and unworthiness
— Feel God has abandoned them

— Feel God has ascribed no value to them

Fear of God's anger and displeasure
— See God as impossible to please
— See God as condemning, punitive, and vindictive

Projection of the attributes of the abuser onto God
— Believe God is hurtful, insensitive, and unpredictable
— Believe God is selfish, controlling, and inconsistent

Knowledge of God but little personal experience of God
— Know God is all-powerful, all-knowing, and all-present
— Know God is a force to be reckoned with
— Know God is eternal and sovereign

Pursuit of God's approval
— Hope God will bless them for their church-related activities
— Hope God will bless them for their service to others

Difficulty forming an intimate relationship with God
— Struggle with being honest and open with God
— Struggle with giving their hearts and lives to God

> *"I am not ashamed of the gospel, because it is the power of God*
> *for the salvation of everyone who believes...Here I am! I stand*
> *at the door and knock. If anyone hears my voice and opens*
> *the door, I will come in and eat with him, and he with me"*
> (ROMANS 1:16; REVELATION 3:20).

IS HEALING FROM VICTIMIZATION POSSIBLE?

Yes, but it will not come instantaneously. As you walk the path to recovery, the old ways of thinking about yourself are replaced with truths about how God sees you and your circumstances. The following steps will help you move from victim to victor, enabling God to direct your steps along the Road to Transformation.

— Accept that pain is a part of this life, common to everyone, and you are one among many victims.

— Begin to see your life from God's perspective—He is in control and wants to bless you and conform you to the image of His Son, Jesus.

— Seek appropriate help from those whom you trust—those who are spiritually and emotionally mature and skilled enough to help you.

— Learn to relax and allow yourself time to meaningfully connect with God and significant persons around you.

— Believe in and trust in the promises of God's Word. Allow His Word to "reprogram" your thought processes to replace the lies of your past with His eternal truth.

> *"Trust in the LORD with all your heart and lean not on*
> *your own understanding; in all your ways acknowledge*
> *him, and he will make your paths straight"*
> (PROVERBS 3:5-6).

WHY TRUST GOD TO HELP IN YOUR HEALING?

There is no solid solution to the serious side-effects of being victimized apart from the supernatural work of the Spirit of God within the lives of victims. Such a work is based on having a personal relationship with God and seeing Him as He really is—a gracious and compassionate heavenly Father full of tender mercies. This usually requires replacing distorted images of God with the truth about His character. It requires maturing in the Lord, walking with Him on a daily basis, confiding in Him, learning to trust Him for life itself.

> *"Do not conform any longer to the pattern of this*
> *world, but be transformed by the renewing of your*
> *mind. Then you will be able to test and approve what*
> *God's will is—his good, pleasing and perfect will"*
> (ROMANS 12:2).

HOW CAN YOU BREAK FREE FROM A VICTIM MIND-SET?

When you were a child, you did not have control over those in authority over you, but as a grownup, that is no longer the case. You are now able to choose those with whom you associate, and you can certainly control your self-talk. Therefore, you can take an active part in changing the distorted view you have of yourself, with these steps:

— *Accept yourself.* Stop striving for perfection or to be like someone else.

Realize the Lord made you for a purpose, and He designed your personality and gave you the gifts and abilities He wanted you to have in order to accomplish His purpose for you.

> *"Many are the plans in a man's heart,*
> *but it is the LORD's purpose that prevails"*
> (PROVERBS 19:21).

— *Acknowledge and praise God for the abilities He has given you* and the things He has accomplished through you. Engage in encouraging self-talk and silence the critic inside your head.

> *"May our Lord Jesus Christ himself and God our*
> *Father, who loved us and by his grace gave us eternal*
> *encouragement and good hope, encourage your hearts*
> *and strengthen you in every good deed and word"*
> (2 Thessalonians 2:16-17).

— *Release past negative experiences and focus on a positive future.* Refuse to dwell on negative things said or done to you in the past; instead, release them to God. Embrace the work God is doing in your life now.

> *"For it is God who works in you to will*
> *and to act according to his good purpose"*
> (Philippians 2:13).

— *Live in God's forgiveness.* God has extended you forgiveness for all your sins (past, present, and future), so confess and repent of anything offensive to God. Do not set yourself up as a higher judge than God by refusing to forgive yourself. Accept that you will not be made fully perfect and totally without sin until you stand in the presence of Christ and are fully conformed to His image.

> *"Dear friends, now we are children of God, and what*
> *we will be has not yet been made known. But we*
> *know that when he appears, we shall be like him,*
> *for we shall see him as he is. Everyone who has this*
> *hope in him purifies himself, just as he is pure"*
> (1 John 3:2-3).

— *Benefit from past mistakes.* Decide to view your mistakes as opportunities to learn needed lessons. Ask God what He wants to teach you from your mistakes, listen to Him, and learn. Then move forward with a positive attitude.

> *"We know that in all things God works for the good of those*
> *who love him, who have been called according to his purpose"*
> (Romans 8:28).

— *Form supportive, positive relationships.* Minimize the time you spend with negative, critical people, whether family, friends, or coworkers, and seek out those who encourage and support you both emotionally and spiritually.

> *"He who walks with the wise grows wise,*
> *but a companion of fools suffers harm"*
> (PROVERBS 13:20).

— *Formulate realistic goals and plans.* Prayerfully set some reasonable, achievable goals that capitalize on your strengths, and make a plan for how you will accomplish those goals.

> *"Do you not know that in a race all the runners run, but only*
> *one gets the prize? Run in such a way as to get the prize"*
> (1 CORINTHIANS 9:24).

— *Identify your heart's desires.* Make a list of the things you have dreamed of doing but have never attempted because of a fear of failure or a lack of self-assurance. Plan the steps you need to take in order to accomplish your desires.

> *"Delight yourself in the LORD and he will give*
> *you the desires of your heart"*
> (PSALM 37:4).

— *Plan for success.* Anticipate any obstacles to accomplishing your goals and desires, and plan strategies for overcoming them.

> *"May he give you the desire of your heart and*
> *make all your plans succeed"*
> (PSALM 20:4).

— *Celebrate each accomplishment.* Your feelings of self-worth and self-confidence will grow with the acknowledgment of each accomplishment. Rejoice with the Lord and those who are close to you over the things God and you have done together.

> *"In the presence of the LORD your God, you*
> *and your families shall eat and shall rejoice in*
> *everything you have put your hand to, because*
> *the LORD your God has blessed you"*
> (DEUTERONOMY 12:7).

> God heals the broken heart when you give Him all the pieces.
> He washes the wounds…mends the mind…tallies the tears.
> He empowers you to rise above abuse and become all He created you to be.
>
> —JH

Your Scripture Prayer Project

Psalm 62:5-6

Psalm 34:18

1 Peter 2:19,21

Psalm 107:20

John 8:36

Romans 12:2

Luke 4:18

Colossians 3:13

For additional guidance on this topic, see also *Anger, Childhood Sexual Abuse, Codependency, Crisis Intervention, Critical Spirit, Cults, Depression, Domestic Violence, Dysfunctional Family, Fear, Hope, Identity, Manipulation, Marriage, Prejudice, Rejection, Salvation, Self-worth, Suicide Prevention, Verbal and Emotional Abuse, Worry.*

50

WORRY

The Joy Stealer

I t can keep you up at night, it can siphon away energy, it can consume your life. Worry comes so naturally—that's why it needs to be dealt with *supernaturally*. The cares and concerns that weigh you down are to be cast upon Jesus, through prayer. Then His peace, not worry, will characterize your life. Philippians 4:6-7 says, "Do not be anxious about anything, but in everything, by prayer and petition, with thanksgiving, present your requests to God. And the peace of God, which transcends all understanding, will guard your hearts and your minds in Christ Jesus."

IS WORRY A SIN?

Worry can keep us stuck in the ditch of doubt and therefore is displeasing to God. Worry is sin when it keeps us stuck in…

Disbelief

Worry reveals you don't believe God when He says He will provide all that you need.

> "*The LORD will guide you always; he will satisfy your*
> *needs in a sun-scorched land and will strengthen*
> *your frame. You will be like a well-watered*
> *garden, like a spring whose waters never fail*"
> (ISAIAH 58:11).

Disobedience

Worry reveals you are taking on personal responsibility and concern for things that God has already promised to provide.

> *"I tell you, do not worry about your life, what you will eat or*
> *drink; or about your body, what you will wear. Is not life*
> *more important than food, and the body more important*
> *than clothes? Look at the birds of the air; they do not sow*
> *or reap or store away in barns, and yet your heavenly*
> *Father feeds them. Are you not much more valuable than*
> *they? Who of you by worrying can add a single hour to*
> *his life? And why do you worry about clothes? See how the*
> *lilies of the field grow. They do not labor or spin. Yet I tell*
> *you that not even Solomon in all his splendor was dressed*
> *like one of these. If that is how God clothes the grass of the*
> *field, which is here today and tomorrow is thrown into*
> *the fire, will he not much more clothe you, O you of little*
> *faith?…Do not worry…about tomorrow, for tomorrow will*
> *worry about itself. Each day has enough trouble of its own"*
> (MATTHEW 6:25-31,34).

Destruction

Worry destroys your physical body, which is the "temple of the Holy Spirit." It can bring about a host of physical ailments, such as high blood pressure, heart trouble, headaches, colds, and stomach disorders.

> *"Do you not know that your body is a temple of the*
> *Holy Spirit, who is in you, whom you have received*
> *from God? You are not your own; you were bought*
> *at a price. Therefore honor God with your body"*
> (1 CORINTHIANS 6:19-20).

Dishonor

Worry shifts the focus of attention from the all-sufficient power of Christ to your human insufficiency and insecurity. Ultimately, worry can undermine your Christian witness to others by presenting God as impotent and unworthy of praise.

> *"Let your light shine before men, that they may see*
> *your good deeds and praise your Father in heaven"*
> (MATTHEW 5:16).

WHAT ARE THE DIFFERENCES BETWEEN DESTRUCTIVE WORRY AND CONSTRUCTIVE CONCERN?[1]

Destructive Worry	Constructive Concern
paralyzes	motivates
decreases creativity	increases creativity
prevents initiative	promotes initiative
results in anxious fretting	results in calm focusing
attempts to control the future	attempts to improve the future
fears the worst	hopes for the best
appears negative to others	appears positive to others
distracts the mind from what is important	directs the mind to what is important
"I'm so worried that my child might drown that I'm never going to let her anywhere near the water."	"I'm so concerned that my child can't swim that I've made arrangements to give her swimming lessons."

"Set your minds on things above, not on earthly things"
(COLOSSIANS 3:2).

HOW YOU CAN LIVE WORRY-FREE

God's Word reveals the following steps for breaking free from the ditches of worry. As you travel the path toward anxiety-free living, it will converge into the Road to Transformation. Here, your faith and God's power will intersect to produce the peace He promises for sojourners who cast their cares on Him.

Desire to be free of all that chokes out the will of God.

— Express your heart's desire to do God's will (Psalm 40:8).

— Admit you have sinned and chosen to go your own way (Psalm 51:4).

— Give Christ control over your life, allowing Him to be your Lord (Mark 8:34-36).

— Tell God you want Him to do His will in and through you.

"The worries of this life, the deceitfulness of wealth and the desires for other things come in and choke the word, making it unfruitful"
(MARK 4:19).

Recognize God's presence in your life.
— The Lord is your life (Colossians 3:4).
— The Lord is your security (Romans 8:38-39).
— The Lord is your provider (Philippians 4:19).
— The Lord is your protector.

> *"Do not fear, for I am with you; do not be dismayed,*
> *for I am your God. I will strengthen you and help you;*
> *I will uphold you with my righteous right hand"*
> (ISAIAH 41:10).

Eliminate worry-producing demands.
— "I *can't* stand to be rejected!"
— "I *should* meet all their expectations."
— "I *must* not fail."
— "I *have to* have excellent health."

> *"How long must I wrestle with my thoughts*
> *and every day have sorrow in my heart? How long*
> *will my enemy triumph over me?"*
> (PSALM 13:2).

See your worry-producing situations as opportunities for character building.
— Initiate new relationships, even at the risk of being hurt.
— Have confidence that the Lord is directing your life, even if circumstances don't work out the way you had hoped.

> *"I make known the end from the beginning, from*
> *ancient times, what is still to come. I say: My*
> *purpose will stand, and I will do all that I please"*
> (ISAIAH 46:10).

Expect the Lord to make positive changes in you even when you fail.
— Let your life be an example of growing gracefully.

> *"Being confident of this, that he who began a good work in you*
> *will carry it on to completion until the day of Christ Jesus"*
> (PHILIPPIANS 1:6).

Cultivate contentment with prayer.
— "Lord, I want to be accepted, but if I'm not, I won't be robbed of my joy. You accept me unconditionally."

— "Lord, rather than worry about the welfare of my family, I'll trust them to Your sovereign care."

— "Lord, instead of becoming anxious about my job, I choose to trust You with my future."

— "Lord, I want to have excellent health, but if I don't, I am willing to learn contentment and refuse to worry."

> *"Jesus told his disciples...they should*
> *always pray and not give up"*
> (LUKE 18:1).

Implant God's promises in your heart.

Read and memorize God's promises for...

— contentment (Philippians 4:11-13)

— hope (Jeremiah 29:11)

— strength (Isaiah 41:10)

— confidence (2 Timothy 1:7)

> *"Through these he has given us his very great and*
> *precious promises, so that through them you may*
> *participate in the divine nature and escape the*
> *corruption in the world caused by evil desires"*
> (2 PETER 1:4).

Thank God for what He is doing.

Thank the Lord for...

— His comforting presence in the midst of your pain (Psalm 34:18).

— what He will teach you through your trials (James 1:2-4).

— His compassion you now have toward others in similar trials (2 Corinthians 1:3-4).

— His sovereignty over yesterday, today, and tomorrow.

> *"He causes his sun to rise on the evil and the good, and*
> *sends rain on the righteous and the unrighteous"*
> (MATTHEW 5:45).

Nourish your body with the right physical activities.

— If you don't get enough sleep, small problems become insurmountable.

— If you don't eat healthy foods, you can feel fatigued and frazzled.

— If you don't make time to exercise, you can feel down and depressed.

— If you don't know where to start, get a thorough medical checkup.

> *"In vain you rise early and stay up late, toiling for*
> *food to eat—for he grants sleep to those he loves"*
> (Psalm 127:2).

Nurture your mind with spiritual music.

— Listen to uplifting praise music.

— Meditate on the words of the songs.

— Sing songs about God's promise to provide what you need.

— The moment worry begins to surface, counteract it with a song of God's faithfulness.

> *"The Lord is my strength and my shield; my heart*
> *trusts in him, and I am helped. My heart leaps*
> *for joy and I will give thanks to him in song"*
> (Psalm 28:7).

Commit to doing the following every day for the next four weeks.

— Focus on living in the present, not in the past or future (James 4:13-15).

— Emulate the godly examples of people whom you know (Proverbs 13:20).

— Ask God to direct you in performing at least one unexpected act of kindness (Matthew 7:12).

— Believe God's promises. You have the peace of God surrounding you and the God of peace within you.

> *"Blessed is the man who trusts in the Lord, whose confidence*
> *is in him. He will be like a tree planted by the water that*
> *sends out its roots by the stream. It does not fear when*
> *heat comes; its leaves are always green. It has no worries*
> *in a year of drought and never fails to bear fruit"*
> (Jeremiah 17:7-8).

When worries sprout, weed them out.
Don't fret over the future—God is already there.
—JH

Your Scripture Prayer Project

Philippians 4:6-7

Matthew 13:22

Luke 12:22-24

1 Peter 5:7

Psalm 139:23

Jeremiah 17:7-8

Matthew 7:9-11

Matthew 6:34

Philippians 4:11-12

Psalm 37:7-8

For additional guidance on this topic, see also *Alcohol and Drug Abuse, Anger, Codependency, Critical Spirit, Depression, Domestic Violence, Fear, Financial Freedom, Hope, Illness, Marriage, Overeating, Rejection, Self-worth, Stress Management, Suicide Prevention, Verbal and Emotional Abuse, Victimization.*

Notes

1. Counseling

1. See American Heritage, Electronic Dictionary (New York: Haughton Mifflin, 1992).
2. Robert S. McGee, *The Search for Significance,* 2nd ed. (Houston, TX: Rapha, 1990), 27-30.

2. Abortion Recovery

1. Material prepared by Abortion Recovery Ministry (ARM) of Hope for the Heart.
2. Teri K. Reisser and Paul Reisser, *Help for the Post-Abortion Woman (*Grand Rapids: Zondervan, 1989), 26.
3. Reisser and Reisser, *Help for the Post-Abortion Woman,* 39-40.

3. Adultery

1. See Kay Marshall Strom, *Helping Women in Crisis: A Handbook for People Helpers* (Grand Rapids: Zondervan, 1986), 90-91.
2. J. Allan Peterson, *The Myth of the Greener Grass* (Wheaton, IL: Tyndale, 1983), 75.
3. See Strom, *Helping Women in Crisis,* 93-96.
4. See Strom, *Helping Women in Crisis,* 93-96.
5. Strom, *Helping Women in Crisis,* 90-91.
6. Peterson, *The Myth of the Greener Grass,* 145.

4. Alcohol and Drug Abuse

1. For this section see Jeff VanVonderen, *Good News for the Chemically Dependent and Those Who Love Them,* rev. and updated ed. (Nashville: Thomas Nelson, 1991), 21-22.
2. Elizabeth J. Taylor, ed., *Dorland's Illustrated Medical Dictionary,* 27th ed. (Philadelphia, PA: W.B. Saunders, 1988), 848.
3. For this section see Ronald Rogers and Chandler Scott McMillin, *Under Your Own Power: A Guide to Recovery for Nonbelievers…and the Ones Who Love Them* (New York: G.P. Putnam's Sons, 1992), 140-43.
4. See *American Heritage Electronic Dictionary,* s.v. "Disease" (Houghton Mifflin, 1992).
5. For this section see Robert S. McGee, Pat Springle, and Susan Joiner, *Rapha's Twelve-Step Program for Overcoming Chemical Dependency: With Support Materials from The Search for Significance,* 2d ed. (Houston, TX: Rapha, 1990); Stephen Van Cleave, Walter Byrd, and Kathy Revell, *Counseling for Substance Abuse and Addiction* (Nashville: W Publishing Group, 1988), 103-10.
6. For this section see Van Cleave, Byrd, and Revell, *Counseling for Substance Abuse and Addiction,* 116-17.
7. For this section see Van Cleave, Byrd, and Revell, *Counseling for Substance Abuse and Addiction,* 116-17.

5. Anger

1. Ray Burwick, *The Menace Within: Hurt or Anger?* (Birmingham, AL: Ray Burwick, 1985), 18; Gary D. Chapman, *The Other Side of Love: Handling Anger in a Godly Way* (Chicago: Moody, 1999), 17-18.
2. Gary Jackson Oliver and H. Norman Wright, *When Anger Hits Home: Taking Care of Your Anger Without Taking It Out on Your Family* (Chicago: Moody, 1992), 84.
3. H. Norman Wright, *Anger* (Waco, TX: Word, 1980), audiocassette.
4. For the three God-given inner needs, see Lawrence J. Crabb, Jr., *Understanding People: Deep Longings for Relationship* (Grand Rapids: Zondervan, 1987), 15-16; Robert S. McGee, *The Search for Significance,* 2d edition (Nashville: W Publishing Group, 1990).
5. Oliver and Wright, *When Anger Hits Home,* 97.

6. Wright, *Anger.*

7. McGee, *The Search for Significance,* 27; Crabb, *Understanding People,* 15-16.

8. Wright, *Anger.*

9. McGee, *The Search for Significance,* 27; Crabb, *Understanding People,* 15-16.

10. Chapman, *The Other Side of Love,* 21; Russell Kelfer, *Tough Choices: Secrets to Bringing Self Under Control from the Book of Proverbs* (San Antonio, TX: Into His Likeness, 1991), 59-73.

11. Kelfer, *Tough Choices,* 65-73; Oliver and Wright, *When Anger Hits Home,* 97.

6. Anorexia and Bulimia

1. Peggy Claude-Pierre, *The Secret Language of Eating Disorders: The Revolutionary New Approach to Understanding and Curing Anorexia and Bulimia* (New York: Times, 1997), 23.

2. Claude-Pierre, *The Secret Language of Eating Disorders,* 98.

3. For this section see Raymond E. Vath, *Counseling Those with Eating Disorders,* vol. 4, Resources for Christian Counseling, ed. Gary R. Collins 14 (Waco, TX: Word, 1986), 39-44; Pam W. Vredevelt, Deborah Newman, Harry Beverly, and Frank Minirth, *The Thin Disguise: Understanding and Overcoming Anorexia and Bulimia* (Nashville, TN: Thomas Nelson, 1992), 33-45.

4. See Pam W. Vredevelt and Joyce Whitman, *Walking a Thin Line: Anorexia and Bulimia, the Battle Can Be Won* (Portland, OR: Multnomah, 1985), 69-72.

5. See Claude-Pierre, *The Secret Language of Eating Disorders;* Vredevelt and Whitman, *Walking a Thin Line: Anorexia and Bulimia, the Battle Can Be Won,* 208-14.

7. Childhood Sexual Abuse

1. For the following section see Grant L. Martin, *Counseling for Family Violence and Abuse,* Resources for Christian Counseling, ed. Gary R. Collins, vol. 6 (Dallas: Word, 1987), 165-71.

2. For this section see Grant Martin, *Please Don't Hurt Me* (Wheaton, IL: Victor, 1987), 52-53.

3. For this section see Martin, *Please Don't Hurt Me,* 51-59.

8. Codependency

1. For this section see Robert Hemfelt, Frank Minirth, and Paul Meier, *Love Is a Choice* (Nashville: Thomas Nelson, 1989), 180-84.

2. For this section see Pia Mellody, Andrea Wells Miller, and J. Keith Miller, *Facing Love Addiction,* (New York: Harper One, 2003), 196-98.

10. Critical Spirit

1. J. Grant Howard, *The Trauma of Transparency: A Biblical Approach to Inter-Personal Communication* (Portland, OR: Multnomah, 1979), 56-59.

2. On the three God-given inner needs, see Lawrence J. Crabb, Jr., *Understanding People: Deep Longings for Relationship* (Grand Rapids: Zondervan, 1987), 15-16; Robert S. McGee, *The Search for Significance,* 2d ed. (Houston, TX: Rapha, 1990), 27-30.

11. Cults

1. Brigham Young, *Journal of Discourses,* 26 vols. (Liverpool, England: F. D. and S. W. Richards, 1854-86), 8:115.

2. See Reverend Sun Myung Moon, *Overview of the Divine Principle,* "The Hidden Dimension of History," http://www.unification.org/overview_DP3.html.

3. See Herbert W. Armstrong, "Why Christ Died and Rose Again," *The Plain Truth,* vol. 28, no. 4 (Pasadena, CA: Radio Church of God), April 1963.

4. Ruth A. Tucker, *Another Gospel: Alternative Religions and the New Age Movement* (Grand Rapids: Zondervan, 2004), 222-23.

5. Watchtower Bible and Tract Society, *Should You Believe in the Trinity?* (Brooklyn, NY: Watchtower Bible and Tract Society, 1989), 20-22.

6. See Joseph Smith, Jr., Article #8 of *The Articles of Faith* and preface to the *Book of Mormon,* "The Testimony of Three Witnesses." The claim is that many mistakes were made in the translation of the Bible, but the *Book of Mormon* was translated by divine intervention, making it flawless and superior to the Bible.

7. See Steven Hassan, *Combating Cult Mind Control* (Rochester, VT: Park Street, 1988); Robert Jay Lifton, *Thought Reform and the Psychology of Totalism* (New York: W.W. Norton, 1961); Margaret Thaler Singer, *Cults in Our Midst* (San Francisco: Jossey-Bass, 1995); Madeleine Landau Tobias and Lalich Janja, *Captive Hearts Captive Minds: Freedom and Recovery from Cults and Abusive Relationships* (Alameda, CA: Hunter House, 1994).

8. Joan Carol Ross and Michael D. Langone, *Cults: What Parents Should Know: A Practical Guide to Help Parents with Children in Destructive Groups* (New York: Carol, 1988), 21-22. See also Hassan, *Combating Cult Mind Control;* Singer, *Cults in Our Midst.*

9. Rachel Andres and James R. Lane, *Cults & Consequences* (Los Angeles: Jewish Federation Council of Greater Los Angeles, 1988), 4:30. See also Tobias and Janja, *Captive Hearts Captive Minds,* 86-200.

10. Andrew F. Ehat and Lyndon W. Cook, eds., *The Words of Joseph Smith: The Contemporary Accounts of the Nauvoo Discourses of the Prophet Joseph* (Provo, UT: Grandin, 1994), 84; Bruce R. McConkie, *The Promised Messiah* (Salt Lake City, UT: Deseret, 1978), 134.

11. For this section, see Andres and Lane, *Cults & Consequences,* 6:23-30.

12. Andres and Lane, *Cults & Consequences,* 6:13.

12. Dating

1. For the following section see Scott Kirby, *Dating: Guidelines from the Bible* (Grand Rapids: Baker, 1979), 111-21; Diane Eble, *The Campus Life Guide to Dating* (Grand Rapids: Zondervan, 1990), 177-83.

14. Depression

1. Frank Minirth, *In Pursuit of Happiness* (Grand Rapids, MI: Fleming H. Revell, 2004), 25.

2. For this section, see Archibald Hart and Catherine Hart Weber, *Unveiling Depression in Women: A Practical Guide to Understanding and Overcoming Depression* (Grand Rapids: Fleming H. Revell, 2002), 49-65.

3. Hart and Weber, *Unveiling Depression in Women,* 55.

4. Hart and Weber, *Unveiling Depression in Women,* 56.

5. *Merriam-Webster Online Dictionary,* s.v. "Repression," http://www.m-w.com.

6. Roy W. Fairchild, *Dictionary of Pastoral Care and Counseling,* ed. Rodney J. Hunter, et al. (Nashville: Abingdon, 1990), s.v. "Sadness and Depression."

15. Domestic Violence

1. *What Every Congregation Needs to Know About Domestic Violence* (Seattle, WA: Center for the Prevention of Sexual and Domestic Violence, 1994), n.p.

2. For this section see Patricia Riddle Gaddis, *Battered But Not Broken: Help for Abused Wives and Their Church Families* (Valley Forge, PA: Judson, 1996), 27-29; Kay Marshall Strom, *In the Name of Submission: A Painful Look at Wife Battering* (Portland, OR: Multnomah, 1986), 44-46; Lenore E. Walker, *The Battered Woman* (New York: HarperPerennial, 1979), 55-70.

3. For this section see Texas Young Lawyers Association, *Family Violence: Legal Choices for Battered Women* (n.p.: Texas Department of Human Services, 1985). Be sure to check the current laws in your area. For this paragraph see Cawthon, *Getting Out,* 123.

4. On the three God-given inner needs, see Lawrence J. Crabb, Jr., *Understanding People: Deep Longings for Relationship* (Grand Rapids: Zondervan, 1987), 15-16; Robert S. McGee, *The Search for Significance,* 2d ed. (Houston, TX: Rapha, 1990), 27-30.

5. For this section see Strom, *In the Name of Submission,* 20-26.

6. S.R. McDill and Linda McDill, *Shattered and Broken Tarrytown, NY: Fleming H. Revell,* 76-82; Ginny Nicarthy and Sue Davidson, *You Can Be Free: An Easy-to Read Handbook for Abused Women* (Seattle: Seal, 1989), 16-19; Kay Marshall Strom, *In the Name of Submission,* 35-39.

7. Marie Marshall Fortune, *Keeping the Faith: Questions and Answers for the Abused Woman* (New York: Harper SanFrancisco, 1987), 15-17.

16. Dysfunctional Family

1. For this section see Robert Hemfelt, Frank Minirth, and Paul Meier, *Love Is a Choice* (Nashville: Thomas Nelson, 1989), 157-59; H. Norman Wright, *Always Daddy's Girl: Understanding Your Father's Impact on Who You Are* (Ventura, CA: Regal, 1989), 163-71; Nancy LeSourd, *No Longer the Hero: The Personal Pilgrimage of an Adult Child* (Nashville: Thomas Nelson, 1991), 38-45.

2. For this section see David Field, *Family Personalities* (Eugene, OR: Harvest House, 1988), 19-29.

3. For this section see LeSourd, *No Longer the Hero*, 198-204.

4. For this section see Jim Conway, *Adult Children of Legal or Emotional Divorce* (Downers Grove, IL: InterVarsity, 1990), 127-240.

5. LeSourd, *No Longer the Hero*, 175-77.

6. LeSourd, *No Longer the Hero*, 175-77.

7. David Field, *Family Personalities*, 153-54.

17. Evil and Suffering...Why?

1. For this section, see Norman L. Geisler and Ronald M. Brooks, *When Skeptics Ask* (Wheaton, IL: Victor, 1990), 68; C.S. Lewis, *The Problem of Pain* (New York: Collier, 1962), 27.

2. For this section, see Geisler and Brooks, *When Skeptics Ask*, 63-64.

3. For this section see Peter Kreeft and Ronald K. Tacelli, *Handbook of Christian Apologetics* (Downers Grove, IL: InterVarsity, 1994), 128-29.

18. Fear

1. *American Heritage Electronic Dictionary* (Houghton Mifflin, 1992), s.v. "Fear."

2. W.E. Vine, Merrill Unger, William White *Vine's Complete Expository Dictionary of Biblical Words,* electronic ed. (Nashville: Thomas Nelson, 1996), s.v. "Fear."

3. American Psychiatric Association, *Diagnostic and Statistical Manual of Mental Disorders: DSM-III-R,* 3d ed. (Washington, DC: American Psychiatric Association, 1987), 432.

4. Phobia Center of the Southwest, "Agoraphobia," 1990.

5. See Karen Randau, *Conquering Fear* (Dallas: Rapha, 1991), 44.

6. Shirley Babior and Carol Goldman, *Overcoming Panic Attacks: Strategies to Free Yourself from the Anxiety Trap* (Minneapolis, MN: CompCare, 1990), 59-62.

20. Forgiveness

1. Robert Jeffress, *When Forgiveness Doesn't Make Sense* (Colorado Springs: WaterBrook, 2000), 47-49.

2. David Augsburger, *The Freedom of Forgiveness*, rev. and exp. ed.(Chicago: Moody, 1988), 47-50.

3. For this section see Lewis B. Smedes, *Forgive and Forget: Healing the Hurts We Don't Deserve* (San Francisco, CA: Harper & Row, 1984), 21-26.

4. Augsburger, *The Freedom of Forgiveness*, 44-46.

5. For the following section see Smedes, *Forgive and Forget*, 31-37.

21. Grief Recovery

1. See Gary R. Collins, *Christian Counseling: A Comprehensive Guide,* rev. and updated ed. (Dallas: Word, 1988), 352-53; H. Norman Wright, *Crisis Counseling: What to Do and Say During the First 72 Hours,* updated and expanded ed. (Ventura, CA: Regal, 1993), 154-56; H. Norman Wright, *Recovering from the Losses of Life* (Tarrytown, NY: Fleming H. Revell, 1991), 53-61.

22. Guilt

1. Larry Richards, *Expository Dictionary of Bible Words* (Grand Rapids: Zondervan, 1985), 322.

2. See the Hebrew dictionary entry in James Strong, *Strong's Exhaustive Concordance of the Bible* (Nashville: Abingdon, 1986), 17.

3. Robert S. McGee, *The Search for Significance: Book & Workbook,* 2d ed. (Houston, TX: Rapha, 1990), 19.

4. Brent Curtis, *Guilt,* ed. Tom Varney (Colorado Springs: NavPress, 1992), 14.

5. See Curtis, *Guilt,* 17-29.

6. Erwin W. Lutzer, *How to Say No to a Stubborn Habit* (Wheaton, IL: Victor, 1979), 40.

7. Lutzer, *How to Say No to a Stubborn Habit,* 37.

8. For the following section, see Lutzer, *How to Say No to a Stubborn Habit,* 37-41.

23. Habits

1. See *Dictionary of Basic English* (Springfield, MA: Merriam-Webster, 2000).

2. On the three God-given inner needs, see Lawrence J. Crabb, Jr., *Understanding People: Deep Longings for Relationship* (Grand Rapids: Zondervan, 1987), 15-16; Robert S. McGee, *The Search for Significance,* 2d ed. (Houston, TX: Rapha, 1990), 27-30.

3. William Backus, *Finding the Freedom of Self-Control* (Minneapolis: Bethany House, 1987), 160.

4. Erwin W. Lutzer, *How to Say No to a Stubborn Habit* (Wheaton, IL: Victor, 1986), 112.

5. Backus, *Finding the Freedom of Self-Control,* 36.

6. Backus, *Finding the Freedom of Self-Control,* 153.

7. Lutzer, *How to Say No to a Stubborn Habit,* 21-24.

8. Backus, *Finding the Freedom of Self-Control,* 43-44; Lutzer, *How to Say No to a Stubborn Habit,* 48-49.

9. Lutzer, *How to Say No to a Stubborn Habit,* 52-53, 100-08.

10. Neil T. Anderson, *A Way of Escape* (Eugene, OR: Harvest House, 1994), 117-33.

11. Lutzer, *How to Say No to a Stubborn Habit,* 76-77

12. Lutzer, *How to Say No to a Stubborn Habit,* 98-108.

13. Lutzer, *How to Say No to a Stubborn Habit,* 131-40.

24. Homosexuality

1. Joe Dallas, *Desires in Conflict* (Eugene, OR: Harvest House, 1991), 91.

2. These figures assume four million homosexual men (a high figure, since it also includes boys), and 111 million heterosexual men age 15 years and older. These statistics are based upon the AIDS statistics from the Centers for Disease Control and Prevention, *HIV/AIDS Surveillance Report,* 2001, vol. 13, no. 2, 14; http://www.cdc.gov/hiv/stats/hasr1302.pdf (accessed August 12, 2003); and the United States population statistics available from the Central Intelligence Agency, *The World Factbook* (2003); http://www.cia.gov/cia/publications/factbook/index.html (accessed August 13, 2003).

3. See Edward O. Laumann et al., *The Social Organization of Sexuality: Sexual Practices in the United States* (Chicago: University of Chicago Press, 1994). Cited in U.S. Supreme Court legal brief 02-102 *Lawrence v. Texas,* 16, note 42; http://www.hrc.org/publications/eu/letters/lawrence_brief.pdf (accessed June 20, 2003).

4. Centers for Disease Control and Prevention, *Sexually Transmitted Disease Surveillance 2001 Supplement: Gonococcal Isolate Surveillance Project (GISP) Annual Report—2001* (October 2002); http://www.cdc.gov/std/GISP2001/GISP2001Text&Fig.pdf (accessed June 23, 2003).

5. Centers for Disease Control and Prevention, *Tracking the Hidden Epidemics: Trends in STDs in the United States in 2000* (n.d.); http://www.cdc.gov/nchstp/dstd/Stats_Trends/Trends2000.pdf (accessed June 23, 2003).

6. Centers for Disease Control and Prevention, *HIV/AIDS Update: A Glance at the HIV Epidemic* (n.d.); http://www.cdc.gov/hiv/pubs/facts/wsw.pdf (accessed June 23, 2003). This statistic is for male homosexuals.

7. *HIV/AIDS Surveillance Report, 2001,* 14; http://www.cdc.gov/hiv/stats/hasr1302.pdf (accessed August 12, 2003). This statistic is for male homosexuals.

8. R. Dotinga, "*US:* 1 in 3 Gay Men have Incurable STD", (March 6, 2002; http://uk.gay.com/headlines/1923.

9. Dotinga, "*US:* 1 in 3 Gay Men Have Incurable STD."

10. Gary Glenn, "Homosexual 'Love Crimes' Pose 50,000% Higher Risk of Violence than 'Hate Crimes'" (March 15, 2001); http://www.afamichigan.org/releases 20010315a.htm.

11. Gregory L. Greenwood, et al., "Battering Victimization Among a Probability-Based Sample of Men Who Have Sex with Men," *Am J Public Health* 92, no. 12 (2002).

12. For this section see Anne Petrov, *10 Things Gay Men Need to Know* (January 2, 2003); www.gaywired.com.

13. "Study: Gay Men at Greater Risk for Eating Disorders", (April 15, 2003); http://www.gayhealth.com.

14. Theo G.M. Sandfort, et al., "Same-Sex Sexual Behavior and Psychiatric Disorders: Findings from the Netherlands Mental Health Survey and Incidence Study (NEMESIS)," *Arch Gen Psychiatry* 58, no. 1 (2001).

15. Robert S. Hogg, et al., "Modeling the Impact of HIV Disease on Mortality in Gay and Bisexual Men," *International Journal of Epidemiology* 26, no. 3 (1997): 660.

16. Hogg, et al., "Modeling the Impact of HIV Disease," 657.

17. For this section see Joanne Highley and Ronald Highley, *Life Ministry Counselor Training Syllabus* (New York: Living in Freedom Eternally, n.d.).

18. Highley and Highley, *Life Ministry Counselor Training Syllabus.* Used by permission.

19. Grace Ketterman, *Depression Hits Every Family* (Nashville: Oliver-Nelson, 1988), 132.

20. Joe Dallas, *Desires in Conflict,* (Eugene, OR: Harvest House, 1991) 127-28.

25. Hope

1. W.E. Vine, Merrill Unger, William White, *Vine's Complete Expository Dictionary of Biblical Words,* electronic ed. (Nashville: Thomas Nelson, 1996), s.v. "Hope."

2. *Merriam-Webster Collegiate Dictionary* (2001); http://www.m-w.com, s.v. "Hope."

26. Identity

1. Adapted from Anabel Gillham, *Wheat & Tares* (Fort Worth, TX: Gillham Ministries, 1994), audiocassette.

27. Illness

1. For this section see Collins, *Christian Counseling* (Nashville: W Publishing Group, 1986), *331-35;* Ruth Kopp and Stephen Sorenson, *When Someone You Love Is Dying: A Handbook for Counselors and Those Who Care* (Grand Rapids: Ministry Resources, 1980) 167-89.

2. See Kopp and Sorenson, *When Someone You Love Is Dying,* 190-97.

3. See Shelley Chapin, *Within the Shadow* (Wheaton, IL: Victor, 1991), 109-22.

4. For this section see Collins, *Christian Counseling,* 331-35; Ruth Kopp and Stephen Sorenson, *When Someone You Love Is Dying,* 167-89.

5. For this section see Kopp and Sorenson, *When Someone You Love Is Dying,* 201-23.

28. Lying

1. For this section see Doug Sherman and William Hendricks, *Keeping Your Ethical Edge Sharp* (Colorado Springs: NavPress, 1990), 158-64.

2. For this section see Jerry White, *Honesty, Morality & Conscience,* (Colorado Springs, NavPress, 1979), 79-81, 175, 202, 206.

29. Manipulation

1. Lori Thorkelson Rentzel, *Emotional Dependency* (Downers Grove, IL: InterVarsity, 1990), 14; *Merriam Webster Collegiate Dictionary,* http://www.m-w.com.

2. Tim Kimmel, *Powerful Personalities* (Colorado Springs: Focus on the Family, 1993), 30. Kimmel calls this kind of manipulator the "Manager."

3. See Rentzel, *Emotional Dependency,* 14-15.

4. Barbara Sullivan, *The Control Grip* (Minneapolis, MN: Bethany House, 1991), 68-69. See Sullivan, *Control Grip,* 63.

5. See Sullivan, *Control Grip,* 67-68; Paul S. Schmidt, *Coping with Difficult People,* ed. Wayne E. Oates, vol. 6 (Philadelphia: Westminster, 1980), 101.

6. Accessed at www.coping.org/control/manipul.htm.

7. Henry Cloud and John Townsend, *Boundaries: When to Say Yes, When to Say No, to Take Control of Your Life* (Grand Rapids: Zondervan, 1992), 199-201.

8. See Rentzel, *Emotional Dependency*, 22.

9. See Cloud and Townsend, *Boundaries,* 241-43.

10. Rentzel, *Emotional Dependency*, 25.

11. See Schmidt, *Coping with Difficult People*, 103.

12. See Cloud and Townsend, *Boundaries*, 245.

13. See Shostrom and Montgomery, *Manipulators,* 61.

30. Marriage

1. H. Norman Wright, *The Secrets of a Lasting Marriage* (Ventura, CA: Regal, 1995), 149-70; Charles M. Sell, *Achieving the Impossible* (Portland, OR: Multnomah, 1982), 145-56.

2. Lawrence J. Crabb, Jr., *The Marriage Builder: A Blueprint for Couples and Counselors* (Grand Rapids: Zondervan, 1982), 29-30.

3. On the three God-given inner needs, see Lawrence J. Crabb, Jr., *Understanding People: Deep Longings for Relationship* (Grand Rapids: Zondervan, 1987), 15-16; Robert S. McGee, *The Search for Significance,* 2d ed. (Houston, TX: Rapha, 1990), 27-30.

4. Crabb, *The Marriage Builder,* 33-34. The following section is from Willard F. Harley, Jr. *His Needs, Her Needs: Building an Affair-Proof Marriage* (Grand Rapids: Revell, 2001).

31. The Occult

1. See W.E Vine, Merrill Unger, William White, "To Divine, Practice Divination" in W.E. Vine, *Vine's Complete Expository Dictionary of Biblical Words,* electronic ed. (Nashville: Thomas Nelson, 1996), and "Occult, the," in *The HarperCollins Dictionary of Religion,* ed. Jonathan Z. Smith (New York: HarperCollins, 1995), 806; James Walker, "What Is the Occult?" *The Watchman Expositor* 9, no. 8 (Dallas: Watchman Fellowship 1992).

2. See Russ Parker, *Battling the Occult* (Downers Grove, IL: InterVarsity, 1990), 29-52.

3. *New Oxford Dictionary of English,* electronic ed. (Oxford University Press, 1998), s.v. "Occult."

4. See Josh McDowell and Don Stewart, *Demons, Witches, and the Occult* (Wheaton, IL: Tyndale House, 1986), 20-26.

5. Kenneth Boa, *Cults, World Religions and the Occult* (Wheaton, IL: Victor, 1979), 158-61.

6. *The HarperCollins Dictionary of Religion,* ed. Jonathan Z. Smith (New York: HarperCollins, 1995), s.v. "Black magic."

7. *The HarperCollins Dictionary of Religion,* s.v. "White magic."

8. McDowell and Stewart, *Demons, Witches, and the Occult,* 71.

9. See Bob Passantino and Gretchen Passantino, "Satanism," *Zondervan Guide to Cults & Religious Movements,* ed. Alan W. Gomes (Grand Rapids: Zondervan, 1995), 7-8.

10. *Merriam-Webster's Collegiate Dictionary* (electronic edition) (Merriam-Webster, 2001).

11. *Merriam-Webster's Collegiate Dictionary;* American Heritage Electronic Dictionary (Houghton Mifflin, 1992).

32. Overeating

1. *New Oxford Dictionary of English* (electronic ed.) (Oxford University Press, 1998).

2. *Merriam-Webster Online Dictionary;* http://www.m-w.com.

3. Raymond E. Vath, *Counseling Those with Eating Disorders,* Resources for Christian Counseling, ed. Gary R. Collins, vol. 4 (Waco, TX: Word, 1986), 58.

4. *Merriam-Webster Online Dictionary.*

5. For this section see Frank Minirth, Paul Meier, Robert Hemfelt, and Sharon Sneed, *Love Hunger* (Nashville: Thomas Nelson, 1990), 21; Neva Coyle and Marie Chapian, *The All-New Free to Be Thin,* rev. ed. (Minneapolis, MN: Bethany House, 1993), 34-36.

33. Parenting

1. Kevin Huggins, "Institute of Biblical Counseling: Counseling Adolescents," seminar at Fellowship Bible Church Park Cities, Dallas, TX, March 3, 1990. See also Kevin Huggins, *Parenting Adolescents* (Colorado Springs: NavPress, 1989), 132-40.

2. For this section see Lou Priolo, *The Heart of Anger* (Amityville, NY: Calvary, 1997), 30-51; Wayne A. Mack, "Developing Marital Unity Through a Common Philosophy of Raising Children," *The Journal of Biblical Counseling* 3, no. 4 (1979): 37-56.

3. See June Hunt, *Bonding with Your Teen Through Boundaries* (Nashville: Boradman & Holman, 2001).

4. See Marilyn McGinnis, *Parenting Without Guilt* (San Bernardino, CA: Here's Life, 1987), 101-13.

5. Erma Bombeck, "Children Are Like Kites," *Forever Erma: Best Loved Writing from America's Favorite Humorist* (Riverside, NJ: Andrews McMeel, 1997), 44-45.

34. Phobias

1. Kevin R. Kracke, "Phobic Disorders," *Baker Encyclopedia of Psychology & Counseling,* 2d ed., eds. David G. Benner and Peter C. Hill (Grand Rapids: Baker, 1999), 871-72. Kracke renames the simple phobia as specific phobia.

2. Karen Randau, *Conquering Fear* (Dallas: Rapha, 1991), 44.

3. See Leslie Parrott, III, "Systematic Desensitization," *Baker Encyclopedia of Psychology & Counseling,* 2d ed., 1193.

35. Pregnancy—Unplanned

1. For this section see Henrietta VanDerMolen, *Pregnant & Alone: How You Can Help an Unwed Friend* (Wheaton, IL: Harold Shaw, 1989), 2-3; Frederica Mathewes-Green, *Real Choices: Offering Practical, Life-Affirming Alternatives to Abortion* (Sisters, OR: Multnomah, 1994), 131-34.

2. American Pregnancy Association, "My Three Choices," http://www.americanpregnancy.org/unplanned pregnancy/my3choices.html; Sylvia Boothe, *No Easy Choices: The Dilemma of Crisis Pregnancy* (Birmingham, AL: New Hope, 1990), 23-56; Carolyn Owens and Linda Roggow, *Pregnant and Single,* rev. ed. (Grand Rapids: Pyranee, 1990), 31-43; VanDerMolen, *Pregnant & Alone,* 35-88.

36. Prejudice

1. *Merriam-Webster Collegiate Dictionary,* s.v. "Prejudice."

2. *Merriam-Webster Collegiate Dictionary* (2001); http://www.m-w.com.

3. *Merriam-Webster Collegiate Dictionary.*

4. For this section see James E. Dittes, "Prejudice," in *Dictionary of Pastoral Care and Counseling,* eds. Rodney J. Hunter, H. Newton Malony, Liston O. Mills, and John Patton (Nashville: Abingdon, 1990), 946.

5. For this section see Jim Conway, *Making Real Friends in a Phony World* (Grand Rapids: Zondervan, 1989), 71.

6. For this section see Dolphus Weary and William Hendricks, *I Ain't Comin' Back* (Wheaton, IL: Tyndale House, 1990), 134.

37. Premarital Counseling

1. H. Norman Wright, *So You're Getting Married* (Ventura, CA: Regal, 1985), 248.

38. Rape Recovery

1. *Merriam-Webster Collegiate Dictionary* (2001); http://www.m-w.com.

2. *Merriam-Webster Collegiate Dictionary* (2001); http://www.m-w.com.

3. For this section see Jennifer Botkin-Maher, *Nice Girls Don't Get Raped* (San Bernardino, CA: Here's Life, 1987), 74-77.

4. For this section see Botkin-Maher, *Nice Girls Don't Get Raped,* 18-22.

5. Botkin-Maher, *Nice Girls Don't Get Raped,* 23-41.

39. Reconciliation

1. Don Baker, *Restoring Broken Relationships* (Eugene, OR: Harvest House, 1989), 115-16.

2. *Merriam-Webster's Collegiate Dictionary,* electronic edition (Merriam-Webster, 2001).

3. Myron Rush, *Hope for Hurting Relationships* (Wheaton, IL: Victor, 1989), 119.

4. See Ken Sande, *The Peacemaker* (Grand Rapids: Baker, 1991), 21-25.

5. See Sande, *Peacemaker,* 93-109.

6. See Rush, *Hope for Hurting Relationships,* 123.

7. *What Do You Do with a Broken Relationship?* (Radio Bible Class, [cited August 28, 2002]); http://www.gospelcom.net/rbc/ds/q0703/0703.html#page5.

8. *What Do You Do with a Broken Relationship?;* http://www.gospelcom.net/rbc/ds/q0703/q0703.html#page5.

9. *What Do You Do with a Broken Relationship?,* http://www.gospelcom.net/rbc/ds/q0703/q0703.html#page5.

10. See Sande, *Peacemaker,* 197-204, and *What Do You Do With a Broken Relationship;* http://www.gospelcom.net/rbc/ds/q0703/q0703.html#page5.

40. Rejection

1. Adapted from *Merriam-Webster's Collegiate Dictionary,* s.v. "Reject."

2. For this section see Marshall Bryant Hodge, *Your Fear of Love* (Garden City, NY: Doubleday, 1967), 26.

3. For this section see Robert McGee, *The Search for Significance* (Nashville: W Publishing Group, 1990), 137-53.

41. Salvation

1. Charles C. Ryrie, *The Ryrie Study Bible: King James Version* (Chicago: Moody, 1978), 1599.

2. W.E. Vine, Merrill Unger, William White, *Vine's Complete Expository Dictionary of Biblical Words,* electronic ed. (Nashville: Thomas Nelson, 1996), s.v. "Sanctification."

3. Earl D. Radmacher, *Salvation* (Nashville: Word, 2000), 5-6, 219-22.

4. Charles Caldwell Ryrie, *The Holy Spirit* (Chicago: Moody, 1965), 52-54.

43. Sexual Addiction

1. For this section see Patrick Carnes, *Out of the Shadows: Understanding Sexual Addiction* (Minneapolis, MN: CompCare, 1983), 9.

2. On the three God-given inner needs, see Lawrence J. Crabb, Jr., *Understanding People: Deep Longings for Relationship* (Grand Rapids: Zondervan, 1987), 15-16; Robert S. McGee, *The Search for Significance,* 2d ed. (Houston, TX: Rapha, 1990), 27-30.

44. Sexual Integrity

1. W.E. Vine, Merrill Unger, William White, *Vine's Complete Expository Dictionary of Biblical Words,* electronic ed. (Nashville: Thomas Nelson, 1996).

2. For this section, see Marilyn Morris, *ABC's of the Bird and Bees for Parents of Toddlers to Teens,* 2d ed. (Dallas: Charles River, 2000), 297-300. Used by permission.

45. Singleness

1. Ron Lee Davis and James C. Denney, *The Healing Choice: Finding God's Grace in Discouragement, Conflict, Mistreatment, Illness, Loss, Loneliness, Failure, Inferiority, Doubt, and Fear* (Waco, TX: Word, 1986), 78.

46. Stress Management

1. See Lloyd John Ogilvie, *Making Stress Work for You: Ten Proven Principles, with Built-in Study Guide* (Waco, TX: Word, 1985), 25-26.

2. See Kristine C. Brewer, *The Stress Management Handbook* (Shawnee Mission, KS: National Press, 1989), 9-10; Peter Meadows, *Finding Peace Under Pressure* (San Bernardino, CA: Here's Life, 1990), 48.

47. Suicide Prevention

1. Bill Blackburn, *What You Should Know About Suicide* (Waco, TX: Word, 1982), 82, 87-88, 96-99.

2. Blackburn, *What You Should Know About Suicide,* 90-96.

48. Verbal and Emotional Abuse

1. Andre Bustanoby and Fay Bustanoby, *Just Talk to Me* (Grand Rapids: Zondervan, 1981), 159-60.

2. For this section see Robert Burney, "Setting Personal Boundaries;" http://victimbehavior.com/boundaries/setting.html.

3. See Susan Forward, *Toxic Parents: Overcoming Their Hurtful Legacy and Reclaiming Your Life* (New York: Bantam, 1989), 236-74.

4. Patricia Evans, *The Verbally Abusive Relationship: How to Recognize It and How to Respond* (Holbrook, MA: Bob Adams, 1992), 164.

49. Victimization

1. *Merriam-Webster's Collegiate Dictionary,* electronic edition (Merriam-Webster, 2001).

2. For this section see Malcolm Smith, *No Longer a Victim* (Tulsa, OK: Pillar, 1992), 9-10.

3. Candace Walters, *Invisible Wounds* (Portland, OR: Multnomah, 1987), 62.

4. Rich Buhler, *Pain and Pretending* (Nashville: Thomas Nelson, 1991), 65.

5. Ellen Bass and Laura Davis, *The Courage to Heal: A Guide for Women Survivors of Child Sexual Abuse* (New York: Harper & Row, 1988), 49.

6. For this section see Bass and Davis, *The Courage to Heal,* 213, 217-19; Joyce Meyer, *Beauty for Ashes: Receiving Emotional Healing* (Tulsa, OK: Harrison House, 1994), 29-30.

50. Worry

1. For this section see David Stoop, *Self Talk: Key to Personal Growth* (Old Tappan, NJ: Fleming H. Revell, 1982), 94.

About the Author

June Hunt is an author, singer, speaker, and founder of Hope for the Heart, a worldwide biblical counseling ministry featuring the award-winning radio broadcast by the same name heard daily across America. In addition, *Hope in the Night* is June's live two-hour call-in counseling program that helps people untie their tangled problems with *biblical hope and practical help*. Hope for the Heart radio broadcasts currently air in more than 25 countries.

Early family pain was the catalyst that shaped June's compassionate heart. Later, as youth director for more than 600 teenagers, she became aware of the need for sound biblical counseling. Her work with young people and their parents led June to a life commitment of providing *God's Truth for Today's Problems*.

After years of teaching and research, June began developing scripturally based counseling tools called *Biblical Counseling Keys,* which address definitions, characteristics, causes, and solutions for 100 topics (such as marriage and parenting, anger and abuse, guilt and grief). Recently these individual topics were compiled to create the landmark *Biblical Counseling Library*.

The *Counseling Keys* have become the foundation for the Hope Biblical Counseling Institute initiated by The Criswell College. Each monthly conference in the Dallas-based institute provides training to help spiritual leaders, counselors, and other caring Christians meet the very real needs of others.

June has served as a guest professor at colleges and seminaries, both nationally and internationally, teaching on topics such as crisis counseling, child abuse, wife abuse, homosexuality, forgiveness, singleness, and self-worth. Her works are currently available in 60 countries and more than 20 languages, including Russian, Romanian, Ukrainian, Spanish, Portuguese, German, Mandarin, Korean, Japanese, and Arabic.

She is the author of *How to Forgive...When You Don't Feel Like It, How to Handle Your Emotions, Seeing Yourself Through God's Eyes, Caring for a Loved One with Cancer,* and more than 40 topical HopeBooks. June is also a contributor to the *Soul Care Bible* and the *Women's Devotional Bible*.

As an accomplished musician, June has been a guest on numerous national television and radio programs, including the NBC *Today* show. She has toured overseas with the USO and been a guest soloist at Billy Graham crusades. Five recordings—*Songs of Surrender, Hymns of Hope, The Whisper of My Heart, The Shelter Under His Wings,* and *The Hope of Christmas*—all reflect her heart of hope.

Learn more about June and Hope for the Heart at...

Hope for the Heart, Inc.
2001 W. Plano Pkwy, Ste 1000
Plano, TX 75075

1-972-212-9200
www.HopeForTheHeart.org

Other Harvest House books by June Hunt

HOW TO RISE ABOVE ABUSE

Compassionate, practical, hand-on guidance for the toughest issues to talk about—childhood sexual abuse, spiritual abuse, verbal and emotional abuse, victimization, and wife abuse. Filled with the hope and healing only Christ can give.

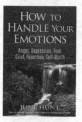

HOW TO HANDLE YOUR EMOTIONS

In Scripture, God gives counsel that helps us process our full range of emotions in a healthy way. Learn how to better navigate your emotions by understanding their definitions, characteristics, and causes, as well as the solutions that lead to emotional growth.

HOW TO FORGIVE...WHEN YOU DON'T FEEL LIKE IT

Though we know God has called us to forgive, we find ourselves asking hard questions: What if it hurts too much to forgive? What if the other person isn't sorry? How can I let the other person off the hook for doing something so wrong? June Hunt speaks from experience as she offers biblical answers, hope, and true freedom through forgiveness.

KEEPING YOUR COOL...WHEN YOUR ANGER IS HOT

This book explores the causes and kinds of anger and the biblical steps toward resolution. You will learn how to identify the triggers of anger, ways of dealing with past angers, what the Bible says about righteous and unrighteous anger, and how to bring about real and lasting change.

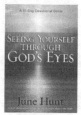

SEEING YOURSELF THROUGH GOD'S EYES

How you view yourself can have a profound effect on your everyday living. The key is to see yourself through God's eyes. Discover the great riches of your identity in Christ in the 31 devotions in this book.